WELFARE REFORM AND POLITICAL THEORY

WELFARE REFORM AND POLITICAL THEORY

LAWRENCE M. MEAD AND CHRISTOPHER BEEM
EDITORS

Russell Sage Foundation • New York

The Russell Sage Foundation

The Russell Sage Foundation, one of the oldest of America's general purpose foundations, was established in 1907 by Mrs. Margaret Olivia Sage for "the improvement of social and living conditions in the United States." The Foundation seeks to fulfill this mandate by fostering the development and dissemination of knowledge about the country's political, social, and economic problems. While the Foundation endeavors to assure the accuracy and objectivity of each book it publishes, the conclusions and interpretations in Russell Sage Foundation publications are those of the authors and not of the Foundation, its Trustees, or its staff. Publication by Russell Sage, therefore, does not imply Foundation endorsement.

Library of Congress Cataloging-in-Publication Data
Welfare reform and political theory / Lawrence M. Mead
and Christopher Beem, editors.
p. cm.
Includes bibliographical references.
ISBN 0-87154-595-0
1. Public welfare—United States. 2. Public welfare—Great Britain. 3. Welfare recipients—Employment—United States. 4. Welfare recipients—Employment—Great Britain. 5. United States—Social policy—1993- 6. Great Britain—Social policy—1979- 7. Public welfare—Political aspects. 8. Citizenship. I. Mead, Lawrence M. II. Beem, Christopher.

HV95.W45496 2005
361.973—dc22

2005049000

The paper used in this publication meets the minimum requirements of American National Standard for Information Sciences—Permanence of Paper for Printed Library Materials. ANSI Z39.48-1992.

Text design by Suzanne Nichols.

RUSSELL SAGE FOUNDATION
112 East 64th Street, New York, New York 10021
10 9 8 7 6 5 4 3 2 1

To our children

Contents

Contributors

Lawrence M. Mead is professor of politics at New York University.

Christopher Beem is program officer of Democracy and Community, and Family at The Johnson Foundation.

Alan Deacon is professor of social policy at the University of Leeds, United Kingdom.

William A. Galston is Saul Stern Professor at the University of Maryland School of Public Policy and director of the Institute for Philosophy and Public Policy.

Desmond King is Andrew W. Mellon Professor of American Government at the University of Oxford and fellow of Nuffield College.

Carole Pateman is professor of political science at the University of California, Los Angeles.

Joel Schwartz is an adjunct senior fellow at the Hudson Institute in Washington, D.C.

Amy L. Wax is professor of law at the University of Pennsylvania Law School.

Stuart White is fellow in politics at Jesus College, Oxford, and research director of the Public Policy Unit in the Department of Politics and International Relations at Oxford University.

Foreword

THIS PROJECT began when the two editors met at a Wingspread conference on welfare reform in Wisconsin in December 1999. Christopher Beem remarked that somebody ought to study the effects of reform on politics. After all, PRWORA represented a revolution in social policy. There had to be implications for politics and citizenship, but these had received almost no attention. Lawrence M. Mead was startled by this insight. He sensed that rare thing—a good research question! The conversation grew into a project, and the eventual result is this book.

Our agreement surprised us. Our politics are often at odds, and we continue to have significant disagreements about welfare reform. But we share an interest in theoretical inquiry. Although we have recently focused on concrete policy issues, both of us have a background in political theory. We both believed political theory had become too estranged from policy debate. We thought theory could contribute to the understanding of welfare reform, and be enriched in the process.

This agreement enabled us to learn from each other and work well together. What is more, that spirit extended to our coauthors. They represent the farthest reaches of the political spectrum. Yet from our first meeting (again at a Wingspread conference), collaboration transcended partisanship. That commitment is reflected in the pages that follow. To an extent unusual for an edited volume, our authors address common issues and respond to each other's arguments. Each rendered useful comments on many of the other chapters. We thank them sincerely.

We also thank John Tambornino for astute comments that significantly strengthened our book. A political theorist who has now moved to an academic position, John exemplifies the close engagement of theory with policymaking that we hope to promote.

This project straddles the boundaries between theory and public policy. Our point is to draw those worlds closer together. But this very feature made the effort difficult to fund. Thus, we especially thank our supporters. Besides the Johnson Foundation, they include Joe Dolan of the

Achelis and Bodman Foundations, Eric Wanner of the Russell Sage Foundation, and Michael Laracy of the Annie E. Casey Foundation. We are very grateful for their trust. Finally, we thank everyone at the Russell Sage press for seeing this project quickly and ably through to publication.

We have dedicated this book to our children. We hope they will inherit a world where political issues have constructive outcomes. We believe that controversies like welfare reform, though deeply felt, can give birth to better public policy and also to a more vibrant political order.

Lawrence M. Mead
New York University
New York, New York

Christopher Beem
The Johnson Foundation
Racine, Wisconsin

Introduction

CHRISTOPHER BEEM AND LAWRENCE M. MEAD

IN 1996, UNDER increasing pressure from a Republican Congress, President Clinton signed the Personal Responsibility and Work Opportunity Reconciliation Act (PRWORA) into law, bringing a dramatic shift in welfare policy toward the indigent. The previous policy, Aid to Families with Dependent Children (AFDC), had supported poor families largely on the basis of entitlement, meaning that eligibility was based almost exclusively on financial need. Few questions were asked about whether the parents could support themselves. And, for poor mothers without spouses, AFDC had seemed to many to foster the dissolution of low-income families and communities. Accordingly, PRWORA replaced AFDC with Temporary Assistance for Needy Families. Under TANF, needy families could receive aid only if the parents met far more demanding work and child support requirements. And, in any event, that support was limited to five years.

In 1997 and 1998, soon after the passage of PRWORA, Tony Blair's New Labour government in Great Britain introduced its New Deal.[1] This was a key element in Blair's effort to develop a so-called Third Way between Conservatism and traditional Labour policies. The New Deal moved away from the concept of social welfare, associated with T. H. Marshall, in which aid was given as a right of citizenship with few questions asked (Marshall 1964).[2] As in the United States, critics had argued that income given in this spirit—the dole—had become a way of life that immured recipients in poverty. Building on earlier Conservative reforms, the new policy required youth and the unemployed, after a short period on aid, to look for work or undertake other activities as a condition of further support. The requirements were less drastic than PRWORA, and largely exempted welfare mothers, but the motivations behind them were similar (see Lødemel and Trickey 2001).[3]

This broad shift in the late 1990s from an entitlement to a work-based support system for the indigent is what we mean in this volume by welfare reform.[4] Yet the term reform fails to anticipate the strong disagreement that followed. As many rejoiced at the death of traditional welfare, others damned welfare reform as a moral and political disaster, bound to force thousands of poor families into the streets. Several years later, it is clear that neither the best nor the worst predictions have come to pass. American and British welfare caseloads have sharply declined, and many former recipients are working. However, poverty levels have changed much less, the ability of the new workers to improve their lot over time appears limited, and the long-term implications for families and children are unclear.

These social and economic effects of reform have provoked an ocean of research and commentary. Nevertheless, we believe the assessment of welfare reform is incomplete. More is at stake than the concrete effects of the law. Welfare reform also shifted the foundations of our democracy and, by implication, democratic political theory. By eliminating entitlement and setting behavioral conditions on aid, welfare reform challenges our understanding of citizenship, political equality, and the role and moral cognizance of the state.

Does welfare reform mean that to be a citizen in full standing one must function in certain minimal ways? Is political equality now conditional on making some effort toward economic self-sufficiency? Has the liberal state given up on moral neutrality as even the goal of policy, so that it now explicitly affirms some ways of life and deprecates others? What are now the limits of government intervention in intimate areas of family life, such as marriage and reproduction? These questions have not been answered. In addressing them, this book offers a more complete accounting of the effects of welfare reform.

Policy Analysis and Political Theory

We have a broader agenda, as well—and to further it we use welfare reform as an example of how political theory can contribute to the appraisal of public policy. Currently, political theory has little to do with policy analysis, and vice versa. That reflects the way both fields have recently evolved. We think that by reconnecting theoretical reflection more closely to policy, both will be served.

Especially in the United States, research and analysis about most policy issues is relentlessly technical. The appraisal of policy is dominated by quantitative research aimed at concrete, measurable effects. In policy discourse, pride of place goes to those with hard evidence regarding what sort of policies have worked or not worked in the past, and what might work in future. That tendency is especially strong in social policy, where program evaluations and statistical models dominate. Welfare reform could hardly have occurred in America without a series of experimental studies showing that mandatory welfare work programs were effective.[5]

Everyone recognizes that political values strongly affect what programs get enacted, especially in an area, such as welfare, where feelings run strong. And whether and how programs are implemented shapes what they mean on the ground. But values and implementation are seldom part of systematic policy argument. Experts relegate them to the government process that politicians and bureaucrats are supposed to manage. Policymaking and administration are also studied, but seldom as part of policy argument. Scholars of these subjects know about government, but they are usually not experts on the policies involved, and they rarely take stands on the issues. Policy studies are thus typically bifurcated, with one group examining best policies and another studying policymaking, but with little communication between them. In this way, the stakes that a major issue such as welfare reform might involve for politics or democracy escape systematic attention.

Meanwhile, trends among political theorists keep them from studying policy closely. Historically, the main impetus to theoretical reflection about politics was often controversies in the real world. In recent decades, however, political theory has largely become an academic subject, written by and for academics. Within the university, theory has evolved into a field that is largely detached from concrete government and even from the rest of political science (Gunnell 1983, 1993; Galston 1993). In the postwar era, as the discipline sought to live up to scientific standards, political theory became suspect and its practitioners were marginalized. The most important theorists of that era, including Sheldon Wolin, Eric Voegelin, and Leo Strauss, maintained the standing of political theory. But perhaps because of these disciplinary concerns, they had little to say about public policy. Political theorists, like other political scientists, also became more specialized, with many focusing just on particular writers or historical developments within the corpus.

This development was strongly promoted by the enormous interest aroused by John Rawls's *Theory of Justice*, published in 1971. Rawls meant to free philosophy from logical positivism, a skeptical tradition that had prevented philosophers from speaking forcefully about political issues in earlier decades. But his system was so influential that an army of other theorists reacted to it, then to each other, eventually spawning a new scholasticism. Such Rawlsian topics as the difference principle and public reason became entire fields unto themselves. Also, Rawls wrote in a language of economics and rational choice that proved elusive to all but the cognoscenti, and all too susceptible to over-refinement. Thus, even as Rawls helped to revive political theory, his success left it increasingly self-referential, with theorists reacting to each other and to the literature more than to government's actual problems.

This estrangement, of course, is a matter of degree. We do not suggest that theorists have ceased to pass judgment on questions of political import. Many works in feminist theory, identity politics, discourse ethics, and deconstruction try to tease out the practical implications of their theoretical apparatus, as indeed did thousands of articles that referenced Rawls's work. Theorists have used Rawlsian principles to address issues of domestic and international justice, as did Rawls himself (see, for example, Beitz 2001; Rawls 1999). To mention just two, Norman Daniels used Rawlsian categories to explore issues surrounding health care (Daniels 1985), and Philippe Van Parijs—in an argument that several of our authors mention—argues that Rawls's ideal of public impartiality toward citizens' plans of life requires government to pay a minimum income to all adults (Parijs 1995).

Nevertheless, it is fair to say that all too often political theory today spurns close engagement with public policy. Those theorists who render judgments on public issues are a minority in the field, and even they usually remain at some distance from live political or policy issues. Judging government from a distance—talking about third-world development or environmental policy, say—is not the same thing as arguing for or against specific policies.

Indeed, theorists are sometimes so far removed from policy that they misapprehend the issues. A number of thinkers have attacked the recent welfare reform as a betrayal of progressive or feminist ideals. But some write as if the 1996 law totally abolished the aid once given by AFDC; actually, cash aid for families continues, albeit in a new, work-conditioned form (Mink 1998; Schram 2000). Some also construe welfare reform as a generalized attack on the welfare state, when in fact programs outside AFDC were little affected.[6] Without a sober focus on the facts of policy, political theory cannot contribute to policy assessment alongside the technicians who now dominate.

As theory has largely lost its public voice, so too has it lost its ability to address the political arena in which policy is made. Policy argument is thus compromised and incomplete. As they confront tough choices, policymakers could use hard-nosed analysis of what values are served by this or that option. But to help them, political theorists must have a taste for confronting real problems, and they must know something about the actual issues. Rising scholasticism makes both things less likely.

Just as significant, the abandonment of politics has undermined political theory's ability to achieve its own ends. To state abiding truths about politics, theorists must appreciate the world as it is. Much of the power of the canonical theorists of the past stemmed from their unblinking scrutiny of the political dilemmas of their day. Reality forced them to break with older ways of understanding politics. Political change generates theoretical change.[7] When theory loses contact with government, however, established categories can become stale and irrelevant. Thinking can live on in the academy even after actual politics has moved on to new issues, at which point theory becomes merely historical, detached from the choices politicians must face.

The welfare issue illustrates this. When it first arose in the early 1960s, politics was preoccupied largely with issues of class and race. The union movement was near its apogee as the civil rights movement gathered strength in the South. In that setting, a focus on justice—that is, on the distribution of relative rewards within the society—was natural and desirable. This was the context that produced Rawls and his critics. After the 1960s, however, movement politics declined. The challenge of urban poverty and its associated social problems, including welfare, became more prominent. That concern largely superseded the early focus on justice (Mead 1992). As a result, the traditional Rawlsian discourse became less relevant to practical politics.

Debate about justice tends to be impersonal and ideological, about the relative power or reward of different elements in the society. Debate about welfare and other social problems is more personal and moralistic—about why some groups seem to function poorly, and who or what is to blame for this. In *A Theory of Justice,* Rawls said little about deservingness, which he viewed as an improper basis for justice. But, later, behavioral issues such as whether welfare recipients should work became unavoidable.[8] Accordingly, all our authors address the question of deservingness directly—even those who also have strong views about equality or justice. In so doing, they develop a discourse more aligned with actual politics—and more useful to it—than much of contemporary political theory.

To sum up, conventional policy analysis is limited by its concreteness and its devotion to quantitative methodology, and political theory is limited by its frequent abstraction, its separation from the specifics of politics and policy. Theoretical reflection that focuses initially on policy is an improvement on both counts. It can be a contribution to policy assessment, but at the same time a policy connection can restore realism to theory. A dilemma such as welfare illustrates the potential. By speaking to it, theorists can help address a major issue of our own time while speaking to timeless questions about the meaning of citizenship and democracy.

Contributors

To meet these objectives, we have assembled an accomplished set of contributors. Each was asked to address the question: "How does welfare reform affect the Anglo-American political order and core concepts of political theory such as citizenship and democracy?" Note that this question ties together the specifics of reform with general reflections about the regime.

We deliberately sought out authors with diverse views. Our contributors include those who, politically, stand well to the left and right, and at several positions in between. All are established authors who combine knowledge of welfare policy with sensitivity to the theoretical stakes involved in reform.

Carole Pateman is a democratic political theorist and a critic of welfare reform. She argues that welfare reform has compromised democracy itself: the idea of citizenship now centers on participation in the marketplace. In her view, conditionality, which is the heart of the reform, is contrary to the rights that democratic citizens should enjoy. She would return to entitlement and, indeed, institute a broader form of guaranteed income covering all adults.

Desmond King is a scholar of social policy development who also criticizes reform. He argues that work requirements tend to draw invidious distinctions among citizens. Setting conditions for some citizens and not others destroys any notion of political equality. It leaves welfare recipients less able to participate in democratic politics. Like Pateman, King would reject reform in its current shape and return to entitlement.

Stuart White is a liberal political theorist who begins with a roughly Rawlsian construction of justice. He believes that justice requires a much more egalitarian society than we have. But where Rawls rejected desert as a basis for justice, White contends that conditionality is wholly in keeping with a liberal point of view. He accepts welfare reform as preferable to entitlement, but subject to certain conditions. He doubts that these conditions are met by the current New Deal, which is his main focus.

William Galston is another liberal theorist who supports work requirements. But whereas White grounds that position on fairness to others, Galston sees it as implied by the moral values that he says a liberal society must assume, among them individual responsibility and self-reliance. Galston's chapter argues that American citizenship is already conditioned on good behavior in several respects; welfare conditionality is simply another example.

Alan Deacon is a theorist of social policy who, like White, thinks that justice requires a more egalitarian society than we have. He too accepts conditionality, but finds that appeals to reciprocity or paternalism alone are not enough to justify it. Human relationships involve responsibilities and commitments that can be far-reaching, and which are independent of the state. This implies that liberal theory alone cannot justify morals in social policy. Deacon develops a mutualist, or communitarian, rationale for behavioral requirements. These could extend far beyond work tests, and even into private life. Deacon, like White, focuses mainly on the New Deal.

Christopher Beem is a political theorist who develops the argument, found also in Pateman, that entitlement welfare serves a social function. The original rationale for AFDC was that a single mother should receive social support to provide maternal care outside the market. Beem argues that welfare reform lauds work to the point of denigrating the social value of care. He discusses two experimental state programs that have supported low-income single mothers who leave the workforce to care for their infants.

Lawrence M. Mead is a social policy expert who was an early proponent of work requirements. He argues that work enforcement has occurred at several levels, not all of them focused on welfare recipients or the poor. The new welfare policy seeks to integrate the poor through work, although it also narrows the poor who can be publicly supported. In politics, reform discouraged a politics of complaint, in which the poor appear only as victims. But it also permits a more radical and efficacious politics, because a working poor population has stronger claims to public support.

Amy L. Wax is a law professor who focuses on social policy. Whereas Mead treats behavioral requirements as a political issue, Wax sees them as having deep anthropological roots. Society insists on work in order to enforce social cooperation and deter free-riding. Thus, the work test is really not new. At the same time, Wax argues that society is flexible in enforcing the test, and that the passion for reciprocity may be archaic, even outmoded, in society today.

Joel Schwartz is a historian of social policy who finds today's conditionality reminiscent of the Victorian era. Now as then, welfare policy seeks to inculcate certain virtues such as work effort and prudence. That makes social policy more effective, he argues, but the values are also believed to be true and good in themselves. However, he notes that society is much more willing to enforce work than marriage. That represents a significant limitation to the new moralism.

A Look Ahead

Following this introduction, we begin with Lawrence Mead's assessment of the meaning and effects of welfare reform, which all the contributors have seen, and which simply lays out the facts to which theoretical analyses should respond. He avoids making an argument, outlining only those points that that well-informed experts would agree on, whatever their politics. The discussion centers on PRWORA and its aftermath; more briefly it summarizes the British New Deal.

Chapters 2 through 10 are the individual essays, in the same order as the authors are listed. The sequence is meant to run from the most liberal argument to the most conservative. Of course, our ordering is only rough, and the politics presented in these chapters sometimes confound typical partisan categories. Still, as one proceeds from Pateman to Schwartz, one moves from the defense of entitlement to the defense of conditionality, from the defense of moral neutrality to its rejection, and from an individualist to a communitarian idea of citizenship, among other changes.

In chapter 11, the conclusion, we as editors try to identify the most important themes, or issues, that the essays raise. These we think lie at the bottom of the welfare controversy, in the political arena as well as among commentators. The most profound single difference seems to be over the nature of citizenship. At bottom, liberal critics of welfare reform think the recipients should be seen as rights-bearing claimants of social support, and conservative defenders think they should be seen as accountable for good behavior. That difference suggests profoundly different conceptions of democracy and the good society.

Taken together, these essays illuminate the deep political shifts associated with welfare reform, just as they demonstrate the value of a political theory that is, at once, sophisticated and concrete. A full assessment of policy should consider the political world, not just immediate social impacts. And political theory should not be afraid to address theoretical issues through the lens of specific policy change. The same approach might well be applied to any number of contemporary policy debates—for example, school reform, privacy laws, or criminal justice reform. In each area, different options imply differing economic effects, but also effects on important political values that should be specified.

Whenever policy is made, the background institutions are affected. Politics is the source of policymaking, and the place where its deepest effects are felt. Thus politics can improve the society and, hopefully, be improved in turn. Introducing theoretical concerns into a policy debate is one path by which policy science might return to its ancient tradition as the master science.

Notes

1. Technically, there are several New Deals for different groups of recipients. We use New Deal singular to refer generically to all these.
2. Marshall is usually read to endorse a rights-oriented view of social citizenship, but Stuart White argues below and in other work that he actually accepted conditionality.
3. Moves roughly parallel to those of Great Britain have occurred in Australia and New Zealand. The trend is less advanced in Continental Europe, but it is worth noting that France has created Revenue Minimum d'Insertion (RMI), an aid program where support may also be conditioned on the recipients taking steps to reenter the workforce.
4. Some other need-based benefits—Food Stamps, Medicaid, and Supplemental Social Security—have not seen similar change, and are therefore largely ignored here. For our purposes, welfare means AFDC/TANF or the New Deal in Britain.
5. The most influential of these studies were conducted in the 1980s and early 1990s by the Manpower Demonstration Research Corporation (MDRC).
6. PRWORA did include sharp cuts in eligibility for several programs for aliens, but most of these were later reversed.
7. Consider, for example, the end of the medieval period, when Thomistic political categories failed to anticipate the more ruthless politics of the emerging modern era. Machiavelli and Hobbes abandoned the scholastic tradition in favor of a new realism about conflict and power.

8. In writings after *A Theory of Justice,* Rawls revised his theory so that voluntary nonworkers would no longer have claims on primary goods. In their chapters, Stuart White finds this change sufficient but William Galston does not, a difference that reflects their different approaches to justice in a liberal society.

References

Beitz, Charles R. 2001. *Political Theory and International Relations,* rev. ed. Princeton, N.J.: Princeton University Press.

Daniels, Norman. 1985. *Just Health Care.* Cambridge: Cambridge University Press.

Galston, William. 1993. "Political Theory in the 1980s: Perplexity Amidst Diversity." In *Political Science: The State of the Discipline II,* edited by Ada W. Finifter. Washington, D.C.: American Political Science Association.

Gunnell, John G. 1983. "Political Theory: The Evolution of a Subfield." In *Political Science: The State of the Discipline,* edited by Ada W. Finifter. Washington, D.C.: American Political Science Association.

———. 1993. *The Descent of Political Theory: The Genealogy of an American Vocation* Chicago: University of Chicago Press.

Lødemel, Ivar, and Heather Trickey. 2001. *"An Offer You Can't Refuse": Workfare in International Perspective.* Bristol, U.K.: Policy Press.

Marshall, T. H. 1964. "Citizenship and Social Class." In *Class, Citizenship, and Social Development: Essays by T. H. Marshall,* introduction by Seymour Martin Lipset. Garden City, N.Y.: Doubleday.

Mead, Lawrence M. 1992. *The New Politics of Poverty: The Nonworking Poor in America.* New York: Basic Books.

Mink, Gwendolyn. 1998. *Welfare's End.* Ithaca, N.Y.: Cornell University Press.

Rawls, John. 1971. *A Theory of Justice.* Cambridge, Mass.: Harvard University Press.

———. 1999. *The Law of Peoples.* Cambridge, Mass.: Harvard University Press.

Schram, Sanford F. 2000. *After Welfare: The Culture of Postindustrial Social Policy.* New York: New York University Press.

Van Parijs, Philippe. 1995. *Real Freedom for All: What (If Anything) Can Justify Capitalism?* New York: Oxford University Press.

Chapter 1

A Summary of Welfare Reform

LAWRENCE M. MEAD

IN THIS chapter I summarize both the meaning of welfare and welfare reform as political issues and the effects of reform in recent years.[1] I concentrate mainly on the United States, especially the Personal Responsibility and Work Opportunity Reconciliation Act (PRWORA) of 1996 and its aftermath. More briefly, I also summarize the New Deal in Britain, to which some of our authors refer. I try to avoid saying anything that well-informed observers would dispute, whatever their politics.

Welfare

Welfare connotes support provided by government to people who, for whatever reason, cannot support themselves.[2] Aid or assistance are close synonyms. The terms imply programs that are means tested, are available only to the needy, and are not based on prior payroll contributions. Welfare is usually distinguished from social insurance programs that support workers when they are jobless due to unemployment or retirement, such as Social Security or Medicare; these benefits are contributory and not means tested.

Welfare has existed in the United States since colonial times and before that for centuries in Britain and other European countries. This reflects the wide acceptance in Western culture of a public responsibility for the needy. America inherited from Britain the habit of providing assistance on a local and discretionary basis. In both countries, local boards provided for the indigent using local taxes. An important controversy during the nineteenth century was whether to give such aid to families in their own homes ("outdoor relief") or to insist that they move into a poor house or work house, where the employable would have to labor for their support ("indoor relief"). The latter view gained ground late in the century. But between

1911 and 1919, most states began to support indigent mothers—chiefly widows—in their homes, on the view that society should pay them to raise their children.

During the New Deal, the national government began to support welfare. The Social Security Act of 1935 provided for federal matching funds to support state programs of cash aid to the needy who were aged, blind, disabled, or children in single-parent families. In 1972, aid to the first three of these groups was federalized under the Supplemental Security Income (SSI) program. Single men or childless couples do not qualify for federal cash welfare. Aid programs for these groups, commonly called general assistance, are funded entirely by states and localities.

The 1960s saw the establishment of Medicaid, which funds health care for welfare recipients and other low-income groups, and Food Stamps, or coupons to buy food, which virtually all poor can receive. Because these forms of aid are given in kind rather than in cash, they have not been strongly controversial. They are not central to welfare politics, and I say little about them here.

The program that is central is family welfare. The 1935 program aiding needy children came to be called Aid to Families with Dependent Children. AFDC used both federal and state funding to support needy children and their parents, usually single mothers. It became a national issue in the 1960s and early 1970s, when its rolls grew rapidly. What to do about it has remained the leading issue in social policy for more than three decades. Finally PRWORA radically recast AFDC as Temporary Assistance for Needy Families (TANF), as explained below.

Today, the largest cash welfare program is the Earned Income Tax Credit (EITC), a subsidy for low-paid workers. First established in 1975, it was sharply expanded in the 1990s, displacing AFDC as the major cash subsidy for poor families. Because it is work-connected, it is vastly more popular than older forms of family aid.

Welfare is only part of the welfare state. The social insurance programs just mentioned cost much more than welfare, largely because they serve the bulk of the population rather than just the needy. These programs include not only Social Security and Medicare, which provide retirement and health benefits to the elderly and disabled, but also unemployment insurance, which supports jobless workers, and workers' compensation, which supports employees injured on the job. Social Security and Medicare are by far the most expensive government benefit programs. Of the welfare programs, only Medicaid compares with them in cost, and most of its spending goes toward the elderly in hospitals and nursing homes, not toward the families and children at the center of the welfare debate. In general, the chief disputes in welfare politics are not about money.

Welfare Politics

Throughout its history, welfare has been controversial. It is embarrassing when people—especially working-aged adults and their children—become a public charge.[3] Dispute breaks out over who or what is responsible. The big issue is what is often called deservingness. Government is most willing to give aid to people who are victims of circumstances, such as natural disasters, rather than their 0own behavior. In family welfare, however, the initial cause of dependency is usually that parents have had children without marrying or working to support them. Some observers blame those behaviors on the recipients. Others, however, blame an unjust society and the economy in particular. On this view, poor parents fail to marry or work because they cannot find jobs sufficient to support families, among other problems. Hence, government must intervene to prevent destitution.

The positions reflect different views of the opportunity structure facing the poor. Liberals typically think that the needy have little chance to support themselves and get ahead. They also perceive various barriers that prevent the poor from working and escaping poverty, such as a lack of jobs or child care, or racial bias. Conservatives tend to dismiss such fears as excuses, believing that virtually anybody can get a job and thereby escape poverty. These views of society are closely tied to differing views about the responsibility and the capacity of the poor to cope with their situation. Liberals typically doubt that the poor are responsible, or that they can function without extensive help. Conservatives are readier to demand responsibility because they think that the poor can cope. Hence, they are more willing to criticize recipients' behavior and demand changes (Mead 1992, chaps. 4–7).

In policy terms, the leading issue in welfare is entitlement. Should people be given aid on the basis of impersonal economic criteria such as income, or should aid be conditioned in some way on good behavior? Especially, do the adult poor have to work or take other steps toward independence in return for support? As I use it here, entitlement connotes this issue. A second meaning of entitlement, however, is budgetary. In an entitlement program, government is legally obliged to pay benefits to everyone eligible for them, regardless of available funds. Social Security and Medicaid are in this sense entitlements. In a nonentitlement such as public housing, by contrast, funds are limited, benefits are rationed, and some eligible individuals may not be served.

Until the later nineteenth century, attitudes toward welfare tended to be moralistic. Most people blamed dependency on the needy, whom they admonished to work harder, save more, and avoid promiscuity and drink. A public responsibility to help the needy was still accepted, but much aid was also given by private charitable bodies such as churches. Public assistance was typically less generous and attitudes more severe in the United

States than in Europe, due to the greater individualism of the culture and greater belief that the chance to support oneself was available. These attitudes permitted conditioning aid on good behavior, although the conditioning was done more by private aid donors than by government. Interestingly, attitudes were more severe in Victorian times, when poverty was far more common and more clearly due to impersonal economic causes, than they are today, when conditions appear more favorable (Schwartz 2000, chap. 5).

With the Progressive era, however, the opposed view that poverty and welfare reflected hostile social conditions became dominant among policymakers and experts, and it remained so until around 1980. More aid was provided and fewer conditions were set on it. In addition, in the 1960s some restrictions that did remain were disallowed by the courts. Entitlement triumphed. This was one cause of the rapid expansion of AFDC in the 1960s and early 1970s. Largely, welfare reform is an effort to return to the earlier view—to hold the dependent once again responsible for at least some behaviors, especially employment. Indeed, reform has aptly been called a neo-Victorian social policy (Morone 2003). The current moralism, however, focuses much more on work and other obligations outside the home, and less on family behavior, than that of the Victorian era.

Elites tend to polarize over welfare more than the public does. They also focus more on the economic dimensions of aid. Typically, liberals and Democrats favor higher benefits or coverage in welfare, while conservatives and Republicans favor restrictions. This reflects the general division of left and right over the proper scale of government. Leaders left of center are also more loath to enforce work on recipients (Teles 1996). Liberals do seek to promote work, but typically through new benefits or opportunities, not by requiring effort as a condition of aid; they also would allow recipients to substitute training or education for employment in available jobs. Conservatives insist on enforcing work, refusing to leave it as a choice, and they resist education and training as a substitute.[4]

In contrast to the leaders, the public is less divided about welfare but more ambivalent. That is, ordinary Americans largely agree about welfare, but what they want is complex. Most people accept the principle of aid. They want government to be generous to children and other people in need. But at the same time, they strongly opposed the unreformed aid system, largely because most of the adult recipients appeared to be undeserving. So they want government to aid families in need but also to ensure that poor parents and other adults work in return for support. In short, the voters divide the responsibility for poverty. They affirm a public responsibility for the needy, but they reject entitlement. They insist that the needy work alongside the taxpayers, on whom they rely (Gilens 1999). Notably, this will to enforce good behavior does not extend to marriage, where more tolerant attitudes prevail. The public regrets the decline of the family but is reluctant to enforce marriage or stigmatize single mothers (Thornton 1995).

Deferring to the public, most politicians in both parties have come to accept that welfare should aid families yet demand that adult recipients work. That largely is what the recent reform has required. But some elements of elite opinion remain uncomfortable with this, reflecting the polarization mentioned above. On the right, some libertarians oppose giving aid on any basis, believing that welfare promotes dysfunctional lifestyles (Murray 1984). On the left, some liberal experts and community groups continue to oppose conditionality as a matter of principle. These voices defend entitlement as an ideal, or at least as realistic given the problems that poor families face (Edelman 1997).

Welfare Reform

Welfare reform in the United States largely means the struggle to change AFDC, driven by the beliefs and divisions just mentioned. Those tensions have played out in varying ways over the forty years that welfare has been a leading issue in national politics.

In the 1960s and 1970s, when politics was more liberal than it is today, the focus was mainly on the economic dimensions of welfare. Experts and advocates criticized AFDC for inadequate benefits and a failure to cover most poor people other than single-parent families. In that era, welfare reform chiefly meant raising benefits and expanding welfare coverage (Barth, Carcagno, and Palmer 1974). Yet these plans were defeated, in part because of costs but chiefly because they did not seriously expect employable recipients to work. Conservatives for their part sought mainly to restrain welfare spending. One of their initiatives in the 1970s was to crack down on fraud and abuse in the payment of welfare benefits, a task that was largely accomplished.[5] Another was to improve payment of child support by absent fathers, a task government still finds difficult.

In the 1980s and 1990s, the climate surrounding welfare reform turned more conservative. This reflected the rightward trend in politics generally, a change that was in part driven by worries about rising welfare and crime. The shift began with Richard Nixon's election as president in 1968, intensified with Ronald Reagan's two terms in the White House in the 1980s, and culminated in the election of a Republican Congress in 1994. When Democrats were elected president—Jimmy Carter in 1976 and Bill Clinton in 1992—a key reason was that they were southerners who could appeal to a broad electorate by taking more conservative stands on welfare and crime than much of their party.

After the mid-1970s, reform effort focused less on the economics of AFDC and more on the moral concerns surrounding the program, which were of such concern to the public. Because the work issue had overshadowed plans to expand welfare, liberals in the middle and late 1970s tried to promote employment among the poor through government jobs. But they still opposed strictly enforcing work as a condition of aid. In the later 1980s, they also called for "making work pay," by raising wage subsidies for the low-skilled and providing better child and health care (Ellwood 1988). Another liberal plan was to make child support into a substitute for welfare, using both the support paid by absent fathers and some public funds to guarantee support for needy families whether or not fathers paid (Garfinkel 1992).

In the 1980s, conservatives for their part focused more narrowly on the objectionable behaviors linked to welfare, while doing less to improve benefits or opportunities. As mentioned, some on the far right called for welfare to be abolished. Other conservatives sought mainly to require welfare adults to work, seeing this as the key to getting them off welfare and out of poverty (Mead 1986, 1997). Some others wanted to devolve control of welfare more fully to state and local governments, believing that these jurisdictions had more power than Washington to limit dependency (Butler and Kondratas 1987). The religious right proposed turning welfare administration over to churches and other community groups, the better to restrain unwed pregnancy (Olasky 1992). In the 1990s, some conservatives argued that restoring the family by promoting marriage was the answer to welfare, a view they pressed strongly during the debates on PRWORA (Weaver 2000, chaps. 5, 6, 8, 9).

By the late 1980s, work enforcement came to dominate the reform movement. That was because enforcing work, more than any other reform strategy, proved to be both popular and feasible. It appealed to the public's insistence on the poor doing more to help themselves. At the same time, it was practicable, because government had learned how to enforce work on welfare mothers. In contrast, improving child support was a slower process, and programs able to promote marriage or prevent unwed pregnancy remain a distant prospect.

Efforts to enforce work in AFDC go back to 1967. The initial work programs attached to welfare affected few recipients and expected little of them. Then starting in the Reagan administration, states gained permission to run welfare work programs that were more demanding than normal federal rules permitted. The favorable evaluation of some of these programs by the Manpower Demonstration Research Corporation (MDRC) put the work strategy on the map. In the Family Support Act of 1988 (FSA), Congress toughened and expanded mandatory work programs. However, the majority of welfare mothers were still exempted, and those who did participate usually went into education or training rather than the workplace. Only with PRWORA was a broader and stiffer work test imposed, leading to s sharp shift of single mothers off welfare and into jobs.

Since the 1960s, controversy over welfare has generally been to the political advantage of conservatives and Republicans. Growing dependency, like crime, raises popular concerns about social order, shoving off the agenda those questions liberals and Democrats would like to raise about economic fairness and equality. Conversely, when social problems abate, economic issues return to prominence and the agenda becomes more liberal (Mead 1992, chaps. 1–3, 10, 11). In the last decade, both welfare and crime have fallen. That has shifted social politics somewhat to the left, despite Republican control of the White House and Congress.

Attacks on the antipoverty programs of the 1960s and 1970s were arguably the most conservative aspect of the Reagan administration. George W. Bush is similarly conservative on economics and foreign policy, but on social policy he is more liberal than either Reagan or the Republicans who took control of Congress in 1994. In 2000, Bush did not run against welfare, as previous Republican presidential candidates had done, but rather as a "compassionate conservative." He wanted churches to play a larger role in antipoverty programs, but he did not call for reduced public spending on the poor.

Bush raised federal education aid, as part of the No Child Left Behind testing program, and accepted a costly expansion of Medicare to cover prescription drugs. His administration took a moderate position on TANF reauthorization, maintaining current funding levels despite the fall in the rolls. In the 2004 presidential campaign, the president proposed to expand training programs and community colleges. Admittedly, the cost of these proposals cannot easily be reconciled with Bush's tax cuts, which have reduced revenues and expanded deficits, thus arousing opposition in both parties. But that the proposals were made at all reflects the liberalizing effect that the success of welfare reform in the 1990s had on the social agenda.

PRWORA

The Republicans took control of Congress in 1994 in part due to continuing anxiety about welfare. The AFDC rolls suddenly jumped by about a third between 1989 and 1994, driven by rising unwed pregnancy as well as the recession of the early 1990s (Congressional Budget Office 1993; Blank 1997). The Republicans' victory gave conservatives more power to reshape welfare than they had had in forty years.

PRWORA went beyond the efforts to enforce work and child support and save money that marked earlier conservative reform proposals. The act attempted to promote the family and devolve control of aid to states and localities in radical new ways. These latter aspects were obnoxious to most Democrats and lacked a clear popular mandate. However, President Clinton had a history of criticizing welfare, an issue that had hurt the

Democrats. He also feared that welfare might become an issue in his reelection campaign. He therefore felt bound to sign the bill, and did so. Several academic experts on welfare who had staffed his administration resigned over the issue, and discontent has continued to simmer among some liberal Democrats and advocacy groups (Weaver 2000).

These were PRWORA's main provisions. Their main brunt was to end entitlement in both a behavioral and budgetary sense:

- *Aid was unentitled.* Under AFDC, the federal government shared in the cost of local aid programs regardless of spending level or numbers of eligibles served. Under TANF, federal funding is instead limited to a fixed block grant to each state, conditional only on states' spending at least 75 percent of what they previously spent on welfare. That grant was set at the levels of 1994 and 1995, when caseloads peaked. That turned out to be generous due to the ensuing fall in the caseload, which far exceeded expectations. Child care funding was raised by about $4 billion (Ways and Means 2004, 9.28).
- *Aid was time-limited.* Families are not normally allowed to receive TANF for more than five years, including repeat spells, measured from the signing of PRWORA on August 22, 1996. However, far fewer recipients have been dropped from aid after the time limit than many feared. States may exempt up to 20 percent of cases from the limit. They may also support families beyond five years using their own funding. Some liberal states have done this, including California and New York, which have the largest caseloads.
- *Work requirements were ostensibly toughened.* Cases are supposed to work within two years of going on the rolls even to continue to get aid. States were required to raise the share of their cases that were in work activities in stages, until half qualified by 2002, on pain of cuts in federal funding. However, states were also allowed to count against these targets any percent by which their caseloads fell after 1995. In most states, the fall was enough to meet the new work standards without welfare having to do much to raise work-activity levels.
- *Work policy now stressed work first.* Under the Family Support Act, most welfare adults subject to the work test had gone into education or training rather than taking available jobs. The hope was to qualify them for better jobs later. Under PRWORA, by contrast, the definition of work activities strongly favors actual work or looking for work over remediation. This was partly because evaluations of work programs of the 1990s showed that those that stressed actual jobs outperformed those stressing skill enhancement (Freedman and Friedlander 1995; Riccio, Friedlander, and Freedman 1994).

- *Child support was also toughened.* The state and federal governments were to set up computerized registries to facilitate tracking absent fathers across state lines and attaching their wages. Subsidies previously mandated for welfare mothers who cooperated with child support were repealed. These steps were much less controversial than PRWORA's other provisions.
- *Control of welfare was further devolved.* States already controlled benefit levels under AFDC. Under TANF they gained greater control over eligibility and other details. They could now decide whether and how to cover two-parent families (largely excluded under AFDC) and whether to institute work incentives (allowing recipients who take jobs to keep part of their benefit, to give them more reason to work).
- *Marriage was promoted.* States were allowed, although not required, to deny coverage to unwed mothers under eighteen and to children born on the rolls. If covered, teen parents were required to live with caretakers and go to school. States also received bonus funding if in comparison to other states they reduced the rate of unwed pregnancy, or if they performed well, measured by such criteria as job retention and earnings gains among recipients going to work. States were not, however, penalized for failure in these respects, as in principle they could be for low work activity levels.
- *Other aid was cut.* Legal aliens were largely barred from TANF, Supplemental Security Income (aid for the aged, blind, and disabled), and Food Stamps, and these programs were cut in other ways. PRWORA's budgetary savings were entirely due to these cuts, not the changes in AFDC or TANF. Congress later restored most benefits for aliens who were in this country before PRWORA was signed, but those arriving later remain largely excluded. SSI, Food Stamps, and Medicaid were not otherwise reformed and remain entitlements.

Most states have implemented PRWORA so as to combine continued aid with rising work demands, which the public wants. Most have instituted tougher work requirements, but few have cut benefits, as liberals feared, or paid much attention to the family provisions. That is because promoting marriage is considerably more controversial than enforcing work, and because programs that clearly prevent unwed pregnancy are not yet available (Gais et al. 2001).

The Liberal Side of Reform

Recent welfare policy also has a liberal side that is often overlooked. Congress and the states have acted on many of the recommendations to make work pay made by liberal experts and the Clinton administration. The following steps have enhanced support for poor families, especially when one or more family members are employed:

- *Expanded wage subsidies.* The Earned Income Tax Credit (EITC), mentioned earlier, is a subsidy for the working poor. It was sharply increased in 1990 and 1993. It now subsidizes the earnings of low-income parents by as much as 40 percent. Some states have added wage subsidies of their own.
- *Children's credits.* In 2001 Congress added a tax credit for children that is aimed at full-time workers and is partially refundable to low-income families without tax liabilities.
- *Strengthened work incentives.* Most states liberalized work incentives in TANF. These rules allowed recipients to keep some of their former benefits when they went to work. This raised the benefits available to low-income working families. Families in the typical state can now escape poverty, by the federal definition, even working at the minimum wage, provided they work at least half-time. On the other hand, the subsequent loss of these benefits as earnings rise makes it harder to move up to higher incomes (Acs et al. 1998; Gais and Weaver 2002).
- *Higher minimum wage.* In 1996 and 1997, the federal minimum wage was raised from $4.25 to $5.15 an hour. This enhanced earnings among the low-paid, although only 14 percent of workers at the minimum wage are heads of household (Haugen and Mellor 1990). In real terms, though, the minimum is still well below the levels of decades ago.
- *Expanded child care.* Between 1994 and 1999, federal and related state spending for child care rose by 60 percent, or from $8.9 to $14.1 billion. In 2000, federal spending was projected at over $15 billion for child care under Head Start and several other programs, both in and outside of welfare (Besharov and Samari 2001, 463–64; Ways and Means 2000, 599).
- *Expanded health coverage.* Although the Clinton proposal for a universal health system was defeated, Congress in the 1980s and 1990s expanded coverage for poor children and families under Medicaid. The State Child Health Insurance Program (SCHIP), aimed at children somewhat above the Medicaid level, was added in 1997. Today, poor mothers and children can get at least some coverage whether on or off welfare.

The enactment of these measures reflects the popularity of aiding poor families—provided the adults work. The new benefits already represent a redistribution of advantages toward the working poor, part of the liberalizing shift in social policy mentioned earlier.

Effects of Reform

Effects here means the consequences, not just of PRWORA, but of the fall in the welfare rolls that began in 1994, triggered by earlier welfare reforms and a good economy. To what extent these effects are due to the recent reform rather than to other changes is addressed later.

- *Cash welfare rolls have fallen sharply.* From a peak of 5.1 million cases and 14.4 million recipients in March 1994, AFDC-TANF fell to 2 million cases (5 million recipients) by June 2003. That decline is 60 percent for cases, and 66 percent for recipients. The fall is much the largest in the history of the program and considerably more than experts expected. It more than reversed the welfare growth of the 1989 to 1994 period.[6]
- *States reaped a huge financial windfall,* due both to the fall in the rolls and the fact that TANF's federal grants to states did not decline with caseloads, as the earlier matching funds would have done. Some states found it difficult even to spend the 75 percent of earlier levels necessary to claim all their federal funds. At least through 2002, most states had plenty of money to finance welfare reform. Total federal and state spending per case rose from $6,269 in 1996 to $8,330 in 1999 (Ways and Means, 2000, 417). Many states have recently faced fiscal crises, but that has been due to the recent recession, not to welfare reform.
- *Noncash rolls have fallen less sharply.* The Food Stamps rolls have come down by almost a third since 1994. The Medicaid rolls grew steadily in the 1990s as coverage was broadened, yet not all children and families eligible claimed their benefits (Ways and Means, 2004, 15.24, 15.41–15.45). Many TANF leavers do not receive Food Stamps or Medicaid, even though they remain eligible, either because the bureaucracy fails to offer the benefits or because those leaving TANF prefer to leave other means-tested programs as well. The relative role of these factors is disputed.
- *Work levels on welfare have sharply risen.* The percentage of AFDC-TANF adults working in unsubsidized jobs rose from 8 percent in 1994 to 28 percent in 1999, before falling to 26 percent in 2001, due to the recession. The share meeting work activity requirements within welfare work programs rose from 15 percent in 1991 to 38 percent in 1999. The level then fell to 33 percent by 2002, due to the recession and perhaps the declining employability of the remaining recipients as the caseload fell.[7]
- *Most people who left welfare are working.* According to state studies of families leaving welfare, most did so because of going to work or increased earnings. From 55 to 64 percent of adult former recipients

were employed when surveyed, and from 63 to 91 percent had worked since leaving welfare (Devere 2001, 10–11). These work levels are much above what most experts expected.

- *Nonworking leavers usually have other support.* Those leaving welfare without a job often have benefits from other programs, such as disability. Many appear to have support from spouses or other family members who are employed, although the extent is unclear (Besharov and Germanis 2000, 27–32).
- *Earnings remain low.* In state surveys, average wages among working leavers ran from $5.50 to $8.80 an hour, or somewhat above the minimum wage. Quarterly earnings averaged from $1,999 to $3,868. This is below what one would expect from the wage levels, because few leavers work the full-time hours typical of the population (Devere 2001, 12).
- *Whether reform has raised overall incomes is unclear.* In the short run, leavers' earnings usually exceed prior welfare benefits, but families also tend to lose some noncash benefits. There is some evidence that incomes among the poorest single mothers initially fell, but at the same time, their consumption rose (Haskins 2001; Primus et al. 1999). Most likely, incomes do rise, but not always immediately.
- *Earnings and incomes rise over time.* Earnings tend to increase gradually the longer a family is off welfare. This could bring many above the poverty line eventually. It appears that welfare mothers do gain higher wages with experience—gains proportionally as large as those of better-off women—but only if they work steadily, as many do not (Loeb and Corcoran 2001; Danziger et al. 2002).
- *Promarriage effects appear likely.* Anecdotes suggest that working single mothers have to rely on their spouses more than they did before reform, if only to care for the children when they work. The share of welfare mothers living with a partner rose from 7 to 14 percent between 1997 and 1999 (Zedlewski and Alderson 2001). One evaluation also found positive effects on marriage and less spousal abuse among families exposed to a mandatory work program (Knox, Miller, and Gennetian 2000).
- *Hardship appears little changed.* As many as 59 percent of leavers report problems paying bills or affording food and housing, but many had similar problems before leaving welfare (Devere 2001, 16–18). Most leavers appear to be struggling, but few suffer hardship as acute as homelessness or the need to give children over to foster care.
- *Many social problems remain.* In cities with extreme caseload falls, such as Milwaukee, journalists hear of more people working and filing tax returns (Derus 1998; DeParle 1999; Sherman 2000). Much less change

is apparent in the more private problems common among the poor, such as family conflicts or sexual or substance abuse (DeParle 2004).

Alongside these changes, several recent evaluations of welfare work programs have studied the effects on children. These programs mostly date from the early 1990s, prior to PRWORA, but are enough like the programs states implemented under PRWORA that most experts take this evidence as applying to the current reform:[8]

- *Young children appear to benefit.* When their parents are in welfare work programs, young children tend to show cognitive gains and do better in school. The effects appear stronger for boys than girls. This may be because a working mother is a better parent and role model, or because children receive more stimulation in child care than they would if they stayed home with a nonworking mother.
- *Effects on adolescents are more negative.* Older children tend to have more behavioral problems, such as drinking or school misbehavior, perhaps because more parents are now working and less able to supervise them. However, a more recent statistical study finds largely positive effects on adolescents (Chase-Lansdale et al. 2003).
- *Health coverage falls.* Fewer children have health benefits because families are leaving Medicaid and cash welfare programs. Again, how this happens is unclear, because health eligibility has expanded.

The effects appear most positive with programs that combine work requirements with income supplements such as work incentives (Morris et al. 2001). However, effects on marriage and children also appear to be small or transient: these findings, taken from evaluations, were measured two years after the programs began. Over five years, the effects mostly fade out or become inconclusive. The economic effects of reform are more robust (Adams-Ciardullo et al. 2001).

Reform had an impact on welfare institutions as well. In many states, administrative arrangements became more complicated. More often than before PRWORA, the various services required to move recipients into jobs were contracted out to nongovernmental entities, usually nonprofit organizations but sometimes profit-making firms. In some places, religious agencies played a larger role, in part because PRWORA contained charitable choice provisions that made it easier for such agencies to seek government contracts without changing their religious character. These changes partly reflected the general movement toward the reinvention of government in social administration (Osborne and Gaebler 1992), an idea espoused primarily by conservatives.

Other Social Changes

The welfare changes, in turn, are related in unclear ways to certain positive changes occurring in the society at large:

- *Work levels have risen sharply.* More poor adults are working than before welfare reform, especially single mothers. In 1993, only 44 percent of poor female heads of family with children were employed. The rate jumped to 64 percent by 1999, before falling to 55 percent in 2003, probably due to the recession.[9]
- *Poverty rates are falling more slowly.* The overall poverty rate was 15.1 percent in 1993, felling to 11.3 percent by 2000, then rising to 12.5 percent in 2003. Poverty rates for children fell from 22.7 percent in 1993 to 16.2 percent in 2000, before rising to 17.6 percent in 2003 (U.S. Census Bureau 2004b, tables B1–B2; Haskins 2001, 121–24). Again, the reversals probably reflect the recession.
- *Unwed childbearing is falling.* The share of births out of wedlock leveled off in the 1990s, and pregnancy and births among teenagers declined. Research suggests that if welfare mothers work, their daughters are less likely to become pregnant (Lopoo 2005). These trends, however, are gradual and began in the early 1990s, prior to PRWORA (Sawhill 2002).
- *Child abuse and neglect has fallen since 1993.* Again, trends are gradual and predate PRWORA (Ways and Means 2000, 706–10; 2004, 11.74–11.77). One possible negative effect of TANF may be more out-of-home placement of children. This could reflect an inability of some single mothers to care for their children following a loss of aid (Paxson and Waldfogel 2003).

The Role of Reform

It is uncertain what role welfare reform actually played in these developments. First, as mentioned, PRWORA's bark was worse than its bite. Its severe work standards were largely nullified by the caseload fall credit, and its family goals were not mandatory for states, which have mostly ignored them. It is thus unclear to what extent PRWORA actually produced the changes brought by reform. The vogue for work requirements may really be due more to earlier federal requirements or to state and local decisions.

It is also unclear how important reform, whether due to PRWORA or not, was in producing its apparent social and economic effects. The dramatic fall of the rolls might also reflect the superb economy of the late 1990s, when conditions for poor adults were the best in thirty years—not only low unemployment, rapid economic growth, and plentiful job creation but rising real wages for the low skilled. A third reason was new benefits (work incentives, work subsidies, and others), which made working more possible and more worthwhile. A fourth was improved child support enforcement (Huang, Kunz, and Garfinkel 2002; Mead 1999, 2003). In 2001, 56 percent of poor single mothers had child support judgments, compared to 38 percent in 1978, and the share receiving support from absent parents rose from 18 to 31 percent in the same period (Ways and Means 2004, 8.73). Fifth, and finally, the political climate is less tolerant of dependency than it was before reform. Local officials say that this motivates needy families to leave the rolls or avoid them entirely (Mead 2004, chap. 9).

Most experts agree that all these forces help to explain the dramatic welfare and work changes, but disagree about their relative importance. Some economists argue that the changes were due mostly to the economy and new benefits, especially the expanded EITC, rather than to work requirements (Ziliak et al. 1997; Meyer and Rosenbaum 2001). Other studies give welfare reform the leading role, followed by the economy (Ellwood 1999; Council of Economic Advisors 1999; O'Neill and Hill 2001; Grogger 2004).

Journalistic observations of reform support the latter view. In a study of welfare decline in Wisconsin, officials told me that work requirements and changed expectations were the leading causes, followed by the economy and improving child support; none mentioned the EITC (Mead 2004, 177–81).[10] Journalistic accounts suggest that higher work levels have driven up receipt of the EITC, rather than the other way around (DeParle 1999; Sherman 2000). One reasonable estimate is that 35 to 40 percent of the work rise for low-income single mothers is due to work enforcement, 25 to 30 percent to the economy, and 20 to 30 percent to expanded benefits (Ellwood 1999; Besharov 2003, 9–10).

The principal question hanging over the reform is what would happen if the economy faltered. The decline in the rolls was halted, not reversed, by the recent recession, probably because the economy was in fact secondary to reform in driving the rolls down (Grogger 2004, 686–92). At the same time, no one expects the rolls to fall in future at the rate of the late 1990s.

Future Issues

The reauthorization of TANF was to occur in 2002 but has been delayed by divisions in Congress. There is broad agreement that the caseload credit should be phased out and that the work activity targets required of states should be somewhat raised. But because, among other changes, permissible activities would be broadened, states would have to raise actual activity levels by less than it would appear. Neither party has addressed closing certain loopholes in the original law, by which states have shielded some recipients from the work test and time limits entirely.[11]

Democrats resist raising work standards as much as Republicans want. They also want to allow more forms of education and training to count toward satisfying the work test, and Republicans resist. Democrats also demand more funding for child care than the Bush administration thinks necessary (Haskins and Offner 2003). The differences reflect the long-standing partisan divide over how to deal with poverty and welfare.

The range of disagreement, however, has been narrowed compared to 1996 because of the success of reform to date. Among members of Congress, there are no serious proposals from the left to repeal work requirements, nor from the right to abolish aid. In its reauthorization proposals, the Bush administration has not attempted to promote marriage much more than PRWORA already does. The administration is developing programs to promote or preserve marriage among low-income Americans. But, in TANF reauthorization, it does not insist that states pursue marriage as a condition of federal funding.

Most experts think that welfare reform is a success, but also that it is incomplete. One challenge is to ensure adequate earnings to mothers after they leave welfare. That will require paying them more per working hour through higher wage subsidies or the minimum wage, but also requires getting them to work more consistently at the wages they can already get. The parties may differ about which aspect to emphasize. Once mothers leave welfare, government has no authority to require them to keep working. Programs to promote job retention and advancement for this population have so far proved disappointing.

The second unsolved problem is reaching the absent fathers of welfare families. Welfare reform has helped them far less than it has poor mothers. Although child support enforcement is improving, most absent fathers of poor families still evade their obligations. The goal is not simply to get them to pay up, but to involve them more fully in their families, to their own as well as the mothers' and children's benefit. That requires addressing the problems the fathers have with both employment and relating to their spouses. Government has had little success to date in this, although some special child support programs aimed at fathers have been tested (Mincy and Pouncy 1997).

The New Deal

Although reform has been most drastic and visible in the United States, it is also occurring in Europe (Lødemel and Trickey 2001). The leading instance is the New Deal in Britain.[12]

Background

Work testing has a different basis in Europe than in the United States in that it does not center on welfare mothers. Employment by mothers, while growing, is less common than in the United States, and working is not yet a norm that most people want to enforce in family welfare. It is still accepted that needy single mothers may claim social support to raise children, even if they do not work.

There is more concern about youth and the male unemployed, many of whom live on aid for long periods. These groups have not been a primary focus of welfare reform in the United States mainly because they get little cash aid here. They may qualify for Food Stamps or general assistance (local cash relief), but unemployment insurance (UI), the principal cash benefit for the jobless, covers only some of the unemployed, due to restrictive conditions. Receipt is usually limited to six months. Beneficiaries are supposed to look for work, but the government does not police job search closely, knowing that dependency cannot be prolonged in any event.

In Europe, however, aid to the unemployed is more widely available and commonly open-ended. Initial support may be contributory and time limited, as in the United States. But after it ends, beneficiaries can transition to means-tested aid that can last indefinitely—what in Britain is known as the dole. In addition, youth leaving school without work are eligible for support until they take jobs. Finally, European societies have more generous and accessible benefits for the disabled than the United States does.

As these features suggest, Europe generally accepts a public responsibility to ensure a minimum income to all persons, regardless of why they are needy. This reflects in part a less-individualistic culture and also less confidence that jobs are available for all willing workers. Although jobless benefits usually carry formal requirements to look for work, these strictures have not been widely enforced until recently. This effectively turned aid for the unemployed into an entitlement.

What triggered reform was the persistence of extensive dependency on unemployment benefits even during good economic times. Similarly, disability caseloads rose steadily throughout the 1990s, even though health conditions were improving. The view that jobs were scarce became more questionable in light of significant immigration from non-Western countries. Budgetary pressure from welfare also was more significant in Europe than in America, where aid programs are a minor expense alongside the much larger social insurance programs. And, as in the United States, there were concerns about social cohesion—a fear that the dependent were losing contact with the work force and mainstream society.

British Reforms

The Conservative government of 1979 to 1997 trimmed some benefits and took several steps toward promoting work among recipients of unemployment benefits.[13] The Tories reactivated the work tests that had long been dormant. They required out-of-school youth living on benefits to enter training programs as a condition of aid. In 1996, they shortened the period of unconditional jobless benefit from a year to six months and required recipients to sign agreements specifying the steps they would take toward employment. The long-term unemployed were required to search for jobs, then given unpaid work in government jobs ("workfare"). To "make work pay," tax credits available to low-income working families were increased.

The Labour government elected in 1997 built on these steps with its own, more ambitious New Deal. Of the several programs, the most important—and the most compulsory—is the New Deal for Young People, which covers ages eighteen to twenty-four. Under this scheme, youth living on benefit for more than six months must enter what is known as a gateway, in which they interact intensively with staff and look for work. After four months, if they are still jobless, they must choose among four options: subsidized work arranged through government, self-employment or approved voluntary work, participation in an environmental taskforce, or education or training. Those still jobless after these activities face continued supervised job search. Participation is enforced by cuts in benefits. Jobless people older than twenty-five may draw aid without question for eighteen months, but they then face similar demands, with fewer options other than work. Teenagers under eighteen who have left school must, as a condition of aid, enter training or apprenticeships.

Lone mothers living on aid, however, face a much less demanding regime. Initially, they were offered a personal advisor with whom they could discuss employment; less than a quarter did so. Thus, in 2002, an initial interview with the advisor became mandatory; interviews every six months were later required. But the mothers face no definite demands at present to work or look for work. Similarly, the disabled are asked to seek work on a voluntary basis, and since 2002 they too must attend an initial work-focused interview when they go on aid.

To make work pay more, the government instituted the nation's first general minimum wage. Wage subsidies for low-income families who were working were still further increased. Child care subsidies were increased as well, to ensure that mothers who wanted to would be able to work.

Labour departed from the earlier Conservative measures—and from American policy—mainly in incorporating explicit antipoverty goals. The government committed itself to ending child poverty within twenty years. To this end, children's allowances and other benefits drawn by poor families were raised, independent of whether families worked. The government also combated the social exclusion due to disadvantaged neighborhoods with additional social programs not directly tied to benefits. One of these is Sure Start, an early childhood program akin to America's Head Start.

Effects

The New Deal, like American welfare reform, achieved a substantial reduction in dependency and a rise in work levels by poor parents. But, as in the United States, progress occurred during the late 1990s, when economic conditions were superb. One might doubt how much of the gains were due to social policy. The British do not yet have experimental evaluations to establish the impact of their programs. Statistical studies, however, suggest that at least part of the work increase is due to the recent steps to promote employment.

Poverty reductions were greater than in the United States. That reflected, in part, the antipoverty goal and the enhanced benefits. The downside was that the benefit increases somewhat offset the effort to make work pay, because families could now realize incomes close to the poverty line even without working (Hill and Waldfogel 2004). This inhibits reaching the employment goals of the reform.

Despite this, however, the New Deal for Lone Parents appears to have produced as much work increase among single mothers as TANF, even though it does not strictly enforce work. That might be because mothers on aid were influenced by the other, and mandatory, New Deals aimed at the unemployed. They also seem to have responded quite positively to the attention given to them by work advisors (Hill and Waldfogel 2004; Millar 2003).

In Britain, as in the United States, an ongoing question will be how welfare reform and other policies have affected dependency, poverty, and other social conditions. In the following chapters, however, we ask instead how welfare reform has affected the body politic. Reform is a product of politics and government, but it also has reshaped the democratic process and the very meaning of citizenship.

Notes

1. This is an update and expansion of Lawrence Mead (2001). For a more detailed discussion of PRWORA and its effects, see Rebecca M. Blank and Ron Haskins (2001).
2. The following account draws especially on Michael Katz (1986).
3. The following draws on Gertrude Himmelfarb (1984, 1991); Marvin Olasky (1992); and Joel Schwartz (2000).
4. For an analysis of these separate themes in welfare politics, see Lawrence Mead (2005b).
5. Ineligibility and incorrect grant payments were rife in the 1960s and 1970s, when the welfare rolls grew rapidly. Driven by federal fiscal sanctions, states reduced errors, by the 1990s, to around 6 percent of payments. See U.S. Congress (1998, 466).
6. Data from the U.S. Administration for Children and Families.

7. Ways and Means (2004, 7.81); data from the U.S. Administration for Children and Families.
8. The following draws on Gayle Hamilton with Stephen Freedman and Sharon M. McGruder (2000), and Greg Duncan and Lindsay Chase-Lansdale (2001).
9. Data from the Current Population Survey for March 1994 (U.S. Census Bureau 1994, table 19); March 2000 (U.S. Census Bureau 2000, table 17); Annual Demographic Survey, March 2004 (U.S. Census Bureau 2004a, table POV15).
10. The economic studies probably overemphasize economic causes because these variables are easier to measure than welfare reform.
11. Beside the caseload fall credit, these include sanctioning rules, "child-only" cases, "separate state programs" for TANF eligibles, and waiver programs (see Mead 2005a).
12. There are several New Deals aimed at different populations. Here and throughout this volume, we use New Deal to refer to all these.
13. The following draws on Heather Trickey and Robert Walker (2001), Robert Walker and Michael Wiseman (2003) and John Hill and Jane Waldfogel (2004).

References

Acs, Gregory, Norma Coe, Keith Watson, and Robert I. Lerman. 1998. *Does Work Pay? An Analysis of the Work Incentives under TANF.* Washington, D.C.: The Urban Institute.

Adams-Ciardullo, Diana, Surjeet Ahluwalia, Jennifer Brooks, Stephen Freedman, Anna Gassman-Pines, Lisa Gennetian, Gayle Hamilton, Sharon McGroder, Charles Michalopoulos, Johanna Walter, and Martha Zaslow. 2001. *How Effective Are Different Welfare-to-Work Approaches? Five-Year Adult and Child Impacts for Eleven Programs.* New York: Manpower Demonstration Research Corporation.

Barth, Michael C., George J. Carcagno, and John L. Palmer. 1974. *Toward an Effective Income Support System: Problems, Prospects, and Choices.* Madison: University of Wisconsin, Institute for Research on Poverty.

Besharov, Douglas J. 2003. "The Past and Future of Welfare Reform." *The Public Interest* 150(winter): 4–21.

Besharov, Douglas J., and Peter Germanis. 2000. "Welfare Reform—Four Years Later." *The Public Interest* 140(summer): 17–35.

Besharov, Douglas J., with Nazanin Samari. 2001. "Child Care after Welfare Reform." In *New World of Welfare,* edited by Rebecca Blank and Ron Haskins. Washington, D.C.: Brookings Institution.

Blank, Rebecca M. 1997. "What Causes Public Assistance Caseloads to Grow?" NBER Working Paper No. 6343. Evanston, Ill.: Institute for Policy Research, Northwestern University.

Blank, Rebecca M., and Ron Haskins, eds. 2001. *The New World of Welfare: An Agenda for Reauthorization and Beyond.* Washington, D.C.: Brookings Institution.

Butler, Stuart, and Anna Kondratas. 1987. *Out of the Poverty Trap: A Conservative Strategy for Welfare Reform.* New York: Free Press.

Chase-Lansdale, P. Lindsay, Robert A. Moffitt, Brenda J. Lohman, Andrew J. Cherlin, Rebekah Levine Coley, Laura D. Pittman, Jennifer Roff, and Elizabeth

Votruba-Drzal. 2003. "Mothers' Transitions from Welfare to Work and the Well-Being of Preschoolers and Adolescents." *Science* 299(March): 1548–52.

Congressional Budget Office. 1993. "Forecasting AFDC Caseloads, with an Emphasis on Economic Factors." CBO Staff Memorandum. Washington: Congressional Budget Office.

Council of Economic Advisors. 1999. "The Effects of Welfare Policy and the Economic Expansion on Welfare Caseloads, An Update." Washington: Executive Office of the President.

Danziger, Sheldon, Colleen M. Heflin, Mary E. Corcoran, Elizabeth Oltmans, and Hui-Chen Wang. 2002. "Does It Pay to Move from Welfare to Work?" *Journal of Policy Analysis and Management* 21(4): 671–92.

DeParle, Jason. 1999. "On a Once Forlorn Avenue, Tax Preparers Now Flourish." *New York Times,* March 21, pp. 1, 20.

———. 2004. *American Dream: Three Women, Ten Kids, and the Nation's Drive to End Welfare.* New York: Viking.

Derus, Michele. 1998. "Making the Bus Means Making a Living on W-2." *Milwaukee Journal Sentinel,* June 28, pp. 1, 12.

Devere, Christine. 2001. "Welfare Reform Research: What Do We Know About Those Who Leave Welfare?" Washington, D.C.: Congressional Research Service.

Duncan, Greg J., and P. Lindsay Chase-Lansdale. 2001. "Welfare Reform and Child Well-Being." In *New World of Welfare,* edited by Rebecca Blank and Ron Haskins. Washington, D.C.: Brookings Institution.

Edelman, Peter. 1997. "The Worst Thing Bill Clinton Has Done." *Atlantic Monthly,* March, pp. 43–58.

Ellwood, David T. 1988. *Poor Support: Poverty in the American Family.* New York: Basic Books.

———. 1999. "The Impact of the Earned Income Tax Credit and Social Policy Reforms On Work, Marriage, and Living Arrangements." Cambridge, Mass.: Harvard University, Kennedy School of Government.

Freedman, Stephen, and Daniel Friedlander. 1995. *The JOBS Evaluation: Early Findings on Program Impacts in Three Sites.* Washington: U.S. Department of Health and Human Services and U.S. Department of Education.

Gais, Thomas L., and R. Kent Weaver. 2002. "State Policy Choices Under Welfare Reform." Policy Brief No. 21. Washington, D.C.: Brookings Institution.

Gais, Thomas L., Richard P. Nathan, Irene Lurie, and Thomas Kaplan. 2001. "Implementation of the Personal Responsibility Act of 1996." In *The New World of Welfare,* edited by Rebecca Blank and Ron Haskins. Washington, D.C.: Brookings Institution.

Garfinkel, Irwin. 1992. *Assuring Child Support: An Extension of Social Security.* New York: Russell Sage Foundation.

Gilens, Martin. 1999. *Why Americans Hate Welfare: Race, Media, and the Politics of Antipoverty Policy.* Chicago: University of Chicago Press.

Grogger, Jeffrey. 2004. "Welfare Transitions in the 1990s: The Economy, Welfare Policy, and the EITC." *Journal of Policy Analysis and Management* 23(4): 671–95.

Hamilton, Gayle, with Stephen Freedman and Sharon M. McGruder. 2000. *National Evaluation of Welfare-to-Work Strategies: Do Mandatory Welfare-to-Work Programs Affect the Well-Being of Children? A Synthesis of Child Research Conducted as Part of the National Evaluation of Welfare-to-Work Strategies.* Washington: U.S. Department of Health and Human Services and U.S. Department of Education.

Haskins, Ron. 2001. "Effects of Welfare Reform on Family Income and Poverty." In *New World of Welfare,* edited by Rebecca Blank and Ron Haskins. Washington, D.C.: Brookings Institution.

Haskins, Ron, and Paul Offner. 2003. "Achieving Compromise on Welfare Reform Reauthorization." Washington, D.C.: Brookings Institution.

Haugen, Steven E., and Earl F. Mellor. 1990. "Estimating the Number of Minimum Wage Workers." *Monthly Labor Review* 113(1): 70–74.

Hill, John, and Jane Waldfogel. 2004. "A 'Third Way' in Welfare Reform? Evidence from the United Kingdom." *Journal of Policy Analysis and Management* 23(4): 765–88.

Himmelfarb, Gertrude. 1984. *The Idea of Poverty: England in the Early Industrial Age.* New York: Alfred A. Knopf.

———. 1991. *Poverty and Compassion: The Moral Imagination of the Late Victorians.* New York: Vintage.

Huang, Chien-Chang, James Kunz, and Irwin Garfinkel. 2002. "The Effect of Child Support on Welfare Exits and Re-Entries." *Journal of Policy Analysis and Management* 21(4): 557–76.

Katz, Michael B. 1986. *In the Shadow of the Poorhouse: A Social History of Welfare in America.* New York: Basic Books.

Knox, Virginia, Cynthia Miller, and Lisa A. Gennetian. 2000. *Reforming Welfare and Rewarding Work: A Summary of the Final Report on the Minnesota Family Investment Program.* New York: Manpower Demonstration Research Corporation.

Loeb, Susanna, and Mary Corcoran. 2001. "Welfare, Work Experience, and Economic Self-Sufficiency," *Journal of Policy Analysis and Management* 20(1): 1–20.

Lødemel, Ivar, and Heather Trickey, eds. 2001. *"An Offer You Can't Refuse": Workfare in International Perspective.* Bristol, U.K.: Policy Press.

Lopoo, Leonard M. 2005. "Maternal Employment and Teenage Childbearing: Evidence from the PSID," *Journal of Policy Analysis and Management* 24(1): 23–46.

Mead, Lawrence M. 1986. *Beyond Entitlement: The Social Obligations of Citizenship.* New York: Free Press.

———. 1992. *The New Politics of Poverty: The Nonworking Poor in America.* New York: Basic Books.

———, ed. 1997. *The New Paternalism: Supervisory Approaches to Poverty.* Washington, D.C.: Brookings Institution.

———. 1999. "The Decline of Welfare in Wisconsin." *Journal of Public Administration Research and Theory* 9(4): 597–622.

———. 2001. "Welfare Reform: Meaning and Effects." *Policy Currents* 11(2): 7–13.

———. 2003. "Welfare Caseload Change: An Alternative Approach." *Policy Studies Journal* 31(2): 165–72.

———. 2004. *Government Matters: Welfare Reform in Wisconsin.* Princeton. N.J.: Princeton University Press.

———. 2005a. "The Reauthorization of TANF: Work and Child Care Provisions." Testimony before the Committee on Education and the Workforce, Subcommittee on 21st Century Competitiveness, U.S. House of Representatives, 109th Cong., 1st sess. (March 15, 2005).

———. 2005b. "Welfare Politics in Congress." Paper presented at the conference of the American Political Science Association. Washington, D.C. (September 4, 2005).

Meyer, Bruce D., and Dan T. Rosenbaum. 2001. "Welfare, the Earned Income Tax Credit, and the Labor Supply of Single Mothers." *Quarterly Journal of Economics* 116(3): 1063–1114.

Millar, Jane. 2003. "The Art of Persuasion? The British New Deal for Lone Parents." In *The Welfare We Want? The British Challenge for American Reform,* edited by Robert Walker and Michael Wiseman. Bristol, U.K.: Policy Press.

Mincy, Ronald B., and Hillard Pouncy. 1997. "Paternalism, Child Support Enforcement, and Fragile Families." In *The New Paternalism,* edited by Lawrence M. Mead. Washington, D.C.: Brookings Institution.

Morone, James A. 2003. "American Ways of Welfare." *Perspectives on Politics* 1(1): 137–46.

Morris, Pamela A., Aletha C. Huston, Greg J. Duncan, Danielle A. Crosby, and Johannes Bos. 2001. *How Welfare and Work Policies Affect Children: A Synthesis of Research.* New York: Manpower Demonstration Research Corporation.

Murray, Charles. 1984. *Losing Ground: American Social Policy, 1950–1980.* New York: Basic Books.

Olasky, Marvin. 1992. *The Tragedy of American Compassion.* Wheaton, Ill.: Crossway Books.

O'Neill, June E., and M. Anne Hill. 2001. "Gaining Ground? Measuring the Impact of Welfare Reform on Welfare and Work." New York: Manhattan Institute, Center for Civic Innovation.

Osborne, David E., and Ted Gaebler. 1992. *Reinventing Government: How the Entrepreneurial Spirit is Transforming the Public Sector.* Reading, Mass.: Addison-Wesley.

Paxson, Christina, and Jane Waldfogel. 2003. "Welfare Reforms, Resources, and Child Maltreatment," *Journal of Policy Analysis and Management* 22(1): 85–113.

Primus, Wendell, Lynette Rawlings, Kathy Larin, and Kathryn Porter. 1999. "The Initial Impacts of Welfare Reform on the Incomes of Single-Mother Families." Washington, D.C.: Center on Budget and Policy Priorities.

Riccio, James, Daniel Friedlander, and Stephen Freedman. 1994. *GAIN: Benefits, Costs, and Three-Year Impacts of a Welfare-to-Work Program.* New York: Manpower Demonstration Research Corporation.

Sawhill, Isabel V. 2002. "The Perils of Early Motherhood." *The Public Interest* 146(winter): 74–84.

Schwartz, Joel. 2000. *Fighting Poverty With Virtue: Moral Reform and America's Urban Poor, 1825–2000.* Bloomington: Indiana University Press.

Sherman, Amy L. 2000. "The Lessons of W-2." *The Public Interest* 140(summer): 36–48.

Teles, Steven M. 1996. *Whose Welfare? AFDC and Elite Politics.* Lawrence: University Press of Kansas.

Thornton, Arland. 1995. "Attitudes, Values, and Norms Related to Nonmarital Fertility." In *Report to Congress on Out-of-Wedlock Childbearing.* Washington: U.S. Department of Health and Human Services.

Trickey, Heather, and Robert Walker. 2001. "Steps to Compulsion within British Labour Market Policies." In *"An Offer You Can't Refuse": Workfare in International Perspective,* edited by Lødemel and Trickey. Bristol, U.K.: Policy Press.

U.S. Census Bureau. 1994. *Current Population Survey for March 1994*. Washington: U.S. Government Printing Office.

———. 2000. *Current Population Survey for March 2000*. Washington: U.S. Government Printing Office.

———. 2004a. *Annual Demographic Survey for March 2004*. Washington: U.S. Government Printing Office.

———. 2004b. *Income, Poverty, and Health Insurance Coverage in the United States: 2003*, Series P-60, No. 226. Washington: U.S. Government Printing Office.

U.S. Congress, House [Ways and Means]. 1998. *Green Book: Background Material, and Data on Programs Within the Jurisdiction of the Committee on Ways and Means*. Washington: U.S. Government Printing Office.

———. 2000. *Green Book: Background Material, and Data on Programs Within the Jurisdiction of the Committee on Ways and Means*. Washington: U.S. Government Printing Office.

———. 2004. *Green Book: Background Material, and Data on Programs Within the Jurisdiction of the Committee on Ways and Means*. Washington: U.S. Government Printing Office.

Walker, Robert, and Michael Wiseman, eds. 2003. *The Welfare We Want? The British Challenge for American Reform*. Bristol, U.K.: Policy Press.

Weaver, R. Kent. 2000. *Ending Welfare as We Know It*. Washington, D.C.: Brookings Institution.

Zedlewski, Sheila R., and Donald W. Alderson. 2001. "Before and After Reform: How Have Families Changed?" Washington, D.C.: Urban Institute.

Ziliak, James P., David N. Figlio, Elizabeth E. Davis, and Laura S. Connolly. 1997. "Accounting for the Decline in AFDC Caseloads: Welfare Reform or Economic Growth." Madison: Institute for Research on Poverty, University of Wisconsin.

Chapter 2

Another Way Forward: Welfare, Social Reproduction, and a Basic Income

CAROLE PATEMAN

Workfare has nothing to do with economics. It is about citizenship, and whether able-bodied adults who do not earn anything actively can be regarded as full citizens.
—Judith Shklar, *American Citizenship* (1991, 98)

Like capital, an individual moves faster when unencumbered.
—Teresa Brennan, *Globalization and Its Terrors* (2003, 87)

IN THE United States, as many commentators have noted, welfare had an extremely narrow meaning. In the 1980s and 1990s it came to refer not merely to residual, means-tested programs but to one such program in particular, Aid to Families with Dependent Children (AFDC), which provided benefits to single mothers with children. Welfare is separated from social insurance, which in other countries is treated as part of welfare, and divorced from other claims on the public purse that provide assistance to private individuals, whether tax allowances for mortgages or subsidies to private business. The Personal Responsibility and Work Opportunity Reconciliation Act of 1996 (PRWORA) abolished AFDC and replaced it with Temporary Assistance for Needy Families (TANF).

"Welfare" was replaced by workfare.[1] Recipients of assistance are now expected to find employment and time limits have been set on how long they can receive benefits.[2] It was generally agreed that the 1996 legislation was necessary to resolve a crisis about "welfare." Although preceded by attempts to introduce workfare, notably the Family Support Act of 1988, TANF marked a historic shift. Until 1996, "welfare" had provided support for single mothers to care for children at home, but workfare implies that all able-bodied adults should be in the labor force, even mothers with small children. The implication of the legislation is thus that universal employment is now required.

The United States is not alone in introducing workfare—for example, Britain has taken a similar course—but is unusual in the focus on single mothers (for some details of British policy see, for example, chapter 4; King 1999, 246–55).[3] More generally, the United States stands apart from other rich countries in the extent of reliance on the labor market and other private sources to provide for the welfare of citizens. Employment is important in all welfare systems in the sense that wages are subject to a special tax, misleadingly seen as insurance, to help fund programs, but social insurance in the United States is remarkably limited compared to Western European countries. Older citizens enjoy Social Security (retirement pensions) and Medicare (medical insurance)—two very popular programs, unlike "welfare"—but there is no national health insurance even for children, and about 44 million people are currently uninsured. Medical insurance is largely provided through employment, with availability and coverage depending on employers' discretion. Most comparable countries also provide parents with assistance with the cost of child rearing, but the United States lacks a universal child endowment.

A crucial question in understanding and discussing any reform is the reason why it was implemented. PRWORA was designed to solve a problem about "welfare" that arose, it was argued, because too many citizens (in this case, single mothers) had been reduced to dependency by receiving their subsistence from welfare rather than from employment. The attributes of a citizen and the respect due to citizens can be gained, it was claimed, only through employment. Supporters of workfare also assume that employment is the social contribution owed by citizens.

At one level of my argument I discuss a number of issues about single mothers. Feminist scholars have criticized claims about dependency, the neglect of motherhood and women's caring work as a contribution to citizenship, and the identification of employment with "work." Part of my discussion will be along similar lines. These criticisms, however, depend on the deeper level of my argument: that the connection between employment and democratic citizenship, taken for granted by supporters of workfare, can be questioned and that, rather than solving anything, PRWORA exacerbates a major problem about social reproduction that has been growing since the late 1970s.

Social reproduction refers to a great deal more than motherhood, although motherhood is central to political life and public policy, whether or not this is explicitly acknowledged. It is about welfare in a very broad sense, about the maintenance and future of the public or common weal and the care of citizens. New generations must be produced and reared if a society is to reproduce itself, so women have to have babies, but if a society is not merely to continue but to flourish, and flourish as a democracy, social reproduction extends far beyond parenting. Each new generation has to be kept healthy, educated in appropriate ways, and exposed to cultural life. Just as important, however, existing generations, which include the parents of the new generation, must also be cared for: their welfare and development is critical to a flourishing society and democracy. Social reproduction is not something that can be undertaken by mothers or fathers alone, or through purely individual endeavors, but requires public provision. To be concerned with democratization, that is, with the creation of a more democratic society in which citizenship is of equal worth to all so that every citizen enjoys full standing, necessarily involves an interest in welfare and the requirements for social reproduction.

The controversy over "welfare" and PRWORA has focused on only one group of citizens, single mothers, and the narrow meaning of "welfare" diverts attention from the implications of current public policy for social reproduction. Democratic social reproduction requires public resources if time is to be available for parenting, if citizens are to be educated and cared for, if they are to develop and take part in social and political life and enjoy a dignified old age, and if the welfare of all citizens is to be treated as of equal worth. The problem is that social reproduction has been undercut by the direction of public policy for the past quarter century. Workfare and universal employment not only diminish the time available to citizens to be parents, but more generally, domestic and international economic policy emphasizes the market and privatization. Allocating public resources to the task of social reproduction, to the welfare and care of citizens, runs counter to the demands of prevailing (global) neo-liberal ideology and economic doctrines (Brennan 2003).

Another way of formulating this level of the problem, following but adapting T. H. Marshall, is that it is a contemporary manifestation of the conflict between two different logics—democracy and the Poor Law. Since the 1970s the balance of the conflict between the two logics has shifted toward the Poor Law. In his famous essay "Citizenship and Social Class," Marshall stated that in the twentieth century "citizenship and the capitalist system have been at war" (1963, 87). The conflict existed because citizenship, or more specifically what Marshall called social rights—all that is necessary "to share to the full in the social heritage and to live the life of a civilized being according to the standards prevailing in the society"—placed limits upon and regulated the market, and placed some goods outside of it altogether (1963, 74).[4] My argument is narrower: it is not about capitalism or the market but one market, the labor market. Lawrence Mead noted in 1992 that in the contemporary United States "the equivalent [of the

Poor Law] would be to abolish AFDC or transform it into workfare" (255).[5] That has been achieved through TANF.

The logic of the Poor Law is part of the making and expansion of labor markets and the creation of the institution of employment. Able-bodied poor adults unwilling to participate in this institution are designated as undeserving and then receive public assistance only in exchange for employment (workfare). But to deem an individual as undeserving and so open to the coercion of workfare is to mark her out as lacking certain capacities and thus she is unlikely to be accorded the respect due to a fellow citizen.[6]

The logic of democracy is universalist and part of the making of citizenship. Citizenship is not necessarily democratic. Historically it has been a privilege reserved for only part of the population (the males, the propertied, those with white skins). When citizenship ceases to be a privilege and becomes universal, a matter of rights, it becomes democratic and in most countries today one universal element, the suffrage, is present.[7] Democracy is commonly given a minimal meaning as the institutional infrastructure required for free and fair elections. Universal suffrage is necessary but is set apart from other rights, especially those involved in the welfare of citizens. A more robust interpretation, which I follow here, takes universal suffrage, an entitlement of citizens, as the model for other rights necessary for democratic social reproduction and full citizenship.

I also offer an alternative policy and challenge some claims about workfare, free riding, and reciprocity. To solve the problem of social reproduction and the welfare of citizens it is necessary to move back to the universalism of democracy. I argue that an unconditional basic income for all citizens is a step in this direction.

TANF, Employment, and Citizenship

The two "attributes of an American citizen," Judith Shklar states, are "voting and earning" (Shklar 1991, 3). The connection between voting and being a citizen is fairly straightforward, but it is not so obvious why earning, being employed, is so closely connected with citizenship. To be sure, there are some general ideas, notably individual freedom and equality, that are necessary to both labor markets and democracies, and historically the establishment of civil and political rights (for white males at least) and the consolidation of employment have been associated. But the interpretation and deployment of these ideas and rights has been very different in the case of citizenship from that of employment.

The premise that individuals are "born free and equal" lies at the heart of arguments for democracy, and such individuals are necessarily self-governing; if self-government is to be maintained they must become citizens with rights. The right to vote, and other associated civil and political rights required for free and fair elections, upholds and expresses collective self-government. The influential minimalist view of democracy stops at that point and treats the citizen as another face of the consumer, spending votes rather than dollars.[8] However, although participation in the market depends on dollars, standing as a democratic citizen is not determined by an individual's income, wealth, or other particular attributes. Consumers look only to their own advantage or interest, but citizens often do more than this and are concerned with justice, equality or the public good. Martin Gilens, for example, argues that empirical data shows that when American citizens think about welfare they ask which policy is best overall and not just for themselves (Gilens 1999).

The minimalist view sees democracy in terms of the suffrage and collective self-government, but an alternative conception looks further to individual self-government (individual freedom or autonomy). To participate fully as citizens—that is, to participate in social and political life beyond periodically casting a ballot—individuals need a certain level of resources. Poor material circumstances can also lead to denial of respect by fellow citizens. To maintain and enjoy individual autonomy requires that individuals interact with one another within authority structures that enhance rather than diminish their self-government (see also Pateman 1970, 2002). But in contemporary democracy the scope of citizens' autonomy is circumscribed and confined to a narrowly conceived political arena. A sharp line has been drawn between government and the undemocratic structure of authority in workplaces.

Proponents of "welfare" reform see employment as the key to citizenship but ignore lack of democracy in the workplace. Yet employment was once regarded with suspicion in the United States because it was seen as antithetical to self-government and therefore as a threat to free citizenship. In the past, in both political theory and practice, categories of the population deemed dependent and subordinate (such as wives) were excluded from citizenship. For a time in the United States, during the nineteenth century, the employed were seen as dependent (see Shklar 1991, chap. 2; Sandel 1996, chap. 6). Workers were instructed what to do by a boss, depended on the wages he paid, and could lose their jobs at will if their employer no longer wanted them. They lacked the independence demanded of citizens. More recently, political theorists of starkly different political persuasions, such as Friedrich Von Hayek and G. D. H. Cole, have seen the employed as undermining freedom because they are trained in subordination and so do not develop the characters required of free citizens. The employed, Hayek wrote, are "in many respects . . . alien and often inimical to much that constitutes the driving force of a free society" (1960, 119).

Virtually nothing remains today (despite the vogue for Hayek's theories in the 1980s and 1990s) of the suspicion of employment. On the contrary, advocates of "welfare" reform see employment as the mark of independence and necessary for full citizenship. Mead, for example, has argued in the name of citizenship that nonworkers (that is, employable individuals who are neither employed or seeking employment) in receipt of "welfare" must be compelled to find employment, even if the wages are very low: "Low-wage work apparently must be mandated, just as a draft has sometimes been necessary to staff the military. Authority achieves compliance more efficiently than benefits, at least from society's viewpoint" (1986, 84).

The argument that employment, even coerced employment, is necessary for citizenship is not as convincing as proponents suggest. I have not, for example, come across any discussion of why and how participation, including coerced participation, in an undemocratic workplace creates the qualities needed for democratic citizenship. Joel Schwartz argues that, in the same spirit as nineteenth-century moral reformers, PRWORA promotes virtue and good behavior. Such virtues as thrift, frugality, punctuality, civility, or reliability may be required for employment, but further argument is needed to show that precisely the same set of virtues are central to democratic citizenship (see chapter 10).[9]

The identification of independence with employment reflects adherence to the logic of the Poor Law rather than a demonstration of how self-government is promoted in workplaces. The British Poor Law was about the making of a national labor market, not about democratic citizenship. The major concern of the *Poor Law Report* of 1834, with its conception of the deserving and undeserving poor and doctrine of less eligibility, was the problem of the able-bodied male head of a household who received outdoor relief (Dean 1991, chapter 9). The report declared that "the great source of abuse is the outdoor relief afforded to the able-bodied on their own account, or on that of their families" (cited in Dean 1991, 159). These men were undeserving because they were potentially independent. Their condition, as the *Poor Law Report* stated, had been brought about by their own failings: it "originated in indolence, improvidence, or vice, and might have been averted by ordinary care and industry" (cited in King 1999, 228).

The solution was to put able-bodied men to work—just as Locke had recommended in 1697, declaring that "the true and proper relief of the poor . . . consists in finding work for them, and taking care they do not live like drones upon the labour of others" (1697/1997, 189). Men able to enter the labor market and earn a wage, even if not enough to raise them above poverty, must be compelled to do so. The "incentive" to enter employment was that relief would be given only under the less eligible conditions of the workhouse, so that employment would always be seen as the preferable alternative. Relief was, therefore, reserved for the deserving indigent individual (a pauper) who was "a person unable to labour, or unable to obtain, in return for labour, the means of subsistence" (cited in Dean 1991, 176).[10]

The marginal status of the "dependents" who entered the workhouse was underlined by depriving them of the standing of full citizens. Until 1918 in Britain, the condition of receiving relief in workhouses was forfeiture of political rights. The Poor Law, the abolition of outdoor relief, and loss of citizenship rights were carried to the United States: "as late as 1934, fourteen states' constitutions removed relief recipients' right to vote or hold public office" (King 1999, 266).

The Poor Law was about men, who were assumed to be heads of families. By the 1840s in Britain the idea that wives, properly, were their husbands' economic dependents had gained a firm foothold, and employment for the male breadwinner was established as the only respectable way for all those outside the aristocratic or pauper classes to find a livelihood. Widows were seen as deserving and were assisted, and it appears that women with children were viewed more generously than men. The implication of the Poor Law for single mothers is less clear, but they constituted only around 5 percent of the pauper population (Dean 1991, 167–71). PRWORA, in an historic shift, brought women (single mothers) within the logic of the Poor Law. Single mothers were the only remaining major category of able-bodied adults explicitly exempt from participation in the labor market. Some married women still remain outside the paid labor force but most wives were employed by 1996, and the social expectation that wives should remain at home has lost most of its force (I shall return to these points). The implication of arguments about employment and citizenship is that all able-bodied adults should be employed. Receipt of "welfare" no longer entails being stripped of rights in a formal sense, but workfare involves diminution of freedom and standing; recipients are deemed undeserving, seen as free riders who are legitimately open to coercion, and conditions are imposed on their citizenship.

Supporters of TANF would respond that this is the wrong way to look at the reform. Employment is central to citizenship for two reasons. First, when they leave welfare for employment former recipients cease to be dependent and thus become more free, not less; even if they are still below the poverty line they become independent. Second, they also appear more deserving to other citizens because they have ceased to be free riders (getting something for nothing).

The first part of this response relies on the peculiar meaning of dependence in the debates about "welfare"and the fact that only one category of beneficiaries of the public purse have been labeled as dependents. Dependence is a social relationship—and more often than not a euphemism for a relationship of superiority and subordination—but in the controversies in the 1980s and 1990s "dependence" referred not to a social relationship but to characteristics of individuals.[11] In the tradition of the Poor Law, the need for "welfare" is held to be the consequence of individual flaws of character. The assumption underlying TANF is that the individual attributes signifying dependence are present if a citizen is reluctant to seek work, that is, employment. The reluctance is treated as a form of individual pathology, yet there are a variety of reasons why someone may wish not to enter employment. Nonwork stemming from problems such as drug abuse or individual incapacity,[12] is very different from a refusal to accept a job with below poverty wages or poor conditions, or a desire to be a full-time mother to a small child.

It is not obvious that single mothers caring for their children are dependent merely because they gain their subsistence from public provision. They may remain on the rolls (many cycle on and off) not because of the small payment but from "the lack of anything else (such as education, training in high-tech skills, or child care)." Their confidence, too, can be eroded by the general hostility toward recipients combined with the conditions under which "welfare" is given, including "endless waiting, unhelpful and even exploitative caseworkers who refuse to provide advice or guidance, and the contempt that many in social services barely hide for their 'clients' " (Hirschmann 2003, 153).[13] Single mothers on "welfare" can be seen as endeavoring to be independent, or as independent as a small benefit would allow. "Welfare" offers women freedom from dependence on men's wages, and enables them, if necessary, to leave an abusive or unsatisfactory relationship with a man.

PRWORA contains provisions to encourage marriage, but the assumption that marriage encourages independence can be questioned; another view is that this provision reflects unease about too much independence for women. Women usually earn less than men, and since the earnings of husbands tend to be seen as the primary earnings, wives are still perceived as partially dependent. Marriage can actually add to women's burdens because it is far from guaranteed that husbands will contribute their fair share of daily caring work.[14] "Welfare" reform is also seen as a means of decreasing the incidence of births to women on their own. Murray, for example, states that the "main reason for scrapping welfare is to reduce the number of babies born to single mothers" (Murray 1994, 29). However, evidence from experiments in the 1990s is inconclusive about the effects of welfare reform on the birth rate. Rates of births out of wedlock began to decline in the 1990s, but this began before PRWORA, and the contribution, if any, of the legislation to the decline is unclear.[15]

Motherhood, whether single or married, illustrates graphically that dependence is an inescapable feature of human relationships. All infants depend completely on mothers and other adults, we all become dependent on others during serious illness, and many adults become dependent to a greater or lesser extent in their old age. Husbands still largely depend on their wives to take care of their daily needs and their children so that they can appear, ready for the day, at the workplace door. We all rely on the complex webs of interdependence or reciprocity that constitute social life.

This interdependence is reflected in the arguments of the early modern theorists of an original contract who make mutual aid and forbearance, which is the web of social life, the primary law of nature.

This brings me to the second reason why supporters of "welfare" reform see employment as central to citizenship. The assumption is that "welfare" creates a category of citizens who weaken the web of interdependence and undermine reciprocity (I will return to reciprocity). Citizens who are not employed are free riders; they are nonworkers who fail to do their duty and make the necessary social contribution. Mead argues that if these citizens are to do their social duty "they must be made *less* free in certain senses rather than more" (1986, 4).

Like the language of dependence, the language of nonwork is also odd. To put single mothers into the category of nonworkers is possible only because "work" has become identified with employment. This narrow meaning of work was reinforced by the structure of the Social Security system set up in 1935 and the reforms in Britain in the 1940s. "Going out to work," that is, engaging in paid employment, was what counted for citizenship. Single mothers and other able-bodied individuals outside of the labor force can thus be seen as avoiding the duties of citizens—because they are not employed.[16]

But this raises a very basic question: what counts, or should count, as a contribution of a citizen or toward standing as a citizen? This is not an easy question to answer, as T. H. Marshall's discussion reveals. He notes that the requirement to give "such service as one can to promote the welfare of the community" is vague (1963, 123).[17] Moreover, it is not clear in which direction, so to speak, one should begin to look to give it more content.

Citizenship as a formal political status is a vertical relationship between an individual and the state. Thus Marshall noted that two specific duties were the performance of military service and payment of taxes.[18] Similarly, in a list of social obligations, Mead includes law-abidingness (1986, 243; and see William Galston's comments on required performance and obeying the law, chapter 5, this volume). With the introduction of TANF, the state mandates that in return for subsistence a certain duty must be performed. But citizenship can also be seen as a horizontal relationship between citizens; that is to say, it becomes part of the social web of interdependence. This view makes it much harder to distinguish activities that fulfill specific duties of citizens from those that contribute to general social well-being, to democratic social reproduction (see Pateman 1985). Much of the discussion of "welfare" suggests that the dereliction involved in dependency is failure to perform a duty owed to fellow citizens. Universal employment seems to fit more easily into the horizontal view; are not individuals outside of the labor force, it can be asked, "harming others by failing to fulfill their obligations to their fellow citizens?" (Gutmann and Thompson 1996, 278). Marshall concluded that the only clear general duty of citizens is the duty to work, that is, to be employed (he confined this duty to male breadwinners).

But why should employment be given special status as the contribution of citizens? The institution of employment is one way of organizing the production of goods and services required for the welfare of citizens, and in that sense to be in paid employment is to make a social contribution. However, the institution of employment lies at the center of the capitalist system of production, a form of undemocratic organization that has as its aim not a social contribution but private profit. As Schumpeter clearly saw, if a social function was performed, if a social contribution was made, that was merely a happy by-product of profit-seeking. In his comparison of economic competition and the electoral competition for political office he wrote that "the social function [of the latter] is fulfilled, as it were, incidentally—in the same sense as production is incidental to the making of profits" (Schumpeter 1943, 282). The connection of employment to citizenship is at best indirect.

A more direct argument is that employment is the basis of social respect and thus equal standing. Citizens have a duty to participate and thus a duty "to develop their capacities to do so. One of these capacities is the acquisition of the social respect that work [that is, employment] brings" (Gutmann and Thompson 1996, 203).[19] But, again, capacities developed through employment are fostered within an undemocratic structure. How then do they contribute to democratic citizenship? Moreover, this argument begs the question of why employment should be so crucial for social respect. Why should other contributions not bring respect?

There are many ways of contributing to social life and duties other than employment are involved in the network of mutual aid and forbearance. The reproduction, education, and care of the population—social reproduction—is a basic social necessity and crucial for citizenship. Citizens, young and old, must be cared for, their welfare must be addressed, and thus there is much work to be done in addition to the work central to the Poor Law. Many aspects of the welfare state in the European sense can be seen as a public solution to the problem of caring for citizens. Yet public provision has always rested heavily on the private, unpaid welfare provided by wives, mothers and daughters. Much of the work of care has been seen as women's work—husbands, and men in general, typically are free riders in these tasks.

Universal employment and cuts in public provision have created a major problem of democratic social reproduction. From the Poor Law until the 1970s the problem was not so urgent. Wives were available for the much of the caring work and the development of Western welfare states, as Marshall emphasizes, shifted the political balance away from the Poor Law toward citizenship. Today, economic policies of structural adjustment and privatization have swung the balance back again to the Poor Law and most women, including mothers, are now in the paid workforce.[20] TANF both reflects this new context and exacerbates it, and symbolizes the distance from earlier arrangements.

International trade and the extraction of resources by imperial powers from around the globe existed, of course, at the time of the Poor Law, but the scope and rapidity of expansion, extraction and production has increased and now includes the construction of (integrated) labor markets around the world (that is, global "work"). The problem is that reproducing and providing for the welfare of the population cannot be speeded up in the same way. Social reproduction requires time and human and other resources. Yet "welfare" reform demands that all able-bodied adults be employed at the same time that public provision is reduced. The costs of, and time needed for, the replenishment, education and care of the population have become a drag on profit-making in the new economic order: "Time spent on human reproduction is time spent away from the speedy pursuit of profit across space" (Brennan 2003).[21]

Motherhood and Welfare

The recent controversies over "welfare" give little indication that marriage, motherhood and fatherhood have been at the heart of the development of welfare. The standard view, which goes back at least to Hegel, is that the major aim of public provision is to remedy damage to male workers from the operation of the labor market. Assistance is given to those who cannot find employment, who are sick, injured or retired. Welfare rescues workers from poverty and so from becoming "undeserved exile[s] from society" (Moon 1988, 29). From the time of the Poor Law, however, the wage was much more than a payment to an individual that enabled him to continue to participate in the institution of employment. It was a family wage that in principle (the practice was often very different) was sufficient to enable a man, as a husband and father, to maintain his wife and children without his wife entering paid employment.

"The laws of marriage," Nancy Cott has written, "sculpt the body politic" (2000, 5).[22] For most of the twentieth century, the institutions of marriage, employment, and citizenship were firmly locked together. Married women's political standing was still shaped by coverture,[23] by their private status as wives and their tasks as mothers. As wives, they had a legal entitlement to support from their husbands and so most, it was assumed, would not "work." But, as feminist scholars pointed out from the 1970s onward, this was connected to lesser citizenship. In the Social Security Act (1935), wives were treated primarily as the economic dependents of their husbands whose tasks were to be fulfilled—unpaid—at home. Male breadwinners made a contribution through their wages to social insurance, and were, therefore, full citizens entitled to benefits. Their wives typically received benefits as the dependents of citizens, not as citizens in their own right.[24]

European countries, too, usually structured social insurance systems around the male breadwinner, but the United States stood apart in having no national measure to support child-rearing. Europe and the Antipodes established universal support for children, and in Britain and Australia the allowance was paid directly to the mother, who was much more likely than her husband to spend it on the children. Debate over these measures did not pass entirely unnoticed in the United States, but child endowment was never on the political agenda.[25]

On the one hand, the lesser citizenship of married women was part of the structure of social insurance. On the other hand, the earlier arrangements looked to social reproduction in the assumption that wives would not be employed but would bear and rear children. There was thus at least an implicit recognition that mothers were performing significant work, albeit that it was not seen as a relevant contribution for social insurance. This was made explicit by William Beveridge in his report, which laid the foundation for the major reforms in Britain in the 1940s. He wrote that "the great majority of married women must be regarded as occupied on work which is vital though unpaid, without which their husbands could not do their paid work, and without which the nation could not continue." Husband and wife are "a team, each of whose partners is equally essential." In particular, mothers "have vital work to do in ensuring the adequate continuance of the British race and of British ideals in the world" (1942, §107, §117).

As Christopher Beem emphasizes, the conceptual framework was then still available through which mothers could be seen as making a civic contribution. He calls this framework republican motherhood, but the label is misleading. Feminist historians have devised the term to refer to the eighteenth-century argument that women's task was to bear and rear the next generation of citizens even though women were at the same time regarded as naturally unfit for, and so excluded from, citizenship. By the 1940s, husbands and wives may, for Beveridge, have been a team in which both members were doing important work, but only the husband's employment was the work that counted as part of full citizenship. In contrast, the feminist argument, as Beem notes, was that women should be included as full citizens and that motherhood should count as contributing to, or even as part of, their citizenship.[26] One aspect of the current problem of social reproduction (on which I shall comment shortly) is that women have won all the formal rights of citizens but motherhood in the United States is seen as a private undertaking.

Some of the earliest welfare measures in both Europe and the United States were concerned with motherhood. In 1883, for example, Germany introduced very modest and optional benefits for maternity leave, and maternity benefits were introduced in Britain 1911, in Italy in 1910, and in France and the Netherlands in 1913. In the United States there was concern about single mothers from the 1880s; public support began early in the twentieth century and was reasonably popular until the 1960s.

The first Mothers' Aid legislation to assist women raising young children on their own was passed in 1911, and by 1920 forty states had enacted similar measures (see Gordon 1994, chaps. 3 and 4; Skocpol 1992, chaps. 6, 8, and 9). The recipients of mothers' pensions were not, significantly, the welfare mothers who came to haunt the popular political imagination of the late twentieth century. They were predominantly widows (80 percent of recipients by 1931); only fifty-five unmarried mothers were granted pensions nationwide. The great majority was white: only 3 percent of recipients were African American and only 1 percent members of other minority groups (Skocpol 1992, 471; Nelson 1990, 139). Funding for the program was never adequate, many mothers were not assisted, and the payments were meager (see Gordon 1994, 189).[27] Single mothers who received aid were therefore likely to be in paid employment: a study in 1923 of urban areas found that over half were employed and that their children were more likely than those of other mothers to be in the labor force (Skocpol 1992, 476; Nelson 1990, 142).

The white widow left alone with her children to struggle to manage was seen as eminently deserving. Indeed, the women's organizations that had campaigned for mothers' pensions supported tests of moral fitness, which were common for other programs at the time, and mothers were monitored to ensure that they maintained eligibility. Thus the mothers' pension programs were much closer to charitable poor relief (though many charities had opposed them) and to the spirit of the Poor Law than to the workers' compensation schemes established in forty-two states by 1920.[28]

The Mothers' Aid model was brought to Washington and into the Social Security Act in the form of Aid to Dependent Children (ADC) through a network of women activists who worked largely through the Children's Bureau, set up in 1912 and staffed by women, which drafted the proposal for ADC (see Gordon 1994, chaps. 6, 9, and 10; Skocpol 1992, chap. 9; and Michel 1993). They brought with them the social work perspective, moralistic criteria and monitoring practices of the state programs. ADC was thus set apart from the social insurance side of the 1935 legislation, foreshadowed by the workers' compensation schemes. From the beginning, ADC resembled "welfare."

Southern politicians determined to maintain very low wages for their workforce opposed the 1935 legislation in Congress. Agricultural, domestic, educational and hospital workers were not covered, thus excluding most black, Latino, and women workers, and vagrancy laws were also used to compel black individuals into employment. Under ADC, like mothers' pension programs, African American and other minority women were largely excluded from assistance, and nonwhite women were considered "employable mothers" (see Kerber 1998).[29] Moreover, the work of single mothers caring for their young children was already being devalued as a contribution of citizens; "mothers' monthly entitlement was only half that of other categorical recipients of public assistance" (Mink 1990, 112).

ADC was relabeled as AFDC in 1962, but by then the popularity of the program had begun its rapid decline (Teles 1996, 43–45).[30] From the end of the 1970s, government support for many forms of public provision declined as neo-liberalism ascended politically.[31] The public, however, were more discriminating, and though not as supportive of welfare as Europeans, are by no means opposed to it. Americans "not only support most of the welfare-state programs that currently exist, but they also think that in most areas the government is not doing enough to help its citizens" (Gilens 1999, 27; see also Teles 1996, chap. 3). Public hostility was focused on "welfare," on AFDC and single mothers. Other programs for the poor, such as Food Stamps and Medicaid, did not suffer the same level of opprobrium and Social Security remained extremely popular.

A number of factors contributed to the opposition to AFDC. By the 1970s the number of beneficiaries of the program had greatly expanded and their composition had changed. From 1939 many (white) widows were included under the survivors provisions of Social Security, and the remaining mothers were the most impoverished—"divorced, or not married, or widows of men without histories of wage earning in occupations covered by social insurance" (Skocpol 1992, 536).[32] Many more mothers from minority sections of the population were receiving AFDC by the 1960s. The increase in nonwhite beneficiaries was important for two reasons. First, Gilens's evidence shows that many white Americans overestimate by a wide margin the percentage of African Americans both in the population and among "welfare" recipients. Second, the hostility to "welfare" arose from the perception of moral failure on the part of the mothers in AFDC. "Welfare" recipients are seen as unwilling to help themselves, and, above all, to be unwilling to seek employment; blacks, in particular, are perceived as lazy. Thus welfare mothers became emblematic of the undeserving poor.[33]

The other major element in the rise of antagonism toward welfare was the change in the position of women (see also chapter 7). The proportion of married women in the paid labor force increased rapidly, especially from the 1960s: 70 percent of households in 1940 had only one breadwinner; by 1980, 28 percent did (Orloff 2001, 150). Some wives have always, due to economic necessity, had to be employed, but changing conceptions of masculinity and femininity meant that "going out to work" became respectable. Women were also able to gain educational qualifications, and many were keen to enter the paid labor force at a time when the rise of service industries had increased the availability of women's employment. More recent structural economic change has taken a different, global form; old economy jobs for male breadwinners are being swept away, and the new jobs are often casual or with no benefits and low wages, even as the spread of downsizing and economic insecurity mean that for many families there is now little choice whether both spouses will be in the labor force.

By 1996 the situation of single mothers who received "welfare" to look after their children full-time at home was thus at odds with that of most other mothers, who were in the paid work force. This, Orloff argues, explains why there was little opposition to PRWORA among women's organizations (2001, 151–53). Welfare reform made the circumstances of all mothers more similar. As Mead reports in chapter 8, the result of the introduction of TANF was that the numbers of recipients of welfare dropped by 62 percent from 1994 to 2001, and many more single mothers are now employed.

In addition, by 1996, thanks to the success of the women's movement in bringing about legal reforms, coverture had finally ended (that is, wives were no longer official economic dependents of their husbands), women had achieved formal civil and political equality, and discrimination was squarely on the public agenda. But in the individualistic political culture of the United States, in contrast to other Western countries, such equality is widely seen as incompatible with support for women as mothers. Maternity leave (which depends primarily on arrangements of employers), for example, had to be treated as a disability, like a man's loss of an arm in a piece of machinery, to rescue it from legal rejection as special treatment for a privileged group. The result is that mothers in the United States are employed "with less public support, such as child allowances, child care, or paid leaves, than . . . their counterparts in other parts of the West" (Orloff 2001, 152). In short, motherhood and child rearing are seen as purely private matters that women themselves must find the time and resources to undertake.

Time is also in short supply. As Juliet Schor pointed out over a decade ago, Americans work longer hours than their counterparts in other rich countries (1991), they take fewer and shorter holidays, and have fewer public holidays. Women adopt familiar strategies to make time; notably, they are more likely to be employed part-time than men so that they can also shoulder their unpaid work of care. But this pattern of employment, the fact that women earn less than men, and the persistence of men's and women's jobs, have perpetuated the moral hazard of men avoiding their fair share of the work of care. Increasingly, mothers who can afford to do so employ women from poor countries to care for their children, who, in turn, often leave their own children with relatives—so adding to the global problem of care. On the other hand, because TANF includes funds for child care, former welfare mothers are able to avoid some of these problems.

The assumption in the United States today is that mothers (parents) need little public provision to care for children. The implications for social reproduction, especially when combined with universal employment, tend to be avoided. The two At-Home Infant Care programs that Christopher Beem discusses in chapter 7 are one attempt to mitigate the problems being generated. Beem suggests that these programs might provide a model for a universal policy of paid parental leave for low-income families. Such a move away from the logic of the Poor Law to the logic of democracy is to be welcomed, but would leave untouched the wider problem of social reproduction. One difficulty is that only mothers who are in paid employment are eligible for the Infant Care programs, and Beem proposes to retain this feature if the programs were extended. But this is to cling to the logic of the Poor Law and to the principle that benefits should be given to the able-bodied only in exchange for employment. The figure of the undeserving (poor) citizen thus still looms large in the background.

Another difficulty is that social reproduction, the task of providing for the welfare and care of citizens, is much broader than the work of mothers or fathers, but in Beem's discussion, as in many feminist arguments about care, the wider public problem disappears. This disappearance makes it all the more easy to overlook that the preoccupation with employment is part of the problem of social reproduction in all its dimensions. Caring for citizens takes second place to employment and the logic of the Poor Law. The time and resources required for social reproduction are being sacrificed to the demands of global labor markets and capitalism.

The alternative is to move away completely from the logic of the Poor Law to the logic of democracy. A basic income for all citizens—which would open up time and resources to citizens and help put social reproduction at the forefront of debate—would be a crucial step in this direction.

A Basic Income and Reciprocity

In *Citizenship and Social Class,* T. H. Marshall saw the British legislation of the 1940s as abolishing the Poor Law and the Poor Law mentality. Marshall wrote that the "significance of [the] final removal" of the disenfranchisement of those receiving relief "has, perhaps, not been fully appreciated" (1963, 83). His words are still apt. The provision of benefits without loss of rights is a major step forward in the process of democratization. Citizenship ceases to be conditional, a privilege, and the maintenance of a minimum standard of living through public provision becomes a universal right or entitlement. Marshall writes of a "universal right to real income which is not proportionate to the market value of the claimant" (100).[34] In other words, welfare becomes part of citizenship; the care of citizens is part of public policy.

But Marshall was too optimistic. The Poor Law mentality has persisted, and over the past quarter century has gained new influence at the expense of the universalist logic of democracy. The proponents of workfare argue that full citizenship is conditional on employment, and that respect depends on that particular contribution. In the United States universalism has received much less support than in some European countries and has generally been outweighed by the Poor Law mentality and a minimalist view of democracy. Nonetheless, it animated Social Security (though this is sometimes seen as a reward for life-time employment), and in the 1960s Charles Reich argued that public provision should be seen as a form of property right that represented "part of the individual's rightful share in the commonwealth, and provided a basis for individual well-being and dignity in a society where each man cannot be wholly the master of his own destiny" (1964, 785–86). Marshall also took for granted that husbands were breadwinners and wives were available to provide care in the household. Thus, to fulfill his hope of abolishing the Poor Law, a new approach to the care and welfare of citizens and to their self-government and standing is required. This must follow the logic of democracy: that citizenship is unconditional and that respect is owed because an individual is a citizen.

A basic income for all citizens, a policy that has been receiving attention in recent years, would be a significant step forward in keeping with the logic of democracy and would help recapture the time and resources needed for social reproduction. By a basic income I mean the regular payment of a sum of money by a government to each adult citizen with no conditions attached.[35] A basic income differs from the generous income replacement policies in some European countries precisely in being unconditional; marital and household status, and employment history are irrelevant.[36]

While there are few people who are now opposed to universal suffrage, there is widespread reluctance to see a decent living standard as an analogous democratic right. Nonetheless, a basic income can be compared to the suffrage. If the vote is essential for participation in collective self-government, then a decent standard of life is essential for individual self-government and participation in social life more generally. Universal suffrage is the emblem of equal citizenship, and underpins an orderly change of government through free and fair elections, so enhancing citizens' security. A basic income is the emblem of full citizenship, and provides the security required to maintain that political standing and individual self-government. Both the vote and a basic income can be seen as fundamental rights in Henry Shue's sense of rights that "specify the line beneath which no one is to be allowed to sink." Rights are fundamental "if enjoyment of them is essential to the enjoyment of all other rights" (1996, 18, 19). A basic income provides the life-long security that helps safeguard other rights, ensures that citizens are able—that is, have the opportunities and means—genuinely to enjoy their freedom and helps promote respect (compare Gaffaney 2000, chapter 5).

Hayek argued that the deleterious effect of employment on freedom could be combated if there were sufficient gentlemen of private means (1960, 125). One way of looking at a basic income is as a democratization of this argument at a lower standard of living. The idea of a basic income does not, in itself, specify an appropriate income level. This is a crucial question, and the subject of considerable debate. In part, the different levels advocated depend, of course, on evaluations of cost, but I shall leave these aside to highlight some of the implications of the logic of democracy. If cost proves a decisive obstacle, then we need to be clear about what is being given up and what that means for citizenship and democratization.[37] Arguments for specific levels of a basic income also depend on the reasons for an interest in the policy. If it is supported as a means to relieve poverty or a way to promote flexible labor markets, the suggested level is likely to be lower than if the concern is social reproduction and democratic citizenship.

The logic of democracy requires that a basic income be set at a level sufficient to ensure that citizens can enjoy what I call a modest but decent standard of life. That is, a standard sufficient to provide them with a meaningful degree of choice about how they live their lives and the ability to participate in social, cultural, economic, and political life to the extent they wish. A basic income would provide citizens with a wide range of opportunities, because ex hypothesis they could live on it, including the opportunity not to be employed. A basic income would therefore make it possible for mothers—and fathers—to care for their children full-time if they wished. The opportunity would be universal, available to all citizens, and so would begin to provide some remedy for the problem of social reproduction. But a basic income in itself could not solve the wider problem, which can only be addressed by other areas of public policy.

One of the most significant consequences of a basic income would be for women's self-government. For the very first time all women could be economically independent. Mary Wollstonecraft argued in 1792 that if women were to enjoy freedom and the rights of citizens they must have economic independence—whether married or single. In the interwar years in Britain, some feminists hoped that a child endowment could break the nexus between men's wages and mothers' standard of living and "once for all, cut away the question of the maintenance of children and the reproduction of the race from the question of wages" (Rathbone 1927/1986, 219).[38]

Not all contemporary feminists support a basic income; some have argued against the idea on the grounds that it would reinforce the status quo. Given the existing private and public sexual division of labor and occupational structure, women's lesser earnings, and lingering beliefs about the proper tasks of men and women, a basic income might merely give women an incentive to undertake more unpaid caring work and bolster free riding by men. Would men take advantage of the new opportunity? Whether the work of care would be shared more fairly, or feminist fears realized, is an empirical question. However, the outcome depends in part on how a basic income is argued for. Men would more likely begin to do their fair share if the debate about its introduction drew attention to their free riding; that is to say, if questions are asked about the relationship between marriage, income, and citizenship; about caring for citizens and time; about the relation between paid and unpaid work and thus the meaning of "work"; about the place of employment in a democracy; and about social reproduction. Only then would questions begin to be raised about the institutional restructuring necessary for a solution to the problem of democratic social reproduction.

These questions have received little attention so far in discussions of basic income because, as in the controversies over "welfare," employment has remained a major focus. Ironically, despite the fact that a basic income stands at the opposite pole from welfare, the continuing grip of the logic of the Poor Law is evident in the discussions. The unconditional character of a basic income has provoked a great deal of apprehension and anxiety, and, in particular, much criticism has centered on two related questions; first, idleness and, second, the question already raised earlier, the practice of reciprocity and citizens' contributions. So let me begin with some comments about a basic income, free riding, idleness, and employment.

I have seen little evidence to suggest that the outcome of the introduction of a basic income would be a large number of idle citizens. That most people do not want to be idle is indicated by the extent of unpaid voluntary contributions of time and work, particularly from women. Significantly, Hayek did not expect his gentlemen of independent means to be idle. They would be indispensable in using their resources "in the service of aims which bring no material return," and which "the mechanism of the market cannot adequately take care of" (1960, 125). In debates about basic income it is not work in general or motherhood (usually ignored) that is the concern, but male employment, illustrated by the figure of a male surfer as the symbol of the free rider.[39] Significant numbers of men, it is assumed, would turn away from employment if given a basic income. The major problem of male free riding in caring work is rarely acknowledged.

The effect on employment of a basic income is another empirical question, and there is little evidence to draw on. One source is the five negative income tax experiments conducted in the United States and Canada between 1968 and 1980. Karl Widerquist has recently reanalyzed the evidence from these, and concludes that limitations of the experiments mean that no definitive answer is available about the effect on employment. There was some disincentive effect (most noticeable among married women and teenagers living with their parents) but there was no wholesale withdrawal from the labor market. Despite the enormous amount written about the experiments there is no consensus about policy implications, and whether the disincentive effect is seen as acceptable or not largely depends on the political views of commentators.[40]

It is sometimes forgotten that the unconditional character of a basic income means that it would act as an incentive for employment as well as a disincentive. Individuals could choose to supplement their income through employment, even low-paid employment, and so it could act as a subsidy for low wages. Alternatively, individuals might refuse to accept very low pay and unsafe or unsanitary working conditions and take advantage instead of the other opportunities a basic income provides.

Other questions rarely asked in either debates over welfare or basic income are whether universal employment is feasible (especially with jobs that pay a living wage with good benefits and conditions),[41] or, even more important, why in the twenty-first century, with high productivity levels and rapid labor-saving advances, universal employment is required. There is some evidence to suggest that it is not. Robert Goodin, for example, has argued that the Netherlands can be regarded as post-productivist. Citizens there seem to "spend very substantially less time in paid labour and unpaid household labour combined than do people in any of the other nine OECD countries . . . they experience very low rates of poverty. . . . Both their temporal autonomy and their economic autonomy are thus well-served" (2001a, 30–31).[42]

I now turn to the second major anxiety about an unconditional basic income, the issue of reciprocity, or the social web of interdependence, and making a contribution. Like "welfare," a basic income, it is argued, breaches the principle of reciprocity—the principle of doing "one's fair share [in] a cooperative scheme from which one expects to benefit" (Gutmann and Thompson 1996, 303)—because recipients get something for nothing.

Stuart White has considered the reasons for making public assistance conditional, and he concludes that doing so is neither unjust nor illiberal (see chapter 4 this volume and White 2003). In part, his argument rests on empirical outcomes (for example, individuals' human capital will be increased, teenaged parents' child-rearing capacities improved, or the claims of the poor will be legitimized) that cannot be definitively assessed at present. It also rests on the claim that, because societies such as Britain and the United States are unjust in many respects, both reciprocity and employment requirements must be fair in themselves so that existing disadvantages are not consolidated. Thus, in *The Civic Minimum,* White sets out four criteria for a fair work-test, one of which is income adequacy (2003, 134–35).[43] Gutmann and Thompson also propose fair workfare, including the requirement that employment must pay enough "to enable adults to lift their families out of poverty" (1996, 296).[44] Such criteria pose problems for reciprocity because in low-wage economies, such as the United States or Britain, employment often leaves families below the poverty line. For example, from 1995 to 2000 the proportion of poor children in the United States living in working poor families rose from 32 to 43 percent; in 2001 it fell to 40 percent (Child Trends 2004).[45] Increases in the Earned Income Tax Credit have helped to combat poverty but reciprocity would be better served by higher wages, or, better still, by a basic income.

White presents his argument in a Rawlsian framework emphasizing moral reasoning. Moral reasoning is important but is not synonymous with political argument. Self-government and full standing for citizens, and the relationship between employment, labor markets and social reproduction, are political issues. In the present political climate, as White notes in chapter 4, the danger is that disadvantage would be further entrenched and lesser citizenship would result from the imposition of unfair conditions. However, the danger runs deeper still: lesser citizenship cannot be avoided when conditions are imposed.

The debate about conditional benefits is not confined to "welfare." A variety of proposals that introduce conditions into receipt of a basic income have been made; Anthony Atkinson's participation income is the best known (1996, 67–70). These proposals often extend the contribution required to include, for example, looking after children as well as employment. However, the democratic problem is not only a matter of widening what counts as a contribution or the fairness of the conditions, but goes back to Marshall's difficulty in sorting out what counts as a task of citizenship. Which tasks are to count and how it is to be decided if the criteria for performing them have been met? Is there to be another large, intrusive bureaucracy to police the fulfilling of contributions and exacting penalties? More fundamentally, the problem is that there would undoubtedly be some individuals who did not, or refused to, make the designated contributions even if these were broadly defined. Imposing conditions on some citizens for provision of benefits already divides the population into the more or the less deserving, those who are free and those who must be coerced. Some citizens are thus already set apart from others. What, then, would be the standing of those who made no designated contribution? Conditional benefits inevitably reinstate lesser citizenship; the old undemocratic notion of citizenship as a privilege rather than a universal right is still alive in arguments about public provision, contributions, and reciprocity.

Another variant of the reciprocity argument is that to call for an unconditional basic income as a democratic right is to ignore duties. Citizens who benefit from the cooperative scheme that is social life have a duty to contribute their fair share in return. Workfare is a way of ensuring that there are no free riders, that all citizens do their duty (I leave aside the question of why the idle rich are not similarly coerced into their duty). Indeed, the claim has been made that "if there are duties, then there has to be some element of conditionality in citizenship."[46] However, it does not follow from my argument, that a decent standard of life is a democratic right, that duties are unimportant or irrelevant. To argue against workfare or for an unconditional basic income implies nothing about rights or duties in a general sense. There only seems to be a connection because of the narrow understanding of reciprocity in the claims about benefits, reciprocity, and contributions.

A narrow, contractual or economistic sense of reciprocity is presupposed in discussions of both workfare and a conditional basic income.[47] The assumption is that a specific contribution is owed directly and immediately in return for a benefit, rather like a wage in employment. Or, to put this in terms of rights and duties, if there is a right (say, to TANF), then there is a correlative duty (employment or another form of contribution) attached directly to that right. It needs to be emphasized, first, that no such duty is demanded of other beneficiaries of public provision. Second, to see every right as having a correlative duty directly attached is only one conception of the relationship between rights and duties. Furthermore, in social life, outside of the market, few areas of reciprocity operate in such a narrow, contractual fashion.

I have already referred to the broader understanding of reciprocity; social life is a web of mutual aid and forbearance, a dense network of interdependence or reciprocity, which includes rights and duties which have no strict correlation with each other.[48] The narrow, contractual view of reciprocity echoes the idea of an original contract and the move from a state of nature to civil (that is, political) society. The claim is that the move takes place because humans benefit from political society. But there are two ambiguities here. The first is that if the state of nature is not a social state (so the benefits are those of social life itself) the problem arises that, as Hobbes and Rousseau show, the natural condition is not human either. If the state of nature is portrayed as social then reciprocity, the web of mutual aid and forbearance, is already in place (and what exactly are the benefits?).[49] Social life is the network of reciprocity, the cooperative scheme, but nothing follows from this conceptual point without much further argument.

Social life can be organized in many ways, and to posit a specific form of social order is go far beyond a conceptual point. A great deal more discussion and specification of principles, values, and institutional arrangements is then needed to decide what is a just or democratic society. And here the second ambiguity comes to the fore. To maintain social life, contributions have to be made. But in which direction do they flow? I earlier raised the question of vertical and horizontal contributions, but this is a problem only in civil society—that is to say, in a modern state—because only then are duties owed vertically to the state as well as horizontally among citizens. Workfare is mandated by the state in return for benefits and the benefit and the duty are directly linked. Yet arguments about schemes of cooperation, free riders, and duties seem instead to refer to failure to give what is owed (horizontally) to fellow citizens or to do what is necessary to maintain the general well-being—but then the problem of specifying what counts as duty of citizenship reappears. For example, if the tasks of motherhood are seen as a contribution in return for workfare or a conditional basic income does that imply that such tasks are those of a citizen rather than a private individual? If motherhood is brought into citizenship, then what are the implications for the familiar, minimalist view of democracy that separates public citizenship from private motherhood (and fatherhood)? There are other problems, too, in deciding what constitutes doing one's fair share; do the duties, for example, depend on the distribution of benefits? The latter question is not usually raised in debates about welfare, but perhaps poor citizens, rather than being open to coercion, owe less than the better off.

We all rely every day, to a large extent implicitly, on countless acts that look forward to other reciprocal acts that we expect in the future, or reflect actions that have assisted us in the past; we rely, that is, on the performance of duties. Reciprocity stretches over time and space. Neither mothers nor all those engaged in caring work or education demand an immediate reciprocal contribution from, for example, young children, the sick, infirm, elderly, or pupils in return for benefits; their work is not conditional upon a contribution. Indeed, love, not expectation of reciprocity, is seen as motivating the work of wives and mothers. Providing for the welfare of citizens and the work of, and time devoted to, the social reproduction of citizens who can actively participate in a democratic polity cannot depend on immediate reciprocal contributions.

One of the lessons from great political theorists such as Hobbes or Hegel is that narrow, contractual views of reciprocity always depend on the wider web of social interdependence and, if extended too far, contractual practices undermine their own social grounding. The social reproduction of citizens includes careful attention to ethics, but moral education is all the harder when the welfare of citizens is subordinated to the labor market and the logic of the Poor Law takes precedence over the logic of democracy. The rapid changes now taking place provide the opportunity not only to rethink current policies but also to consider how to put employment in its democratic place. Societies in which time for motherhood and fatherhood becomes a luxury, economic insecurity is widespread, inequality is growing, and public provision for the welfare of citizens is under continuous threat are unlikely to be stable in the longer term.

A basic income is, I have argued, a necessary step forward—but it is not sufficient. The social reproduction of citizens goes well beyond the private caring work of wives and mothers and equitable sharing of that work by husbands and fathers. Public provision is also needed to sustain and strengthen democratic citizenship. A basic income cannot in itself provide good quality education in well-equipped schools, affordable housing, access to health care, violence free neighborhoods, access to cultural amenities, or the cultivation of individual capacities within the democratized institutions of a robust democracy. Reforming welfare requires the elimination of the Poor Law; reforming the relationship between employment and the social reproduction of citizens is part of a much bigger process of democratization.

I am grateful to Larry Mead and Chris Beem for their careful reading of drafts of this chapter, for criticisms and helpful suggestions. I also thank Mary McThomas for her assistance and Gary Chartier for discussions. I dedicate this chapter to the memory of my old friend and former student (who wrote her honors thesis on motherhood): Teresa Brennan 1952–2003.

Notes

1. I shall use "welfare" to indicate the circumscribed usage of the term in the United States, in contrast to the much broader welfare provision in most other rich Western countries. Workfare means that assistance is conditional upon employment in either the public or private sector.
2. States now receive a fixed grant for the program from the federal government and are able to set most eligibility rules for beneficiaries.
3. In 1997 only 17 percent of British social expenditure went to means tested benefits but by 1995 it was 36 percent (Wilding 1997, 722). Sweden's active labor policy is often cited too, but, unlike the United States and Britain, Sweden has few means-tested programs and has very generous income replacement policies and support for parents, so the context is different.
4. Marshall equivocated about social rights, and his argument about citizenship was thus more complex than these quotations suggest; in places, especially in his later writings, his argument points towards recent claims that social rights are outdated (see Pateman 1996).
5. Though this is not exactly as Mead envisaged: by workfare he was referring to employment in the public sector.
6. Workfare is one element in the wider category of means-tested policies that create the paradox that a given group "must first be singled out as *different* from ordinary citizens. But if the group is that different, how can they ever by any social policy initiative become like 'ordinary citizens' " (Rothstein 1998, 159).
7. Universal suffrage has been much harder to achieve than is usually supposed. For example, women won the vote in Switzerland only in 1971, they still lack the franchise in Kuwait, and neither men nor women have the franchise in Saudi Arabia. In the United States voting was only democratized in practice after the Civil Rights Act of 1965 ensured that African Americans could freely cast a ballot, and in a few states felons are still disenfranchised for life.
8. Minimalist and economic theories of democracy owe a good deal to Joseph Schumpeter (1943).
9. Moreover, virtues such as frugality and thrift sit uneasily with an economy that depends on continuous consumption and high levels of individual indebtedness.

10. In fact, there were too many men and families to fit into the workhouses and outdoor relief survived in the form of a system of Labour Yards (where half the relief was paid in kind), and here is "the historical origins of a workfare principle . . . in exchange for receiving assistance recipients must undertake some work activity" (King 1999, 229; on the Labour Yards, see 229–32).
11. This view is associated in particular with the work of Charles Murray, but it is hardly new (on dependency, see Fraser and Gordon 1994).
12. These problems need to be tackled through the appropriate therapeutic channels, whether they derive from illiteracy or health problems (though the war on drugs is a singular failure) and lie outside my concerns here. If criminal behavior is involved there are numerous laws to deal with it.
13. A small-scale study from 1996 to 1998 in New Jersey of single mothers who were sanctioned for noncompliance found that they were confused about why they had been penalized, and no significant differences existed between those who then complied and those who did not. It is reported that in other research caseworkers were also found to be confused about the new laws (Smith and Gunn 2002).
14. Based on data from the 2000 census, the U.S. Census Bureau found that in 400 fields full-time, year-round women workers earn only 74 cents compared to the dollar earned by their male counterparts.
15. President G. W. Bush has also introduced a Healthy Marriage Initiative. Leaving aside religious objections to childbirth out of wedlock, it is hard to see why single motherhood, in itself, is a problem, even though it is a difficult task when women are mired in poverty. If mothers lack parenting skills then that is a problem to be tackled directly. In Sweden, over half of all births were to unwed mothers by 1990 but conditions for, and social perceptions of, unmarried mothers are very different from those in the United States. Reference in often made to empirical research to show that children fare poorly in the absence of an intact two-parent family. However, the methodology of much of this research can be questioned (see Lister 2001).
16. Nor does so-called nonwork count in a more literal sense. Nonmarket activities are not calculated in estimates of GDP. There are now efforts to remedy this, but the division between public work in the labor force (primarily male) and private activities in the household (primarily female) was built into the United Nations System of National Accounts (see Waring 1988).
17. Marshall goes on to say, "but the community is so large that the obligation appears remote and unreal."
18. He ignored the problems this raised about women citizens in 1949, when he first presented the lectures that became his essay. They were not subject to postwar conscription, and, if they were married, were regarded as under coverture (that is, as part of the legal person of their husband) for tax purposes and not allowed to make a tax return as individuals.
19. Gutmann and Thompson draw on Judith Shklar's argument about earning. I am not sure that acquiring respect is a capacity.
20. Structural adjustment and privatization are often seen as applying only to developing countries, but New Zealand provides perhaps the most complete example of the application of these economic dogmas. Other rich countries are beginning to follow this example, but at least in the countries of The Com-

monwealth, there is a considerable gap between the views of citizens about the responsibilities of governments and current government policy (see Knight, Chigudu, and Tandon 2002).

21. In the final chapter Brennan discusses the prime directive; that is "we shall not use up nature and humankind at a rate faster than they can replenish themselves and be replenished" (164).
22. Cott also notes that in 1996 a report "from the U.S. General Accounting Office found more than *one thousand* places in the corpus of federal law where legal marriage conferred a distinctive status, right or benefit" (2; see also Pateman 1988).
23. The common law doctrine under which (in Blackstone's words) "the husband and wife are one person in law; that is, the very being, or legal existence of the woman is suspended during the marriage, or at least is incorporated and consolidated into that of the husband" (Blackstone 1765/1899, 442).
24. In 1996, "65 percent of elderly female Social Security recipients received benefits based at least in part on their husbands' work histories" (Ackerman and Alstott 1999, 145; see also Pateman 1989).
25. In Australia, a child endowment scheme was introduced in New South Wales in 1927 and at federal level in 1941; family allowances were introduced in Britain in 1946, and continue as a universal child benefit; a child tax credit has also been introduced (either can be paid to the custodial parent).
26. It is the feminist, not the republican, view of motherhood that generates (my formulation of) Wollstonecraft's dilemma, on which Beem draws (see chapter 7).
27. Under the Federal Emergency Relief Act (1934) "three times as many children and almost three and a half times as many single-mother families were receiving federal emergency relief as had received any mothers' aid."
28. These replaced a tort liability system, and the programs were based on standardized criteria and eligibility, and realized risk (Nelson 1990, 141).
29. In the late nineteenth and early twentieth centuries there was also a welfare system for Civil War veterans: "After 1890, what amounted to disability and old-age pensions were paid quarterly from the federal Treasury to all applicants who could claim to be Union veterans, as well as to others who could claim to be dependents of soldiers who had died during or after the war." Between 1880 and 1910 a quarter of federal expenditures were allocated to such pensions (Skocpol 1992, 65). Military service, along with employment, have been the contributions required of men, and are seen as primary political obligations. But political theorists have rarely paused to consider the political obligations of women, or, indeed, if they have any.
30. Support dropped especially between 1960 and 1973, and 1991 and 1993.
31. Religious fundamentalism also became increasingly influential. Campaigns were launched for family values and against single motherhood, but opposition to abortion (and also in some cases contraception) contradicts the goal of lowering the incidence of births out of wedlock. The administration of G. W. Bush has promoted partnership between religious organizations and government in delivering welfare services.
32. In 1974 Old-Age Assistance and aid to blind and disabled people were absorbed into SSI, but these were not seen in quite the same way as AFDC.

33. Gilens (1999) presents evidence about the role of the media in fostering these perceptions, so it is hardly surprising that figure of the African American welfare queen became so prominent.
34. I called this Marshall's strong or democratic view in *Democratization and Citizenship in the 1990s.*
35. The policy has attracted supporters from different parts of the political spectrum for a variety of reasons ranging from social justice to flexible labor markets, and has been supported by Nobel Prize winners James Meade, Herbert Simon, and James Tobin. Information can be found at www.basicincome.org; for the United States at www.usbig.net; and for Britain at www.citizens income.org. The policy is being widely discussed in Europe and South Africa and has adherents in the United States. In 2002, the Irish government published a Green Paper on Basic Income, and in early 2004 Brazil became the first country to enact legislation for a basic income, to be phased in gradually. The academic discussion was sparked off in earnest by Philippe Van Parijs (1995). There is now a large literature on basic income (for an introduction see Van Parijs 1992; *Boston Review* 2000; see also Pateman 2003, 2004).
36. The idea of a basic income has a competitor; stakeholding, or basic capital, in which a lump sum is paid to each individual on reaching adulthood (see Ackerman and Alstott 1999). In the political culture of the United States a stake is likely to be more immediately appealing than a basic income. In the United Kingdom the Blair government has already taken a step toward stakeholding by instituting a Child Trust Fund. For each child born on or after 1 September 2002 the government is providing £250 which is invested and will be available to the child at age eighteen. At age seven, the government will make a further contribution (the amount not yet determined) and parents and others can add up to £1200 per year to the child's Trust Fund account. Such measures are welcome, but, still, I believe that if democracy and citizenship is the concern a basic income is to be preferred (see Pateman 2003).
37. The net cost of a basic income is less than it may appear at first sight. It would replace means tested and some other programs, and the tax-transfer system would still operate. In the last analysis, cost is a political question. Since 2000 many hundreds of billions of dollars have been devoted to tax cuts, to subsidies to the agricultural and steel industries, sent up in space and spent on warfare. In the 1960s, the proportion of GDP comprising public spending, mostly welfare programs, in United States and the Scandinavian countries was roughly the same. By the 1990s, the latter were spending twice as much as the United States, and some other European countries fifty percent more (Rothstein 1998, 18). And Sweden in 2003 had a budget surplus and seemed to be in good economic shape.
38. Rathbone also hoped that child endowment would open the way for men and women workers to be paid the same for the same work. But the feminist case was overshadowed by pro-natalist arguments and the more general argument that child endowment was important in the relief of poverty.
39. Rawls used the figure of the surfer to discuss this problem and he appears on the cover of Van Parijs's book.
40. "The experimental results seem to be a scientific Rorschach test in which an observer can see whatever she wants to see." The findings were complex but much of the commentary ignored the complexities. Nor did the experiments

measure the possible long run shift in the labor supply or the demand (Widerquist 2005).

41. Unemployment rates in America are often compared favorably to those in Europe. However, this neglects the very high incarceration rate in the United States; in 1996 1.63 million individuals were in prison, a number that had increased threefold since 1980. In the short run the size of the prison population means tighter labor markets—male unemployment was understated by about 2 percent in the mid-1990s—and means that those imprisoned were more likely to be unemployed in the long run: "sustained low unemployment in the future will depend on continuing expansion of the penal system." (Western and Beckett 1999, 1031). (My thanks to Bob Goodin for alerting me to this article.) Expansion has continued and by mid-2002 there were 2 million inmates.
42. There will, no doubt, always be a few idle drones but a robust democracy can afford them. The use that citizens choose to make of their freedom is open to no guarantees. Self-government entails that they decide for themselves how and when they will contribute or whether they will contribute at all. In the last analysis, if the cost of democratization and a basic income as a fundamental right is the existence of some drones, then it is worth paying.
43. For his five criteria for fair reciprocity and a formulation of the "contributive obligation," see White (2003, 90–91).
44. The other requirements are that governments make employment and child support available. Gutmann and Thompson also argue that if any parents refuse employment they must be coerced into supporting their children. They note that this "comes close to a policy of forced labor," but claim that the "alternatives are morally worse" (300)—not an argument that I find convincing, especially from democratic theorists.
45. A working poor family is one in which in a two-parent family one parent worked at least thirty-five hours per week, or a single parent worked twenty hours, and the family income (in 2001) was still below $18,104.
46. An anonymous reviewer.
47. For a discussion of different models of reciprocity in the context of workfare in Australia, see Robert Goodin (2001b, 579–96). For further criticism of contractual conceptions of welfare see, for example, Robert Goodin (1998, 141–58), and King (1999).
48. For convenience, I am writing of duties here but I should be referring to acts that ought to be performed. For the reasons why I see acts that ought to be performed as distinct from both obligations (self-assumed by individuals) and duties (attached to stations and offices), see Pateman (1985, 27–30, 34).
49. I criticized some earlier versions of the benefits argument in *The Problem of Political Obligation* (1985, 121–25).

References

Ackerman, Bruce, and Anne Alstott. 1999. *The Stakeholder Society*. New Haven, Conn.: Yale University Press.

Atkinson, Anthony. 1996. "The Case for a Participation Income." *Political Quarterly* 67(1): 67–70.

Beveridge, William. 1942. *Social Insurance and Allied Services.* New York: Macmillan.

Blackstone, Sir William. 1765/1899. *Commentaries on the Laws of England,* 4th ed., Book 1. Chicago: Callaghan and Co.

Boston Review. 2000. "Symposium: Delivering a Basic Income." October/November.

Brennan, Teresa. 2003. *Globalization and Its Terrors: Daily Life in the West.* London and New York: Routledge.

Child Trends Databank. Available at: http://www.childtrendsdatabank.org (accessed January 2004).

Cott, Nancy. 2000. *Public Vows: A History of Marriage and the Nation,* Cambridge, Mass.: Harvard University Press.

Dean, Mitchell. 1991. *The Constitution of Poverty: Toward a Genealogy of Liberal Governance.* London and New York: Routledge.

Fraser, Nancy, and Linda Gordon. 1994. "A Genealogy of 'Dependency': Tracing a Key Word of the U.S. Welfare State." *Signs* 19(2): 309–36.

Gaffaney, Timothy J. 2000. *Freedom for the Poor: Welfare and the Foundations of Democratic Citizenship.* Boulder, Colo.: Westview Press.

Gilens, Martin. 1999. *Why Americans Hate Welfare: Race, Media, and the Politics of Antipoverty Policy.* Chicago: University of Chicago Press.

Goodin, Robert E. 1998. "More than Anyone Bargained For: Beyond the Welfare Contract." *Ethics and International Affairs* 12: 141–58.

———. 2001a. "Work and Welfare: Towards a Post-Productivist Welfare Regime." *British Journal of Political Science* 31(1): 13–39.

———. 2001b. "Structures of Mutual Obligation." *Journal of Social Policy* 31(4): 579–96.

Gordon, Linda. 1994. *Pitied but Not Entitled: Single Mothers and the History of Welfare, 1890–1935.* New York: The Free Press.

Gutmann, Amy, and Dennis Thompson. 1996. *Democracy and Disagreement.* Cambridge, Mass.: Harvard University Press.

Von Hayek, Friedrich. 1960. *The Constitution of Liberty.* Chicago: University of Chicago Press.

Hirschmann, Nancy. 2003. *The Subject of Liberty: Towards a Feminist Theory of Freedom.* Princeton, N.J.: Princeton University Press.

Kerber, Linda. 1998. *No Constitutional Right to be Ladies: Women and the Obligations of Citizenship.* New York: Hill and Wang.

King, Desmond S. 1999. *In the Name of Liberalism: Illiberal Social Policy in The United States and Britain.* Oxford: Oxford University Press.

Knight, Barry, Hope Chigudu, and Rajesh Tandon. 2002. *Reviving Democracy: Citizens at the Heart of Governance.* London and Sterling, Va.: Earthscan Publications.

Lister, Andrew. 2001. "Understanding the Burdens of Judgment: Moral Pluralism, Causal Ambiguity, and the Limits of Consequentialist Public Reason." Ph.D. dissertation, University of California, Los Angeles.

Locke, John. 1697/1997. "An Essay on the Poor Law." In *Political Essays,* edited by Mark Goldie. Cambridge: Cambridge University Press.

Marshall, T. H. 1963. "Citizenship and Social Class." In *Sociology at the Crossroads and Other Essays.* London: Heinemann.

Mead, Lawrence M. 1986. *Beyond Entitlement: The Social Obligations of Citizenship.* New York: Free Press.

———. 1992. *The New Politics of Poverty: The Nonworking Poor in America.* New York: Basic Books.

Michel, Sonya. 1993. "The Limits of Maternalism: Policies Toward American Wage-earning Mothers During the Progressive Era." In *Mothers of a New World: Maternalist Politics and the Origins of Welfare States,* edited by Seth Coven and Sonya Michel. New York and London: Routledge.

Mink, Gwendolyn. 1990. "The Lady and The Tramp: Gender, Race, and the Origins of the American Welfare State." In *Women, The State, and Welfare,* edited by Linda Gordon. Madison: University of Wisconsin Press.

Moon, J. Donald. 1988. "The Moral Basis of the Welfare State." In *Democracy and The Welfare State,* edited by Amy Gutmann. Princeton, N.J.: Princeton University Press.

Murray, Charles. 1994. "What to do About Welfare." *Commentary* 98(6): 29–34.

Nelson, Barbara. 1990. "The Origins of the Two-Channel Welfare State: Workmen's Compensation and Mother's Aid." In *Women, The State, and Welfare,* edited by Linda Gordon. Madison: University of Wisconsin Press.

Orloff, Ann. 2001. "Ending the Entitlements of Poor Single Mothers: Changing Social Policies, Women's Employment, and Caregiving in the Contemporary United States." In *Women and Welfare: Theory and Practice in the United States and Europe,* edited by Nancy Hirschmann and Ulrike Liebert. New Brunswick, N.J.: Rutgers University Press.

Pateman, Carole. 1970. *Participation and Democratic Theory.* Cambridge: Cambridge University Press.

———. 1985. *The Problem of Political Obligation,* 2nd ed. Berkeley: University of California Press.

———. 1988. *The Sexual Contract.* Stanford, Calif.: Stanford University Press.

———. 1989. "The Patriarchal Welfare State." In *The Disorder of Women: Democracy, Feminism and Political Theory.* Stanford, Calif.: Stanford University Press. First published in 1988 by Princeton University Press in *Democracy and The Welfare State,* edited by Amy Gutmann.

———. 1996. *Democratization and Citizenship in the 1990's: The Legacy of T. H. Marshall.* The Vilhelm Aubert Memorial Lecture, University of Oslo.

———. 2002. "Self-Ownership and Property in the Person: Democratization and a Tale of Two Concepts." *The Journal of Political Philosophy* 10(1): 20–53.

———. 2003. "Freedom and Democratization: Why Basic Income is to be Preferred to Basic Capital." In *The Ethics of Stakeholding,* edited by Keith Dowding, Jurgen De Wispelaeire, and Stuart White. London: Palgrove Macmillan.

———. 2004. "Democratizing Citizenship: Some Advantages of a Basic Income." *Politics and Society* 32(1): 89–105.

Rathbone, Eleanor. 1927/1986. *The Disinherited Family,* 3rd ed. Bristol, U.K.: Falling Wall Press.

Reich, Charles. 1964. "The New Property." *Yale Law Journal* 73(5): 733–87.

Rothstein, Bo. 1998. *Just Institutions Matter: The Moral and Political Logic of the Universal Welfare State.* Cambridge: Cambridge University Press.

Sandel, Michael J. 1996. *Democracy's Discontent: America in Search of a Public Philosophy.* Cambridge, Mass.: Harvard University Press.

Schor, Juliet. 1991. *The Overworked American: The Unexpected Decline of Leisure.* New York: Basic Books.

Schumpeter, Joseph. 1943. *Capitalism, Socialism and Democracy.* London: Allen & Unwin.

Shklar, Judith N. 1991. *American Citizenship: The Quest for Inclusion.* Cambridge, Mass.: Harvard University Press.

Shue, Henry. 1996. *Basic Rights: Subsistence, Affluence, and U.S. Foreign Policy,* 2nd ed. Princeton, N.J.: Princeton University Press.

Skocpol, Theda. 1992. *Protecting Soldiers and Mothers: The Political Origins of Social Policy in the United States.* Cambridge, Mass.: Harvard University Press.

Smith, Judith, and Jeanne Brooks-Gunn. 2002. "How Mothers Cope When their Welfare Grant is Cut." *Social Policy Journal* 1(4): 63–83.

Teles, Steven. 1996. *Whose Welfare? AFDC and Elite Politics.* Lawrence: University Press of Kansas.

Van Parijs, Philippe, ed. 1992. *Arguing for Basic Income.* London: Verso.

———. 1995. *Real Freedom for All: What (if Anything) can Justify Capitalism?* New York: Oxford University Press.

Waring, Marilyn. 1988. *If Women Counted: A New Feminist Economics.* New York: Harper and Row.

Western, Bruce, and Katherine Beckett. 1999. "How Unregulated is the U.S. Labor Market?: The Penal System as a Labor Market Institution." *American Journal of Sociology* 104(4): 1030–60.

White, Stuart. 2003. *The Civic Minimum: An Essay on the Rights and Obligations of Economic Citizenship.* Oxford: Oxford University Press.

Widerquist, Karl. 2005. "A Failure to Communicate: What (if Anything) Can We Learn from the Negative Income Tax Experiments?" *Journal of Socio-Economics* 34(1): 49–81.

Wilding, Paul. 1997. "The Welfare State and the Conservatives." *Political Studies* 45(4): 716–22.

Chapter 3

Making People Work: Democratic Consequences of Workfare

DESMOND KING

THE SHIFT to workfare is one of the most significant changes to the welfare state observable across advanced industrial democracies. By workfare I mean broadly the range of measures that impose work, training, or educational requirements on some groups of recipients of public assistance.

The reform coincides with the end of the golden age of the social democratic welfare state, meaning the social benefits and services that developed in European countries after World War II, a system that provided generous support for the vulnerable based largely on their need. Workfare now demands that those in need work, or prepare for work, as a condition of aid. The shift is most advanced in those democracies whose liberal roots are more entrenched—the United States and Britain—but it is seen to a lesser extent elsewhere in Europe (see Huber and Stephens 2001; Kitschelt et al. 1999).

Here I focus on the policy changes associated with a sharper conditionality in the United States and Britain since the 1980s. I summarize the political rationale for workfare and the philosophical justification that some authors have given it. I also contest these arguments. Principally, however, I concentrate on the damage workfare does to the status of its clients as citizens. Workfare has reshaped the shared quality we call citizenship—the sense that democratic citizens should hold that they are common members of a political community. The damage occurs because workfare is invidious and discretionary—treating its recipients in different ways from other citizens.

Although a great deal has been written on workfare, much of this literature deals only with empirical issues such as the detailed design of workfare schemes or their effects, or addresses the implications of workfare for the contractualist bases of liberal democracies. I ask here, instead, how workfare affects the identity of citizens in a variety of guises and therefore our conception of membership arising from citizenship. I find that it alters the relationship between the state and claimants, between citizens funding benefits and those in receipt of them, and between state administrators and their clients. It thus diminishes the social bases of democratic participation and inclusion.

America's PRWORA

In 1996 Congress enacted and President Bill Clinton signed the Personal Responsibility and Work Opportunity Reconciliation Act (PRWORA). The principal focus of reform was the decades-old program of Aid to Families with Dependent Children (AFDC), which supported largely single mothers and their children. PRWORA recast AFDC as Temporary Assistance for Needy Families (King 1999; Waddan 2003; Jayasuriya 2002; Weaver 1998; Blank 1997; King and Nou 2003). TANF fundamentally changed the conditions under which families with little or no income received public assistance. Families were limited to five years on the welfare rolls. Adult members faced tougher work requirements, with labor expected in exchange for benefits after two years of income support. Administratively, America's states won enhanced autonomy to design their own welfare programs subject to loose federal rules. At its most extreme—seen in Wisconsin—the new regime confined virtually all cash aid to parents who were employed, in either private or government jobs (Mead 2004).

The numbers receiving welfare have declined rapidly, a trend that began before and continued after TANF was enacted in August 1996. From a peak of 5.1 million cases and 14.4 million recipients in March 1994, the rolls fell to 2 million cases (5 million recipients) by June 2003—a fall of 60 percent for cases, and 66 percent for recipients. This was the largest caseload decline in the history of the program. Not since 1967 have so few people lived in the program.

These figures, however, overstate the decline in dependency. Fremstad and Neuberger point out that states use TANF funds to provide work training and other services to an increasing number of families who are not counted in TANF caseload statistics because they do not receive cash benefits. A cautious estimate reveals that more than one million working families receive TANF-funded services (child care, transportation assistance, and job training) without being counted in the caseload (Fremstad and Neuberger 2002). These supports and other services help former welfare recipients as well as other low-income families to stay off welfare.

Caseload numbers also fail to address the underlying problem of poverty. They ignore those who are not on welfare because they have been rejected for aid or diverted—that is, persuaded not to apply even though they might have been eligible. Under TANF, the majority of states use some form of diversion before granting benefits. In 1999, sixteen states required that applicants search for a job either before applying for benefits or during the application process and that qualified beneficiaries document job searches before being approved for benefits. Twenty-two states offered lump-sum cash payments, designed to meet immediate needs, as an alternative to welfare enrollment. These strategies, though designed to promote work and build economic independence, can also discourage welfare participation by needy families (Zedlewski 2002).

Britain's New Deal

New Labour's workfare measures, called collectively the New Deal, are a pivotal feature of this government's reformulation of the Labour Party's ideology and tradition (for the best account, see Driver and Martell 2002). The government recast and expanded the welfare-to-work programs of the Conservatives, especially the Major government's contractualist approach to unemployment benefits. Under the Jobseeker's Allowance, established by the Tories in October 1996, recipients must sign an agreement with the Employment Service outlining the measures they will take to look for work each week (initiative set out in Department of Employment 1994). Failure to attend biweekly interviews and to be actively seeking work can result in the loss of benefits. The agreement also permits the job seeker's mandatory participation in a workfare program. Finally, the allowance gives discretion to advisers in the Employment Service, which may require job seekers to attend certain potential job interviews. This interventionist and directive system focused mostly on the long-term and young unemployed.

On taking office in 1997, New Labour built this system into the New Deal. Of several programs, the New Deal for Young People, for ages eighteen to twenty-four, is the most important. Budgeted at £5.2 billion, the five-year scheme offered four options to unemployed youth who had lived on benefits for more than six months. The first was a job with the private sector, and employers were offered subsidies to take on former unemployed workers for six-month periods. The second was to enter either full-time or part-time education. The course had to be approved by the Employment Service, but offered an opportunity to acquire training that would enhance clients' employability. Third, participants could take a position in the voluntary sector combined with a day a week in training; voluntary organizations received a fee for participation. Last, an environmental task force was an outlet through which those required to participate in workfare could meet community needs. Refusal to take one of the four options, without good cause, resulted in suspension of the unemployed person's benefit for two weeks, and for longer if noncompliance continued. The option of not participating yet retaining benefits was no longer available.

New Deal programs have been instituted for several other groups, including jobless workers over twenty-four, single parents, and people with disabilities. Plans to extend requirements to the homeless and drug addicts have been aired.

The workfare regime is well ensconced. Unemployed persons must attend job interviews and meetings with their advisers or face sanctions. During its election campaign preceding the May 5, 2005, elections, the Labour Party announced a proposal to legislate fines for those long-term unemployed who violate the rules requiring them to seek alternative employment or retraining. Fines are planned for such offenses as losing a job voluntarily, getting sacked for misconduct, refusing suitable employment, declining to attend training, or refusing to attend relevant interviews. Money would be docked automatically and it would be up to benefit claimants to prove that they had not broken the rules. The scheme proposes that claimants would be refused unemployment benefits of £55 a week for up to a fortnight for a first offense and have benefits stopped for up to twenty-six weeks for persistent malingerers.

Administratively, the benefits agency and Employment Service have been merged to coordinate workfare and related labor market measures. Historically this sort of integration has resulted in job testing overshadowing efforts to place people in work (King 1995).

As in the United States, workfare in Britain has been hailed as a success, but there is continuing debate about how well the New Deal succeeds in placing unemployed people in permanent jobs. In 1998 the New Deal for Young People placed close to 50 percent of participants in sustained jobs, which are defined as those lasting more than thirteen weeks. By the end of 2002, this figure had dropped to 36 percent. How many of these sustained jobs prove durable in the long term is, of course, much less certain. But clearly, the New Deal is successful in terms of its goals that emphasize minimizing dependency. Its effects on the common citizenship are more worrisome.

The Rationale for Workfare

The ways in which workfare is justified reveal how far the goals of welfare have changed. The social democratic system emphasized the generous provision of social rights to all in need and thereby an enhanced sense of shared citizenship for all members of a polity. The new logic is contractualist, linking benefits to new duties for claimants. The emphasis is on the responsibilities and even the malfeasance of the dependent.

Fiscally, workfare programs have the appeal of modifying the incentive structures of job seekers in a way that reduces the public welfare rolls.

Morally or ideologically, reducing welfare numbers and imposing conditions on benefits has long been advocated by opponents of the social democratic welfare state. Such critics allege that welfare creates a dependency culture, erodes self-esteem, and fosters the intergenerational reproduction of dependency. Philosophically, some political and social theorists rest their support for workfare on propositions about the nature of citizenship and claim that work measures strengthen citizenship by providing recipients with sources of self-esteem and self-worth (see, for example, Murray 1984; Mead 1986, White 2003).

Members of Congress used all these arguments to justify PRWORA during its passage, even though there was some dissonance between the aim of curbing welfare and the aim of improving it (Weaver 1998). Some experts on welfare and poverty supported the reform, concluding that the old welfare system had failed. Neil Gilbert, for example, sees in PRWORA a change from a welfare state to an enabling state. Liberated from bureaucracy the enabling state promotes work under an ideology of social obligation (Gilbert 2002; for a comparative context, see Rothstein and Steinmo 2002; Pierson 2000; see also Clasen and Clegg 2003). The apparent success of PRWORA has had wide influence abroad, encouraging policymakers in other advanced industrial democracies to break with historical patterns (Blank 2002).

The U.S. reform might be interpreted as consistent with that country's own liberal individualist political culture—as characterized, for instance, by Louis Hartz or Gunnar Myrdal (Hartz 1955; Myrdal 1944; for the limits of this view see Smith 1993; King and Smith 2005). For Britain, however, workfare meant a larger break with the social democratic tradition. The vision of benefit programs as establishing social rights for citizens, articulated by T. H. Marshall, had largely been achieved by an earlier Labour government (1945 to 1951) led by Clement Attlee (Marshall 1964).[1] Whereas earlier discussions of the welfare state in Britain had emphasized these rights, now the corollary obligations of citizenship were discovered or rediscovered by Blair's New Labour.

The prime minister and colleagues were knocking on a door already pushed well ajar under the preceding Conservative governments. In 1996 the House of Commons' influential Select Committee on Employment issued a report on workfare titled *The Right to Work/Workfare* that endorsed a contractualist framework for administering state benefits. The authors thought it appropriate on moral grounds to expect reciprocal activity from benefit recipients. Psychologically, they also believed, this activity would help keep the unemployed and welfare dependents from drifting into a state of demoralization from which recovery was immensely difficult. The committee also thought workfare would save money, because it would act as a deterrent against false claims for benefits (House of Commons 1996).

Tony Blair and his ministers have repeatedly emphasized, expanded upon, and celebrated this mantra about mutual responsibilities. Blair salutes a new bargain with the unemployed: "The basis of this modern civic society is an ethic of mutual responsibility or duty. It is something for something. A society where we play by the rules. You only take out if you put in. That's the bargain." Elsewhere the prime minister blamed the old Marshallian rights-biased framework for "encouraging dependency, lowering self-esteem and denying opportunity and responsibility in almost equal measure" (the 21st Century Welfare State speech of January 24, 1997, quoted in *The Guardian,* "Blair offers jobless a new bargain," June 3, 1997). The employment minister responsible for designing and monitoring the New Deal in its first years, Andrew Smith, characterized it as "tough but fair" and, ideologically, as balancing "rights and responsibilities" (quoted in *Financial Times,* "Tougher conditions for young in 'welfare-to-work' scheme," July 4, 1997).

New Labour's language and philosophy rapidly reshaped government rhetoric and policy. The language of bargains, contracts, duties, and obligations as a corollary of rights permeates government green and white papers, which set out policy aims and specific measures throughout the welfare state (for instance, in education, health, transport as well as income maintenance). The March 1998 green paper on welfare reform announced that, "at the heart of the modern welfare state will be a new contract between the citizen and the Government based on responsibilities and rights" (Secretary of State 1998). David Blunkett, then secretary of state for Education and Employment, proclaimed workfare—somewhat improbably—to be a central plank of Labour's tradition and ideology: " 'Work not dole' was the cry 60 years ago and that's exactly what the New Deal is all about" (*The Observer,* "Work not Dole," November 1, 1998).

The Philosophy of Workfare

Alongside these political rationales, the case for workfare has drawn on arguments developed by Amy Gutmann and Dennis Thompson, Lawrence Mead, William Galston, and Stuart White, among others (see chapters 1, 4, and 5 in this volume; Gutmann and Thompson 1996; Mead 1997a; Galston 1991; White 2000, 2003). These scholars contend that the type of conditionality introduced by workfare can be made compatible with the expectations we traditionally make about the rights and obligations of citizenship.

In probably the most straightforward defense, political theorist Stuart White concludes that if members of society have obligations toward each other—what he calls the principle of fair reciprocity—then the imposition of some sort of exchange expectation on benefit claimants is well founded: "The work-test can be defended as a necessary device for protecting citizens against the unfair resource claims of those who are unwilling to meet the obligations they have to contribute to the community" (2003, 152).

Another important example is the argument for fair workfare advanced by political scientists Amy Gutmann and Dennis Thompson. This concept is designed to make coercive obligations compatible with liberal democratic values and institutions:

> Fair workfare takes individual responsibility seriously as a requirement in welfare reform. But it is grounded on a value of mutual dependence, which is implied by reciprocity, rather than the value of independence or self-sufficiency, which libertarians stress. The obligations of welfare should be mutual: citizens who need income support are obligated to work, but only if fellow citizens fulfil their obligations to enact public policies that provide adequate employment and child support. (1996, 276)
>
> "Fair workfare" is conditioned on the principle of basic opportunity according to which all citizens are entitled to an "adequate level of basic opportunity goods" such as education, health, income support and work. (273, 292)

Such arguments for workfare are concerned with establishing coherent grounds for having work tests or work requirements or other compulsory measures as features of welfare state programs. They say much less, however, about the effects of such schemes on democratic values, institutions, and beliefs, which we may view as the foundations of a good society. Such advocates seem to hold implicitly that workfare type arrangements will be positive for participants' sense of self worth and common citizenship.

A Reply

The case for workfare may be answered in part by doubting whether it is sincere. In large part, one suspects, politicians use workfare to serve an older ideological agenda of simply reducing the scale of government. Many of workfare's most ardent advocates argue that the severe problems in welfare can be overcome only by severe cutbacks. They also readily move on to other agendas—such as marriage and the family, or the involvement of churches in social policy—that are not immediately about welfare or work. So welfare reform becomes a proxy for deeper ideological debates (see Teles 1996).

Even if we take at face value the proponents' strong concern for reciprocity or social contract, it is not obvious why these values should lead to demands that welfare recipients work in return for benefits at the same time that they are dependent. Clearly someone must assume responsibility for supporting the destitute when they are needy—but why should we expect this of the needy? It might rather mean, as welfare traditionally assumed, that the more fortunate support the less fortunate. Or it might mean, as in social insurance, that people contribute to a benefit system before they draw on it themselves. Reciprocity can have many meanings (Goodin 2002).

The proponents also assume that the responsibility to achieve work rests chiefly on the recipients. But if one thinks that work is central to achieving justice, one might conclude that the state should guarantee employment for all able-bodied unemployed persons unable to find work themselves (Arneson 1990; Palmer 1978). Rather than forcing job seekers into a mandatory scheme, an egalitarian view of welfare justice calls on the state to fund jobs at wages above the minimum wage because this forces private employers to offer better jobs. Taking work seriously should lead to an expanded welfare state, not a smaller one, or at best a welfare state in which the training and educational component of workfare gives participants more than the option of taking minimum wage jobs.

That is the tradition spoken for by other scholars, aghast at the changes since 1996. They renew the call for a generous system of public assistance which rewards and does not penalize claimants. To them, PRWORA signals a further shift in the U.S. welfare state away from the European social democratic model, perhaps even the end of welfare, as recipients face expulsion from public support after five years (Esping-Andersen 2002; Goodin 2002; Stoesz 2002). These voices currently go unheard.

The proponents and opponents of workfare differ on how feasible employment is. Workfare programs assume that opportunities are available for the recipients to support themselves, if they only look for work seriously. The policy assumes, that is, that there is no involuntary unemployment. Unemployed citizens' behavior and attitudes then become the object of reform (for an excellent historical-legal account of how the presumption of the absence of involuntary unemployment has developed, see Deakin and Wilkinson 2005, 110–99). By contrast, the older social democratic view attributed unemployment to the capitalist economy, which is organized for profit rather than for employing all those who need and want work. Workfare defines the welfare problem as high numbers on the rolls, where traditionally the goal was to alleviate poverty and hardship.

The historian Alice O'Connor shows that, over the century since poverty became a serious political issue, experts on the subject have moved steadily away from structural explanations of dependency and need (2001). In the Progressive and New Deal eras, scholars attributed destitution to features of the economy, such as low wages, or, in the case of the black poor, to the racial inequity imposed by Jim Crow. But since then, the focus has been more and more on poor communities, particularly a lifestyle of weak family structures and irregular employment that seems aberrant to the more fortunate.

The shift has been promoted, O'Connor contends, by the quantitative research that now dominates debate about poverty. These statistical studies and evaluations present as objective, yet they are part of the problem in O'Connor's view. By focusing on the individual as the unit of analysis, as they typically do, they operate to conceal the larger structures that create poverty. This framework is congenial to the critics of welfare policy, who examine the same data to extract evidence about behavioral failings and weaknesses.

The poverty research industry is also an alien world whose "technical language and decontextualized, rational choice models of human behaviour . . . [refuse] to acknowledge the value judgments underlying measures of welfare 'dependency' " (O'Connor 2001, 5). This type of expertise, though often refuted empirically, continues to dominate the political agenda. O'Connor calls on researchers to develop language, concepts, and measurements capable of matching the ideological success achieved by the welfare dependency school.

Democratic Consequences of Workfare

I now focus on a neglected dimension of workfare—its adverse effects on our common citizenship. Even if one conceded all of the arguments just reviewed, workfare is I contend incompatible with respect for the recipients as fellow members of the political community. It may seem only fair to expect from aid claimants, if they can work, an effort on their own behalf. But we cannot do this without undermining the values and practices that sustain equal citizenship and democratic institutions. These effects fall into three broad categories: compulsion of the recipients, other citizens' perceptions of the dependent, and administrators' practices.

The Effects of Compulsion

For recipients, public welfare programs can foster or hinder their sense of belonging. This arises in part from the well-known contrast between welfare and social insurance programs, which are more respectable. Joe Soss has investigated the attitudes of participants in means-tested and universal state programs, and argues that participating in either type of program is a learning experience that affects participants as political actors and as engaged citizens. He contrasts the means-tested AFDC with disability insurance (SSDI), a part of the Social Security system. AFDC recipients, he finds, "see government decision making as a directive rather than responsive process," whereas to those receiving SSDI "the government appears to be open and responsive to citizens" (1999, 370; see also 2000).

Welfare always was intrusive because applicants are required to expose their private lives to varying extents to demonstrate eligibility for aid. Assistance paid under social democratic assumptions at least minimized the intrusion. New demands have now arisen due to work testing. The sense that welfare is an intrusive and controlling force, which Soss discovered, may partly reflect the demands to work arising from welfare reform, which had already begun at the time he did his research.

Recipients subject to the work tests are liable to stigma because of the expectations set up in the contractual arrangement between job seekers and the state. If job seekers violate the terms and conditions of their agreement with the Employment Service or benefits agency, they become offenders. The punishment may only be to be denied aid, but the effect is akin to criminalization (see also Moore 1997). Failure to comply with publicly maintained codes of behavior renders the violator a miscreant, just as with any other social norm or code. Thus, although workfare claims to assist job seekers, it becomes instead an expression of an overweening state power.[2]

Some workfare proponents try to make a virtue out of compulsion, and claim that the supervisory character of mandatory work programs, far from alienating participants, provides a means of better integrating them into society (Mead 1997b). In the most developed version of this case, Lawrence Mead argues that given the widespread absence of work-based competences amongst the unemployed and those who depend on welfare, and given that nonwork ensures continuing poverty, the state should enforce work and other civilities. Doing so not only raises income and combats poverty, but also boosts recipients' self-esteem and inculcates a fuller understanding of the world of citizenship and its associated expectations. When asked, recipients usually express support for such policies (1997b, 2004).

But these arguments appeal to the very recent past. A longer view suggests that workfare might well produce a deepening sense of alienation and exclusion among those it claims to help. The main reason that the social democratic tradition of assured welfare arose, we should remember, was disillusionment with setting conditions on aid. Especially in the interwar years in Britain, aid was means-tested and conditioned on the recipients genuinely seeking work; these rules came to be deeply hated in working-class communities (King 1995). This was why the Beveridge reforms that rebuilt the welfare state after 1945 emphasized social insurance and universal benefits, such as the child benefit, that everyone would receive.

Mandatory work tests and requirements have already stigmatized some participants, driving some off the rolls (and thereby exacerbating poverty) and others into a feeling of being second-class citizens. They have this effect for one major reason: participants in workfare are treated differently, and not in a positive sense, from participants in other state-administered benefit programs.

Nonclaiming Citizens and Welfare Others

A second effect that workfare has on citizenship is to promote an unfortunate image of the recipients in the minds of other citizens. How do our attitudes change toward those who are required to undertake mandatory activities simply because they are unemployed and unable to find work? Does this activity increase our sense of their status as equals—or encourage us to treat them as second-class supplicants lucky to receive any assistance?

The advocates of workfare claim to be worried that allowing the dependents to avoid the labor market will cause them and their descendants to be excluded from mainstream society. This is the argument Lawrence Mead developed in *The New Paternalism* (1997b). However, even if one grants that intergenerational poverty is a genuine problem, couching it in terms of welfare dependency retains instead of diminishing this perception that recipients are different from the rest of society.

Mead argues indeed that mandatory participation in work programs will enhance the legitimacy of claimants' demands on the rest of us who fund welfare, thus tending to support a decent welfare system (Mead 1992). However, the services the new paternalism offers to workfare participants rarely provide the sort of comprehensive education or training likely to give them any economic status other than that of the precarious working poor. Thus, rather than making the rest of us feel that workfare participants have a legitimate claim on society, we may instead view them as incompetent, hence lacking in the qualities needed for membership in the polity as equal citizens.

Even before workfare, welfare tended to stigmatize the image of racial groups strongly associated with it. For many Americans, welfare is a code word for African Americans. Political scientist Martin Gilens finds that "the belief that blacks lack a commitment to the work ethic" appears to play an important role in generating opposition to welfare among white Americans. "Images of blacks," he adds, "have come to dominate the public's thinking about poverty and welfare, generating negative perceptions of welfare recipients and fostering demands for cuts in welfare spending" (Gilens 1999, 77, 101; and see Quadagno 1995). Media discussions dominated by experts claiming impartiality often appear highly critical of poor people, especially black women (Flanders and Jackson 1995).

In much the same way, Alice O'Connor argues, academic research on poverty tends to concentrate on blacks. To talk of poverty can appear more race neutral than to talk of race, but it comes to much the same thing. Although the 1960s argument about a culture of poverty was replaced in the 1980s with a focus on the family, inquiry in any event ends up focusing disproportionately on African American communities (2001, 17; see also Schram 2005).

Probing beneath everyday politics, the association of blacks with poverty and welfare is more apparent than real. It is due, not to race per se, but to the link that race has with poverty and its associated disadvantages. Poor people are more likely to become single parents. Thus, if African Americans display more single-parenthood and dependency, this is because they are more often poor. But these trends are commonly discussed in ways which focus on group based distinctions rather than economic class. Determining whether inner-city poverty reflects being born to a minority parent, an unmarried parent, a poor parent, or some combination of these factors is far from simple.

Haya Stier and Marta Tienda's study of Chicago found that both African Americans and Puerto Ricans grow up in more disadvantaged neighborhoods, compared with whites and Mexicans, and that these differences continue from adolescence into adulthood. It is early life circumstances that are critical to these trajectories:

> Racial and ethnic differences in recent welfare use largely reflect group variation in characteristics and early life circumstances that qualify them for public assistance, notably, having been reared in a mother-only family, childhood material deprivation, and the two pivotal life-course events that shape adult well-being: low educational attainment and bearing children out of wedlock. (2001, 131)

These researchers stress the effects of disadvantages among labor market participants that accumulate along racial and ethnic lines. Educational underachievement is a particular handicap which shapes work trajectories negatively. These accumulated weaknesses fall more heavily on blacks and Puerto Ricans than Mexicans or whites. This finding implies that when levels of education and work experience are equalized, the effects of racial and ethnic differences disappear (224).

Racial minorities are thus disadvantaged by the society. Their link with welfare is then a further disadvantage, permitting the better-off to blame them for their need for public support. Workfare intensifies that stigma by blaming the recipients all the more surely for their condition. The goal of racial integration would be served better by forms of social support that reduced the distinctions between some groups of citizens than others.

The Effects on Administrators

Finally, mandatory programs affect program administrators. These street-level bureaucrats are the critical players as society relates to citizens in the time of their greatest need. It was precisely to maintain the dignity of the dependent that the traditional welfare state emphasized the rights of claimants. Caseworkers were advocates for the poor in obtaining needed benefits. Workfare programs, however, advance a strict contractualist approach to recipients and administrators. This emphasis is likely to change how administrators define their jobs and perceive those whom they process through the workfare schemes. Their job now becomes one of behavior modification, especially if there are performance-related incentives attached to clients' successful completion of the program.

The recipients may in essence become instances of an impersonal social condition (rather than human beings) that administrators manipulate to achieve mandated outcomes, namely work. As one sign of this, officials are increasingly required to compile data about welfare clients. Whereas AFDC expected a fairly narrow range of information in delivering benefits, PRWORA requires that states collect detailed data about recipients, and on a broad range of indicators related to state compliance and program evaluation efforts (HHS 1997). Quarterly reports derived from "the use of scientifically acceptable sampling methods approved by the Secretary" are mandated (Wiseman 1996). By employing the language of social science, PRWORA adopts the same stance of antiseptic expertise struck by antipoverty researchers.

Under AFDC, data were distinct to each system of welfare delivery. Information was gathered solely to determine whether individuals met eligibility requirements and to ensure timely and accurate benefits. In addition, managers and staff had little experience in analyzing data beyond these functional needs. In contrast, PRWORA demanded a new level of detail about welfare recipients. For example, establishing five-year limits on benefits implies that total time on welfare has to be added up for each family across multiple spells of receipt, perhaps across different states. That requires that states be able to access and exchange information at a new level (HHS 2003).

Furthermore, under AFDC, opening and closing a case coincided with opening and closing a cash grant. TANF, on the other hand, allows efforts to divert clients from opening a grant. The five-year limit on benefits means that agencies now trace the life of the individual during a longer cycle of support than the current case (HHS 2003). The focus of data gathering under TANF changes from delivering payments to moving people from welfare to work. This entails collecting information beyond eligibility and benefits. Managers and staff now must collect information about "compliance with immigration requirements, fleeing felon status, domestic violence and mental health, dependents' school attendance, probation status, and substance abuse" (HHS 2003, 2).

In addition, management information systems are designed to assess the performance of case managers and supervisors. Such measures may include the percentage of caseload participating in work programs, the numbers satisfactorily completing activities, the numbers placed in jobs, average wage at placement, and the percentage of closed cases still working at certain points or receiving the Earned Income Tax Credit. In short, the new requirements of TANF promise a profusion of data and statistics about welfare reform programs and their effects. This data will in turn promote a managerial, rather than a responsive, stance toward welfare clients in the political arena.

Another feature of staff-client relations under workfare is that they are more variable and discretionary than under the earlier system. Just because of the vulnerability of clients, the old system endeavored to limit discretion by laying down firm rules for how claimants were to be treated.

Past practices that gave staff personal control of whether applicants were given aid were proscribed. Deciding how best to move clients off aid into jobs, however, is necessarily complicated and judgmental. The effect is to bring discretion back into administration. That undermines the rule of law and, with it, the equal respect in which citizens are held.

In short, administrative arrangements under TANF are justified in the name of social science and managerial efficiency. Nevertheless, they raise an Orwellian specter of state management of the dependent. Far from ushering the needy toward fuller membership in the society, workfare drives administrators toward a stance of superiority toward them. That position makes it less conceivable that they could regard those they serve as in any way like themselves. Their doubts only mirror the larger society's condescending stance toward those it is supposed to help.

Conclusion

Workfare encourages both participants and other members of the polity to conceive of themselves as economic participants rather than as citizens. This is dangerous for the sustenance and extension of liberal democratic values and institutions. It brings market criteria—which are distinct from democratic and participatory criteria—into the polity in a new and consequential way. Most significant, perhaps, the workfare participants are not the only ones affected. All of us are encouraged to look on welfare claimants as the others within our societies.

Under mandatory work schemes, the relationship between the state and its members becomes one of contract, not of belonging. The imaginative and educative development necessary to full citizenship—classically expressed by John Stuart Mill and Alexis de Tocqueville—is thus precluded. If the illiberal coercive element were absent, these schemes might have a more positive effect.

Knowledge based on our history calls for great caution about the costs to democracy of taking a workfare approach to welfare claimants. Workfare may well force some members of society into greater marginality and poverty, if they reject the mandatory requirements. It may brutalize administrators, compelled to impose sanctions upon unwilling participants. These are the likely consequences of workfare for democratic engagement, social capital, and senses of inclusion. Political theorists quite rightly worry about these costs.

Notes

1. For further arguments about social rights, see King and Waldron (1988); Fabre (2000); Gaffaney (2000); for broader accounts of welfare rights, see Goodin (1985, 1988).
2. These arguments are pursued legalistically in Mark Freedland and Desmond King (2003).

References

Arneson, Richard J. 1990. "Is Work Special? Justice and the Distribution of Employment." *American Political Science Review* 84(4): 1127–47.

Blank, Rebecca M. 2002. "Evaluating Welfare Reform in the United States." NBER Working Paper 8983. New York: National Bureau of Economic Research.

———. 1997. *It Takes a Nation.* Princeton, N.J.: Princeton University Press.

Clasen, Jochen, and Daniel Clegg. 2003. "Unemployment Protection and Labour Market Reform in France and Great Britain in the 1990s: Solidarity Versus Activation?" *Journal of Social Policy* 32(3): 361–81.

Deakin, Simon, and Frank Wilkinson. 2005. *The Law of the Labour Market.* Oxford: Oxford University Press.

Department of Employment. 1994. *Jobseeker's Allowance.* Cm. 2687. London: HMSO.

Driver, Stephen, and Luke Martell. 2002. *Blair's Britain.* Oxford: Polity Press.

Esping-Andersen, Gosta, ed. 2002. *Why We Need a New Welfare State.* Oxford: Oxford University Press.

Fabre, Cecile. 2000. *Social Rights Under the Constitution.* Oxford: Oxford University Press.

Flanders, Laura, and Janine Jackson. 1995. "Public Enemy Number One? Media's Welfare Debate Is a War on Poor Women." New York: Fairness and Accuracy in Reporting. Available at: http://www.fair.org/index.php?page=1303 (accessed July 2003).

Freedland, Mark, and Desmond King. 2003. "Contractual Governance and Illiberal Contracts: Some Problems of Contractualism as an Instrument of Behaviour Management by Agencies of Government." *Cambridge Journal of Economics* 27(3): 465–77.

Fremstad, Shawn, and Zoë Neuberger. 2002. "TANF'S 'Uncounted' cases: More than One Million Working Families Receiving TANF-funded Services Not Counted in TANF Caseload." Washington, D.C.: Center for Budget and Policy Priorities. Available at: http://www.cbpp.org/4-24-02tanf.pdf (accessed July 2003).

Gaffaney, Timothy J. 2000. *Freedom for the Poor: Welfare and the Foundations of Democratic Citizenship.* Boulder, Colo.: Westview Press.

Galston, William A. 1991. *Liberal Purposes: Goods, Virtues, and Diversity in the Liberal State.* Cambridge: Cambridge University Press.

Gilbert, Neil. 2002. *Transformation of the Welfare State.* New York: Oxford University Press.

Gilens, Martin. 1999. *Why Americans Hate Welfare: Race, Media, and the Politics of Antipoverty Policy.* Chicago: University of Chicago Press.

Goodin, Robert E. 1985. *Protecting the Vulnerable: A Reanalysis of Our Social Responsibilities.* Chicago: University of Chicago Press.

———. 1988. *Reasons for Welfare: The Political Theory of the Welfare State.* Princeton, N.J.: Princeton University Press.

———. 2002. "Structures of Mutual Obligation." *Journal of Social Policy* 31(4): 579–96.

Gutmann, Amy, and Dennis Thompson. 1996. *Democracy and Disagreement.* Cambridge, Mass.: Harvard University Press.

Hartz, Louis. 1955. *The Liberal Tradition in America: An Interpretation of American Political Thought Since the Revolution.* New York: Harcourt, Brace & World.

House of Commons Sessions. 1996. *The Right to Work/Workfare.* Employment Committee Second Report 1995–96, February 13. London: HMSO.

Huber, Evelyne, and John D. Stephens 2001. *Development and Crisis of the Welfare State.* Chicago: University of Chicago Press.

Jayasuriya, Kanishka. 2002. "The New Contractualism: Neo-liberal or Democratic?" *Political Quarterly* 73(3): 309–20.

King, Desmond. 1995. *Actively Seeking Work? The Politics of Unemployment and Welfare Policy in the United States and Britain.* Chicago: University of Chicago Press.

———. 1999. *In the Name of Liberalism: Illiberal Social Policy in the US and Britain.* Oxford: Oxford University Press.

King, Desmond S., and Jennifer Nou. 2003. "American Welfare Reform and the Paradox of Expertise." Unpublished paper. Nuffield College, Oxford University.

King, Desmond S., and Rogers M. Smith. 2005. "Racial Orders in American Political Development." *American Political Science Review* 99(1): 75–92.

King, Desmond S., and Jeremy Waldron. 1988. "Citizenship, Social Citizenship and the Defence of Welfare Rights." *British Journal of Political Science* 28(fall): 415–44.

Kitschelt, Herbert, Peter Lange, Gary Marks, and John D. Stephens, eds. 1999. *Continuity and Change in Contemporary Capitalism.* New York: Cambridge University Press.

Marshall, T. H. 1964. *Class, Citizenship and Social Development.* New York: Doubleday.

Mead, Lawrence M. 1986. *Beyond Entitlement: The Social Obligations of Citizenship.* New York: Free Press.

———. 1992. *The New Politics of Poverty: The Nonworking Poor in America.* New York: Basic Books.

———. 1997a. "Citizenship and Social Policy: T. H. Marshall and Poverty." *Social Philosophy and Policy* 14(2): 197–230.

———, ed. 1997b. *The New Paternalism: Supervisory Approaches to Poverty.* Washington, D.C.: Brookings Institution.

———. 2004. *Government Matters: Welfare Reform in Wisconsin.* Princeton, N.J.: Princeton University Press.

Moore, Michael S. 1997. *Placing Blame: A General Theory of the Criminal Law.* Oxford: Clarendon Press.

Murray, Charles. 1984. *Losing Ground: American Social Policy, 1950–1980.* New York: Basic Books.

Myrdal, Gunnar. 1944. *An American Dilemma: The Negro Problem and Modern Democracy.* New York: Harper and Row.

O'Connor, Alice. 2001. *Poverty Knowledge: Social Science, Social Policy, and the Poor in Twentieth Century U.S. History.* Princeton N.J.: Princeton University Press.

Palmer, John L., ed. 1978. *Creating Jobs.* Washington, D.C.: Brookings Institution.

Pierson, Paul, ed. 2000. *The New Politics of Welfare.* Oxford: Oxford University Press.

Quadagno, Jill. 1995. *The Color of Welfare.* New York: Oxford University Press.

Rothstein, Bo, and Sven Steinmo, eds. 2002. *Restructuring the Welfare State.* London: Palgrave Macmillan.

Schneider, Saundra K., and William G. Jacoby. 2003. "A Culture of Dependence? The Relationship Between Public Assistance and Public Opinion." *British Journal of Political Science* 33(2): 213–31.

Schram, Sanford F. 2005. "Contextualizing Racial Disparities in American Welfare Reform: Toward a New Poverty Research." *Perspectives on Politics* 3(2): 253–68.

Secretary of State for Social Security and Minister for Welfare Reform. 1998. *New Ambitions for Our Country: A New Contract for Welfare.* London: The Stationery Office.

Smith, Rogers M. 1993. "Beyond Tocqueville, Myrdal and Hartz: The Multiple Traditions in America." *American Political Science Review* 87(3): 549–66.

Soss, Joe. 1999. "Lessons of Welfare: Policy Design, Political Learning and Political Action." *American Political Science Review* 93(2): 363–80.

———. 2000. *Unwanted Claims: The Politics of Participation in the U.S. Welfare System.* Ann Arbor: University of Michigan Press.

Stier, Haya, and Marta Tienda. 2001. *The Color of Opportunity: Pathways to Family, Welfare and Work.* Chicago: University of Chicago Press.

Stoesz, David. 2002. "The American Welfare State in Twilight." *Journal of Social Policy* 31(4): 487–503.

Teles, Steven M. 1996. *Whose Welfare? AFDC and Elite Politics.* Lawrence: University Press of Kansas.

U.S. Department of Health and Human Services (HHS). 1997. "Welfare Reform." Press Release dated November 17, 1997. Washington: U.S. Government Printing Office. Available at: http://www.acf.dhhs.gov/news/welfare/regfact.htm (accessed January 2003).

———. Administration for Children and Families. 1999. "Welfare Reform Information Technology: A Study of Issues in Implementing Systems for the Temporary Assistance for Needy Families (TANF) Program. Washington: U.S. Government Printing Office. Available at: http://www.acf.hhs.gov/nhsitrc/writ/overarchingissue.asp.htm (accessed January 2003).

Waddan, Alex. 2003. "Redesigning the Welfare Contract in Theory and Practice: Just What Is Going on in the USA?" *Journal of Social Policy* 32(1): 19–35.

Weaver, R. Kent. 1998. "Ending Welfare as We Know It." In *The Social Divide,* edited by Margaret Weir. Washington, D.C.: Brookings Institution.

White, Stuart. 2000. "Social Rights and the Social Contract: Political Theory and the New Welfare Politics." *British Journal of Political Science* 30(2): 507–32.

———. 2003. *The Civic Minimum: On the Rights and Obligations of Economic Citizenship.* Oxford: Oxford University Press.

Wiseman, Michael. 1996. "Welfare Reform in the United States: A Background Paper." In *Housing Policy Debate,* vol. 7, iss. 4. New York: Fannie Mae Foundation. Available at: http://www.fanniemaefoundation.org/programs/hpd/pdf/hpd_0704_wiseman.pdf (accessed July 2003).

Zedlewski, Sheila. 2002. "Are Shrinking Caseloads Always a Good Thing?" Washington, D.C.: Urban Institute.

Chapter 4

Is Conditionality Illiberal?

STUART WHITE

IS WELFARE reform a repudiation of liberalism? For welfare reform's critics, such as Desmond King, the shift toward increased conditionality in welfare programs, by which eligibility for benefits is made conditional on satisfying prescribed behavioral standards, is a symptom of a new and worrying kind of illiberal social policy (see King 1999 and chapter 3 in this volume). By allegedly subjecting welfare recipients to disciplines from which others are free, conditionality demeans them. For welfare reform's supporters, such as Lawrence Mead, recent reforms also mark a break with liberalism. But this is to be welcomed. Liberalism is defined, in Mead's view, by a strong sense of the fragility of the disadvantaged and by a narrowly structural explanation of nonwork. Hence liberalism has demanded permissive welfare programs that fail to address the real problems of the poor: their limited capacity to function in society on the same terms as everyone else (see Mead 1986, 1992). Thus, while these theorists disagree about the desirability of welfare reform, they nevertheless seem to agree on its philosophical significance: that it marks a definite break with something called liberalism.

In the face of this consensus, I pose and explore the question of whether welfare reform is illiberal. More specifically, I want to consider how far the practice of conditionality, which is so central to welfare reform, is consistent with liberalism. I argue that there is nothing inherently illiberal about conditionality. However, the liberal does have good reason to be wary of conditionality where there is significant background injustice. The justice of welfare reform thus depends on how far it is connected with an agenda of deeper structural change.

Which Liberalism?

Before we can consider the relationship between liberalism and welfare conditionality we must first clarify what we take liberalism to be. It is not hard to show that many past thinkers in the liberal tradition have endorsed conditionality. John Locke, for example, was so keen to make poor relief conditional on work that he called for shirkers on welfare to be pressed into military service (1697/1993). John Stuart Mill supported the Victorian Poor Law and its demanding behavioral requirements (1848/1970, 333–36). British New Liberals at the turn of the twentieth century, such as Leonard Hobhouse, had doubts about the Poor Law, but not about the basic principle of work-conditionality in welfare. Hobhouse argued that the state had a duty to secure a "civic minimum" for the citizen (see 1911/1993, 1912). But he envisaged this as a right to a decent minimum in return for work. Those who refused to work would receive a basic sub-minimum on punitive terms. In Hobhouse's words: "Given the opportunity of adequately remunerated work, a man has the power to earn his living. It his right and his duty to make the best use of this opportunity, and if he fails he may fairly be treated as a pauper" (1911/1993, 79).

William Beveridge, whose wartime report *Social Insurance and Allied Services* (1942) exercised enormous influence over the development of the British welfare state, was similarly emphatic that benefits to the unemployed worker should come with obligations to look for work and to retrain.[1] Critics of conditionality such as Desmond King sometimes cite T. H. Marshall's influential text, *Citizenship and Social Class*, as expressing a quite distinct welfare philosophy based on unconditional "social rights" (1999; and King and Wickham-Jones 1999, 62–74; Marshall 1950). However, as I have explained at length elsewhere, Marshall's text does not clearly break with the contractualist philosophy we find in social liberals such as Hobhouse and Beveridge (see White 2003; Powell 2002).

Nevertheless, it might be argued that all this changes when we come to contemporary Anglo-American liberalism. When the critics and proponents of conditionality referred to in the introduction appeal to, or attack, something called liberalism, I suspect that it is contemporary Anglo-American liberalism that they have in mind. Politically, this variety of liberalism is identified with the mainstream of the Democratic Party in the United States and with the Liberal Democrats and currents within the Labour Party in Britain. Philosophically, it is associated primarily with the work of Ronald Dworkin (see 2000) and John Rawls (see especially 1971/1999). Contemporary conservatives might argue that this contemporary version of liberalism has abandoned many of the key insights and values of its parent tradition and, as a result, has regrettably embraced a much more permissive philosophy of welfare as unconditional entitlement.

On the other hand, critics of conditionality might argue that the liberalism of Locke, Mill, Hobhouse, and Beveridge was distorted by residual class biases. Once liberalism is finally freed from these distortions, as it perhaps is in the work of Rawls and Dworkin, we will see that true liberalism stands firmly opposed to welfare conditionality. Marcel Wissenberg has argued, in this vein, that the welfare-to-work policy of Britain's Labour government "deviates from Rawls's theory" in part because "it lacks impartiality with regard to individuals' theories of the good" by "forcing them to be subject to the dictates of the labour market" and so "probably directly discourages, the development and expression of plans of life and theories of the good that deviate from the ideal of the useful drone" (2001, 233–34). Particularly noteworthy here is the appeal to the idea of impartiality or neutrality between conceptions of the good. This is taken to be a central tenet of liberalism, and one that is violated by conditionality.

It is this variety of liberalism that I shall be concerned with in this chapter. I want to ask, more specifically: Is welfare conditionality consistent with an egalitarian liberalism of a broadly Rawlsian kind? I shall argue that a liberal of this kind does have good reasons to be critical of (at least some forms of) conditionality, but that the picture is a good deal more complicated than that presented earlier.

Let us begin with a brief overview of Rawls's liberalism. Rawls's preoccupation with articulating what he came to call a "political liberalism" in his later work can be understood as an effort to reconcile two intrinsically attractive, but potentially antagonistic lines of thought within the liberal democratic tradition. For the sake of simplicity we might refer to the first line of thought as the quintessentially liberal part of the tradition. It is concerned with the toleration of different religions and lifestyles, with maintaining a framework of expansive freedoms within which people are free to pursue their respective "conceptions of the good." This line of thought suggests a picture of society as ethically pluralistic. The other line, deriving from Rousseau, we might term republican. Its concern is not immediately with the scope of the law, but with whether those subject to the law can see it as an expression of their will. For laws to be collectively willed, however, citizens must share a conception of the common good. This suggests a picture of a society that is ethically integrated. On the face of it, there seems to be a conflict. How can a society be ethically pluralistic as the liberal wants and ethically integrated as the republican wants? Rawls's political liberalism can be seen as an effort to solve this puzzle.[2] Political liberalism addresses the question: What kind of conception of the common good can people share that will underpin liberal institutions given the ethical pluralism that these institutions inevitably produce?

Rawls's answer is that the required conception of the common good must eschew grounding in any specific comprehensive ethical doctrine, but must instead be constructed from certain abstract political ideas, allegedly implicit in the public culture of a democratic society, that can be presented independently of such doctrines. These ideas centrally include the idea of society as a fair scheme of cooperation, for mutual advantage, between citizens who are free and equal (Rawls 2001, 5–8). So what does fair cooperation between free and equal citizens consist in? What principles of justice define fair terms of cooperation? Rawls argues that the most reasonable account of these principles is given by the conception of justice defended in *A Theory of Justice,* "justice as fairness." The basic structure of society must be designed so that, first, each person has "the same indefeasible claim to a fully adequate scheme of equal basic liberties; and, second, "social and economic inequalities are . . . attached to offices and positions open to all under conditions of fair equality of opportunity; and . . . are . . . to the greatest benefit of the least-advantaged members of society" (Rawls 2001, 42–43). I shall assume that Rawls is broadly correct in claiming that these two principles offer the most reasonable account of the terms for fair, mutually advantageous cooperation between free and equal persons. We should note, however, that Rawls does acknowledge that justice as fairness is only one of a number of conceptions of justice that reasonably elaborate this core idea (see 1999, 142).[3]

For the political liberal, argument about public policy, at least when it concerns "constitutional essentials and matters of basic justice" (Rawls 1993, 227–30), must proceed from principles such as these, and related political values, and must eschew reasons that are internal to specific comprehensive ethical doctrines (224–25).[4] What Rawls calls our "duty of civility" requires that we confine the moral reasons we give in public justification for policies to those that appeal to such principles of justice, and associated political values, and that we vote for a given policy only if we genuinely believe it to be supported by moral reasons derived from these principles and associated values.

Demands of Citizenship

I now clarify some of the civic obligations and related virtues of citizenship in an egalitarian liberal state of the kind that Rawls's principles of justice suggest.

The Obligation to Work

In *A Theory of Justice,* Rawls (1971/1999, 64) argues that inequalities in income and wealth that reflect differences in "willingness to make an effort" between individuals should not be treated as inherently deserved. The willingness to work hard is influenced by other and morally arbitrary factors, such as one's endowment of natural ability or class background, and, being so tangled with these other factors, we cannot feasibly separate its influence to make assessments of individual desert (see 1971/1999, 64, 274). These comments naturally give the impression that when Rawls states that economic inequalities must work to the maximum benefit of society's worst-off group he is endorsing a scheme in which the hard-working are allowed to benefit from their hard work only to the extent that this also benefits people who are less well-off, some of whom are badly off simply because they make little or no productive effort.

This reading supports the claim that Rawls's liberalism is the philosophical expression of what Gareth Davies calls entitlement liberalism: a political movement aimed at securing payment of welfare to those in need regardless of willingness to work (1996). Conservative critics have certainly interpreted Rawls in these terms. Thus, Clifford Orwin connects the idea of welfare as entitlement with a rejection of traditional notions of desert, and identifies Rawls's theory of justice as offering intellectual support for this rejection (1983). Brian C. Anderson claims that "Rawls's idea of justice offers us . . . a rather dispiriting world, where individual responsibility and striving have no place" (2003, 50). Although writing from a more sympathetic standpoint, Samuel Scheffler also stresses the way in which Rawls's treatment of desert puts his theory at odds with popular views of distributive justice, a gap that, in Scheffler's view, helps explain the apparent inability of egalitarian liberalism to win more than a small, academic following (1992).

However, the criticism that his theory of justice sanctions the subsidization of the idle is one that was made early on in the academic debate that followed publication of *A Theory of Justice*, and in response Rawls explicitly clarified (or, less generously, revised) his account of justice as fairness to meet this criticism. The response is stated fully in *Justice as Fairness: A Restatement*, though the ingredients of the response were first presented in a 1974 article in the *Quarterly Journal of Economics* (see 2001, 179; 1993, n.9; 1974/1999). Here Rawls seems to accept as self-evident that it would be wrong for working citizens to subsidize the lifestyle of those "who live on welfare and surf all day off Malibu." Those who receive a generous social minimum (or more) under the difference principle must satisfy a basic work requirement in return. This reflects the idea that "all citizens are to do their part in society's cooperative work." Those who choose not to meet the basic work requirement are not entitled to this minimum: "Surfers must somehow support themselves." Involuntary unemployment, of course, is quite another matter.[5] When these comments are taken into account, Rawls's difference principle no longer appears as a principle to guide the distribution of income and wealth without any regard to individuals' productive efforts. Rather, it appears more like a principle to guide differentials in income and wealth amongst those engaged in productive service. It is, one might say, a principle of just differentiation in reward for productive service.

So understood, there is a striking similarity between Rawls's conception of economic justice and the functionalist accounts of economic justice advanced by British social democratic philosophers like Leonard Hobhouse and R. H. Tawney in the first half of the twentieth century. The social democratic functionalists thought that income entitlement is essentially a reward for productive contribution. It was on this basis that theorists such as Hobhouse opposed unconditional welfare payments and called for the abolition of "functionless" property incomes, such as income derived from inherited wealth. Amongst those performing a productive function, the functionalists held that differential rewards could be justified, but only if these inequalities benefit the community as a whole: "Inequality in circumstance is reasonable, in so far as it is the necessary condition of securing the services which the community requires" (Tawney 1931/1964, 112). Rawls's difference principle offers us a clearer account of exactly when inequalities in functional reward serve the common good: when they work to make the functional reward paid to the class of lowest-paid workers as high as possible (for further discussion of the affinities between the functionalists and Rawls, see Jackson 2003).

Thus, we can say that justice as fairness, at least in the later, functionalist form that Rawls articulated, does endorse the idea of a civic obligation to work.[6] What motivates the assertion of such an obligation? Rawls is not very expansive about this, but his language—"all are to do their part in society's cooperative work"—hints at some underlying notion of fair play or reciprocity.[7] The idea can be related to his concern for mutual advantage in economic and social relations. The rules of economic cooperation are, arguably, not sufficiently geared to mutual advantage if they allow surfers to live off the labor of others. This does not imply a simple doctrine of the laborer's right to his product, for this would unfairly reward those who are born with more productive ability than others; but mutual advantage does require that everyone do their bit, given the respective endowments they have.

Education and Parenting

Education plays a crucial role in the political liberal state. It is through education that people develop the two moral powers that Rawls presumes all citizens of the liberal state to have: the power to form, to revise, and rationally to pursue a conception of the good and the power to act from a sense of justice (see 1993, 19). It is also in part through the education system that society seeks to achieve "fair equality of opportunity": the state of affairs in which any two children with similar natural endowments have similar opportunities to develop these endowments regardless of their initial social background (2001, 43–44). It is through education that citizens learn how to be "economically independent and self-supporting members of society over a complete life," a concern that is arguably related to the civic obligation to work (1993, 200).

What obligations or duties do citizens have with respect to the educational goals of the liberal state? Rawls argues that we have a natural duty to help establish and maintain just institutions,[8] and this surely requires of us at least some minimum level of political engagement across the policy areas that bear on social justice, which include education. We should use our political liberties to construct an educational system that will help develop citizens' moral powers to a sufficient extent, and that will also help secure fair equality of opportunity. But are our duties in relation to the educational aims of the liberal state only about political participation? Rawls does not expand on these duties very much, but someone working within the framework of his liberalism might reasonably argue as follows.

First, parents obviously have a duty to see that their children have an education. Parents are trustees of their children's welfare, with a responsibility to act to secure their long-term interests. These interests include developing children's moral powers of citizenship to an adequate extent (given the natural capacity to do so), and starting children's own adult lives on a footing of fair equality of opportunity with their peers. To advance these interests, parents must do their bit to see that their children have an adequate education. In their position of trusteeship, they may not encourage or allow their children to opt out of school.

Parental duties do not necessarily stop here, however. There is growing evidence that children's educational attainment depends to a considerable extent on how their cognitive and related abilities develop in preschool years, and that early years development in turn crucially depends on the quality of parenting and family life.[9] From a liberal point of view, the worry must be that poor parenting in preschool years will impair development of the moral powers of citizenship and scuttle the prospects of fair equality of opportunity before children have even reached the school gates. Given the importance of these public goals, a liberal might argue that the duties of parental trusteeship go further than just making a reasonable effort to see that one's children attend school. They also include a duty to make a good faith effort to nurture one's children's cognitive and related capacities within the home, starting in preschool years. They also include a duty to make a good faith effort to acquire the knowledge and skills necessary to effective nurturing.

In response to this latter point, it might be said that it is no business of a liberal state to go prying into how parents raise their children.[10] This is to violate the public-private distinction that liberalism is meant to protect. However, many forms of intervention in family life are widely endorsed by liberals as essential to protecting children's interests, compulsory schooling being one such intervention. It is hard to see why the line against intervention should be drawn to exclude intervention in parenting skills if these skills are as important for the development of children's cognitive abilities as I have supposed. If bad parenting in a child's preschool years can undermine a child's ability to take advantage of schooling, then there is surely something odd about insisting that parents send their children to school and, at the same time, insisting that preschool parenting is, with the exception of the most extreme cases of abuse, a no-go area for state intervention.

The Neutrality Objection

I have tried to show how, on a reasonable interpretation of political liberalism, citizens have certain obligations or duties in relation to work, education and parenting. Keeping this in mind, let us now turn to the claim that welfare conditionality is illiberal.

Liberals believe that to show equal concern and respect for citizens of different conceptions of the good, the state must adopt a policy of neutrality toward the ways of life grounded in these different conceptions of the good. Now, according to some commentators—some of them friends and some of them foes of welfare conditionality—liberals cannot endorse welfare conditionality because conditionality necessarily violates the required stance of neutrality.

This objection in fact comes in at least two versions. In the first, the objection focuses on the impact that welfare conditionality has on different conceptions of the good. A neutral policy, on this conception of neutrality, is one that burdens or benefits different conceptions of the good to an equal extent. The demands of welfare conditionality will tend to weigh more heavily on some conceptions of the good than others. Thus, it is not neutral. This is the version of the neutrality objection that we saw Wissenberg make. The objection is that the policies in question make it harder for people to pursue leisure-intensive conceptions of the good over employment-based conceptions of the good, and this, in itself, makes the policies objectionably not neutral (hence unRawlsian).

As it stands, however, this objection will not do. Neutrality, in the sense that laws and policies impact or burden different ways of life to an equal extent, cannot be what the liberal primarily means by neutrality. For the liberal believes that we all have certain rights, and the laws that secure these rights will of necessity burden some possible ways of life more than others (see Rawls 1993, 192–94; Barry 2000, 34). The neutrality to which egalitarian liberals such as Rawls and Dworkin are committed is not, in fact, primarily a matter of the burden or impact of laws, but of the sort of reasons that lie behind them.[11] For the neutrality objection to have bite, one would have to show, not that a conditionality policy burdens some conceptions of the good more than others, but that the reasons behind the policy are the wrong sort.

So what are reasons of the right sort? In his *Letter Concerning Toleration,* John Locke distinguishes two projects that the state might use its power to pursue. One project is to protect and advance, in an equitable fashion, its subjects' "civil interests": their shared and, so Locke assumes, urgent interests in life, freedom, and access to material goods. A second (and quite different) project is to try to save subjects' souls: to promote what we might call their spiritual interests. Locke's argument is that the state acts legitimately only when it acts from reasons related to the first of these projects. So, let us imagine that state officials are considering whether to introduce a law that would ban the slaughter of cattle in religious worship (see Locke 1685/1993, 415). If the reason for the proposed ban is a theological claim that such worship is offensive to God, then Locke holds that the ban is illegitimate. But if the reason is, say, that society needs to replenish an important food supply following some disaster that has decimated its cattle stock, then the proposed ban may be legitimate. For this reason reflects a concern to protect one of the key civil interests of the state's subjects, their interest in subsistence.

Contemporary egalitarian liberals such as Rawls and Dworkin work with a similar distinction. On the one hand stand perfectionist reasons, which appeal to the alleged inherent superiority of one conception of the good over another: the equivalent of Locke's reasons based on a theory of subjects' spiritual interests. On the other are what Rawls calls public reasons, which are the equivalent of Locke's reasons based on subjects' civil interests. Like Locke, Rawls wishes to restrict reasons for state action (at least over the range of constitutional essentials and matters of basic justice) to reasons of civil interest. Rawls's theory of justice is, in essence, an effort to identify what our core civil interests are, and to identify a set of principles that define what it means to provide equitable protection for them.[12] The public reasoning that Rawls advocates is neutral in the specific sense that it restricts itself to considerations of this kind, eschewing perfectionist arguments.

The second version of the neutrality objection holds, then, that the reasons for conditionality are not grounded in considerations of justice of the kind admissible in public reason, but are perfectionist. Jonathan Wolff has drawn attention to the way in which perfectionist reasoning seems to play a role in arguments for active welfare policies. He writes:

> Consider . . . the shift in welfare policy away from reliance on simple cash benefits towards greater emphasis on re-education, re-skilling, and guiding people towards gainful employment. . . . I think it is clear that part of the appeal of these policies is . . . attributable to the fact that they trade on a perfectionist ideal of the human good. Consider the slogan "a hand-up not a hand-out." The implication is that a cash "hand-out" is demeaning, a "buying off" of the excluded, while a "hand up" is a route to dignity and self-respect. There is clearly an ideal of "self-reliance" at work here. . . . Consider also the statement that "work is the best route out of poverty." If it all comes down to the same amount of money required to lift someone out of poverty, in what sense is money earned through work "better"? Again, there must be

> some kind of "work ethic" that is making the difference here. Work, according to this view, is good for you. And this is why some people might feel discomfort with the moralising tone of some of this language, because this particular ideal of what a good life for human beings is may be a contestable one. (2003, 16–17)

However, in light of our earlier discussion of civic obligations in a liberal state, it is clear that the rationale for welfare conditionality need not be the perfectionist type that Wolff identifies here.

Consider, as a first example, policies that link benefits to work or to preparation for work. The rationale for this need not be a judgment that work is essential to the good life. It might instead be that there is an obligation to work as a matter of justice, of fair treatment of one's fellow citizens. An analogy can be made with the claim that all should do their bit in support of a just war: the rationale behind such a claim is one of fairness, not that all should fight because war is somehow inherently good for the soul.

Or, to take a second example, consider proposals to link welfare benefits to school attendance or to parenting classes. We have seen how education and parenting are both connected with satisfying one of Rawls's principles of justice—fair equality of opportunity. The rationale for using the welfare system to increase school attendance or to improve the quality of parenting might be that the resulting increases and improvements serve this important demand of justice. Programs aimed at discouraging teen pregnancy or at alleviating its effects can also be defended in these terms. Teen pregnancy disrupts the education of the teens concerned, jeopardizing their own prospects of fair equality of opportunity; and teens may lack the skills to be effective parents, so possibly undermining their children's prospects of fair equality of opportunity.[13] Thus conditionality policies that link assistance to teen parents with participation in programs designed to improve their educational attainment and to improve their parenting skills clearly have a justice-based rationale.

It will not do, then, to reject conditionality policies merely because they supposedly have perfectionist rationales that a liberal must regard as inadmissible in public reasoning. For such policies can clearly be defended in appropriately justice-based terms.

Distributional Objections

We have seen that many conditionality proposals have justice-based rationales that are perfectly admissible within public reason as conceived by liberals such as Rawls. Nevertheless, it does not follow that merely because such policies have a justice-based rationale they are on balance consistent with, let alone required by, justice. For there might be other reasons of justice, not yet considered, that count in the balance against them.

In particular, in contemporary circumstances, liberals will rightly be concerned that conditionality could have undesirable distributional consequences. It is to these distributional objections to conditionality that I now turn. There are a number of concerns that fall under this heading, but here I want to focus on just two that I think have a good deal of force.[14]

Let us begin with what we may call the inequity objection. According to some critics, such as Desmond King, conditionality is illiberal because, when welfare is made conditional on behavior, welfare recipients have to do things, as a condition of receiving welfare, that others are not made to do, and this difference means that the welfare recipients are not being treated as equals. In King's words:

> Defenders of workfare . . . present it as consistent with liberal values, but I argue that this apparent compatibility does not mask its illiberality because of the way in which it differentially treats those affected from other citizens. It aims to direct individuals' behaviour in specified ways. (1999, 9; see also 256)

Now, if King's meaning here is that conditionality necessarily entails some kind of objectionably differential treatment, I am not convinced. Assume we are talking about a work-conditionality rule, and that the rationale for the rule is to enforce respect for a norm of reciprocity. Assume that citizens not on welfare are employed, and so, presumably, are satisfying this norm. The concern is that people on welfare might use welfare to escape their obligations under the norm. To prevent this, the expectation of work is formally introduced into the welfare system. As a result, the welfare recipient may indeed be immediately subject to a coercive structure that the citizen in work is not subject to. But this reflects the fact that the welfare recipient has an immediate opportunity, provided by welfare, to evade an obligation that the worker is already meeting. The point is to make sure that a specific obligation continues to be respected by all. Thus, far from violating the basic idea of citizen equity, as King argues, the work-conditionality rule, under the foregoing assumptions, precisely expresses it.

However, King's criticism has more force if it is understood as a more context-specific criticism of work-conditionality in early twenty-first century Britain and the United States. In these advanced capitalist societies it is simply not true that reciprocity-based obligations to work are generally enforced. Most obviously, those who inherit large sums of wealth can live on its proceeds without supplying any work. In this context, work-conditionality in welfare apparently entails the objectionably differential treatment of the welfare-poor and the inheritance-rich. This is the inequity that John Stuart Mill had in his sights when he wrote that he looked forward to a time when the principle "that they who do not work shall not eat, will be applied not to paupers only, but impartially to all" (1873/1989, 175).

Conservative defenders of work-conditionality, such as Lawrence Mead and Joel Schwartz, argue that there is no objectionable equity here. In their contributions to this volume, both cite statistics showing that the rich generally do work—and, indeed, work relatively long hours (see chapters 8 and 10, this volume). However, I find this observation inadequate as a reply to the inequity objection, for two reasons. First, there is a potentially significant difference between the class of rich people to whom the objection refers and the rich as conceptualized in Mead's and Schwartz's responses to the objection. Both cite statistics concerning the work behavior of people in the highest income quintile. But the objection as I state it refers, not to those who are income rich from whatever source, but to those who are asset rich due to inheritance. It is conceivable that some people who inherit enough wealth to live on without working are nevertheless not in the highest income quintile (perhaps they are living modestly). And clearly it would be rash to assume that all, or even a majority, of those in the highest income quintile inherit so much that they can afford to live without working. They might have inherited nothing and be working really hard to maintain their income-intensive lifestyles. Thus the statistics that Mead and Schwartz refer to simply do not show unequivocally that the class of people identified in the objection as potential free riders are in fact working.[15]

Let us waive this point, however, and assume, for the sake of argument, that the relevant class of people do in fact tend to work. Even if this were so, the point that Mead and Schwartz make would still fail to defuse the charge of inequity. For even if the inheritance-wealthy do choose to work, it is still of the utmost significance that they choose to work. If one class of citizens has no choice but to meet the obligation to work, yet members of another class are free to ignore this obligation, then there is still some injustice even if people in the latter class do work.

I turn now to a second distributional objection to conditionality, which we may call the consolidation objection. Against a background of significant (and unjust) inequality of opportunity, there is an understandable fear that welfare conditionality will consolidate the disadvantage suffered by those who suffer unjustly limited opportunity. In a permissive, unconditional system, welfare can serve as an alternative to work. Those who have been unjustly disadvantaged in the initial distribution of assets and opportunities are in this way given some power to refuse participation in the economic system. They can, in principle, use this power to extract improvements in wages and working conditions that partially compensate for their unjust disadvantage. However, if welfare is made conditional—for example, on energetic job search—then this power of refusal is apparently reduced. This, in turn, weakens the general bargaining position of the education- and inheritance-poor, so that they go to work at lower wages and in poorer conditions than they otherwise would (Piven and Cloward 1993).

In reply, it might be said that if conditionality is concerned with the enforcement of civic obligations, the government should press on with conditionality. If citizens have an obligation to work in return for a share of the social product, for example, then surely they should work, and the government should accordingly enforce work norms within the welfare system. But, aside from the inequity problem we have just discussed, it is not obvious that the government should vigorously enforce this obligation if the predictable consequence of doing so is to consolidate unjust disadvantage in the way described. Indeed, do the victims of unjust disadvantage even have the same obligation to work as they would have in a just society? If mainstream society is reneging on one part of the social contract, how can it justify holding those disadvantaged by this to the full contract? (Daniels 1981, 160–62).

Applying the Liberal Perspective to Britain's New Deals

I have described some of the main ideas that I think should frame the way a liberal approaches the issue of welfare conditionality. I now consider how a liberal might assess one actual set of welfare reforms: the New Deal programs introduced by Britain's Labour government since 1998.

The New Deals are welfare-to-work programs covering a range of recipients that include the young unemployed and lone parents.[16] The programs differ considerably, however, in terms of how they address their target groups. The New Deal for Young People (NDYP) applies to youths under twenty-five receiving Jobseeker's Allowance, the main cash benefit in Britain for the unemployed.[17] All those in the target group who have already been on this benefit for six months are required to participate in the NDYP. Participation begins with a four-month Gateway period in which the benefit recipient meets regularly with a personal advisor to discuss his or her progress in finding a job. As with any recipient of Jobseeker's Allowance, the participant may be sanctioned for refusal to take a job without good cause. If the recipient has not left welfare for work by the end of this Gateway period, he or she moves into the Options stage. He or she is then required to take up one of four options including subsidized employment in the private sector, full-time education or training, work in the voluntary sector, or work on the Environmental Task Force. All options provide at least one day a week of vocational training leading to an accredited qualification. If participants have still not found a job at the end of this period, they return to intensive job search. Participants can be sanctioned for not meeting the program's requirements, and though the sanctions are not that severe (a short suspension of benefits in the first instance, though rising to a twenty-six-week suspension for repeated violations), they have been used in the case of more than one in ten participants.[18]

The New Deal for Lone Parents (NDLP) is very different. At present, all lone parents receiving basic means-tested assistance are required to attend periodic interviews to discuss their prospects of finding a job. At these interviews, they are invited to join the NDLP, which provides further, personalized advice on moving into employment, including advice on education and training. They are not, however, required to participate. Indeed, provided that their youngest child is under the age of sixteen, there is no requirement that they do anything with a view to finding a job, aside from attending the interview. As one might expect, there is a lively debate about the effectiveness of these schemes. There is some research that indicates that the programs have been modestly effective in increasing the employment of their participants and, indeed, equilibrium employment in the economy as a whole.[19] But the critics argue that the effects of the schemes are too modest and, in some respects, might be perverse. One particular concern is that the NDYP might pressure some disadvantaged young people off welfare altogether and thereby marginalize them even further.[20]

These New Deal programs represent only one side of the government's active labor market policies. The other side consists of various initiatives designed to make work pay and so increase financial incentives to work. These include the introduction of a national minimum wage and a system of more generous in-work benefits. The latter includes the Working Families Tax Credit (now Working Tax Credit, WTC), akin to the Earned Income Tax Credit in the United States, and a Childcare Tax Credit, which provides a refundable tax credit to the value of 70 percent of child care costs for families without a nonworking parent (up to a maximum of £135 a week for one child, £200 a week for more than one child). The Childcare Tax Credit is part of a National Childcare Strategy that also includes (at present, rather modest) efforts to increase directly the supply of preschool child care places.[21]

Turning now to the task of evaluating these programs, I find it to hard to see what a liberal critic could object to in the NDLP. The element of conditionality here is modest, requiring only an interview about work, with no compulsory follow-up in terms of job search, work experience, education, or training. As Jane Millar notes, the NDLP relies wholly on the "art of persuasion" (see 2003).[22] The emphasis is almost wholly on carrots rather than sticks, with the compulsory interview and voluntary NDLP serving to make lone parents more aware of the improved financial incentives to work that some recent reforms provide. For all the talk of Britain's welfare-to-work programs representing an illiberal policy import from the conservative United States, there is a stark contrast here between the voluntary approach of the NDLP and the compulsory job search of the post-reform U.S. welfare regime.

The NDYP, however, is more likely to give the liberal pause. The element of conditionality here is much stronger. In considering this program, therefore, the liberal must factor in the distributional concerns we have discussed. How far is the NDYP vulnerable to the consolidation and inequity objections?

Let us begin with the consolidation objection. It is important first to note that the NDYP is not being introduced in isolation, but as part of a package of measures that, as we have seen, also include new initiatives to lift the incomes of the low-paid. Research on the distributive impact of these measures indicates that they have substantially improved the social wage accessible to people in Britain's lower income deciles (see Brewer and Gregg 2003, 92–96). Thus, taking the reform package in its entirety, it can be argued that the net effect is to improve the prospects of the (unjustly disadvantaged) worst-off, rather than to consolidate their disadvantage. However, this observation will not do as a reply to the critic as it stands. For the critic can simply say that things would be going even better for the most disadvantaged groups in British society if the social wage-enhancing reforms had been introduced without programs like the NDYP.

One reply to this criticism is to argue that the NDYP itself helps to combat unjust disadvantage. To some extent, unjust disadvantage is manifested in low levels of human capital. To the extent that participation in the NDYP increases such capital, then it can be seen as partial rectification of this form of unjust disadvantage, enhancing the opportunities of otherwise unjustly disadvantaged workers, rather than consolidating their disadvantage.[23]

However, this rectification defense of the NDYP, as we might call it, can be challenged on a number of grounds. First, even if the factual premise of the argument is true (participation in the NDYP increases human capital), it can be objected that this does not provide justification for the controversial element of coercion in this program. Surely, the critic will say, it would suffice to offer people the opportunity to participate in skills-enhancing programs. If the programs really do offer such opportunity, why would it be necessary to coerce people into participating in them? Isn't such coercion essentially paternalistic, and thus essentially illiberal?

There is certainly a presumption against paternalism within liberalism. However, this presumption is not absolute. Paternalism is sometimes based on perfectionist reasons internal to a specific conception of the good life. In this case, it violates the liberal commitment to state neutrality. But if, as in the case we are considering, paternalistic interventions are directed toward rectifying unjust disadvantage in people's capacity to access primary goods, such as income and wealth, then the intervention is not perfectionist. Rawls, for one, explicitly allows for some paternalism of this kind by a liberal state (1971/1999, 218–20; see also White 2004a for relevant discussion). The case for paternalism in this context is particularly strong because it is plausible (but would require careful empirical research to confirm) that a background of severe disadvantage is demotivating for many people, so that, in the ordinary course of events, they simply would not choose to participate in programs even if they do have clear benefits in terms of increased employability.[24] Such people may need a push—indeed, in Mead's terms, some hassle—if they are to overcome the motivational deficits that can accompany severe disadvantage from an early age. The more permissive NDLP might be criticized precisely for failing to apply this paternalistic approach.[25]

A second challenge to the rectification defense of NDYP also concedes that on average the program will raise the human capital of its participants, but questions whether this improvement can be justified given the likely costs to some individual members of the NDYP target group. Imagine two people who enter the NDYP, Alice and Bob. Alice gets on well with her personal advisor, finds a training program that she really enjoys, and leaves NDYP for a moderately good job. In this job she qualifies for in-work benefits and, let us imagine, thereby qualifies for generous training vouchers that she uses to attend some computing classes in the evenings after work. She ends up in a job she enjoys in the solid middle of the earnings distribution.

Bob, however, finds his advisor patronizing and cannot really engage with the program. He is repeatedly sanctioned and eventually leaves welfare altogether. He drifts into a life of petty crime. Let us say, for the sake of argument, that without the NDYP, Alice would not have ended up having such a good life, and that Bob would not have ended up leading such a bad life. We should recall that some critics of the NDYP are precisely concerned that it may be marginalizing some young people in the way I have described in the case of Bob (see Willetts, Hillman, and Bogdanor 2003, 24). The second objection I wish to consider can then be put as follows: even if the vast majority of NDYP participants have Good Stories like Alice's, can the program be justified if there are also Bad Stories like Bob's?

I am not sure that the Rawlsian framework that I have used here offers much in the way of direct guidance. The Rawlsian framework conceptualizes problems of justice in interclass terms, as a matter of ensuring that the worst-off class (roughly speaking, the class of low-skilled manual workers) is sufficiently well off relative to other social classes. However, in the case of welfare conditionality, the main impact will sometimes be on the intraclass distribution of advantage and opportunity. A policy might increase the aggregate or average prospects of people who are in disadvantaged social classes, but at the price of worsening those of some people born into these social classes. Rawls's view seems to be that we should focus on the average prospects of people in different social classes.[26] However, the very concerns that lead Rawls to reject utilitarianism as a basis for thinking about questions of interclass distribution—that we should take seriously "the distinction between persons" and the inviolability of individuals (1971/1999, 24, 163–64)—might be thought also to justify our rejecting it as a basis for assessing questions of intraclass distribution. On the other hand, it seems implausibly extreme to say that we can never enact a policy to improve the average position of people in society's most disadvantaged group if it will worsen the position of an individual within the group.

The difficult, tragic problem of how to balance these intraclass interests cannot be eliminated. But liberal agonizing might be reduced to some extent by intelligent policy design. It is not as if Bob's first spell on the NDYP has to be his one and only chance at a better life. One can readily imagine a range of programs for those with severe handicaps—drug addiction, homelessness, illiteracy, a history of crime—that offer more chances to people who fail the first (or second, or nth) time. The NDYP is itself set up in a way that is sensitive to these handicaps, and personal advisors can offer clients services geared to these needs. It is perfectly possible, moreover, for people who have been sanctioned in the past on the NDYP, and who may even have drifted off welfare, to come back into the program later and benefit from these services. Indeed, the most recent stage in the evolution of the New Deals has been toward a Jobcentre Plus system in which all out-of-work (working age) benefit claimants have a personal advisor on the NDYP model who can offer such services to claimants where they seem appropriate (though at present it is not envisaged that all benefit claimants will be subject to the same degree of compulsion as those on the NDYP).[27] In short, the program can, and does, provide substantial rescue strategies for people like Bob in our imaginary example.

Third, and finally, however, our critic might argue that the key factual premise of the rectification defense of the NDYP is untrue: the program does not significantly raise the human capital of most participants. Is this fair criticism?

In aspiration at least, there clearly is a significant human capital investment element within the NDYP. This is evident not only in the education and training component of the Options stage of the program (on which participants can remain full-time for up to a year), but in the fact that all four of the original options in the program contain a training element intended to lead to a qualification. In addition, personal advisors can intervene earlier, in the Gateway stage, to direct clients with serious weaknesses in basic skills to appropriate assistance. Moreover, in the last couple of years, some interesting new schemes have been added to the New Deal framework.[28] There is now, for example, a New Deal for Musicians. If the NDYP client can convince her personal advisor that she is genuinely interested in working as a musician, she may be enrolled in a six-month training scheme covering relevant musical and business skills. The musical skills covered by the program can range from opera through chamber music to Trip Hop.[29] Another set of recent initiatives are the Ambition schemes. These are industry-specific, designed in consultation with employers in the relevant industries, addressed to their perceived skill shortages, and deliberately targeted at disadvantaged groups within the workforce. There are Ambition schemes in retail, construction, information technology, and energy, providing training to employer specifications and six months of support after training. This is all quite some way from a simple work-first approach.

That said, one must concede that not all New Deal participants will benefit from these sorts of scheme. Some may participate in training schemes but simply fail to complete the training successfully; a recent study by the Adult Learning Institute found, for example, that only 31 percent of those on the full-time education and training option of the NDYP actually gain a qualification (see Willetts, Hillman, and Bogdanor 2003, 24).[30] Moreover, we must not forget that benefit recipients do not move onto the NDYP until they have been on Jobseeker's Allowance for six months, during which time they can be sanctioned at any time with benefit cuts for refusing a job offer without good cause. To a considerable extent, the existing welfare-to-work policy is surely about pushing low-skilled workers into the low-waged work for which they are equipped.

Hence, the rectification defense of the NDYP against the consolidation objection probably fails. Moreover, there is the basic inequity that the program helps to enforce work by some citizens while other, more fortunate citizens remain free to share in the social product without working. Given the character of the background economy in Britain, the inequity objection that I pressed so insistently against Mead and Schwartz also holds for programs like the NDYP. Thus, the liberal must probably conclude that the NDYP is unjust: or, at least, that it does not do enough in itself to convert an essentially unjust welfare-to-work system, grounded in the Jobseeker's Allowance, into a just one.

What would it take to defuse the consolidation and inequity objections? So far as the consolidation objection is concerned, the challenge is to find ways of boosting the pay and job quality of all those in the New Deal's target groups. This may require providing new opportunities to acquire skills for these groups, and new forms of pressure on employers to develop product market strategies that call for skilled work. On the one hand, perhaps those who have been working full-time and receiving WTC for a minimum period could be eligible for generous training vouchers, or for generous matched savings schemes in which they can accumulate sums that they can then use to buy training. The government has already taken some steps in this direction. In 2000 it implemented Individual Learning Accounts (ILAs), essentially a modest training voucher, targeted at specific groups of workers. The scheme was canceled the following year, however, due to problems of fraud.[31] The government has said it would like to introduce a reformed ILA scheme in the future. In the meantime, it has piloted a matched saving program for low-income groups, the Saving Gateway.[32] To ensure a corresponding increase in the demand for skilled workers, there may be a role for government, trade unions, and other workforce intermediaries in encouraging employers to develop more skills-intensive product-market strategies where competitive advantage is sought through high quality rather than merely low cost (see White 1998; Rogers and Streeck 1994; Cohen and Rogers 1995, 82–87; Dresser and Rogers 2003).[33]

Turning to the inequity objection, one way of mitigating the problem would be to introduce a compulsory citizens' service scheme in which all young people are required to provide, say, two years of service to society.[34] This would at least ensure that the inheritance rich put something back to the community at some point in their lives. It is also conceivable that the experience could help to strengthen their attachment to the community in a way that discourages their free riding in later life. However, this would still be a rather limited response to the problem, leaving lucky inheritees with plenty of time after citizens' service to free ride if they wish.

To effectively address the problem, there seems no option but to tax inheritances. The political problem, of course, is that this is unpopular.[35] It comes as no surprise, then, that Britain's Labour government has not made any effort as yet to increase inheritance tax. The character of the debate surrounding the recently announced Child Trust Fund policy provides clear evidence of the government's caution on the issue. Under this scheme every child in Britain will receive a grant at birth that will be held in trust and accumulate as he or she grows up, providing a modest capital sum on maturity.[36] The policy seems clearly inspired by recent academic work on stakeholding and asset-based welfare (see Sherraden 1991; Ackerman and Alstott 1999; Nissan and Le Grand 2000). However, in the academic literature, the universal stake proposal tends to be discussed in the same breath as inheritance tax reform. Reform is seen as providing some of the revenue for the universal capital grant, the combination of the tax and grant representing a new model of socialized inheritance. By contrast, not a whisper of this idea was mentioned in the government's discussion of the Child Trust Fund.

A case for a reformed inheritance tax could be made within the framework of a social reform strategy akin to that of the present government. The government argues that the central, unifying goal of its social policy is to eliminate child poverty within a generation (defined as twenty years).[37] Child poverty is understood not simply in income terms, but in terms of the cognitive and psychological development that is so crucial to life-prospects. To this end, the government has introduced a number of policies aimed at preschool development, such as Sure Start, a program aimed at newborns and infants in Britain's most disadvantaged communities.[38] These initiatives could be further developed with the aim of establishing a nationwide system of child care centers providing free or subsidized child care for all parents. The cost of this system could be met, in part, through a reformed inheritance tax. Although opinion polls find that inheritance tax is unpopular, recent research shows that people do tend to support the tax more if it is explicitly linked to initiatives such as child development policies (see Lewis and White forthcoming).

However, the same research suggests that public attitudes would not countenance a radical reform of inheritance that would prevent the free riding and inequity with which we are concerned. If this is so, and we are hence left with some free riding inheritees, can a liberal support government going ahead with NDYP-type schemes that embody strong work conditionality?

In responding to this we need to separate the questions: "What is demanded by justice?" and "What ought the government to do?" In the situation I have envisaged, there would be a residual injustice in that some citizens are effectively required to meet a civic obligation to work by NDYP-style programs even as others are able by virtue of an inheritance to evade it. However, it is not obvious that this residual injustice would necessarily make it undesirable for the government to run schemes akin to the NDYP. If the schemes do work on balance to improve the prospects of otherwise unjustly disadvantaged workers, and there is no other politically feasible way of achieving similar gains for such workers, then I would argue that the government ought to enact such schemes, notwithstanding the inequity that they involve.[39]

Here one should also mention Lawrence Mead's argument that moves toward conditionality build the competencies of the poor, thus establish their credentials as deserving, and so makes it easier to win support for other initiatives that address the structural sources of their disadvantage (see Mead 1992, 10–11; Glenn 2001, 101–5). These are, however, thoroughly pragmatic defenses of NDYP-style schemes, a matter of making the best of an inherently bad situation. In the politics of contemporary capitalist democracy, there are many things that a liberal might have to concede as a matter of political feasibility that do not fully meet the demands of justice. In such cases, it is important to acknowledge the price or shortfall in terms of justice, and to beware of making a virtue out of necessity. In Britain today (and, I suspect, in the United States as well), the worry must be that politicians of the so-called center left who espouse increased conditionality do not really acknowledge such shortfalls. They adopt a rhetoric about rights and responsibilities that makes too much of a virtue of political necessity.

Conclusion: An Agonistic Position

At the level of ideal theory, liberal neutrality does not exclude conditionality in the welfare system. There can be good, justice-based reasons for conditionality. In the much less than ideal circumstances of our own societies, however, conditionality—in particular, work-conditionality—will properly give the liberal pause because it might well lead to inequity in the enforcement of civic obligations or to a consolidation of unjust labor-market disadvantage, or perhaps both. My discussion of the New Deals in

Britain has illustrated some of the concerns a liberal will have about conditionality policies in the circumstances of contemporary capitalist societies such as Britain, and has indicated some of the programs and policies that, as a matter of justice, seem necessary as a complement to conditionality.

There is clearly some affinity between this liberal position and the Third Way of New Labour and the New Democrats. But they are not the same. Although I have sympathy with the Third Way's dual emphasis on opportunity and responsibility, Third Way thinkers tend to elaborate the demand for opportunity in ways that fall short of what an egalitarian liberal would, quite correctly in my view, regard as just (see White 2004b). Third Way theorizing about social justice is, for the most part, superficial and overly driven by perceptions about what is politically feasible in the course of the next electoral cycle. The challenge to liberals in present circumstances is to try to reawaken the egalitarian ambition that the Third Wayers seem all too keen to damp down. It is to imagine ways in which the rather narrow, potentially punitive politics of something called welfare reform can be expanded into a new, more expansive politics of economic citizenship. In this new politics of economic citizenship, welfare conditionality can (and I think should) have a place. But it will be just one element in a politics aimed at creating a society in which, if citizens do their part in society's cooperative work, they will do so under considerably fairer conditions. In Britain, the policy agendas now emerging around early years intervention, work-life balance, and asset-based welfare, perhaps offer some of the traction needed to move on from welfare reform in this more liberal direction.

I would like to thank all the participants in the conference on "Welfare Reform and Political Theory," Wingspread, Wisconsin, October 16 to 17, 2003, and particularly Larry Mead, Christopher Beem, and Alan Deacon, for their comments on an earlier draft of this chapter. Thanks also to two anonymous readers for Russell Sage for their helpful comments and to Selina Chen, Joshua Cohen, Amy Gutmann, and Christopher Lake for past conversations on this topic that have helped to clarify my ideas (which is not to say, of course, that any of them would necessarily agree with my conclusions).

Notes

1. "[The] correlative of the State's undertaking to ensure adequate benefit for unavoidable interruption of earnings, however long, is enforcement of the citizen's obligation to seek and accept all reasonable opportunities of work [and] to co-operate in all measures designed to save him from habituation to idleness" (Beveridge 1942, 52).
2. In suggesting this interpretation, I am indebted to Joshua Cohen (see 1994, 1516).

3. "Political liberalism . . . does not try to fix public reason once and for all in the form of one favored political conception of justice. . . . the forms of permissible public reason are always several" (Rawls 1999, 142).
4. This stipulation is relaxed somewhat in *The Idea of Public Reason Revisited* (Rawls 1999, 144), where Rawls asserts that we may appeal to our comprehensive doctrine in political discussion at any time, provided that in due course we also present appropriately public reasons for our preferred option.
5. In the brief discussion of this point in *Political Liberalism*, Rawls (1993, 182) says that the exclusion applies to those "unwilling to work under conditions where there is much work that needs to be done (I assume that positions and jobs are not scarce or rationed)." This formulation is confused. In a classic Keynesian slump there can be "much work that needs to be done" even though "positions and jobs" are "scarce or rationed" (Rawls 1993, 182). I think what Rawls is trying to say here is that people who would like to work but can't find a job will not be excluded from the social minimum. Those who would choose not to work even if jobs were available do not have a right to receive the social minimum: "So those who surf all day off Malibu must find a way to support themselves and would not be entitled to public funds" (Rawls 1993, 182).
6. How this functionalism is to be squared with Rawls's skepticism towards the claims of "willingness to make an effort" in his earlier work is not immediately clear to me, and some egalitarian liberals may stand with the early Rawls on this point in opposition to the later Rawls. But my concern here is merely to show how certain ideas about civic obligation can find a place in a political liberalism of the type that Rawls advocates. The specific functionalist version of justice as fairness I have described can certainly be seen as one reasonable conception of justice amongst the family of reasonable conceptions of justice that may play a role in the public reason of a political liberal state. I do not need to claim anything more than this for present purposes.
7. Rawls has a discussion of the individual's obligation of fair-play in *A Theory of Justice.* He never explicitly links his discussion of the duty to work with the obligation of fair-play, though a connection is perhaps intimated when he characterizes the obligation of fair-play as an obligation "not to gain from the cooperative labors of others without doing our fair share" (see Rawls 1971/1999, 93–98; see also Van Parijs 1995, 96–7, 261 n.10).
8. We have an unconditional duty "to support and to comply with just institutions that exist and apply to us. . . . [and] to further just arrangements not yet established, at least when this can be done without too much cost to ourselves" (see Rawls 1971/1999, 99).
9. For a helpful overview of some recent research in this area, see Gosta Esping-Andersen, (2003, 111–16). See also Leon Feinstein, (2003, 213–18), that British children's test-scores at twenty-two months closely predict their final educational achievement.
10. This concern was raised—though not clearly endorsed—by William Galston in discussion at the conference for which this paper was initially written.
11. I would not say that liberals ought to be wholly indifferent to non-neutrality of impact. A liberal case for attention to impact can arguably be made, for instance, on grounds that such sensitivity is sometimes a justified expression of respect for freedom of religion.

12. Rawls's list of "primary goods," encompassing such things as liberties, income, wealth, and the "social bases of self-respect," is an account of our civil interests, and his two principles of justice give us an account of what the equitable protection of these interests consists in. In thinking about the affinities between Locke and contemporary liberals such as Rawls, I have benefited from conversations with Selina Chen.
13. See Rebecca Maynard, that children of teenage mothers in the US "exhibit worse health, greater use of medical care, greater poverty, and poorer school performance than counterparts born to older mothers" and that only 43 percent of this difference "is attributable to the fact that the teenage mothers came from more disadvantaged backgrounds" (1997, 93).
14. One type of distributional argument I do not consider here is the argument we find in the "left-libertarian" tradition to the effect that certain external resources represent a common inheritance of which each citizen has some rightful share. This argument can be developed into a case for a universal, unconditional basic income grant. For a sophisticated example of such an argument, see Van Parijs (1995); and, for a superb response, see Gijs Van Donselaar (1997). See also White (2003, chapter 7).
15. Mead tells us that the figures for work are lower for the top 5 percent in the income distribution than for the top quintile as a whole, which is consistent with the presence of a small class of especially rich, non-working inheritees.
16. The range of target groups has gradually been extended and now includes the long-term unemployed, partners of the unemployed, unemployed people aged twenty-five to forty-nine, unemployed people aged fifty and above, and the disabled. For an overview of the various New Deals, see Martin Hewitt, (2002, especially 192–95, 199–201), and Rajiv Prabhakar (2003, 139–41).
17. Being "unemployed" here means being out-of-work and registered as actively seeking work. Many out-of-work benefit recipients are not unemployed in this sense, and so are not on Jobseeker's Allowance. For most people on the benefit, Jobseeker's Allowance is means-tested, though recipients with a sufficient record of National Insurance Contributions can claim it for up to six months without a means-test.
18. Some 13 percent of participants at the Options stage of the NDYP have been sanctioned. For an overview of the program, see Bruce Stafford (2003).
19. For an authoritative account of the impact of the NDYP, see Richard Blundell et al. (2003). The authors' research shows that the NDYP modestly increases the outflow of young unemployed workers into employment (outflow rates are increased by around 5 percentage points relative to comparison groups). They also calculate that the net gains from the program outweigh its net costs.
20. For criticism along these lines, see David Willetts MP, Nicholas Hillman, and Adam Bogdanor (2003, 20–24). They conjecture that the NDYP "may" be an explanation for why around one in ten of young people is neither in work, full-time education nor registered as unemployed, though they provide no firm evidence to support this conjecture.
21. The details of the various in-work benefit schemes, which now include a Working Tax Credit, Child Tax Credit and Childcare Tax Credit, need not detain us, but for a helpful overview, see Mike Brewer and Paul Gregg (2003).

22. It should be noted, however, that a piece of recent enabling legislation, the 1999 Welfare and Pensions Reform Act, allows "availability for work" requirements to be extended to all claimants at some future time. See Anne Gray (2001, 191).
23. I owe this point to Selina Chen.
24. If this consideration does apply, then paternalism in this context might well satisfy Rawls's stipulation that "paternalistic intervention must be justified by the evident failure or absence of reason and will" (1971/1999, 219).
25. A second reply to the paternalism objection is to shift the original argument from one about how NDYP affects the human capital of its participants, to one about how it and similar programs are likely to affect the human capital of participants' dependents. If children's attainment in school is positively affected by having a parent in work, then even if participation in the NDYP does nothing to improve the participant's human capital, it could have positive effects on her children's educational performance in later years simply by keeping her attached to the labor market. This type of consideration is clearly part of the rationale for the New Deals (see Brewer and Gregg 2003, 89–90).
26. This is how I interpret Rawls's remarks about how we are to judge the justice of social systems from the standpoint of "representative men" occupying "relevant social positions" (see Rawls 1971/1999, 56, 81–6, especially discussion of relevant positions and free trade at 85).
27. In addition to the NDYP, the New Deals for the long-term unemployed and for those aged 25–49 involve significant degrees of conditionality.
28. Information on the latest developments can be found at the websites of the New Deals and the umbrella organization, Jobcentre Plus: http://www.newdeal.gov.uk, http://www.jobcentreplus.gov.uk.
29. The Labour government may have been responding here to criticisms of the original NDYP from within the British pop music industry. When the NDYP was first introduced some influential figures in the industry, such as Alan McGee of Creation records, complained that it would dry up the supply of innovative British rock and pop musicians who, so it was said, had previously used the benefit system to finance their early years of musical experimentation.
30. Blundell et al. also report that: "As far as we know there is no convincing evidence on the impact of the options in raising human capital" (2003, 30).
31. For a helpful overview of the ILA scheme and its demise, see Prabhakar (2003, 143–45).
32. The Saving Gateway is a matched saving program for low-income households very similar to the Individual Development Account advocated by Michael Sherraden, which has been piloted in a number of local experiments in the United States (see Sherraden 1991; Paxton 2003).
33. Joel Rogers is currently preparing a manuscript on his ideas about high road capitalism for the Real Utopias seminar series run under the direction of Erik Olin Wright at the University of Wisconsin-Madison.
34. See discussion of possible schemes for the United States at the Progressive Policy Institute (www.ppionline.org), and for the British context, James McCormick (1994), though it should be noted that McCormick rejects compulsion.

35. The Fabian Society organized an opinion poll on the subject for its recent Commission on Taxation and Citizenship. Fifty-one percent of those surveyed agreed with the proposition that "no inheritances should be taxed" (see Jacobs 2000, 54–55).
36. Children in poorer families will receive £500 at birth, all other children £250, with further payments from the government on the children's 7th and 11th birthdays. Parents and family may also pay into the accounts up to an annual ceiling of £1,200. The accounts may not be accessed until children reach the age of 18, at which point the account holders may use the accumulated funds as they wish (see HM Treasury and Inland Revenue 2003).
37. In his 1999 Beveridge lecture, Tony Blair declared: "Our historic aim will be for ours to be the first generation to end child poverty" (cited in Brewer and Gregg 2003, 81).
38. Sure Start is partly inspired by the Head Start program in the United States. In its original form, it offered activities to promote children's preschool development in over 200 disadvantaged communities. A wider roll-out of the scheme is now planned, though there are concerns that its original aims have been diluted.
39. Some might argue that if there is this inequity, then the scheme can't possibly raise the prospects of unjustly disadvantaged workers because the inequity will damage their self-respect which, since self-respect is such a crucial good, will make them worse off. This is a serious point, but it is also one that demands empirical confirmation, which may or may not be forthcoming.

References

Ackerman, Bruce, and Anne Alstott. 1999. *The Stakeholder Society.* New Haven, Conn.: Yale University Press.

Anderson, Brian C. 2003. "The Antipolitical Philosophy of John Rawls." *The Public Interest* 151(spring): 39–51.

Barry, Brian. 2000. *Culture and Equality.* Oxford: Oxford University Press.

Beveridge, William. 1942. *Social Insurance and Allied Services.* London: HMSO.

Blundell, Richard, Howard Reed, John Van Reenan, and Andrew Shephard. 2003. "The Impact of the New Deal for Young People on the Labour Market: A Four-Year Assessment." In *The Labour Market Under New Labour: The State of Working Britain,* edited by Richard Dickens, Paul Gregg, and Jonathan Wadsworth. Basingstoke, U.K.: Palgrave Macmillan.

Brewer, Michael, and Paul Gregg. 2003. "Eradicating Child Poverty in Britain: Welfare Reform and Children Since 1997." In *The Welfare We Want?* edited by Robert Walker and Michael Wiseman. Bristol, U.K.: The Policy Press.

Cohen, Joshua. 1994. "A More Democratic Liberalism." *Michigan Law Review* 92(6): 1503–46.

Cohen, Joshua, and Joel Rogers. 1995. "Secondary Associations and Democratic Governance." In *Associations and Democracy,* edited by Joshua Cohen and Joel Rogers. London: Verso.

Daniels, Norman. 1981. "Conflicting Objectives and the Priorities Problem." In *Income Support: Conceptual and Policy Issues,* edited by Peter G. Brown, Conrad Johnson, and Paul Vernier. Lanham, Md.: Rowman and Littlefield.

Davies, Gareth. 1996. *From Opportunity to Entitlement: The Transformation and Decline of Great Society Liberalism.* Lawrence: University Press of Kansas.

Dresser, Laura, and Joel Rogers. 2003. "Part of the Solution: Emerging Workforce Intermediaries in the United States." In *Governing Work and Welfare in a New Economy,* edited by Jonathan Zeitlin and David M. Trubek. Oxford: Oxford University Press.

Dworkin, Ronald. 2000. *Sovereign Virtue.* Cambridge, Mass.: Harvard University Press.

Esping-Andersen, Gosta. 2003. "Against Social Inheritance." In *The Progressive Manifesto,* edited by Anthony Giddens. Oxford: Polity.

Feinstein, Leon. 2003. "Not Just the Early Years: The Need for a Developmental Perspective for Equality of Opportunity." *New Economy* 10: 213–18.

Glenn, David. 2001. "I Thought You Said She Worked Full Time." *Dissent* 2001(summer): 101–5.

Gray, Anne. 2001. " 'Making Work Pay'—Devising the Best Strategy for Lone Parents in Britain." *Journal of Social Policy* 30: 189–207.

Hewitt, Martin. 2002. "New Labour and the Redefinition of Social Security." In *Evaluating New Labour's Welfare Reforms,* edited by Martin Powell. Bristol, U.K.: The Policy Press.

HM Treasury and Inland Revenue. 2003. *Detailed Proposals for the Child Trust Fund.* London: HMSO.

Hobhouse, Leonard T. 1911/1993. *Liberalism and Other Essays,* edited by James Meadowcroft. Cambridge: Cambridge University Press.

———. 1912. *The Labour Movement.* New York: Macmillan.

Jackson, Ben. 2003. "Equality of Nothing? Social Justice on the British Left, c.1911–31." *Journal of Political Ideologies* 8(1): 83–110.

Jacobs, Michael. 2000. *Paying for Progress: A New Politics of Tax for Public Spending.* A report from the Commission on Taxation and Citizenship. London: Fabian Society.

King, Desmond S. 1999. *In the Name of Liberalism: Illiberal Social Policy in Britain and the United States.* Oxford: Oxford University Press.

King, Desmond S., and Mark Wickham-Jones. 1999. "From Clinton to Blair: The Democratic (Party) Origins of Welfare to Work." *The Political Quarterly* 70(1): 62–74.

Lewis, Miranda, and Stuart White. Forthcoming. "Inheritance Tax: What Do the People Think? Evidence from Deliberative Workshops." In *The Citizen's Stake: Exploring the Future of Universal Asset Policies,* edited by Will Paxton and Stuart White, with Dominic Maxwell. Bristol, U.K.: The Policy Press.

Locke, John. 1685/1993. *A Letter Concerning Toleration.* In *John Locke: Political Writings,* edited by David Wootton. Harmondsworth, U.K.: Penguin.

———. 1697/1993. "Draft of a Representation Containing a Scheme of Methods for Employment of the Poor." In *John Locke: Political Writings,* edited by David Wootton. Harmondsworth, U.K.: Penguin.

Marshall, T. H. 1950. *Citizenship and Social Class.* Cambridge: Cambridge University Press.

Maynard, Rebecca A. 1997. "Paternalism, Teenage Pregnancy Prevention, and Teenage Parent Services." In *The New Paternalism: Supervisory Approaches to*

Poverty, edited by Lawrence M. Mead. Washington, D.C.: The Brookings Institution.

McCormick, James. 1994. *Citizens' Service.* London: Institute for Public Policy Research.

Mead, Lawrence M. 1986. *Beyond Entitlement: The Social Obligations of Citizenship.* New York: Free Press.

———. 1992. *The New Politics of Poverty: The Nonworking Poor in America.* New York: Basic Books.

Mill, John Stuart. 1848/1970. In *Principles of Political Economy,* edited by David Winch. Harmondsworth, U.K.: Penguin.

———. 1873/1989. *Autobiography.* Harmondsworth, U.K.: Penguin.

Millar, Jane. 2003. "The Art of Persuasion? The British New Deal for Lone Parents." In *The Welfare We Want? The British Challenge for American Reform,* edited by Robert Walker and Michael Wiseman. Bristol, U.K.: The Policy Press.

Nissan, David, and Julian Le Grand. 2000. *A Capital Start: Start-Up Grants for Young People.* London: Fabian Society.

Orwin, Clifford. 1983. "Welfare and the New Dignity." *The Public Interest* 71(spring): 85–95.

Paxton, Will, ed. 2003. *Equal Shares? Building a Progressive and Coherent Asset-Based Welfare Policy.* London: Institute for Public Policy Research.

Piven, Frances Fox, and Richard A. Cloward. 1993. *Regulating the Poor: The Functions of Public Welfare,* rev. ed. New York: Vintage Books.

Powell, Martin. 2002. "The Hidden History of Social Citizenship." *Citizenship Studies* 6(3): 229–44.

Prabhakar, Rajiv. 2003. *Stakeholding and New Labour.* Basingstoke, U.K.: Palgrave, Macmillan.

Rawls, John. 1971/1999. *A Theory of Justice: Revised Edition.* Cambridge, Mass.: Harvard University Press.

———. 1974/1999. "Reply to Alexander and Musgrave." *Quarterly Journal of Economics* 88(4): 633–55. Reprinted in *John Rawls: Collected Papers,* edited by Samuel Freeman. Cambridge, Mass.: Harvard University Press.

———. 1993. *Political Liberalism.* New York: Columbia University Press.

———. 1999. *The Law of Peoples; with, The Idea of. Public Reason Revisited.* Cambridge, Mass.: Harvard University Press.

———. 2001. *Justice as Fairness: A Restatement,* edited by Erin Kelly. Cambridge, Mass.: Harvard University Press.

Rogers, Joel, and Wolfgang Streeck. 1994. "Productive Solidarities: Economic Strategy and Left Politics." In *Reinventing the Left,* edited by David Miliband. Oxford: Polity.

Scheffler, Samuel. 1992. "Responsibility, Reactive Attitudes, and Liberalism in Philosophy and Politics." *Philosophy and Public Affairs* 21(4): 299–323.

Sherraden, Michael. 1991. *Assets and the Poor: A New American Welfare Policy.* New York: M.E. Sharpe.

Stafford, Bruce. 2003. "Beyond Lone Parents: Extending Welfare-to-Work to Disabled People and the Young Unemployed." In *The Welfare We Want? The British Challenge to American Reform,* edited by Robert Walker and Michael Wiseman. Bristol, U.K.: The Policy Press.

Tawney, R. H. 1931/1964. *Equality*. London: Allen and Unwin.
Van Donselaar, Gijs. 1997. *The Benefit of Another's Pains: Parasitism, Scarcity, Basic Income.* Amsterdam: University of Amsterdam.
Van Parijs, Philippe. 1995. *Real Freedom for All: What (if Anything) Can Justify Capitalism?* New York: Oxford University Press
White, Stuart. 1998. "Trade Unionism in a Liberal State." In *Freedom of Association*, edited by Amy Gutmann. Princeton, N.J.: Princeton University Press.
———. 2003. *The Civic Minimum: An Essay on the Rights and Obligations of Economic Citizenship*. Oxford: Oxford University Press.
———. 2004a. "The Citizen's Stake and Paternalism." *Politics and Society* 32(2): 61–78.
———. 2004b. "Welfare Philosophy and the Third Way." In *Welfare State Change: Towards a Third Way?* edited by Jane Lewis and Rebecca Surender. Oxford: Oxford University Press.
Willetts, David, Nicholas Hillman, and Adam Bogdanor. 2003. *Left Out, Left Behind: The People Lost to Britain's Workforce.* London: Policy Exchange.
Wissenberg, Marcel. 2001. "The 'Third Way' and Social Justice." *Journal of Political Ideologies* 6(2): 231–35.
Wolff, Jonathan. 2003. *The Message of Redistribution: Disadvantage, Public Policy and the Human Good.* London: Catalyst.

Chapter 5

Conditional Citizenship

WILLIAM A. GALSTON

MY POINT of departure in this chapter is the proposition that the Personal Responsibility and Work Opportunity Reconciliation Act of 1996 (PRWORA) brought about two fundamental changes in the U.S. welfare system. First, it shifted the basis of that system from entitlement to benefits conditioned on specific behavior. Second, it officially ratified the view, which had been gathering support since the mid-1980s, that full-time employment—coupled with work-conditioned benefits—should enable workers to lift themselves and their families out of poverty. Government has a responsibility to supplement market wages, if necessary, to meet that standard, as the Clinton administration indeed did with a historic expansion of the Earned Income Tax Credit (EITC).

I argue that these changes in welfare took place against a backdrop in which most aspects of citizenship in the United States are in fact conditional, even if that fact is not always well understood. Thus, welfare reform, far from creating either an anomaly or a new conception of citizenship, is actually rendering welfare policy more consonant with a preexisting (if largely tacit) understanding of what I call conditional citizenship.

The conception of citizenship as conditional and the proposition that fulfilling those conditions creates binding claims on the polity draw upon an understanding of a good society that we should endorse. Specifically, if political communities are systems of social cooperation for mutual advantage and endowed with coercive authority, then conditionality understood as performance and reciprocally binding claims emerges as the preferred conception of citizenship.

Arenas of Conditionality

I begin with two conceptual points.

A Property-Citizenship Analogy During the past century, the U.S. legal system has moved away from the notion of property as a unified entity to which an agent stands in an all-or-nothing relation of ownership, and toward an understanding of property as an ensemble of rights and privileges that the law can disaggregate to promote specific public purposes. For example, although laws concerning historic preservation and environmental protection need not transfer ownership of property from private to public hands, they do restrict owners in the exercise of some rights of property that they would otherwise have enjoyed.

In this regard, citizenship resembles property: rather than being a unified all-or-nothing status, it is an ensemble of rights, privileges, and immunities, some of which may stand forfeited or restricted without restricting the rest. Depending on context and circumstances, conditionality may attach to some attributes of citizenship but not others.

Varieties of Conditions It may well be the case that all attributes of citizenship are conditional in that they may be altered or abrogated in particular circumstances. A classic instance occurred during the Civil War, when President Lincoln suspended the writ of habeas corpus in states threatening rebellion. Lincoln described the background of his action in vivid terms: "The whole of the laws which were required to be faithfully executed, were being resisted, and failing of execution, in nearly one-third of the States." And he defended his action with two rhetorical questions:

> Must [the laws] be allowed to finally fail of execution, even had it been perfectly clear, that by the use of the means necessary to their execution, some single law . . . should, to a very limited extent, be violated? . . . are all the laws, *but one,* to go unexecuted, and the government itself go to pieces, lest that one be violated? (cited in Neely 1991, 12, italics in original)

The crux of Lincoln's argument was that the enjoyment of any particular right depends on the existence of institutions capable of securing rights in their totality, and that preserving such institutions may require the suspension of some rights for the duration of the threat.

I want to distinguish between conditionality based on background circumstances, such as the ones President Lincoln faced, and conditionality based on features of individuals. During the depths of the Great Depression, many states reduced their programs of general relief, not because the poor and unemployed had done anything to disqualify themselves for support, but because the background circumstances of declining revenues could no longer sustain the full programs. The welfare reform of the mid-1990s was different. The changes were brought about, not by background circumstances, but by a changing understanding of the attributes of individuals that should be established as qualifications for participation.

From the outset, of course, federal relief programs established eligibility conditions, such as age, employment status, income, and marital circumstances. Some of these programs (the Civilian Conservation Corps and the Works Progress Administration, for example) focused on public employment. Others, including what became AFDC, provided income to individuals depending on their status. (By the 1950s, state provisions of the original AFDC that laid down moral character qualifications for participation had been set aside as discriminatory.)

Against this backdrop, PRWORA can be seen not as creating conditionality where none had previously existed, but rather as shifting the basis of welfare eligibility from status-centered attributes of individuals back to conduct-centered attributes, although some status requirements, such as low income, still applied. From a broad historical perspective, the period from the 1960s through the first half of the 1990s was an aberration, while the 1996 reforms represent a return to the status quo ante of conduct-centered conditionality.

Conditions on Rights

Although we often think of rights as absolute, they may be conditioned or limited on a number of grounds having to do with the behavior or status of the citizen.

Conditionality Tied to Behavior

Here I discuss a number of cases, unrelated to welfare, in which citizenship may be denied, revoked, or abridged because of malfeasance or nonfeasance.

Naturalization I begin with the clearest case. Adult citizens of other nations who wish to become U.S. citizens must meet a number of conduct-related conditions. They must reside in the United States as lawful permanent residents for five years before applying. They must be proficient in English and demonstrate a working knowledge of U.S. history and civics by passing an examination. They must take an oath to renounce foreign allegiances, support and defend the Constitution and laws of the United States, and serve the United States in military or civilian capacities as required by law.

Perhaps most significant for our purposes, they must demonstrate a record of good moral character in the five years preceding the application for citizenship. While U.S. immigration and naturalization laws do not attempt an affirmative definition of good character, they do enumerate criteria that create a presumption of its absence. Among them are being involved in or convicted of habitual drunkenness, polygamy, prostitution, the use of forbidden narcotics, fostering the illegal entry of aliens, illegal gambling, immigration fraud, failure to pay court-ordered child support or alimony, and the failure to complete probation, parole, or a suspended sentence. Conduct such as murder or aggravated felony, terrorism, or persecution based on race, religion, national origin, or membership in a particular social group results in mandatory denial, as does any conduct that has resulted in a valid deportation or removal order.[1]

In addition, U.S. law establishes grounds for individuals previously granted citizenship to be deprived of it. The most frequently invoked basis is fraud or misrepresentation (about past conduct) committed during the naturalization process. There are only two grounds for denaturalization based on subsequent conduct, however: refusing to testify before a congressional committee within ten years of naturalization, or becoming a member of a proscribed subversive organization within five years after naturalization. (Although these latter provisions, adopted in an era of intense anti-communism, have never been enforced, it is not hard to envision their use during the current war on terrorism.)[2]

Enemy Combatant Status U.S. law enumerates acts that constitute voluntary relinquishment of citizenship if performed with that intent. One may formally renounce one's citizenship before duly constituted officials of the U.S. government, at home or abroad. But law provides no grounds on which the government can subject native-born citizens to involuntary revocation of citizenship. In the lead case of Afroyim v. Rusk [387 U.S. 253 (1967)] the Court's majority declares that "we reject the idea . . . that . . . Congress has any general power, express or implied, to take away an American citizen's citizenship without his assent" (257).

At the same time, it must be said that the issue remains somewhat unsettled. For example, U.S. law continues to cite, as grounds for revocation of citizenship, committing acts of treason and entering or serving in the armed forces of a foreign state when such forces are engaged in hostilities against the United States (see USC, Title 8, chapter 12, subchapter III, part III, section 1481). To the best of my knowledge, the Supreme Court has never explicitly invalidated these legislative provisions. If litigation on this point ever occurs (and given current conditions, that hardly seems unlikely), the decision may well turn on the question of whether certain acts imply assent without explicitly expressing it.

There are circumstances, however, in which native-born citizens may forfeit fundamental rights without their consent. To take one example, if a person intentionally joins a military force that the United States engages in armed conflict and is captured on the battlefield, he may be deprived of otherwise applicable legal protection such as habeas corpus. In the case of Hamdi v. Rumsfeld, the U.S. Fourth Circuit Court of Appeals ruled that a native-born citizen captured while fighting with the Taliban in Afghanistan could be held as an enemy combatant, inside or outside the United States, without being charged or tried, until the cessation of hostilities. If a U.S. citizen takes up arms against his country, he places himself by that act under the jurisdiction of the executive branch's sweeping constitutional powers over military affairs and removes himself from many procedural protections afforded by civilian courts.[3] As the Court put it, "the safeguards that all Americans have come to expect in criminal prosecutions do not translate neatly to the arena of armed conflict."[4]

In a subsequent review of this case, the Supreme Court overruled the Fourth Circuit to the extent of allowing Hamdi some review of his claims that his detention was improper. This review might still fall somewhat short of the scrutiny normally given to a habeas corpus petition. So to that extent the normal rights of citizenship are still subordinated to the needs of national security.[5]

Criminal Convictions While unfamiliarity may make the link between law-abidingness and rights less visible, it is a key feature of our legal system. Both the Declaration of Independence and the U.S. Constitution make liberty a fundamental right. Nonetheless, even critics of the criminal justice system do not question the principle that serious violations of law warrant the deprivation of liberty. So liberty is both fundamental and conditional.[6]

In fact, those convicted of serious crimes may lose a wide range of important rights, temporarily or permanently, even when they are no longer incarcerated. Consider the issue posed in the case of Griffin v. Wisconsin.[7] Griffin, previously convicted of a felony and other criminal charges, was out of prison on probation. Under Wisconsin law, probationers are subject to the rules and regulations established by the state's department of health and social services. One of those rules permits a probation officer to search a probationer's home without a warrant as long as there are reasonable grounds to believe that contraband is present. After receiving a tip that Griffin might be in possession of a firearm (a serious violation of probation), a supervisor in the probation department searched his residence and found a handgun. After Griffin challenged the admissibility of the handgun as evidence, first a lower court and then the Wisconsin Supreme Court affirmed his conviction on the grounds that probation status diminished otherwise applicable privacy rights and rendered a warrantless search without probable cause consistent with the Fourth Amendment.

The U.S. Supreme Court agreed. The majority's opinion declared that,

> a State's operation of a probation system, like its operation of a school, government office or prison, or its supervision of a regulated industry . . . presents "special needs" beyond law enforcement that may justify departures from the usual warrant and probable-cause requirements.[8]

More broadly, the Court declared that,

> to a greater or lesser degree, it is always true of probationers (as we have said it to be true of parolees) that they do not enjoy "the absolute liberty to which every citizen is entitled, but only . . . conditional liberty properly dependent on observance of special [probation] restrictions."[9]

I turn now to the much-disputed question of whether convicted felons should have voting rights. Clearly, the Fourteenth Amendment permits the states to disenfranchise felons, and state constitutions have long embraced a link between law-abidingness and voting rights.[10] Forty-six states and the District of Columbia prohibit inmates serving felony convictions from voting. While most states restore felons' voting rights after they complete their terms of prison and probation, eight states permanently bar ex-felons from voting. According to some estimates, nearly 3.9 million people are prohibited from voting, a majority of whom are former convicts who have completed their sentences (see Knowles 2000).

These facts do not settle the question of whether this linkage is appropriate, or whether its effects are acceptable. On the one hand, it is at least not unreasonable to argue that participating in the making of laws presupposes a willingness to be bound by them, which a felony conviction calls into question. Only two states allow convicted felons to vote while incarcerated. On the other hand, is hard to contemplate with equanimity a practice that disenfranchises 13 percent of black males.[11]

Many people believe (and I concur) that the most reasonable position is to restore voting rights to felons after the completion of their sentences. This position is endorsed by, among others, the Reverend Jesse Jackson, who argues that "once you serve your sentence to society, you should have your vote restored. If you don't, it's a lifetime sentence" (quoted in Bennett 2004, para. 57).

I would suggest, however, that it is a mistake to view deprivation of voting rights simply as an aspect of the felon's sentence. It is a proxy, rather, for a deeper conviction about the appropriate moral conditions for the exercise of the franchise. Restoring voting rights after the completion of the sentence expresses the optimistic presumption that the ex-felon has internalized the importance of law-abidingness. Indeed, the fact that a former inmate is released into the community expresses the same presumption. Like most presumptions, this one is rebuttable; multiple felony convictions (say, three or more) may plausibly be taken as evidence that individual in question will never develop the requisite commitment to the rule of law. In such circumstances, permanent disenfranchisement (or permanent incarceration) does not seem unreasonable.

Whatever one thinks about the most desirable policy, the point remains that the right to vote, which is among the most basic attributes of citizenship, is conditioned on conduct as well as age. That this remains the case throughout the United States after the elimination of restrictions based on property, race, gender, the poll tax, civic knowledge, among others, testifies to the enduring intuition that voting is not an unconditioned entitlement but rather presupposes a pro-civic orientation.

Conditionality Tied to Benefits

I now examine the normative appropriateness of conditions on the receipt of public benefits and address the longstanding jurisprudential debate about unconstitutional conditions. As Kathleen Sullivan explained, this doctrine holds that "government may not grant a benefit on the condition that the beneficiary surrender a constitutional right, even if the government may withhold that benefit altogether. It reflects the triumph of the view that government may not do indirectly what it may not do directly" (1989, 1415).[12] This doctrine helped to defend property rights during the Lochner era. Then, starting with the Warren Court, it was applied to hold that "government may not condition tax exemptions or government jobs on political silence or conformity, public unemployment compensation on the acceptance of work on one's sabbath day, or public broadcasting subsidies on abstinence from editorializing" (Sullivan 1989, 1416)

The Supreme Court did not begin applying the unconstitutional conditions doctrine to cases involving public assistance until the early 1960s. In a review of the first three decades of the Court's activity in this arena, Lynn Baker examines twenty-three cases (1990). The Court sustained conditions on receipt of benefits in thirteen of the cases and overturned them in ten. Baker finds a consistent, if poorly articulated, principle guiding these decisions. The Court begins by asking "whether the challenged condition involves a constitutionally protected activity. If not, the condition is sustained" as legitimate (1217). If the challenged condition does involve a constitutionally protected right, the Court then poses a second question on whether the effect of the condition is to "require persons unable to earn a subsistence income . . . to pay a higher price to engage in that constitutionally protected activity than . . . persons earning a subsistence income" (1220). If it does, then the Court overturns the challenged right. The reason is that the Constitution seeks to establish a zone of legal equality within which government may not unequally burden individuals beyond the background inequalities that exist in a market economy.

To illustrate this test, consider two of the cases Baker examines. Dandridge v. Williams [13] concerned a challenge to a Maryland AFDC regulation that imposed a ceiling on the monthly amount of money that any one family unit could receive. The effect was that a family of nine would receive the same amount as a family of six, arguably burdening recipients' constitutional right to procreate. The Court disagreed and sustained the regulation. Baker argues that the Court implicitly compared the welfare recipient with a subsistence wage-earner: in both cases, having an additional child would reduce per capita resources. Thus the regulation does not establish an additional burden on the constitutional right to procreate (Baker 1990, 1235–36).

Compare this to the outcome in Shapiro v. Thompson,[14] which involved state statutes making otherwise eligible residents ineligible for welfare if they had not lived within those states for at least a year before applying for assistance. The Court struck these statutes down. In Baker's analysis, both prongs of the unconstitutional conditions test were met: the condition both implicated a constitutional right (in this case, the right to travel) and had the effect of making it more expensive for welfare recipients than for other low-income wage earners to exercise that right (Baker 1990, 1240–42).

Some scholars argue that the doctrine of unconstitutional conditions is in disarray (see, for example, Sunstein 1990, 593), but let us assume arguendo that Baker's positive analysis of the unconstitutional conditions test is correct. The question remains whether the test, so understood, merits normative endorsement. Baker's answer strikes me as powerful. The test, she suggests, encodes core norms of social equality and of individual dignity and worth. The reason is that in any society, "the formal distribution of rights serves important symbolic and descriptive functions." It may seem to be less offensive for the government to attach a surtax to some citizens' exercise of rights than to deny them those rights altogether. It is, nonetheless, to "create a system of constitutional caste and relegate that group to the lower levels" (1990, 1251–52).

Entitlement Rights and Liberty Rights

So far, so good. But why limit the reach of constitutional equality to burdens the government directly creates? Don't market-induced background inequalities affect the exercise of rights as much, if not more? And isn't that equally unacceptable from a moral point of view?

In some respects, the answer is yes, and that is the Constitution's answer as well. Consider, for example, the Sixth Amendment's guarantee of the assistance of counsel for all criminal defendants. As interpreted by the Court, this provision does more than forbid the government from impeding a defendant's acquisition and use of a lawyer; it requires the government to act affirmatively, using public resources, to provide counsel to indigent defendants. The right to counsel is more than a liberty; it is an entitlement.[15]

Compare this to the right to travel. This is a liberty-right, in that under ordinary circumstances the government may neither prohibit some individuals from travelling nor burden some more than others in the exercise of that right.[16] But though background inequalities of resources make it more difficult for a minimum wage worker than for Bill Gates to fly across the country, it does not follow that the government is under an affirmative obligation to issue low-income individuals air travel vouchers. Travel is a liberty right but not an entitlement right.

Legal controversy over abortion provides another example of this distinction. As Bridget Remington summarizes the situation, the Supreme Court has consistently held that although a woman has a right to have an abortion without direct government interference, the government is under no obligation to subsidize that right, even if it subsidizes other pregnancy-related medical services. In the lead case of Maher v. Roe, the Court emphasized that it had not made the right to abortion an entitlement-right in Roe v. Wade but rather had recognized a constitutionally protected liberty-right to make certain important and intimate decisions without government interference (Remington 2002, 229).

To be sure, the line separating these categories of rights is neither clear nor fixed. The Supreme Court's decision in Gideon v. Wainwright moved the assistance of counsel from one side to the other,[17] and it is not unlikely that subsequent decisions will further widen the zone of entitlement by requiring publicly provided lawyers to display at least basic competence in their defense of poor clients. Nor is constitutional adjudication the last word; it is perfectly possible for an established practice to pass constitutional but not moral muster.

It is suggestive, however, that a generation of advocacy and litigation failed to constitutionalize welfare benefits as an entitlement right.[18] In 1970, the Supreme Court established that welfare benefits could not be revoked in advance of due process, but within the same decade also denied that Congress was constitutionally obliged to provide benefits.[19] In the absence of a compelling general moral theory of welfare entitlement, national differences of political culture will (and should) express themselves in divergent approaches to public policy.

In this context, let us turn to the PRWORA's work requirement. Clearly, those who regard welfare benefits as entitlement rights will reject work requirements in principle. Given the failure of efforts to constitutionalize welfare benefits as an entitlement, whether benefits can be conditioned on work becomes a legislative question, which PRWORA answers in the affirmative.

One could imagine an alternative line of constitutional argument, however. Although not explicitly spelled out in the Constitution, there would seem to be a protected right to not work, at least in the sense that a statute criminalizing voluntary nonwork would surely be struck down as a violation of the Fourteenth Amendment's liberty guarantee. (Compare this to the now-defunct communist regimes that did criminalize nonwork as parasitism.) So it seems reasonable to say that the work requirement does meet the first prong of Baker's test: a constitutional right is implicated. The question then becomes whether the requirement burdens the exercise of that right by making it more costly. The answer is no. To be sure, the nonworker whose time limit has expired receives no cash income, but neither does the low-income wage earner who stops working.[20]

This is hardly the end of the discussion. One may well wonder whether any reasonable moral or political theory would allow some members of a community but not others to go without the means of subsistence, at least when the aggregate resources of the society suffice to prevent this. That is an argument to have welfare. But if we have it, the Baker test argues that conditioning aid on work is fair.

We also assume that those who are required to work have the opportunity to do so. It would be unreasonable to impose work as a condition of public support if the number of needy individuals exceeded the number of available jobs. In these circumstances, the government would incur an obligation either to fill the gap with public sector jobs or to relax the work requirement for those who remain involuntarily unemployed. PRWORA has no such provisions, but it does allow states to create public jobs for recipients if they choose (as New York City and Wisconsin have done), and it promises added money to pay for aid in the event of a recession.

The previous effort at welfare reform in the United States, the Family Support Act of 1988, was hobbled by the recession of 1989 to 1991 and the long jobless recovery that followed it. By contrast, the PRWORA took effect at the beginning of one of the most favorable employment markets in U.S. history. This good fortune allowed the potential contradiction between work requirements and a shortage of private sector jobs to remain latent and masked the law's failure to guarantee public sector employment as a safety net.

The recession of 2001, followed by a slack labor market, has changed this equation. If the emerging tension between public law and private markets persists, it will become morally necessary either to relax the law's strictures or for government to become the employer of last resort. In short, work requirements would ultimately expand the economic responsibility of the U.S. welfare state.

Another key provision of the PRWORA requires women seeking public assistance to cooperate in establishing the paternity of their children. States are given latitude in outlining the terms of cooperation. In Florida, for example, a woman must provide the identity or location of all the men who could possibly be her child's father, consent to DNA tests, and return to the state any support she receives from the father outside the context of a support decree. By contrast, the state of Wisconsin allows such a mother to keep the entirety of her support payments. For the most part, however, the benefits of official support payments stemming from paternity establishment will not flow to the mother and dependent child but goes instead to repay the states and the federal government (Remington 2002, 216).

Does this provision of PRWORA violate the unconstitutional conditions test? The threshold question is whether it implicates a constitutional right. There are recognized rights to marriage[21] and procreation.[22] In addition, unmarried women have the right to initiate abortions or adoptions without the consent of the biological father (in adoptions, unless the father has established paternity).[23] To the best of my knowledge, no state directly requires all unmarried women to (help) establish the paternity of their children, and I infer from existing case law that such a provision would be struck down as a violation of constitutionally protected privacy rights. Indeed, this would seem to be a more direct breach of privacy, understood in its core and common sense, than are many other proscribed state acts.

If I am right about this, we have identified a constitutional right that is affected by the paternity establishment requirement of the PRWORA. The question then becomes whether the second prong of the unconstitutional conditions test is also met—that is, whether this condition illegitimately raises the price of exercising the protected right. The answer, I would argue, is that it does not. Consider that an unmarried woman who is not seeking public financial assistance cannot receive a court-ordered child support award without paternity being established, through either the biological father's voluntary acknowledgment or a mandatory procedure. Given this, conditioning public assistance on good faith efforts to establish paternity does not make women inside the welfare system worse off than comparable women outside it.

Conditionality as a Norm of Citizenship

I have just demonstrated that conditionality, suitably circumscribed, not only enjoys an established place within the U.S. constitutional tradition but appeals to general moral norms that we have good reason to endorse. I now extend the moral analysis by linking conditionality to a morally appealing understanding of politics and citizenship.

Begin with a conception of political community as an association for mutual advantage and the common good.[24] Whatever content the members of a particular political community may give to these goals, experience shows that achieving them requires institutions and public goods as well as cooperative enterprises and sound policies. Call these the requisites of effective political communities.

Experience also shows that the requisites of effective political community do not drop from heaven like manna. They must be produced and sustained through the appropriate kinds of human endeavor, provided primarily by the members of such communities—that is, their citizens. One kind of needed endeavor (not the only kind) is work that helps produce the resources needed for both public and private goods. This leads to a normative conception of citizenship as the willingness to do one's fair share to uphold the requisites of community, in return for full participation in the system of mutual advantage and the common good. So understood, citizenship is an ensemble of benefits and burdens, involving both performance and reciprocity.

Obviously, the content of required performance and reciprocal claims will vary from community to community. Two generalizations seem to apply, however, to most if not all communities. First, citizens are expected to do their part to uphold the rule of law. This means a strong presumption in favor of obeying duly authorized and promulgated law. It also means a willingness to serve as an active participant in the legal system—for example, as a witness or as a member of a jury.

Second, citizens are expected to do their part to generate resources. For reasons of disease or disability, some will be able to do little if anything. That is why any defensible conception of social justice must make a place for claims based on need as well as desert (see also Galston 1980, chapter 5). But most will be mentally and physically able to make some kind of contribution to the material basis of life, individual and communal. And the community is justified in requiring them to do so, in return for participating in the advantages of the common life. To put this point differently: in the case of individuals able to make a contribution, the community honors need-claims by ensuring to each the opportunity to make a contribution and to receive in return remuneration at least sufficient to provide for basic needs.

This argument is abstract, and deliberately so. The concept of contribution acquires specificity within particular communities and circumstances. In principle, the PRWORA could have defined contribution more broadly than it did, to encompass education, training, and care work. The arguments against this broader conception were both practical and normative. Education and training are linked to contribution, not intrinsically, but rather to the extent that they prepare individuals for higher value-added occupations. In too many cases, however, education and training postponed or substituted for employment. In principle, care work is a crucial contribution to community well-being, a fact reflected (albeit inadequately) in the U.S. tax code. In practice, however, for reasons of youth, immaturity, and lack of connection with the norms and practices of the wider society, too many mothers in the pre-1996 welfare regime proved unable to perform care work in a socially acceptable manner.

One may call the work test unfair because in practice it is imposed only on needy aid recipients. Affluence may give some a choice about whether to work, and government does not take this choice from them. Several other papers in this collection wrestle with the problem of the idle rich. The correct response to it is not to give aid without a work test but rather to subject the rich to a more progressive income tax and an inheritance tax. The fact that today's Republican leaders seek instead to reduce the tax burden on the rich is not an objection of principle to the work test, although it surely raises the issue of equal treatment and basic fairness.

I have left the concept not only of contribution but also of participation vague because I am skeptical that any distributional norm can be both richly specified and equally applicable to all communities. One thing is clear, however: every community must work toward internal consistency between norms and practices.

Ought implies can. To make a contribution, individuals must enjoy social circumstances within which ability can be exercised. Any community that makes contribution a condition of access to valued resources incurs an obligation to ensure that every individual has some venue for productive endeavor—that is, a job. As noted, PRWORA does not force states to guarantee jobs, yet some localities have done so, and to date jobs in the private economy have been sufficient.

The concept of reciprocity also requires substantial equality of developmental opportunity—that is, a fair chance to develop the talents and abilities that enable individuals to make a meaningful contribution to their community. Substantial equality of education and training opportunities, and of the background conditions that help develop core intellectual and social competences, is essential if the principle of reciprocity is to be applied fairly and consistently.

The requirement of reciprocity also points toward a social minimum. It is both unrealistic and unfair to expect the requirement of contribution to be honored if the rewards of contribution are demonstrably inadequate. Those who meet legitimate behavioral expectations (such as law-abidingness, acceptance of personal responsibility, and a reasonable work effort) should be able to obtain the basics of a decent life. To the extent that a society's economic system does not fulfill this requirement, other institutions must fill the gap.

In policy terms, if work is required, it must yield enough to achieve decency. Some combination of minimum wage requirements and public wage (or in-kind) supplements is a normative necessity. From this standpoint, the massive expansion of the Earned Income Tax Credit early in the Clinton administration to what is now a $30 billion dollar annual program represents a significant step toward social justice.

The Veil of Ignorance Test

I have long been critical of the Rawlsian enterprise, in part on the grounds that stripping away human particularity, diverse conceptions of the good, and the concept of desert for purposes of determining principles of justice deprives political philosophy of resources essential to its success. In chapter 4, Stuart White maintains that Rawls shifted his position to exclude the voluntary nonworker (the Malibu surfer) from claims to support by society. But the fix is superficial, because Rawls did not alter his fundamental view that justice should take no cognizance of individualized details about desert.[25]

Nonetheless, it is useful to subject my proposal to the Veil of Ignorance test. Suppose, as Rawls does, that we grasp broad facts about society and human life. Among them are that abilities are diverse and unequally distributed, some individuals are born severely disabled while others are rendered so through accident and disease, some individuals are rationally self-interested without being willing to honor reasonable terms of social cooperation, most individuals are willing to honor such terms if most others do, and much of what is needed to sustain both individual lives and social institutions is created through human endeavor.

Given this understanding, rational individuals would be unlikely to choose principles of social organization that fully condition access to individual and social goods on socially beneficial exercise of abilities, because they might find themselves among those who are unable to do so. Nor, on the other hand, would they choose principles that entirely sever the connection between contribution and access to goods. For if some contribute and others who could choose not to, not only will resources needed to provide individual and public goods be less plentiful, but also over time, those who begin by making a contribution will be less and less willing to do so.

Rather, rational individuals would endorse principles that link rewards to doing one's part, loosen the connection between the exercise of specific natural endowments and the quantity of reward, and make provision for the possibility that some may be unable to make a contribution.[26] In addition, because they understand the corrosive effects of free riders, they would choose to endow the political community with the power needed to make their preferred principles of social distribution binding on all members of the community, through coercion if necessary. The enforcement of work as a condition for the enjoyment of certain material and social goods is an example (not the only one) of societal efforts to prevent free riding.

I conclude, then, that the conception of morality and politics encoded in the basic structure of the PRWORA does not require significant revisions in our conception, legal or normative, of citizenship. Instead, the practice of delinking public assistance from behavioral expectations emerges as an anomaly that the welfare reform efforts of the mid-1990s have helped eliminate.[27]

Notes

1. Public Law No. 103-416 Statute 4305 (October 25, 1994). For a discussion, see http://www.unitedstatesvisas.gov (accessed July 22, 2005).
2. The U.S. Patriot Act criminalizes various forms of association with, and contributions to, ostensibly charitable organizations that may also be supporting

individuals or activities defined as terrorist. In principle, this could create grounds for revocation of citizenship.

3. 316 F.3d 450, decided January 8, 2003.
4. 316 F.3d 450, at 465.
5. Case no. 03-6696, decided June 28, 2004.
6. The current debate over the death penalty revolves in part around the question of whether the right to life is similarly conditional. Significantly, many principled opponents of the death penalty advocate life imprisonment without possibility of parole as the morally appropriate alternative. It is hard to imagine a greater deprivation of liberty.
7. 483 U.S. 868 (1987).
8. 483 U.S. 868, at 873–74.
9. 483 U.S. 868, at 874 (citing and quoting its decision in Morrissey v. Brewer, 408 U.S. 471 [1972], at 480).
10. This issue was reached and settled in Richardson v. Ramirez, 418 U.S. 24 (1974).
11. Even stern critics of current practices do not argue that this disparate impact amounts to a constitutional violation. To find such a violation, binding court decisions require evidence of discriminatory intent as well as effect, which state laws do not contain (see Bennett 2004, 1, fn. 1).
12. It is much easier to state the doctrine abstractly than to explain its underlying rationale or apply it to specific cases (for detailed discussions of these difficulties, see Sullivan 1989; Kreimer 1984; Sunstein 1990; Berman 2001).
13. 397 U.S. 471 (1970).
14. 394 U.S. 618 (1969).
15. The locus classicus is of course Gideon v. Wainwright, 372 U.S. 335 (1963).
16. Imagine the legal response if the TSA required men but not women to undergo inspection before boarding airplanes. I say under ordinary circumstances because if public authorities can show compelling reasons to scrutinize some categories of individuals more carefully than others, at least some differences of treatment may well be constitutionally acceptable.
17. Gideon v. Wainwright, 372 U.S. 335 (1963).
18. The best-known legal presentations of this view are Charles Reich (1964) and Albert M. Bendich (1966). Some philosophers and students of jurisprudence labored hard (if not wisely) to find John Rawls's Difference Principle in the penumbra and emanations of the Fourteenth Amendment!
19. Procedural welfare rights were established in Goldberg v. Kelly, 397 U.S. 254 (1970). Substantive welfare rights were denied in Dandridge v. Williams, 397 U.S. 471 (1970) and several other cases.
20. To simplify the analysis, I ignore the possible effects of unemployment insurance.
21. Loving v. Virginia, 388 U.S. 1 (1967); Zablocki v. Redhail, 434 U.S. 374 (1978).
22. Skinner v. Oklahoma, 316 U.S. 535 (1942).
23. Planned Parenthood v. Danforth, 428 U.S. 52 (1976); Quilloin v. Walcott, 434 U.S. 246 (1978).
24. Theorists as various as Aristotle, Thomas Aquinas, and John Rawls have affirmed versions of this proposition.
25. For my critique of Rawls, see William A. Galston, *Liberal Purposes* (1991, chaps. 4–7). For Rawls's altered position, see *Justice as Fairness* (2001, 179). For his original position rejecting desert, see *Justice as Fairness* (72–78).

26. This is more than mere speculation. The most systematic attempt to determine the principles of justice that would be chosen in an experimental situation that models the Veil of Ignorance found that groups almost unanimously rejected Rawls's Difference Principle in favor of an ensemble of principles that gave considerable weight to individual contributions but limited the impact of differences of ability (see Frohlich and Oppenheimer 1992).
27. Lest this position seem insufficiently compassionate and charitable, I should note its consistency with the religious tradition I know best. In Deuteronomy 15:11 the children of Israel are commanded to "open your hand to the poor and needy kinsman in your land." (Fulfilling this commandment requires, not only individual charity, but also a mandatory annual tithe and the septennial remission of debts.) While this would seem to establish an unconditional system of public aid, rabbinic interpretations brought in the dimension of personal conduct. In the Babylonian Talmud (Pes. 113a) we read, "Better to flay carcasses in the marketplace than to depend on public assistance because you feel the available work is beneath your dignity." Accepting public assistance because individual incapacity or social circumstances leave you with no choice is permissible and honorable; spurning work (even low-income or low-status work) is not. The principles of self-help and social contribution, suitably delimited, find their place in religion as well as political philosophy.

References

Baker, Lynn A. 1990. "The Prices of Rights: Toward a Positive Theory of Unconstitutional Conditions." *Cornell Law Review* 75(September): 1105–1257.

Bendich, Albert M. 1966. "Privacy, Poverty, and the Constitution." *California Law Review* 54(2): 407–42.

Bennett, Scott M. 2004. "Giving Ex-Felons the Right to Vote." *California Criminal Law Review* 6(1). Available at: http://www.boalt.org/CCLR/v6/v6bennett.htm (accessed July 18, 2005).

Berman, Mitchell N. 2001. "Coercion Without Baselines: Unconstitutional Conditions in Three Dimensions." *Georgetown Law Journal* 90(November): 1–112.

Frohlich, Norman, and Joe A. Oppenheimer. 1992. *Choosing Justice: An Experimental Approach to Ethical Theory.* Berkeley: University of California Press.

Galston, William A. 1980. *Justice and the Human Good.* Chicago: University of Chicago Press.

———. 1991. *Liberal Purposes: Goods, Virtues, and Diversity in the Liberal State.* Cambridge: Cambridge University Press.

Knowles, Bryan. 2000. "Should Convicted Felons Have Voting Rights?" In *Crime, Law, and Justice Issues.* Washington, D.C.: Speakout.com. Available at: http://speakout.com/activism/issue_briefs/1289b-1.html (accessed July 18, 2005).

Kreimer, Seth F. 1984. "Allocational Sanctions: The Problem of Negative Rights in a Positive State." *University of Pennsylvania Law Review* 132(July): 1293–1397.

Neely, Mark E., Jr. 1991. *The Fate of Liberty: Abraham Lincoln and Civil Liberties.* New York: Oxford University Press.

Rawls, John. 2001. *Justice as Fairness: A Restatement,* edited by Erin Kelly. Cambridge, Mass.: Harvard University Press.

Reich, Charles. 1964. "The New Property." *Yale Law Journal* 73(5): 733–87.
Remington, Bridget. 2002. "It Takes a Father? Conforming with Traditional Family Values as a Condition of Receiving Welfare: Morals Reform and the Price of Privacy." *Stetson Law Review* 32(fall): 205–40.
Sullivan, Kathleen M. 1989. "Unconstitutional Conditions." *Harvard Law Review* 102(May): 1415–1506.
Sunstein, Cass R. 1990. "Why the Unconstitutional Conditions Doctrine is an Anachronism (with Particular Reference to Religion, Speech, and Abortion)." *Boston University Law Review* 70(4): 593–621.

Chapter 6

An Ethic of Mutual Responsibility? Toward a Fuller Justification for Conditionality in Welfare

ALAN DEACON

THE ABOLITION of a "right to welfare" has been at the heart of welfare reform in the United States. Entitlement is no longer determined by an assessment of financial needs, but is instead conditional on the willingness of claimants to meet specific requirements regarding their behavior. Such conditionality has also been a central theme of the New Labour government's attempts to restructure the British welfare state. In both countries, it is a tenet of public policy that welfare can best serve the common good not only by relieving hardship, but also by shaping the lives of those who receive public assistance.

The end of entitlement in welfare has been the subject of an extended and sometimes heated debate. In general, welfare conditionality has been justified in two ways. The contractualist justification views welfare as a contract, the terms of which obligate public agencies to provide services but also obligate recipients to make the most of those services and the opportunities they create. If public agencies keep their side of the bargain, then claimants should keep theirs. The second justification is paternalist, viewing welfare as a means whereby recipients are required to change their behavior in ways that serve their own longer-term interests. Government knows better than the claimants themselves how their behavior must change.

Here I argue that the contractualist and paternalist justifications for conditionality are powerful but incomplete. Consideration should be given to a third justification that I call mutualist. This conception has not been set out so fully or so explicitly as the contractualist and paternalist arguments, but it can be derived from the writings of communitarian theorists, especially Philip Selznick. It begins with the premise that people have responsibilities and commitments to each other that arise independently of the claims they make on the state. It views welfare as a mechanism for reflecting and affirming the interdependence of human beings, and for enforcing the obligations that flow from this.

I do not claim that mutualism alone provides a full justification for conditionality, but suggest instead a pluralist justification. This is grounded in mutualist arguments but also draws on the contractualist and paternalist justifications. I show that welfare conditionality informed by a mutualist perspective is more compatible with the pursuit of greater equality, and more consistent with an ethic of care.

Shortly after taking office in 1997, Britain's Prime Minister Tony Blair spoke of an "ethic of mutual responsibility or duty" ("Blair offers jobless a new bargain," *The Guardian*, June 3, 1997). It is highly probable that this term was born of a need for an arresting sound bite, rather than philosophical reflection. Yet it captures well what is required. Creating a more just and well-ordered society requires both reducing the social and economic inequalities now in Britain and the United States, and that citizens be more willing to recognize and fulfill their obligations to each other.

What are these obligations that should be fostered and sometimes enforced through welfare? Does the addition of this mutualist rationale broaden the objectives of welfare reform beyond those already implied by contractualist and paternalist thinking? And if so how?

Three Justifications for Ending Entitlement

There are three broad justifications for ending entitlement.[1] Each must state its own case and rebut two major criticisms that have been made of conditionality in welfare. The first criticism is that conditionality rests on a false analysis of the causes of the problems it seeks to remedy. These critics charge that conditionality fails to recognize the structural causes of pathologies such as worklessness and deprivation, and so blames and punishes those who are already the victims of social and economic injustice.[2] The second criticism acknowledges that the analysis underlying welfare reform may have some merit, but still argues that imposing sanctions will worsen rather than alleviate the problems. This second criticism is voiced most forcefully when the sanctions are believed to have an impact on the dependents of welfare recipients.[3]

Contractualist

The core of this argument is that it is reasonable to use welfare to enforce reciprocal obligations. If the government keeps its part of the bargain, then the claimants should keep theirs. It is hard to imagine a clearer expression of this idea than that given by then Governor Bill Clinton in 1987. Speaking of the blueprint for welfare reform produced by the National Governors Association, he explained:

> we believe that every welfare recipient should sign a contract with the [s]tate, making a personal commitment in return for benefits to pursue an individually-developed path to independence. That includes education, training and eventually work. (cited in King 1999, 276)

Contractualist arguments such as this dominated political and academic debates about welfare in the 1980s and early 1990s. As David Ellwood wrote in *Poor Support*,

> [the] notion of mutual responsibilities is not controversial anymore. . . . It seems that in both the liberal and conservative policy making communities, there is widespread acceptance of the notion that it is legitimate to ask people to fulfill some obligations and that, in return, the government must provide some training, jobs or other programs. (1988, 226)

As Desmond King notes in chapter 3, the consensus proved to be less deep-rooted than Ellwood supposed. It is true that all agreed that contractualism was more than an administrative procedure, and that there was a widespread rejection of what the Working Seminar on Family and Welfare called a "misdirected compassion, in which benefits are offered without reciprocity" (Novak et al. 1987, 114).[4] There was little agreement, however, about what this reciprocity involved. Some, like Ellwood, thought that governments should provide job guarantees and generous in-work benefits. Others, such as Lawrence Mead, formulated their arguments in contractualist terms but placed far more emphasis on what should be required of recipients.

Contractualism is also the most familiar justification for conditionality in Britain. As early as 1995, Tony Blair declared that if a Labour government succeeded in creating new opportunities, it could then demand responsibility in return. It would not, he said, be "squeamish" about passing judgment on those who failed to fulfill their obligations to their families or communities (1995, 7). In 1998 the recently elected government's green paper on welfare reform, titled *A New Contract for Welfare,* declared that at "the heart of the modern welfare state will be a new contract between the citizen and the government, based on rights and responsibilities" (Department of Social Security 1998, 80).

The twin ideas of the welfare contract and the need to strike a new balance between rights and responsibilities have become recurrent themes of New Labour rhetoric. This has not, however, been matched by a rigorous exploration of what that balance should be. For all the attention paid to the New Deal programs, there has been little sign of the broader "redefinition of rights and responsibilities" (Giddens 1998, 65) that was called for by New Labour's "court theorist" Anthony Giddens (Klein and Rafferty 1999, 35). How much opportunity has to be created before responsibility can be demanded in return?

This is the question that Stuart White has sought to answer in *The Civic Minimum.* At the heart of his argument is the notion of justice as fair reciprocity. This is grounded in a philosophy of economic citizenship that citizens do have "definite, potentially enforceable obligations to make a productive contribution to the community." These obligations, however, arise only in a society that offers all its citizens "a sufficiently generous share of the social product" (2003, 17). Specifically, White argues that the institutions that govern economic life must be structured so as to satisfy a number of core commitments. These include the elimination of brute luck poverty, adequate protection against market vulnerability, the reduction of inequalities of opportunity, and protection against discrimination (90). These constitute the civic minimum, which he defines as,

> the concrete rights and obligations of economic citizenship, embodied in specific institutions and policies, necessary to make a market economy acceptably (though not absolutely) just. (2)

In the absence of such institutions and policies, "those who are unjustly disadvantaged by this have a proportionately reduced obligation to contribute" (91).

Where they are in place, however, the obligation stands. White is particularly clear about the need to ensure that parents fulfill their obligations to their children and the wider community. Parents, he argues, are entitled to financial and other support from the community, but in return they should see themselves as responsible "for raising children in ways that serve the public good." Specifically, they "have a duty to work to provide for the basic material needs of their children" and the state "may rightfully enforce this duty" (146).

> Certainly if the state, on behalf of the wider community, supports parenting in view of the contribution it can make to specific public ends, then it is appropriate to expect those receiving such support to commit themselves to these ends. (111)

White is, however, more troubled by the "risk of harm to innocent third parties." He acknowledges that there are no sanctions that can be imposed upon parents who refuse to work that do not threaten "to penalise children and other dependants for decisions over which they have no control" (144). In the final analysis, however, this is a problem that has to be lived with. If other conditions are met, the policies required to ensure justice as fair reciprocity should not be abandoned because of the irresponsibility of a relative handful of people. Welfare contractualism is part of a broader package of policies that together work to satisfy the conditions of fair reciprocity (2000, 521).

Paternalist

The most straightforward justification for conditionality is that it is in the best interests of the claimants. Lawrence Mead has provided the fullest and most influential statement of this, the paternalist justification. Initially, he made the contractualist argument that the obligation to work has to be enforced much more strictly. The main problem with traditional social policy, he wrote in 1986, "lies not with the poor themselves but with the political authorities who refuse to govern them firmly" (248).

He subsequently developed this call for firm government into a new paternalism, on the argument that the poor are less competent than he had previously assumed. He now starts with the view that the long-term dependent poor are "dutiful but defeated" (1992, 133). They are not competent self-regarding individuals who can be assumed to act rationally in pursuit of their own interests. This means that they will not necessarily respond to financial incentives. "No incentive has shown a power to pull many people across the line from nonwork to work. For that, stronger medicine is required" (162). This stronger medicine means not only clear-cut obligations tied to welfare but also a "tutelary regime [in which] dependants receive support of several kinds on condition of restrictions on their lives" (181).

The essence of paternalism, then, is the exercise of authority. Not only is an individual's entitlement to welfare subject to conditions as to his or her behavior, but the fulfillment of those conditions is enforced through direction and surveillance. Those who depend on welfare are told how to conduct themselves—in at least some aspects of their lives. Mead argues further that the effectiveness and legitimacy of such regimes lies in the fact that they are making people do what they want to do anyway. The problem is not that the dependent poor do not want to work or care for their families, but that they fail to do so, and that failure is in turn condoned by public policy. The task, then, is close the gap between the aspirations of the poor and their lifestyle (1997, 64).

This is not a matter of blaming the victims, but of providing the combination of help and hassle that they need to escape from what Mead calls victimhood. Moreover, once they have acquired the necessary competence, once they have begun to meet the obligations of citizenship, then they can begin to claim those rights. "When competence is no longer at issue, then justice can be" (1992, 239).

Mead is untroubled by the criticism that the penalties and sanctions required to enforce conditionality have a severe impact on children. On the contrary, the "main task of social policy" is now to "restore the authority of parents and other mentors who shape citizens," and the only way to do that is to make sure that they fulfill their obligations. Only parents who work can have the self-respect needed to command the respect of their children. "Functioning parents," he concludes, are "worth [twenty-five] Head Start programs" (2002, 15).

The central difference between the contractualist and paternalist arguments lies in expectation of government. The level of supervision to which welfare recipients are subject in a paternalist regime makes heavy demands upon the skills and resources of welfare agencies. What paternalism does not do, however, is insist that governments first create jobs or increase the benefits paid to low-paid workers before they can enforce work. Recipients are obligated to meet the conditions imposed on them because they and their dependents will benefit from those conditions, not to reciprocate what the government is doing for them. It is in this sense that the 1996 act represented a shift from contractualism to paternalism. Indeed, this is why President Clinton's decision to sign the Republican bill was condemned so fiercely by some of his former aides. David Ellwood, for example, described PRWORA as appalling. It offered claimants, he said, not "two years and you work" but two years followed by nothing—no welfare, no jobs, no support (1996, 26).

To date there has been no comparable shift toward paternalism in Britain. It will be seen that there have been a number of initiatives that are markedly authoritative in approach. Their rationale, however, has been mutualist rather than paternalist.

Mutualist

This justification starts from the premise that people have commitments and responsibilities toward each other that arise independently of the claims they make on government. Unless citizens recognize and fulfill these obligations it will be impossible to create the social and cultural conditions within which individuals can fulfill their potential and help others to realize theirs. This justification for conditionality, then, is grounded in communitarian arguments about the right of communities to collectively establish the common good and "to articulate the responsibilities they expect their members to discharge" (Etzioni 1998, xxxvii).

The understanding of obligations and commitments that underpins mutualism is thus deeper than that assumed by welfare contractualism. In the words of the communitarian Philip Selznick, it is not just a matter of a bargain between individuals and governments, but of responsibilities "that arise from social involvements or commitments. Our lives touch others in many ways, for good or ill, and we are accountable for the consequences" (1998, 62; see also Deacon 2002 for a discussion of communitarian thinking on welfare).

This is not, of course, to deny the importance of public or collective responsibility. Indeed Selznick is anxious to disclaim any "selective concern [with] personal responsibility, personal morality, personal virtues." It is important, he argues, to also pay heed to the responsibilities "[of] the affluent, or of business leaders," and to those of the community.

> *Personal responsibility is most likely to flourish when there is genuine opportunity to participate in communal life.* These conditions require substantial investment by the community and its institutions. At the same time, how much the community invests, and what kind of investment it makes, will depend on the prevalence of a sense of personal responsibility for the common good. (63, italics in original)

For Selznick, however, the responsibilities that people have as parents, neighbors, and citizens are not contingent on what the government is or is not doing to redistribute resources and to lessen material inequalities. This is the central difference between the mutualist and contractualist justifications for conditionality.

In Britain there are echoes of mutualist arguments in much of New Labour's rhetoric. Indeed, following its second landslide victory in the election of 2001, New Labour began to open up an important debate about the ways in which conditionality may be used to enforce the obligations of parents, and to reduce antisocial behavior. In doing so it has come to pay more attention to mutualist arguments. Tony Blair himself has spoken of the need for "something deeper than a merely contractual relationship between us as citizens" (speech to CPU Conference, Cape Town, October 14, 1996). Similarly, James Naughtie has noted that Finance Minister Gordon Brown's upbringing in a Scottish manse taught him that self-improvement was an obligation and so too was a commitment to the community around (Naughtie 2001, 4). Brown himself has acknowledged in a speech that "growing up in a town with strong community and voluntary organisations at its heart" he learned that people were not just self-centered but also sociable and cooperative, and as interdependent as independent (Annual Conference of the National Council for Voluntary Organisations, February 9, 2000). This helps to explain why the Treasury's 2001 pre-budget report *Tackling Child Poverty* devoted more pages to the government's measures to support parenting, develop communities and strengthen the family than it did to measures to raise low incomes and reduce worklessness (HM Treasury 2001).

Nonetheless, New Labour's mutualism is most pronounced when it is talking about antisocial behavior and about families. The white paper

Respect and Responsibility—Taking a Stand Against Anti-Social Behaviour, for example, argued that,

> [the] common element in all antisocial behaviour is that it represents a lack of respect or consideration for other people. . . . [It] shows a failure to understand that one person's rights are based on the responsibilities we have towards others and towards our families and our communities. . . . This is a web of rights and responsibilities that involves the whole society; every individual and every community. Communities need to be empowered and everyone must play their part in setting and enforcing standards of behavior. (Home Office 2003, 17)

Mutualists, then, regard those being blamed not as victims but as people who have rejected the moral claims the community has made on them. They are subject to welfare conditions and sanctions, not because of factors beyond their control, but because of their own lack of civic responsibility. The danger that harm will be done to innocent third parties is real, but that threat will be much greater if citizens are allowed to flout collective norms of acceptable conduct.

The Justifications: Strengths and Limitations

Each of the arguments outlined is a powerful justification for conditionality. Each gives a different response to the charge that conditionality blames the victim, and each presents a view of those who would be subject to sanctions and penalties. In effect, contractualism sees the sanctioned as people who are calculating free riders on public goods and services. Welfare conditionality prevents them from making a claim upon the public purse without making a productive contribution in return. Paternalism sees them as people who may be well intentioned but lack capacities and motivation. In this understanding, welfare conditionality requires them to have more regard for their own well being and that of their dependents. Mutualism sees them as people who are irresponsible and have no concern for others. The role of welfare conditionality is to pressure them to honor the commitments and virtues that are essential to the health of civil society.

It is important to emphasize, however, that these are arguments about why some obligations should be enforced, not about how they should be enforced. It is true that contractualism rests on a clear linkage between eligibility for benefits and the fulfillment of particular conditions, while paternalism involves the exercise of authority. In other cases, however, there is not such a ready correspondence between justification and mode of implementation. Sanctions to enforce a welfare contract could include the forms of surveillance and supervision associated with paternalism. Conversely, mutualist objectives might be pursued by requiring tenants in social housing to sign acceptable behavior contracts. The logic of doing so was expressed by a "Sociable Neighbourhoods Co-ordinator" in Scotland.

> Acceptable behaviour contracts are individualized but seek to get people to recognize they are within a community and to think how they behave will have an effect in the community. (cited in Flint 2003, 10)

As this suggests, the three justifications are not mutually exclusive. Indeed, there are significant commonalties between them.[5] At the same time, each has particular limitations.

The most important of the contractualist justification is that the contract is possible only when a claim is made upon the state. This means that it applies only to the disadvantaged. Welfare contractualism, for example, can enforce standards of behavior upon tenants of social housing but not upon those who own their own homes. As a leading British authority on antisocial behavior has commented,

> it seems inconceivable that an owner-occupier whose teenage son is convicted of burglary in the surrounding area should be evicted from his home. Yet, this is what happens to tenants in social housing. (Hunter 2001, 234)

A further limitation of the egalitarian form of contractualism put forward in *The Civic Minimum* is that conditions are legitimate only if they are imposed alongside other measures to reduce inequalities. There are some obligations, however, that are not contingent in this sense. Indeed it could be argued that there are some circumstances in which the enforcement of obligations should come first. To what extent, for example, can programs of neighborhood renewal improve people's lives unless steps are first taken to tackle antisocial behavior?

The paternalist justification faces three limitations. The first is scope. By definition, paternalism can only justify the imposition of conditions that are in the interests of the person subject to them. It has little force in respect of antisocial neighbors or people who fail to ensure that their children attend school. The second is the capacity of public or private agencies to exercise direction and control with the requisite skill and sensitivity. The more this capacity is stretched, the more conditionality is vulnerable to the charge that it will worsen rather than improve the situation.

The third limitation, however, is the most fundamental. Paternalism assumes that the experience of direction and surveillance will in itself bring about long-term changes in the behavior of those subject to it. What, however, if it has the opposite effect? As Mark Kleiman has acknowledged, treating people as children may "exacerbate the deficits in self-command that gave rise to the need for such intervention in the first place" (1997, 191).[6]

The most obvious limitation of the mutualist justification is its high generality. By itself it does not provide a means of determining which obligations should be enforced and which behaviors should be penalized. The areas in which the mutualist justification has been articulated most clearly—such as antisocial behavior—are also those in which the problems are hardest to define and in which success is most difficult to measure.

The three justifications can be seen as complementary. They can be viewed as akin to pieces of a jigsaw, which would provide a complete picture if they were fitted together in the correct way. Such a view would be accurate in respect of the scope of conditionality. The justifications characterize those who would incur penalties or sanctions in different ways, and it is not hard to see how these characterizations could be applied to different behaviors, and to different groups of welfare recipients. It would not be accurate, however, in respect of the critical question of how far the justification for conditionality is contingent on other areas of public policy. Contractualism and paternalism assume that government must do something for the poor to gain its authority over them, whereas mutualism asserts that the collectivity already has authority over its members without any further action.[7] Any attempt to develop a fuller justification for conditionality must begin by considering this issue.

Conditionality, Equality, and Care

The mutualist case for conditionality cannot be made in isolation from broader questions of social and economic justice because the authority mutualism claims cannot be justified without some increase in social equality. Philip Selznick suggests that the responsibilities of the affluent are limited to establishing a "baseline equality of condition" (1998, 64). But that is setting the bar too low. Indeed, unless public policy provides more than the "minimum of nurture and opportunity" that he describes, it will be impossible to realize the conception of the good society that underpins mutualism.

Irrefutable evidence indicates that some children will struggle to flourish if they grow up in families and communities blighted by social exclusion, however responsible their parents may be. Caregivers will struggle if the need to balance work and care makes impossible demands upon their resources, however committed they may be. More broadly, establishing social relations based upon mutual regard is at best more difficult and at worst impossible in the context of gross disparities of income and wealth.

The most compelling statement of why equality matters for community is still one the British Christian Socialist Richard Tawney made. As a Christian, Tawney started from the premise that all are entitled to equality of respect by virtue of their common relationship with the Creator. Such equality of respect, Tawney argued, was "incompatible with the existence of sharp contrasts between economic standards and educational opportunities of different classes." For Tawney, the "fact of human fellowship [should not be] obscured by economic contrasts," and a good society is one that uses its "material resources to promote the dignity and refinement of the individual human beings who compose it" (cited in Reisman 1982, 24, 26). As David Reisman has documented, it was in the work of Tawney and his intellectual heir Richard Titmuss that a concern for a common culture "became translated into a demand for social welfare firmly rooted in shared social values" (1982, 75). Thus, because mutualism starts with a deeper concept of social responsibility, it also sets higher demands on both the recipients of aid, and the society that offers it.

Conditionality and the Ethic of Care Debate

Both Tawney and Titmuss were men of their time. Both failed, as Ann Oakley has observed, to notice the deep fissure in the vision of an equal society created by men's and women's different social experiences. The "discovery of differentiation by gender," she added, "had to await its own historical moment" (Oakley 1991, 188). One of the most significant consequences of this historical moment has been the contribution of feminist philosophers and sociologists to the ethic of care debate.

The literature on the ethic of care extends well beyond the scope of this discussion (see in particular Tronto 1993; Sevenhuijsen 1998, 2002; Williams 2001). It would also be something of an understatement to say that much of the literature is unsympathetic to welfare conditionality. Nonetheless, two features of this debate are highly relevant. First, the ethic of care illustrates the inadequacies of the reciprocal justification of welfare reform, even as it challenges the understanding of dependency that underpins the mutualist arguments considered so far. Second, it offers a compelling vision of the implications for both political theory and social policy of any attempt to respond fully to those dependencies. Both of these themes are articulated most powerfully in a recent Eva Feder Kittay (2001) essay.

Kittay begins by observing that communitarianism seeks to project a stronger base for community in the desire for affiliation and the "need for shared moral values."

> There is, however, another sort of necessity that is still more fundamental and that issues in relationships with the most compelling bonds. This is the need that results from inevitable human dependencies, that is, from our dependency in our young years, in our frail old age, during illness, or from significant impairment. At these times we need care, frequently total care, care so extensive that the people who care for us cannot attend to their own needs. (2001, 527)

These all consuming demands thus induce a kind of dependency in the one who does the caring, the dependency worker. The bonds that form through relations of dependency are "deep and count amongst those we most cherish." Despite this, caring lacks the social standing and financial rewards of what is commonly regarded as work. As a result, the dependency worker is both susceptible to poverty and denied full citizenship. At the same time both public policy and political theory continue to assume that "society is an association of equals, of those who can function independently and who are equally situated with respect to power" (Kittay 2001, 528). This means that the notion of reciprocity that underpins communitarian thinking (and many of the mutualist arguments discussed in this chapter) "is plausible as long as we think of community as consisting of independent persons who are all capable of reciprocating" (531).

Due to the realities of care, however, this conception is not plausible. We therefore require a conceptual framework that moves "beyond interactions between independent and fully functioning persons who are capable of being self-supporting." We need to consider what social cooperation and reciprocation mean for the dependent person and those who care for him or her. The ethic of care demands that we acknowledge that dependency is part of the human condition. All of us have received care, and if we live long enough, all of us will receive it again. As Carole Pateman suggests in chapter 2, a fully informed sense of reciprocity extends across time. It is on this basis that Kittay argues for a "public ethic of care by which we acknowledge the social responsibility to care for the caregiver" (2001, 533).

Such an ethic does not negate the case for conditionality in welfare, but it does increase significantly what must be demanded of public policy if conditionality is to be justified. Kittay's essay leaves no room for doubt that conditionality demands a notion of equality that includes far more acceptance of dependency and far more support and choices for caregivers. Such provision is essential if responsibility for the well being of both dependents and caregivers is to be shared fairly across the community (2001, 547).

Yet Kittay's work, broadly considered, does raise the question of whether the caregiver can be held accountable for the support she or he receives. Should public policy take it as read that all caregivers will be able and willing to fully discharge their responsibilities to those who depend on them? It is beyond dispute that caregivers should not be exploited, but does this mean that the support they receive should be unconditional?

Kittay does not address this issue in her essay.[8] In earlier work, however, she argues strongly that the dependency worker is accountable only to the dependent. This holds even though it is the public that provides the money that enables her or him to care for that dependent person.

> The point is only that when a larger structure is the provider, being such a provider is not the same as being the employer to whom a worker is responsible. Such a duty is not an open ticket to intrude upon the relationship or to regulate the life of the dependency worker. The duty of the public provider

> remains the duty of the state at present: to insure that a child is neither neglected nor abused nor denied provisions of a fundamental sort. (1999, 144)

There are two responses that can be made to this argument. The first is that provisions of a fundamental sort may include enforcing responsibilities to the child such as school attendance. The second and more important is that Kittay's argument here rests on a distinction between the public and the private domain that is at odds with the understanding of interdependency that infuses her essay. She writes that "an individual in need of care is like a stone cast in the water." The larger society may "delegate the responsibility for the care[—but] cannot evade the moral responsibility to assure that care is provided" (2001, 535). It is difficult to see how this moral responsibility can be discharged by providing a cash allowance and leaving be.

The third and perhaps most important response is to ask whether it is reasonable for Kittay to assert that "the care of dependants must be recognised as work" and "given the same status and social standing as any legitimate employment," and yet deny any accountability to the wider community that funds such care (2001, 544). To be sure, it is not a question of requiring dependency workers to do something such as take a job or attend a course. They are already providing the care, often at great cost to their own health and well-being. Nevertheless, it is still possible that there are circumstances in which public authorities might reasonably exert their right to hold caregivers accountable for the performance of their civic labor.

What Obligations Should Be Enforced Through Welfare?

Those whom Kittay calls dependency workers command public support on the grounds that they are contributing to the attainment of specific public ends. That support, however, brings with it an obligation to commit to those ends. In the great majority of cases that commitment will be self-evident. The immediate question here, however, is just how much can society demand of dependency workers in the light of our financial support?

Conditionality and the Limits of Redistribution

A similar question arises in the context of New Labour's pledge to end child poverty by 2019. In a stimulating essay David Piachaud, a center-left British commentator, argues that child poverty must be eliminated if the lives of poor children are to be improved, but that doing this will not be sufficient. What matters is not "low family incomes in themselves, but their consequences—for nutrition, stress, lack of stimulating childhood experiences, exclusion from normal social activities" (2001, 449). Higher incomes will not necessarily lead to an enhanced quality of life for children. The impact on nutrition, for example, may be minimal if "families are bombarded with disinformation promoting processed junk foods, crisps and soft drinks" or if "many parents know next to nothing about nutrition having learned nothing from their parents or from their schools" (450). Piachaud wants to limit the commercial pressures on children. This in turn would require a greater degree of corporate responsibility on the part of the food industry and the media regarding the content and advertising of food targeted at children.

The most important point, however, is that higher incomes would not necessarily ensure the "socialisation of children into humane, respectful, and tolerant human beings." This means, Piachaud argued, that,

> the boundary between the private and the public must be reassessed. . . . The influence of family and environment—physical, social and cultural—on opportunities is so important that if opportunities are to become more equal, then family and environment must become of more public concern. (452; see also Mayer 1997)

Taken at face value, this suggestion is scarcely contentious. There is now, for example, a remarkable measure of agreement that the decisions that people take regarding their parenting and partnering practices can no longer be regarded as a purely private matter. As Wade Horn and Isabel Sawhill put it, they not only have social consequences but "social determinants as well, including messages embedded in public policy and in the popular media" (2001, 429). That is, what people accept as their responsibilities in public life will depend in part on what they are told by public authorities and the wider society.

On the other side of the Atlantic, Britain's leading center-left think tank has recently claimed that public policy "must be more readily prepared to cross the threshold into the private world of the family, although this is a step that must be taken with great care." The Institute for Public Policy Research (IPPR) argues that hitherto policy "has paid too little attention to the impact that the social and familial context has on a child's development. A strategy that focuses solely on money as the means to reduce inequality will fail" (Harker and Kendall 2003, 3, 48).

The two areas highlighted by both Piachaud and IPPR—the family and the immediate context in which children are raised—are also those into which New Labour has proposed to extend the scope of welfare conditionality. Prime Minister Blair has insisted that his government would "not hesitate to encourage and even enforce . . . [the obligation] to bring up children as competent, responsible citizens, and to support those—such as teachers—who are employed by the state in the task" (Blair 1998, 12).

There is no doubt that such a use of welfare conditionality is fraught with difficulties. A recent study of *Government and Parenting* in Britain, for example, concluded that there is a "fundamental and inevitable tension" between New Labour's interest in conditionality and the need for any government to "preserve parents' autonomy to a sufficient degree to enable them to willingly shoulder the caring responsibilities that are expected of them" (Henricson 2003, 39). Moreover, conditionality required the government to stipulate "standards of behaviour by and within families . . . as preconditions of receiving benefits," even though defining "responsibilities, or even expectations, in this area is a minefield" (41).

Functional Traditionalism

One way of traversing this minefield has been suggested by William Galston. It is now over ten years since his influential book *Liberal Purposes* set out the case for what he termed functional traditionalism (1991, 288). In essence, his argument was that public policy should promote more traditional family forms if there was clear evidence that those forms produced better outcomes for children and for the wider community. Galston hoped that functional traditionalism's insistence that arguments be grounded in evidence would "create the largest possible space for public discussion among men and women of good will," and would stake out a common ground between the "partisans" of individualism and the "proponents" of duty (288). This hope has not been realized in respect of his own proposal that public policy should privilege the intact two-parent family. Neither the American public nor its politicians are persuaded that the merits of two-parent families are sufficient to warrant penalizing single parents.

But Galston's proposal leaves open the possibility of an empirically grounded debate about the use of welfare to enforce commitments that arise irrespective of family form. Indeed this point was made by one of the strongest critics of Galston's proposal, Iris Marion Young. She argued that "the state can properly intervene in or punish particular actions or inactions within families," but that this is quite different from punishing or favoring families based on their composition alone (1995, 553).

Morality as Social Practice

Such an approach would still be open to the charge that it is too top down. It may reflect the assessments of policy makers, analysts, and administrators, yet not demonstrate an understanding of how the issues are perceived by those on welfare. One response to these criticisms is to draw on sociological studies of the moral practices through which people determine their commitments and obligations to family and friends.

It was in the 1980s that Janet Finch began her study of kin relations with the question: what is the nature of duty, responsibility and obligation? Are they feelings and emotions, or intellectual ideas? Perhaps, she suggested, they might be moral evaluations, "based on a person's assessment of right and wrong" (1989, 7). Her answer was that they should be understood as commitments that emerged out of negotiations between kin. People did not decide what was and what was not the proper thing to do on the basis of fixed rules. The normative guidelines and principles to which they did refer were "more concerned with how to work out what to do, than with specifying precisely what you should do in particular circumstances" (241).

> In reality, the "sense of obligation" which marks the distinctive character of kin relationships is nothing like its image in political debate, where it appears as a set of ready-made moral rules which all right-thinking people accept and put into practice. It is actually much less reliable than that. It is nurtured and grows over time between some individuals more strongly than between others, and its practical consequences are highly variable. It does have a binding quality, but that derives from commitments built up over time between real people, not from an abstract set of moral values. (Finch 1989, 242)

There is no suggestion here that these commitments constitute some kind of trump card. Nor that it is sensible to derive principles about people's rights and responsibilities directly from the moral practices they have themselves developed. That would be to confuse is with ought and would be self-defeating insofar as the purpose of conditionality is to cause some people to change their behavior. Conversely it would be illiberal in the extreme to impose a particular set of commitments upon everybody simply because they appear to be accepted by a majority.

Instead the purpose would be to inform the policy debate with an understanding of how people reach decisions about their partnering, or how they try to balance their commitments to work and to care. As Fiona Williams has noted,

> what is important about this approach is that it moves the moral subject out of the world of moral philosophy in which "he" has a given, or pre-social, moral identity into a sociological world in which (s)he forms and reforms her/his moral identity, and engages in moral activity as a social practice. (2000, 6)

It is, of course, this sociological world in which conditionality has to be implemented and in which it will either succeed or fail.

Conditionality and Parenting

To date New Labour ministers have made the case for conditionality in respect of parenting on contractualist grounds. In the spring of 2002, for example, Blair suggested that child benefits be withheld from parents who failed to ensure that their child attended school. He told BBC News that his government was "examining the issue of when people are paid substantial amounts of benefits by the state and their children are persistently truanting." Is it really fair, he asked, "that they owe no sense of responsibility in return?" ("Blair defiant over child benefit plan," April 29, 2002). In part this was a response to an apparent upsurge in street crime. Official figures indicated that children between the ages of ten and sixteen were responsible for 40 percent of such crime, as well as 33 percent of car thefts, 25 percent of burglaries, and 20 percent of criminal damage. Moreover, much of this crime was allegedly committed during school hours, whilst other evidence suggested that many parents colluded in their children's truancy. This led then Education Secretary Estelle Morris to talk of a "hard-core of feckless parents who have a corrosive effect on the rest," and who caused a "cycle of disrespect starting in school and lasting throughout these children's" lives ("Parents face benefits axe over unruly children," *Observer*, 24 March 2002; "Q&A Parenting Orders," *BBC News*, 27 March 2002).

In this respect, a powerful case can be made that welfare conditionality is necessary if the government is to achieve its objective of reducing inequalities of opportunity. All but New Labour's most trenchant critics acknowledge that it has made a genuine attempt to fulfill its pledge to reduce child poverty by a quarter between 1999 and 2004, itself part of a unique commitment to end it completely by 2019 (Sutherland, Sefton, and Piachaud 2003). It is also widely acknowledged that this is part of New Labour's effort to tackle the "cycle of disadvantage." Longitudinal studies have demonstrated that educational attainment is at the heart of this cycle.

> Childhood disadvantage frequently leads to low educational attainment, low educational attainment leads to low pay and low employment, which in turn leads to low income and denial of opportunity for the next generation. (HM Treasury 1999, 27)

In this context, the responsibility of parents is to do all that they can to see that their children attend and benefit from school. This obligation follows not from some benefit they claim from government but rather from the duty they have to their children and to the larger society.

The responsibilities of parents extend far beyond ensuring that their children turn up at school. It is equally true that the ways in which these responsibilities are exercised are a critical factor in the development of children. All the evidence suggests that parenting matters, and this cannot be ignored by any policy that seeks to improve the life chance of disadvantaged children. This does not mean that these broader responsibilities can and should be enforced through welfare. But as Stuart White argues in chapter 4, neither can we regard parenting as a "no-go area for state intervention." It is possible to justify the imposition of benefit sanctions on parents who collude in the truancy or antisocial behavior of their children.

Whether to do this through benefit sanctions, authoritative programs, or simply legal sanctions is a matter for detailed determination on an issue by issue basis. But what is of critical importance is the signals that such measures send to all parents. As the *Observer* commented in its May 5, 2002, leader column in support of Blair's original proposal, public policy must provide "some overt statement of the obligation that all parents have to ensure that their children are properly educated."

Conditionality and Antisocial Behavior

New Labour has recently been described by one commentator as having an "apparent obsession with anti-social behaviour" (Hunter 2001, 221). Like the concern with truanting, this is in part a response to popular fears and anxieties. An alleged upsurge in harassment, vandalism, graffiti and noise has generated real public anger and the specter of the "neighbor from hell" is now readily invoked in British political debates (Field 2003). Despite this, New Labour's approach has been attacked as being essentially disciplinary in nature, and as an attempt to regulate and punish the behavior of marginalized groups that fail to conform to socially constructed norms (Haworth and Manzi 1999; Card 2001).

There can be no doubt that antisocial behavior represents the clearest possible breach of the obligation to respect one's fellow citizens. Nor is it a matter of serious dispute that many of those who experience this disrespect are themselves disadvantaged. As Malcolm Harrison has written, those who identify control measures as authoritarian landlordism fail to acknowledge that "tenants themselves are disempowered by violent, racist or criminal neighbours" (2001, 103; Li, Pickles, and Savage 2004). Moreover, the effects go beyond the immediate neighbors to the larger community. Recent research on social capital has shown that people living in deprived areas especially need good neighborly relations; they depend on the security and well-being that comes from being able to call upon one's neighbors in times of need. This is precisely what is destroyed by the antisocial behavior of a relatively small number of households (Li, Savage, and Pickles 2003).

The key policy issue is whether to withhold housing benefits from those guilty of perpetrating antisocial behavior. Of course, to do so might be to make the perpetrators homeless. This outcome, while surely regrettable, could be defended on contractualist grounds. In his speech in 1995, for example, Tony Blair claimed that if tenants do not fulfill their side of the bargain, particularly after repeated warnings, the contract is broken (9). It could also be argued that enforcing such sanctions is essential if the measures were to be effective. The recent white paper, for example, insisted that "it was vital that perpetrators understand that keeping their home is dependent upon their behaviour not ruining whole communities" (Home Office 2003, 59). Such a policy would also be in line with the approach adopted by some housing associations.[9]

The obvious difficulty is of course, that it would have the most severe impact on children and other dependents. Moreover, it is unlikely that the experience of being homeless would itself change behavior. As the director of Shelter, the leading British charity for the homeless, put it,

> Shelter's primary argument is that making people homeless does not solve antisocial behavior and works directly against strategies to tackle poverty and homelessness. . . . And where there are children, making them homeless causes damage across all aspects of their lives. (Sampson 2003, 6)

Early in 2004, as reported in *The Guardian,* the government announced that it was shelving plans to withhold housing benefits ("U-turn on benefit cut for neighbours from hell," January 28). Attention has since been focused upon other, still more authoritative responses. A number of projects, for example, are being developed by local authorities and housing associations that subject their tenants to the kinds of surveillance and direction associated with new paternalism. One such scheme in Manchester offers those responsible for antisocial behavior a choice between court proceedings for eviction and admission to a family support unit. The latter involves living in a designated block of apartments that is staffed twenty-four hours a day. The duties of the staff, *The Guardian* reported nearly a month later, include making sure that everyone gets up in the morning, that the children have breakfast and go to school on time, that they do their homework in the evening and do not wander the streets at night" ("Peace Process," February 18, 2004).

Such schemes seem to work. An evaluation of the longest established project in Dundee found that there were significant improvements in the behavior of the majority of tenants.[10] After antisocial charges have been proven, then, there is a strong case for making continued receipt of housing benefits conditional upon a willingness to live in such a project.

Conclusion: An Ethic of Mutual Responsibility

Private behaviors have public consequences, and personal qualities are also civic virtues. As the Working Seminar on Family and Welfare noted nearly twenty years ago, the rules that determine entitlement to welfare serve,

> both as signals of the basic values of a free society and as guides to self-development. . . . The underlying principle is that the welfare system must

> be infused with a sense of obligation in order to build a sense of reciprocal bonds. (Novak et al. 1987, 114)

The justification for conditionality outlined here is grounded in this understanding of reciprocity and mutual obligation, but also recognizes the myriad ways in which personal and collective responsibilities are interlinked. On the one hand, it asserts the central importance of economic redistribution and of supporting those who accept responsibility to care for others. On the other, it also asserts that public policy cannot assume that providing support will be sufficient on its own.

There are circumstances in which the case for conditionality can be expressed most readily and most persuasively in contractualist terms. The argument that someone is obligated to make the most of opportunities created for them by others is one that accords with basic sentiments of fairness and reciprocity. In other circumstances the paternalistic rationale is equally persuasive. Why should not someone who has been robbed of confidence and motivation by prolonged unemployment be required to take steps that offer a good prospect of restoring both? Ultimately, however, these are different applications of a broader and deeper argument about the need for people to accept responsibility for themselves, and for others—as parents, neighbors and taxpayers. In the words of the British Christian Socialist—and former government minister—Frank Field,

> right political activity is about supporting at every opportunity the age-old verities of civic responsibility at the expense of the darker side of human nature, i.e. to provide an environment where those values crucial to a civil society can flourish. (1997, 20)

This means that welfare has to play a dual role. It has to be a mechanism through which support is provided and resources redistributed, but it also has to delineate, reaffirm and at times enforce the obligations that people have to their families, to their neighbors, and to the wider communities in which they live. A good society requires both a more equitable distribution of material resources, and a greater affirmation of mutual care than currently exists in either Britain or the United States. A welfare system grounded in an ethic of mutual responsibility is essential to the achievement of both of these objectives.

This chapter has benefited from the helpful comments and suggestions of all the participants in the conference Welfare Reform and Political Theory at Wingspread, Wisconsin, on October 16 and 17, 2003. I am particularly grateful, however, to Christopher Beem, Larry Mead, and Stuart White. I am also grateful to Pat Deacon and Marie Leake, who read an earlier draft and made helpful suggestions regarding grammar and presentation. The chapter draws on work undertaken as part of the ESRC Research Group on Care, Values and the Future of Welfare (Grant M5664281001).

Notes

1. It may be argued that a further justification for conditionality is that it serves to reassure the voters that money is not being spent on those whose lifestyles they may disapprove. Such an argument is not made in this chapter.
2. The classic condemnation of the ignorant smug moralisms of those who pontificate about the behavior of the poor is still that of Michael Harrington (1997, 14).
3. The late Daniel Moynihan, for example, argued in 1996 that welfare reform in the U.S. had come to rest upon the assumption that the "behavior of certain adults can be changed by making the lives of their children as wretched as possible" (cited in Bryner 1998, 198).
4. The Working Seminar consisted of academics and practitioners with a wide range of perspectives. Several members expected that the numbers moving from dependency to work would be modest at first (Novak et al. 1987, 113).
5. It could be argued that both the paternalist and contractualist justifications are rooted in mutualist sentiments. Mead, for example, writes that "a tutelary role for government is more accepted" in Wisconsin because of its dutiful culture in which people define themselves in terms of the commitments they have made to others (2004, 257). Similarly, White draws upon Becker's discussion of reciprocity as an encompassing personal virtue and an action-guiding disposition that ought to manifest itself in all areas and types of social interaction (2003, 65).
6. It may be objected that any authoritative measure shares this limitation.
7. It is possible that a welfare contractualist such as White would agree that some obligations should be enforced whatever the level of social injustice. A paternalist, however, could not agree that any form of conditionality should be contingent upon economic redistribution.
8. She does discuss the obligations of the dependent to those who pay the caregiver, which are "generally discharged through paying taxes when we have an income" (Kittay, 1999, 537).
9. A good example of welfare contractualism in this area is the Gold Service Scheme pioneered by Irwell Valley Housing Association in Manchester. This provides a range of benefits, such as quick repairs and discounts in local shops, which are withdrawn from tenants who begin to behave in an anti-social manner (Flint 2003, 13).
10. Interestingly, it also found that some parents had "difficulties in adjusting after the projects very structured support had ended" (Dillane, Hill, Bannister, and Scott 2001).

References

BBC News. "Q & A: Parenting Orders." March 27, 2002. Available at: http://news.bbc.co.uk/1/hi/education/1892556.stm (accessed July 18, 2005).

BBC News. "Blair Defiant over Child Benefit Plan." April 29, 2002. Available at: http://news.bbc.co.uk/1/hi/uk_politics/1957279.stm (accessed July 18, 2005).

Blair, Tony. 1995. "The Rights We Enjoy Reflect the Duties We Owe." Spectator Lecture. March 22, 1995.

———. 1996. Speech to Commonwealth Press Union conference, Cape Town. October 14, 1996.

———. 1998. *The Third Way: New Politics for the New Century.* London: Fabian Society.

Brown, Gordon. 2000. Speech to Annual Conference of the National Council for Voluntary Organisations. February 9, 2000. Available at: http://www.hm-treasury.gov.uk/newsroom_and_speeches/speeches/chancellorexchequer/speech_chex_90200.cfm (accessed July 18, 2005).

Bryner, Gary. 1998. *Politics and Public Morality.* London: W. W. Norton.

Card, P. 2001. "Managing antisocial behavior—inclusion or exclusion?" In *Two Steps Forward: Housing Policy into the New Millennium,* edited by D. Cowan and A. Marsh. Bristol, U.K.: Policy Press.

Deacon, Alan. 2002. *Perspectives on Welfare: Ideas, Ideologies and Policy Debates.* Buckingham, U.K.: Open University Press.

———, ed. 2001. *From Welfare to Work: Lessons from America.* London: Institute for Economic Affairs.

Department of Social Security. 1998. *A New Contract for Welfare.* Cm 3805. London: HMSO.

Dillane, Jennifer, Malcolm Hill, Jon Bannister, and Suzie Scott. 2001. *Evaluation of the Dundee Families Project.* Final Report. Glasgow: Centre for the Child & Society and Department of Urban Studies University of Glasgow. Available at: http://www.scotland.gov.uk/library3/housing/edfp-00.asp (accessed July 18, 2005).

Ellwood, David T. 1988. *Poor Support: Poverty in the American Family.* New York: Basic Books.

———. 1996. "Welfare Reform As I Knew It: When Bad Things Happen to Good Policies." *The American Prospect* 26(May–June): 22–29.

Etzioni, Amitai. 1998. "The Responsive Communitarian Platform: Rights and Responsibilities." In *The Essential Communitarian Reader,* edited by Amitai Etzioni. Lanham, Md.: Rowman and Littlefield.

Field, Frank. 1997. *Reforming Welfare.* London: Social Market Foundation.

———. 2003. *Neighbours from Hell: The Politics of Behaviour.* London: Politico's Publishing.

Finch, Janet. 1989. *Family Obligations and Social Change.* Cambridge: Polity Press.

Flint, John. 2003. "New Methods of Reconfiguring Agency and Responsibility in the Governance of Social Housing." Paper to Autumn Conference of the Housing Studies Association, Bristol, U.K. (September 2003).

Galston, William A. 1991. *Liberal Purposes.* Cambridge: Cambridge University Press.

Giddens, Anthony. 1998. *The Third Way: The Renewal of Social Democracy.* Cambridge: Polity Press.

Guardian. "Blair Offers Jobless a New Bargain." June 3, 1997.

———. "U-turn on Benefit Cut for Neighbours from Hell." January 28, 2004.

———. "Peace Process." February 18, 2004.

Harker, Lisa, and Liz Kendall. 2003. *An Equal Start?* London: Institute for Public Policy Research.

Harrington, Michael. 1997. *The Other America,* rev. ed. New York: Touchstone Books, New York.

Harrison, Malcolm. 2001. *Housing, Social Policy and Difference.* Bristol, U.K.: Policy Press, Bristol.

Haworth, Anna, and Tony Manzi. 1999. "Managing the Underclass: Interpreting the Moral Discourse of Housing Management." *Urban Studies* 36(1): 153–65.

Henricson, Clem. 2003. *Government and Parenting.* York, U.K.: Joseph Rowntree Foundation.

HM Treasury. 1999. *Tackling Poverty and Extending Opportunity.* London: HMSO.

———. 2001. *Tackling Child Poverty: A Pre-Budget Report Document.* London: HMSO.

Home Office. 2003. *Respect and Responsibility: Taking a Stand Against Anti-social Behaviour.* London: HMSO.

Horn, Wade F., and Isabel Sawhill V. 2001. "Fathers, Marriage and Welfare Reform." In *The New World of Welfare,* edited by Rebecca Blank and Ron Haskins. Washington, D.C.: Brookings Institution.

Hunter, Caroline. 2001. "Antisocial Behavior and Housing—Can Law Be the Answer?" In *Two Steps Forward: Housing Policy into the New Millennium,* edited by David Cowan and Alex Marsh. Bristol, U.K.: Policy Press.

King, Desmond. 1999. *In The Name of Liberalism.* Oxford: Oxford University Press.

Kittay, E. Feder. 1999. *Love's Labor: Essays on Women, Equality and Dependency.* New York: Routledge.

———. 2001. "A Feminist Public Ethic of Care Meets the New Communitarian Family Policy." *Ethics* 111(April): 523–47.

Kleiman, Mark. 1997. "Coerced Abstinence: A Neopaternalist Drugs Policy Initiative." In *The New Paternalism,* edited by Lawrence M. Mead. Washington, D.C.: Brookings Institution.

Klein, Rudolf, and Anne Marie Rafferty. 1999. "Rorshach Politics." *American Prospect* 10(45, June/July): 35.

Li, Yaojun, Andrew Pickles, and Mike Savage. 2004. "Social Capital Dimensions, Social Trust and the Quality of Life in Britain in the Late 1990s." Unpublished paper. Department of Sociology, University of Birmingham, 2004.

Li, Yaojun, Mike Savage, and Andrew Pickles. 2003. "Social Capital and Social Exclusion in England and Wales (1972–1999)." *British Journal of Sociology* 54(4): 497–526.

Mayer, Susan E. 1997. *What Money Can't Buy: Family Income and Children's Life Chances.* Cambridge, Mass.: Harvard University Press.

Mead, Lawrence M. 1986. *Beyond Entitlement: The Social Obligations of Citizenship.* New York: The Free Press.

———. 1992. *The New Politics of Poverty: The Nonworking Poor in America.* New York: Basic Books.

———, ed. 1997. *The New Paternalism: Supervisory Approaches to Poverty.* Washington, D.C.: Brookings Institution.

———. 2002. "From Welfare to Work." In *From Welfare to Work: Lessons from America,* edited by Alan Deacon. London: Institute for Economic Affairs.

———. 2004. *Government Matters: Welfare Reform in Wisconsin.* Princeton, N.J.: Princeton University Press.

Naughtie, James. 2001. *The Rivals.* London: Fourth Estate.

Novak, Michael, John Cogan, Glanche Bernstein, Douglas J. Besharov, Barbara Blum, Allan Carlson, and Michael Horowitz. 1987. *The New Consensus on Family and Welfare.* Washington D.C., and Milwaukee, Wisc.: American Enterprise Institute and Marquette University Press.

Oakley, Ann. 1991. "Eugenics, Social Medicine and the Career of Richard Titmuss." *British Journal of Sociology* 42(2): 165–94.

Piachaud, David. 2001. "Child Poverty, Opportunities and Quality of Life." *Political Quarterly* 72(4): 446–53.

Reisman, David. 1982. *State and Welfare.* London: Palgrave Macmillan.

Sampson, Adam. 2003. "The Antisocial Behavior Bill: Will It Deliver for Communities?" *Poverty* 115(summer): 6–8.

Selznick, Philip. 1998. "Social Justice: a Communitarian Perspective." In *The Essential Communitarian Reader,* edited by Amitai Etzioni. Lanham, Md.: Rowman and Littlefield.

Sevenhuijsen, Selma. 1998. *Citizenship and the Ethics of Care.* London: Routledge.

———. 2002. "A Third Way? Moralities, Ethics and Families." In *Analysing Families,* edited by Alan Carling, Simon Duncan, and Rosalind Edwards. London: Routledge.

Sutherland, Holly, Tom Sefton, and David Piachaud. 2003. *Poverty in Britain: The Impact of Government Policy Since 1997.* York, U.K.: Joseph Rowntree Foundation.

Tronto, Joan. 1993. *Moral Boundaries. A Political Argument for an Ethic of Care.* New York: Routledge.

White, Stuart. 2000. "Social Rights and the Social Contract: Political Theory and the New Welfare Politics." *Journal of Political Science* 30: 507–32.

———. 2003. *The Civic Minimum: An Essay on the Rights and Obligations of Economic Citizenship.* Oxford: Oxford University Press.

Williams, Fiona. 2000. "A Conceptual Chart for CAVA." Workshop Paper 16. ESRC Group on Care, Values and the Future of Welfare. Leeds, U.K.: University of Leeds.

———. 2001. "In and Beyond New Labour: Towards a New Political Ethics of Care." *Critical Social Policy* 21(4): 467–93.

Young, Iris Marion. 1995. "Mothers, Citizenship and Independence: A Critique of Pure Family Values." *Ethics* 105(April): 553–79.

Chapter 7

Restoring the Civic Value of Care in a Post–Welfare Reform Society

CHRISTOPHER BEEM

IN LIBERAL political theory, citizenship, politics, even society itself begins with labor. For John Locke, mixing one's labor with nature creates property and the need to preserve that property is the reason why humans leave the state of nature and create political society.[1] To labor is thus to create a status and a claim within liberal society. Labor is the point of entry into citizenship and its accompanying political rights.

But this political conception has always had to deal with a host of complicating realities. First, the claim of human equality confronts differences, both natural and cultural, that surround gender. Second, individuals do not enter this existence with the ability to labor or to exercise political rights; children require care, and it is only after many years that they can be expected to contribute to society as full citizens. Finally, the care that children require in order for them to reach adulthood is a form of labor that does not result in property. It is therefore at best unclear how care fits within the Lockean-liberal conception.

Here I explore how these issues manifest themselves in the history of welfare and, more recently, welfare reform. I argue that welfare was driven originally by a conception of republican motherhood that lauded care by single mothers—widowed and otherwise—as a form of civic labor equivalent to economic labor. Yet almost from its inception, this concept of care ran up against a competing conception of feminism that sought full citizenship for women through the economic sphere. This second notion led to a cultural shift in which mothers increasingly began to seek compensated employment. As a result, our society developed a new conception of gender equality that made Aid to Families with Dependent Children (AFDC) appear ever more anachronistic, and the welfare mothers who were supported by these funds ever more estranged from the body politic. Temporary Assistance to Needy Families (TANF), and its accompanying demand for work as a condition for receiving assistance, is the result.

But society's need for care work has not gone away. While welfare reform has helped to move our society beyond the exclusion of women from full citizenship, it has simultaneously denigrated the notion of care as civic work. My question is whether it is possible for American society to restore the civic status it once afforded to parental care and especially motherhood. I conclude by examining and endorsing the concept of At-Home Infant Care, a pilot project developed in Minnesota and Montana, which not only acknowledges the essential connection between labor and citizenship, but also strains to acknowledge and sanction parenthood as worthy civic work.

Republican Motherhood

As Carole Pateman has noted, "the fact that only women have the capacity to become pregnant, give birth and suckle their infants is a mark of difference par excellence. Childbirth and motherhood have symbolized the natural capacities that set women apart from politics and citizenship" (1992, 18). For most of American history, the problem of balancing labor and care was solved by giving men and women different and indeed separate responsibilities. Men were to labor in the public marketplace, and women to raise children and, more generally, tend the private sphere of family life.[2] Although their absence from the world of compensated labor meant that they were separated from economic self-reliance, and from the world of politics and full citizenship, mothers were touted as performing an essential civic task. Indeed, their work in caring and raising the next generation of Americans was often lauded as more important than compensated labor. Combining elements of liberal and republican ideals, this consensus developed into a distinctively American understanding of republican motherhood.[3]

During the founding, Dr. Benjamin Rush argued that "a principal share of the instruction of children naturally devolves upon the women. It becomes us therefore to prepare them by a suitable education, for the discharge of this most important duty of mothers" (1787/1973, 259). Similarly, James Wilson argued that women were to serve as republican mothers, fostering the democratic values and dispositions that were necessary to sustain the fledgling nation" (see Zagarri 1992). In *Democracy in America,* Alexis de Tocqueville both noted and celebrated this division of labor. De Tocqueville was convinced that women were seen as equals in American society—the fact that they were educated along with boys demonstrated as much. Nevertheless, de Tocqueville also saw that this equality did not mean women were free to enter the economic realm. Their responsibilities were equal, but separate. Women's job was to nurture and mold the values and attitudes that were needed to sustain a democratic society (1835/2000, 573–76).

The aftermath of the Civil War (in which many women were widowed and left without financial support), along with the rise of urbanization and industrialization, placed severe strains on poor Americans, and especially widowed mothers. The social programs developed in the late nineteenth and early twentieth centuries were meant to enable widows to provide for their children and thereby better ensure that their children would grow up to be responsible and productive members of society.[4] By the early 1920s, Theda Skocpol notes that "forty-four states passed laws to protect women workers and also 'mothers' pensions' to enable poor widows to care for their children at home" (1997, 110; 1995).

Through these policy changes, American political leaders thus affirmed the popular belief that the more important job for mothers was to stay home and raise children. These programs were usually justified by an appeal—often made by women themselves—to the civic sacrifice that women made, and the civic work they performed. Skocpol goes on to say "programs for mothers were justified as supports for the services of women who risked life to bear children and devoted themselves to raising good citizens for the future" (1997, 112).[5]

Introduction of the federal welfare program was grounded on the same appeals. Established in 1935, Aid for Dependent Children provided support to widows so that they would not need to work outside the home and thereby compromise their civic status as the primary caregiver. Steven Teles quotes a Senate report:

> Through cash grants adjusted to the needs of the family it is possible to keep the young children with their mother in their own home, thus preventing the necessity of placing the children in institutions. This is recognized by everyone to be the least expensive and altogether the most desirable method for meeting the needs of these families. (1996, 34)

Obviously, child care for a working mother was not considered a viable alternative. Rather, for financial and moral reasons, lawmakers concluded that the mother must stay home to avoid the only other option: placing the child in an institution.

To be sure, the language of the act did not focus on widows alone. Title IV defined dependent child as any child under the age of sixteen who "has been deprived of parental support or care by reason of the death, continued absence from the home, or physical or mental incapacity of a parent" (U.S. Congress 1935). Yet in the beginning, only widows were deemed worthy of assistance; any other reason for single motherhood was, at best, ignored. Linda Gordon rightly points out that in the context of the law, widow simply functioned as a generic term for single mothers and a necessary accommodation to the contemporary political realities (1994, 20). But by singling out widows as the stated beneficiaries, the act also set up an implicit distinction between more and less deserving mothers.

This distinction became particularly relevant only four years later, for in 1939, survivors benefits for widows were added to the larger, more mainstream Social Security program and the ADC program was left almost exclusively for "less deserving" single mothers. Thus, although the program and the objective of keeping mothers in the home remained unchanged for several decades, over the years single motherhood came to focus more on divorced, deserted or never-married mothers rather than widows.[6] Indeed, one might say that during the 1950s and 1960s, the application of the law came to more closely resemble its universal mandate: to help all single mothers, regardless of circumstance, stay home (out of the paid work force), and concentrate on their duties within the private sphere.

Pateman's (Wollstonecraft's) Dilemma

The link between compensated labor and citizenship in liberal society, and yet the accompanying exclusion of women from the labor market, set the terms for the relationship between work and care in American society. Not surprisingly, it likewise set the terms for the feminist response. As Carole Pateman has argued, these two possible responses constitute what she calls the Wollstonecraft dilemma:

> On the one hand, they [women] have demanded that the ideal of citizenship be extended to them, and the liberal-feminist agenda for a "gender-neutral" social world is the logical conclusion of one form of this demand. On the other hand, women have also insisted, often simultaneously, as did Mary Wollstonecraft, that *as women* they have specific capacities, talents, needs and concerns, so that the expression of their citizenship will be differentiated from that of men. The dilemma is that the two routes toward citizenship that women have pursued are mutually incompatible within the confines of the patriarchal welfare state, and, within that context, they are impossible to achieve. Their unpaid work providing welfare could be seen, as Wollstonecraft saw women's tasks as mothers, as women's work *as citizens,* just as their husbands' paid work is central to men's citizenship. (1998, 196–97, italics in original)[7]

Early supporters of ADC embraced the second or care option that Pateman outlines. Doing the work of care was understood to be the way that women as women could best meet their responsibilities and solidify their status as citizens. Thus, feminists believed that by supporting that effort through government they were reinforcing that status for all women caregivers. But, as Pateman (1998) also noted, things did not quite work out that way.

> An official nod of recognition to women's work as "vital" to "the nation" is easily given; *in practice,* the value of the work in bringing women into full membership in the welfare state was negligible. The equal worth of citizenship and the respect of fellow citizens still depended on participation as paid employees. "Citizenship" and "work" stood then and still stand opposed to "women." (196, italics in original)

Despite rather dramatic advances (including the development of ADC but also the establishment of universal suffrage), feminists maintained that these changes had not altered their second-class status. The tactic of pursuing feminist goals through maternal feminism was at best inadequate, if not ultimately counterproductive. As a result, women increasingly began to choose the other, work horn of the dilemma, challenging the notion of republican motherhood and demanding equal freedom to enter the labor market. Beginning in the 1960s, millions of women and mothers began to do just that.[8]

The problem for welfare policy was that these changes mostly affected the population off welfare. They were not manifested and indeed were often contradicted by AFDC recipients. Blank and Blum note that "between 1960 and 1970 [just as mothers were starting to enter the workforce in droves] the AFDC caseload almost doubled" (1997, 30). In Kent Weaver's words, "more than 90 percent of AFDC mothers in the early 1990s were not in the paid labor force [and] a growing majority of non-AFDC mothers were working" (2000, 20). Feminists were inclined to defend AFDC recipients, yet by embracing the path of economic freedom and entering the labor market, they implicitly rejected the notion of republican motherhood. This cut the conceptual legs out from under the program, ensuring its ultimate demise.

As Stuart White has written, the increased participation of women in the workforce made a gendered notion of civic labor look "increasingly anachronistic." In some countries, and particularly the United States, he notes, "civic labour is more or less identified with paid employment to the exclusion of unpaid care work." Hence, White concludes, "it becomes harder to explain why those only performing care work should be in receipt of public support" (2003, 109). Viewing these changes in hindsight, the eventual collapse of AFDC seems inevitable.

As these cultural changes took effect, public support for the old welfare slowly evaporated. Beginning in the 1960s, "Congress moved away from the principle of providing support to enable mothers to stay at home, toward the theory that adults who received welfare benefits should make good-faith efforts to become economically self–sufficient" (Blank and Blum 1997, 31). For example, in 1967 and 1971, the federal government decided that welfare mothers could remain at home "only until their children entered elementary school." (Weaver 2000, 31). During debates on the Nixon Family Assistance Plan in 1972, Senator Wallace Bennett asked, "can this Nation treat mothers of school-age children on welfare as though they were unemployable and pay them to remain at home when more than half of mothers with school-age children in the general population are already working?" (quoted in Mead 1986, 223). In 1977, the Carter administration proposal Program for Better Jobs and Income called for mothers with children ages seven to thirteen to work part-time during school hours so that they might remain in the upper tier of income support (Weaver 2000, 62). Both programs stopped short of demanding work of all mothers, and PBJI did not become law. But both show the general movement toward enforcing greater consistency between welfare mothers and other mothers. As women began to opt for inclusion in the liberal social contract by entering the labor market, welfare recipients were increasingly seen as social parasites.

The Family Support Act of 1988 took a further step in acknowledging changing social mores, exempting the mother from participation in work programs only if her youngest child was under the age of three. The contradictions within AFDC were again reflected in the congressional debate surrounding this bill. Senator Moynihan's 1987 statement echoes Senator Bennett's: "a program that was designed to pay mothers to stay at home with their children cannot succeed when we now observe most mothers going out to work" (Weaver 2000, 70). In its final version, the Family Support Act strained to move from a welfare program that rewarded nonwork to one that encouraged and facilitated work. FSA "made relatively generous provisions for education, job training, and medical and child care services for welfare recipients making the transition to work" (Heclo 2001, 20). Yet though the law expanded welfare work activities, these changes were not funded or implemented at the level intended. Work levels on welfare rose somewhat, but most welfare mothers remained nonworking. The shift to a work-based social welfare system was still incomplete and the stage was set for a more fundamental shift in welfare policy.

TANF and Motherhood

Between 1960 and 1990, policymakers whittled away at the American conception of republican motherhood. With the advent of TANF in 1996, they abandoned the notion entirely. Instead, they at once argued and acknowledged that in American society, the burdens of care were no longer sufficient grounds for single mothers to opt out of the labor market and demand public support. Personal Responsibility and Work Opportunity Reconciliation Act (PRWORA) decreed that welfare was no longer an entitlement but rather a temporary and strictly limited, state-run, work-based program. After TANF, a family could receive assistance without working for no more than two years, and no more than five years total.[9] Assistance was predicated on the notion that recipients would show due diligence in securing work, or they could be sanctioned, and even eliminated from financial assistance. In short, after PRWORA, governmental assistance required that a single parent accept the burdens of compensated labor.

Rhetorically, at least, PRWORA does not understand work as the only viable pathway out of poverty. Correctly or not, welfare reform was driven by the belief that AFDC had contributed to the collapse of the two-parent family, especially in the inner city. The act therefore purported that increasing work and increasing stable marriages were both commensurate and essential strategies for moving families out of poverty. However, for a host of reasons well documented in this volume, states have been largely reluctant to develop policy initiatives regarding marriage. In terms of implementation, PRWORA has focused almost entirely on promoting work, including work for the single mother. As mentioned, ADC was established to allow mothers to stay home with their children and thereby keep families together. The fact that PRWORA sees work requirements as part of a pro-family agenda bespeaks the extent to which our society has changed.[10]

But if this mother is expected to look for work, what is she to do about her children? Under TANF, funding for child care increased substantially. Between 1994 and 1999, more than $5 billion of new funding was budgeted and about 1.2 million children were added to child care subsidy programs (Besharov and Samari 2001, 467). Nevertheless, like welfare itself, child care under TANF is not an entitlement. At most, the law provides that single parents with children under age six cannot be sanctioned for failure to participate in work activities if care is unavailable.[11]

If, on the other hand, a mother gives birth to a child, TANF allows states to exempt her for up to a year from work activities. Twenty-three states have one-year exemptions in place. In some states, the exemption is significantly shorter. Indeed, in eleven states, women must look for or return to paid labor once newborns are twelve weeks old. This twelve-week period is similar to the limit available to many working women, and is based as much on the woman's needs as the child's. The disabilities associated with delivery, and in some states, the burdens associated with care of a newborn, justify a mother's temporary exemption from the labor market, but no more than that (see chapter 9).[12]

With the passage of TANF, American society fully embraced the work horn of the Wollstonecraft dilemma. But by so doing, it abandoned the framework in which care and motherhood—absent some form of independent financial support—were understood as a worthy form of civic work. The feminist strategy of pursuing gender equity through the labor market succeeded in universalizing the liberal connection between labor and citizenship. To be sure, the civic value of motherhood remains viable for those households that are able to pay their way.[13] The so-called mommy wars notwithstanding, mothers who raise their children while the father engages in compensated labor are still considered citizens in full standing. But for the single mother, there are precious few options; short of engaging in compensated labor, there is no longer any way for her to fully meet her civic responsibilities.

In his 1986 book *Beyond Entitlement,* Lawrence Mead argued in precisely these terms. He claimed that by condoning nonwork, welfare set recipients (men and women) apart from the necessary conditions of full citizenship. "The moral lessons most people learn, that they must work and take care of their families if they are to prosper, were blocked for much of the underclass by federal policy. Society normally exacts work or other contributions from its members in return for support" (Mead 1986, 67). This argument ultimately carried the day.

But it is worth focusing for a moment on notion of other contribution. For that was exactly what society used to expect, and what it used to support financially, in the many decades before welfare reform. Mothers were indeed understood to be contributing, but through care rather than work. The collapse of that notion meant that staying out of the workforce and demanding financial support was now seen as a fairly egregious form of social parasitism. Welfare reform meant that poor, single mothers had to join the labor force if they were to enjoy the status of citizen and receive the financial support of the state.

Child Care and the Welfare of Children

It is simple enough to acknowledge that welfare reform represents a profound shift in American social policy. It is far more difficult to judge the effects of that change. Again, welfare's very existence derives from a past in which many children grew up without adequate care. And there were certainly those who predicted that the abandonment of the principle of stay-at-home motherhood would lead to a similar predicament. But the facts are far more complicated. In this section, I survey the data on motherhood, child well-being and welfare reform.

If one can conclude anything about the effects of welfare reform, it is that work by former welfare recipients appears to benefit school age children. After an exhaustive consideration of the available data, Duncan and Chase-Lansdale offer this conclusion:

> We find strong evidence that welfare reform can be a potent force for enhancing the achievement and positive behavior of children in preschool and elementary school. . . . Above all, children are seen to benefit from maternal employment, which is presumed to enhance mothers' self-esteem,

as well as from the discipline and structure of work routines, in contrast to welfare dependence, impose on family life. (2001, 392)

Seen in this light, a welfare system premised on work appears to operate very much along the lines that advocates predicted. Work helps to bring families into the social and political mainstream, inculcating the habits and dispositions necessary for them to escape poverty. Children are proud that their mother holds a job and perhaps come to see more possibilities for themselves. Moreover, child care placements may offer children opportunities for developmental stimulation that their mothers, for whatever reason, were unable to provide. As long as opportunities for work remain, there is little ground for condemning welfare reform because one fears that the school age child is worse off as a result.

But these positive findings are not so readily applicable to children who are not in elementary school or preschool. Evaluations also show that teenagers are more likely to get in trouble after school because working parents are less available to supervise them (see, for example, Duncan and Chase-Lansdale 2001, 397). The data are also at best unclear when it comes to newborns and infants. Almost concomitant with the welfare reform debate, scientific data emerged that showed the critical importance of the first three years of life for the child's development and the unique importance of the mother in providing care. The research confirmed that babies need to form attachments with some adult if they are to develop feelings of security and self-worth, and that building those attachments required time and consistency (for a useful summary, see Board on Children, Youth, and Families 2000).[14] Individuals other than a child's mother can become a primary attachment, but "the security of attachment between a mother and her child is more influential on early psychosocial growth than are the relationships a child has with other caregivers at home or outside the home, and even children in extensive child care continue to show an overwhelming preference for their mothers" (235). Conceivably, such ties might be harmed if mothers have to work full-time, especially during the first year of life.

Research has been decidedly mixed regarding this question. Shields and Behrman conclude that, "on the one hand, some evidence suggests that when a family's income increases, young children benefit, especially young children living in families below poverty level. . . . On the other hand, other studies indicate that parent-child interaction may be harmed when infants spend extended lengths of time in child care" (2002, 10). For their part, Duncan and Chase-Lansdale acknowledge that "infants and toddlers rely on parents or 'attachment figures' to provide a secure base from which they actively explore the environment and an important emotional foundation for later development." But while "mothers' entry into the labor force could compromise children's attachment, research tends to show that this does not happen" (2001, 396). Both studies thus conclude that the data on outcomes for very young children due to maternal employment show few large changes either positive or negative. However, they, like most researchers, also acknowledge that any conclusions here must be held with diffidence. Even Stephanie Coontz (no fan of gender segregation), acknowledges that "the jury is still out on full-time day care for . . . infants" (1992, 219). What is more, these data are from a general population. Effects on lower income families, where mothers are more likely to be single, and use family members or neighbors for child care rather than centers, are even less well understood.

One recent survey by Ermisch and Francesconi of the Institute for Economic and Social Research in Britain maintains that the lack of consensus that characterized the early cognitive development literature seems to have been replaced by a somewhat more consistent set of results. Most relevant, the authors conclude, "early maternal employment is likely to have long-term consequences on children's wellbeing"—including negative effects on "emotional and cognitive outcomes" (2005, 173) But they also acknowledge that even this consistency is not as clear-cut when considering poor, single-parent families. On the one hand, the study notes that any negative effects are less apparent in children of better-educated and higher-earning mothers. For poor, single mothers, the loss of parental time is particularly difficult to overcome. On the other hand, they say that some of the negative effects associated with first-year maternal employment are not present for black and Latino families. One could speculate that the problems with nonmaternal day care are less pronounced when the mother is especially poor because the quality of maternal care is lower. And therefore, provided that there is sufficient quality day care, current TANF policy might well result in a net positive for child outcomes.

But the sufficiency and quality of child care for poor mothers, in the United States and Great Britain, is in question. Duncan and Chase-Lansdale (2001) conclude that "long-lasting beneficial impacts on the achievement and behavior of low-income children" depends on "intensive, education-based preschool programs." If that high quality is absent or unavailable, the impact of child care on developmental outcomes is uncertain (396). For a variety of reasons, children from poor households are less likely to be enrolled in high quality programs than children from wealthier households (Fuller et al. 2002, 107). Another key issue is availability. Despite significant increases in federal funding, Ellen Goodman noted in 2002 that "across the country, there are only enough licensed infant child-care slots for 18 percent of the need" ("Paying Mothers Makes Sense," *Boston Globe,* September 27). Those numbers are even lower for children living in rural areas, or for those children with any kind of special need. Even if one were to stipulate that outstanding child care leads to better developmental outcomes for all children, it means little if such care is frequently unavailable.

This brief review demonstrates that conclusions about the effects of maternal employment on newborns and infants are contestable and uncertain, and these effects for children of former welfare recipients are even less clear. Both the mother who wishes to stay home with her young child, and those who champion her return to work can find support for their positions. At the same time, research has conclusively demonstrated the specific and unique importance of maternal care to the healthy development of children and especially infants—whether she is working or not.

If we live long enough, all of us will live in a society led by today's children. And therefore all of us have a vested interest in how the care of infants and children is delivered and sustained. If research demonstrates the unique importance of maternal care, then the ability of mothers to provide that care is a profoundly important public issue. It also means that when mothers do their job well, they are performing a public service—one that merits public acknowledgment and support. For all its failures, the world of republican motherhood and AFDC understood both of these conclusions better than we do. The question we are left with is whether there is a way to restore the civic value of care given the realities of a post–welfare reform society. More specifically, can we move toward this synthesis in the policy arena?

At-Home Infant Care

Richard Mulder is a family physician in rural Minnesota. In the 1990s, he was also a Republican representative in the Minnesota state legislature. Based on his experience as a physician, his knowledge of research on infant bonding, and his awareness of the lack of out-of-home child care for infants (especially in rural settings), he believed that "in the interests of children's health and emotional development, mothers should stay home with their babies as long as possible" (Melissa Healy, "Mothers Do It All for Love—but Money Helps," *Los Angeles Times,* August 22, 1999, p. 3). He therefore developed a bill establishing a pilot proposal for At-Home Infant Care (AHIC). In 1998, with near unanimous support, that bill was signed into law.

The program provided funds to either parent of a newborn to stay at home to care for their child. The program was available to single parents or couples, but as with TANF and AFDC, almost all the participating caregivers were women. Eligibility required that the parent or parents met income requirements and was employed or involved in some eligible activity (education or training) prior to application. The program was revenue neutral; funds were taken from Minnesota's Basic Sliding Fee Program for child care and the money provided the parents was less than the state would have given to a child care center for the same child. (Most families received between $200 and $299 per month.) Funding was available for up to a year per family. The program coordinated with the state's Healthy Beginnings Home Visiting Program, which offered parenting, infant growth and development, and health and safety information to the parent or parents (see http://www.betterbabycare.org/docs/AHICsummary.doc; accessed July 20, 2005).

Primarily because it addressed the child care shortage in a revenue-neutral way, the program was given an innovative government award in 2001 from the Council of State Governments. For their part, parents who were interviewed said that bonding with their infant was an important benefit of the program, but financial assistance was also cited. Fifty-five percent of participants in the first year were single parents, 45 percent of families were headed by two parents. Although the program provided support for up to one year, the vast majority of families (two-thirds) used it for less than three months, and many used it to extend their maternity leave. In 1999, the program was changed to accommodate the waiting lists that existed in many counties. In 2003, budget shortfalls were so severe that many state programs were cut, and others, like AHIC, were eliminated.

Legislators in Montana modeled a bill on the Minnesota program and introduced it in 2001. That bill was withdrawn when Governor Judy Martz authorized a pilot project. That pilot program was very similar to Minnesota's. It was for families with income below 150 percent of poverty and with infants under the age of two. There was a lifetime limit of twenty-four months for all children. Parents had to be over eighteen and working before applying for coverage. Importantly, program recipients in Montana were also required to complete a child development education plan. This plan had to include activities or information that address the following areas: infant health, safety and nutrition; child growth and development; infant brain development, and child guidance.

According to the Montana Department of Human Development (2001), "child development education plans are designed to be completed in a self-assessment format. They can be highly individualized and contain a variety of activities. Examples of plan elements regarding child development, could be videos such as *I Am Your Child,* consultations with public health nurses, participation in Even start, WIC, [and the like]." As in Minnesota, the program offered minimal support, with a maximum allowance of $384 per month. In March 2003, based on the results of that pilot, an AHIC bill passed the legislature, but again because of the state's budget crisis, no funds were authorized for it.

Assessment

In many ways AHIC resembles the exemptions from the work test permitted under TANF. Both programs allow a low-income single mother to devote herself to caring for her child without working outside the home. Both cost government about the same. The at-home program is, if anything, slightly less expensive than the money that the state would allocate for child care under TANF. Nor is there much difference in the gender make-up of program recipients. TANF, AFDC, and AHIC are all gender neutral, but in practice, almost all adult recipients are women.[15] Finally, the time factor is also not relevant; either way, the mother or father is staying home with the newborn for up to one year, and frequently much less.

But there is a big difference with regard to how this time is perceived. Under TANF, the time a mother spends caring for a newborn is called an exemption; it is the time that the mother can remove herself from the labor market without penalty.[16] But with AHIC, the mother is compensated for the care that she provides for her child. AHIC thus moves beyond questions of flexibility and accommodation toward an older notion of the civic value of care. That difference bespeaks a different valuation of the mother and her labor, and the child and its value to society. The distinction is clearly not lost on recipients. Ellen Goodman notes in a *Washington Post* article that poverty advocates began to lobby for the Montana bill because their constituents (single mothers on assistance) asked them to; they believed that raising their children was "their top priority and their first job." They wanted "caregiving to count as work" ("The Job of Raising Kids," *Boston Globe,* September 29, 2002, p. D11). With AHIC, the mother is able to maintain her claim to full citizenship by being a mother.

Of course, the mothers' desires aren't the only things that should be considered. In their chapters, Wax and Mead argue that responsible parenting begins with having the resources in place to raise a child. It is morally illegitimate, they say, for a poor mother to create a fait accompli by having a child and then expecting government to pay her to raise it. The question then is why caring for a child under these circumstances is any more worthy of public support than any other potentially valuable but uninvited task that individuals might choose for themselves, like tending a public garden or creating graffiti art (see chapter 9). Indeed, Wax notes that some Americans worry that assistance for single mothers risks fostering more single motherhood, thereby ensuring that more children grow up in a less successful family structure.

On the other hand, even if a parent's actions are profligate, the child is an innocent victim of circumstance. Even rudimentary notions of fairness make it difficult to countenance public indifference. What is more, even though it is impossible to prove the point empirically, society's fundamental stake in the well being of every future citizen make a fairly strong a priori case for offering support to the child and family (see chapter 11).

Even if one grants this, however, Wax's larger point about the need for a general theory about compensable labor remains valid. If a post–welfare reform society is to understand care as civic labor, and if the state is to compensate care in a way that reinforces that judgment, then society should be able to expect that providing care yields outcomes worthwhile to society. In Stuart White's words, "if we do include parenting in our account of civic labour, then it is important that as citizens we understand and appreciate the reasons for regarding it as such, and that parenting itself be informed by a commitment to produce these wider public benefits" (2003, 111).

Thus, even if one stipulates that children are public goods, that doesn't mean that parental care automatically qualifies as civic work, for there is no guarantee that at-home parental care offers the best prospects for the child. A mother on public assistance could be a terrible parent, and the mother's child could be far better served by spending all day in daycare.[17] Society will benefit only if children benefit, and one cannot assume that having a mother at home will ensure such an outcome.

But neither is there any reason to assume the opposite. The mothers taking part in AHIC are not separate from American society; they are not part of some forgotten underclass. To qualify for the program, they must either be working or engaged in training or education. They have therefore been exposed to the very same beneficial effects that welfare reform advocates associate with working. Second, this program is not mandatory; mothers can choose not to participate. It is reasonable to assume some self-selection among those who do. And because mothers must be working to qualify, one can also assume that those who select in are interested in bonding with, and providing quality care for, their newborn.

More important, the Montana plan stipulates that the parent work with their social worker to develop an education plan for their new child. Again, these plans focus on child development goals and the parenting skills needed to achieve them. By making a parental care plan conditional to employment, and by having state employees work with the parents to design that plan, the Montana AHIC program differs from the Minnesota plan, and thereby more ably meets these standards. By demonstrating that the parent is being held to certain standards, the state of Montana communicates the notion that it has a stake in the outcome of care, a concern for the recipient of care, and a respect for the caregiver.[18]

To be sure, there is not enough data to judge the effectiveness of the Montana program. And research on programs designed to enhance parenting skills shows that "it is not easy to change parenting." Nevertheless, one can say that "carefully designed intervention programs have proven successful in improving the sensitivity and reciprocity of care that parents give their infants and toddlers, with some programs also succeeding in strengthening the security of attachment in young children as a consequence" (Board on Children, Youth, and Families 2000, 261). It is quite possible that within the limits of a liberal society, we might increase the parenting demands on mothers and the oversight available from social workers.

Even without such claims, however, the fact remains that the child's bond with its mother is critical to the child's development, and that the child overwhelmingly prefers the mother to any other caregiver. Therefore we have no reason to presume that providing mothers the option to stay home will not end up benefiting the society at large. What is more, whatever demands the state makes, it is much better positioned to make them if it accepts that maternal care is valuable and the funds are seen, in the first place, as compensation for that care. If a mother is simply exempted from work activities, the state's demands are much more difficult to sustain.

All this is not to say that all mothers should stay home with their infants, nor is it to denigrate those mothers who choose to place their babies in out-of-home child care, but it is to say that those mothers who want to stay home with their child have good reasons and good grounds for the state to support their decision. And with respect to the child's well-being, there are no compelling reasons for government to insist that infant day care is the only legitimate option for a single mother.

Prospects

This policy debate continues to unfold. Under current law, if a state used federal TANF funds for AHIC programs, it would have to count those mothers as not working in the calculation of the state's work participation rate. Originally, there were hopes that this disincentive might disappear when TANF came up for reauthorization. Indeed, when Max Baucus, Democratic senator from Montana, was head of the U.S. Senate Finance Committee, a provision was written into the Senate's reauthorization bill that would have provided funding for a pilot program similar to the Montana program in up to ten states. With transition of power to Republicans in 2002, Senator Baucus became ranking minority member, and prospects for the provision faded.

In the House, Connecticut Representative Rosa DeLauro introduced the At-Home Infant Care Act of 2004, "which would amend the Child Care and Development Block Grant Act of 1990 to permit infants to be cared for at home by parents." Much like the Minnesota and Montana bills, DeLauro's bill notes research findings regarding the importance of quality care for "the first months and years of life," as well as the shortage of quality child care for infants, especially in rural areas. It stipulates that the parent or parents must be working prior to application, and that financial assistance may not exceed twenty-four months (U.S. Congress 2004).

Advocates for working mothers were pleased that the AHIC concept had been introduced at the federal level, but given the Republican control of the House, the bill had little chance of getting out of committee, let alone passing. One may question why a party that professes such devotion to the family would spurn such a provision. But in light of these prospects, perhaps AHIC should be seen as part of a larger and no doubt longer-term objective.

Conclusions

The problematic relationship between care and citizenship in liberal society is a large and long-standing question. The contemporary dynamics around care within welfare reform policy merely reflect some of these problems. AHIC does not even begin to address these issues adequately, but it may offer a model for adjudicating labor and care in a post–welfare reform society.

In her survey of the history of American social policy, Theda Skocpol concludes,

> the most enduring and popularly accepted social benefits in the United States have never been understood either as poor relief or as mere individual entitlements. From public schools to Social Security, they have been morally justified as recognitions of or as prospective supports for individual service to the community. The rationale of social service in return for service has been a characteristic way for Americans to combine deep respect for individual freedom and initiative with support for families and due regard for the obligations that all members of the national community owe to one another. (1997, 111)

Skocpol makes two points. First, new social benefits in American society are most likely to gain approval if they are made universal, that is, available regardless of income levels. Second, in America, benefits are justifiable only insofar as they can be seen as recognitions of service to the broader society.

Seen in this light, the AHIC Program is perhaps best understood as a paid parental leave program for low-income families. Given the paucity of quality child care in most poor neighborhoods, there is much to recommend such a targeted investment of public funds. But the most conclusive research findings regarding child care relate to the importance of early childhood development and maternal-infant bonding. These findings apply to all infants and mothers, and therefore, the case for a universal policy is compelling.

In September of 2003, the state of California became the first in the nation to establish a paid parental leave program. The program was implemented in July of 2004 and is available to virtually all working parents, providing up to six weeks of partial pay to care for a sick family member of new child. If at-home infant care were to move ahead in other states, or at the federal level, it might foster further efforts toward statewide and even nationwide paid parental leave (see Labor Project for Working Families, 2003). And if more states adopt various paid parental leave programs, it could similarly advance the cause of AHIC.

The Wollstonecraft dilemma reflects the inability of liberalism to accommodate the realities of care. Formerly, American society accommodated this lacuna within liberal theory through a sexist division of labor. Given that labor is the ground for liberal citizenship, it is no surprise that women chose to reject this division and pursued empowerment in the economic sphere. But it is also no surprise that this shift exposed the inadequacies of liberal theory.

AHIC outlines a strategy for developing a new synthesis of care and work. By requiring that recipients be employed or otherwise participating in society prior to application, it acknowledges that participation in the labor market is prerequisite for governmental support and indeed, for full citizenship. It also accepts that the home is not the only place where a child can receive adequate care. But at the same time, AHIC asserts that a mother is indispensable to a child's well being, and that this is especially true when a child is newly born. It also says that when a mother works and then decides to stay home with her infant, she does not therefore cease to perform meaningful work for society. AHIC is one means by which our society might move closer toward a synthesis in which all Americans have the opportunity and, indeed, responsibility to contribute through compensated labor, but also in which care is once again valued as essential civic work.

In addition to the authors in this collection and especially my co-editor, I am grateful to Lissa Bell, Jane Waldfogel, Richard Mulder, and Marco Francesconi for their helpful suggestions.

Notes

1. "But because no political society can be nor subsist without having in itself the power to preserve the property, and, in order thereto, punish the offences of all those of that society, there, and there only, is political society, where every one of the members hath quitted this natural power, resigned it up into the hands of the community" (Locke 1690/1967, 437).
2. The full story is much more complicated, of course. See Stephanie Coontz (1992).
3. The notion of republican motherhood and its relationship to liberal theory is a contested one. Many, including a reviewer of this volume, argue that as the name implies, the notion is fundamentally republican and not liberal. Of course both streams of thought were operative during the American founding. At the same time, I would note that Locke's rejection of primogeniture (and the resultant democratization of the family); his claim that both sexes were rational, and depended on educational experience to fill the tabula rasa; and his explicit references to mothers in an educative and authoritative role; all lend strong support to the claim that liberal/Lockean thought—at minimum—contributed significantly to the unique form of republican motherhood that appeared within the American context.
4. Michael Walzer argues that restrictions on women in the workplace (in addition to child labor laws and the shorter working day) developed during the

Victorian era (that is, mid-nineteenth century) "to protect family ties against the market" and especially rising industrialization (1984, 233).

5. Note that this justification was not confined to the United States. In 1911, Leonard Hobhouse argued that "if we take in earnest all we say of the rights and duties of motherhood, we shall recognize that the mother of young children is often doing better service to the community and one more worthy of pecuniary remuneration when she stays at home and minds her children than when she goes out charing and leaves them to the chances of the street or to the perfunctory care of a neighbor" (1911/1993, 94).
6. The name of the program was changed in 1962 to Aid to Families with Dependent Children (AFDC), but most acknowledge that this change was made primarily to counter charges that the program discouraged marriage.
7. Pateman argues that this dilemma is manifest in the life and writings of eighteenth-century English feminist Mary Wollstonecraft.
8. Coontz argues that changes in economics and culture came before this ideological shift. That is, rising rates of employment among married women and mothers preceded the growth of feminism (see 1992, 162). My colleague Wendy Butler pointed out to me that for many mothers, feminism was not a primary consideration: entering the work force was simply a matter of economic necessity. In this regard, see Elizabeth Warren and Amelia Warren Tyagi (2003). These are important debates, but for my purposes it is enough to note that the historic rise in the rates of working mothers is not controversial.
9. These numbers, while accurate, do not reflect the whole story. The law also provided that a state could keep 20 percent of the number of welfare recipients it had in 1996 on the caseload even after their five years had expired. With the steep and nearly ubiquitous decline in the number of welfare recipients, this had made the five-year limit far less onerous than it might first appear.
10. Some conservatives opposed enforcing work because of concerns about child well-being. In "What to Do about Welfare," Charles Murray voiced skepticism about work as the principal element of reform (1994). I am indebted to Lawrence Mead for pointing this out to me.
11. On the other hand, that period does count against the two years lifetime limit for TANF funds.
12. Regarding these exemptions, Amy Wax writes, "these figures illustrate that . . . many commonplace situations are still regarded as absolving people—and especially mothers—of the responsibility to engage in paid employment, at least temporarily." Though we disagree about the implications, on this point we fully agree.
13. Indeed, William Galston has pointed out to me that this value continues to find expression in public policy. At the same time that American society moved away from Republican motherhood with welfare reform, government moved to restore tax credits for children, in part at least, to make it possible for a parent (usually the mother) to choose to remain home.
14. This document also recommends "lengthening the exemption period before states require parents of infants to work as part of welfare reform."
15. Although as a percentage, more two-parent families participated in the Minnesota program, than in AFDC or TANF. Some feminists will likely blanch at

any program that does not mandate gender equity in the provision of care. They will point to countries like Norway that have instituted "use it or lose it" provisions for new fathers. Leaving aside any questions about innate or socialized differences, I would argue that politics is the art of the possible. Developing a program that is, in principle, gender neutral is possible. Demanding that men take part in that care is, in my judgment, beyond the pale of contemporary American politics.

16. Perhaps not fully without penalty. The time spent in the AHIC program does count against the five-year time limit for TANF funds.
17. Shonkoff and Phillips note "the circumstances that surround parents . . . exert a powerful influence on their capacity to fulfill the responsibilities that are entailed in raising children" (Board on Children, Youth, and Families 2000, 265). For example, studies show that poor mothers are twice as likely to suffer from depression as the nonpoor (251).
18. Note how the Montana plan comports with Stuart White's demands for parental commitment. He notes that "eligibility for public support (specifically for parental labour) might be made conditional on attending parenting classes, or parents might be required to attend such classes shortly after the birth of their first child as an extension of the community's post-natal support services" (2003, 250–51).

References

Besharov, Douglas J., with Nasanin Samari. 2001. "Child Care after Welfare Reform." In *New World of Welfare,* edited by Rebecca Blank and Ron Haskins. Washington, D.C.: Brookings Institution.

Blank, Susan, and Barbara B. Blum. 1997. "A Brief History of Work Expectations for Welfare Mothers." *The Future of Children* 7(1): 28–38.

Board on Children, Youth, and Families. 2000. *From Neurons to Neighborhoods: The Science of Early Childhood Development,* edited by Jack P. Shonkoff and Deborah A. Phillips. Washington, D.C.: The National Academy of Sciences.

Brooks-Gunn, Jeanne, Wei-Jui Han, and Jane Waldfogel. 2003. "Maternal Employment and Child Cognitive Outcomes in the First Three Years of Life: The NICHD Study of Early Child Care." *Child Development* 73(4): 1052–72.

Coontz, Stephanie. 1992. *The Way We Never Were: American Families and the Nostalgia Trap.* New York: Basic Books.

de Tocqueville, Alexis. 1835/2000. *Democracy in America,* translated, edited, and with an introduction by Harvey C. Mansfield and Delba Winthrop. Chicago: University of Chicago Press.

Duncan, Greg J., and P. Lindsay Chase-Lansdale. 2001. "Welfare Reform and Children's Well-Being." In *The New World of Welfare,* edited by Rebecca Blank and Ron Haskins. Washington, D.C.: Brookings Institution.

Ermisch, John F., and Marco Francesconi. 2005. "Parental Work and Child Welfare." In *Women at Work: An Economic Perspective,* edited by Tito Boeri, Daniela Del Boca, and Christopher Pissarides. Oxford: Oxford University Press

Fuller, Bruce, Sharon Kagan, Gretchen Caspary, and Christine A. Gauthier. 2002. "Welfare Reform and Child Care Options for Low-Income Families." *The Future of Children* 12(1): 97–120.

Gordon, Linda. 1994. *Pitied but Not Entitled: Single Mothers and the History of Welfare, 1890–1935.* New York: Free Press.

Heclo, Hugh. 2001. "The Politics of Welfare Reform." In *The New World of Welfare,* edited by Rebecca Blank and Ron Haskins. Washington, D.C.: Brookings Institution.

Hobhouse, Leonard T. 1911/1993. *Liberalism and Other Essays,* edited by James Meadowcroft. Cambridge: Cambridge University Press.

Labor Project for Working Families. 2003. "Putting Families First: How California Won the Fight for Paid Family Leave." Berkeley, Calif.: Labor Project for Working Families. Available at http://www.laborproject.org/publications/pdf/paidleavewon.pdf (accessed July 22, 2005).

Locke, John. 1690/1967. *Concerning Civil Government, Part II. The English Philosophers from Bacon to Mill,* edited and with an introduction by Edwin A. Burtt. New York: Modern Library, Random House.

Mead, Lawrence M. 1986. *Beyond Entitlement: The Social Obligations of Citizenship.* New York: Free Press.

Montana Department of Public Health and Human Services. 2001. "Non-TANF Child Care Eligibility, At-Home Infant Care." Child Care Policy Manual Bulletin. December 1. Available at: http://www.betterbabycare.org/docs/MONTANACC2-3a2001DecAt-HomeInfant.doc (accessed July 20, 2005).

Murray, Charles. 1994. "What to Do about Welfare?" *Commentary* 98(December): 26–34.

Pateman, Carole. 1992. "Equality, Difference and Subordination: the Politics of Motherhood and Women's Citizenship." In *Beyond Equality and Difference: Citizenship, Feminist Politics, and Female Subjectivity,* edited by Gisela Bock and Susan James. London and New York: Routledge.

———. 1998. "The Patriarchal Welfare State." In *Democracy and the Welfare State,* edited by Amy Gutmann. Princeton, N.J.: Princeton University Press.

Rush, Benjamin. 1787/1973. "Thoughts Upon Female Education." In *Theories of Education in Early America: 1655–1819,* edited by Wilson Smith. Indianapolis: Bobbs Merrill.

Shields, Margie K., and Richard E. Behrman. 2002. "Children and Welfare Reform: Analysis and Recommendations." *The Future of Children* 12(1): 1–209.

Skocpol, Theda. 1992. *Protecting Soldiers and Mothers: The Political Origins of Social Policy in the United States.* Cambridge, Mass.: Harvard University Press.

———. 1997. "A Partnership with American Families." In *The New Majority: Toward a Popular Progressive Politics,* edited by Theda Skocpol and Stanley B. Greenberg. New Haven, Conn.: Yale University Press.

Teles, Steven M. 1996. *Whose Welfare? AFDC and Elite Politics.* Lawrence: University Press of Kansas.

U.S. Congress. House. 1935. *The Social Security Act of 1935; Title IV: Grants to States for Aid to Dependent Children,* Public Law No. 271, 74th Congress, 1st sess.

———. 2004. *At-Home Infant Care Act of 2004,* 108th Congress, 2d sess. HR 3595.

Walzer, Michael. 1984. *Spheres of Justice: A Defense of Pluralism and Equality.* New York: Basic Books.

Warren, Elizabeth, and Amelia Warren Tyagi. 2003. *The Two-Income Trap: Why Middle-Class Mothers and Fathers Are Going Broke.* New York: Basic Books.

Weaver, R. Kent. 2000. *Ending Welfare as We Know It.* Washington, D.C.: Brookings Institution.
White, Stuart. 2003. *The Civic Minimum: On the Rights and Obligations of Economic Citizenship.* Oxford: Oxford University Press.
Zagarri, Rosemarie. 1992. "Morals, Manners and the Republican Mother." *American Quarterly* 44(June): 187–205.

Chapter 8

Welfare Reform and Citizenship

LAWRENCE M. MEAD

WELFARE REFORM has changed the meaning of citizenship and democracy in America. By enforcing work on the adult recipients, reform dramatized that citizenship entails obligations as well as rights. Here I show what work enforcement meant and that it occurred at several levels, not all related to welfare. I suggest how work operates to integrate the poor and to reshape politics. Work demands tend to narrow government aid to the poor, but they may also move political outcomes to the left.

I also consider philosophical objections to work enforcement. These arguments have some weight, but they are made at too great a distance from actual politics—a gap we are trying to narrow in this book. If one respects the strong imperative for equal citizenship in American politics, then the need to enforce work to integrate the poor appears overriding.

Welfare Reform

Welfare here means the controversial family aid system once called Aid to Families with Dependent Children (AFDC). Welfare reform means the rapid changes in AFDC that occurred from the late 1980s through the late 1990s. In this period, the federal government enacted the Family Support Act (FSA) of 1988 and the Personal Responsibility and Work Opportunity Reconciliation Act (PRWORA) of 1996. PRWORA reshaped and renamed AFDC as Temporary Assistance for Needy Families (TANF). Along with local decisions, those laws recast welfare policy.

Critics say that reform curbed the aid available to needy families, and it expressed hostility to racial minorities and single mothers. Some of these accounts suggest that welfare was totally abolished (Gans 1995; Mink 1998; Schram 2000). Actually, overt restrictions on aid played little role in reform.[1] States liberalized eligibility rules to allow more two-parent, as well as single-parent, families to qualify.[2] Benefit levels changed little; indeed, support often rose because states liberalized the earnings a family could have and still get aid. Overall spending did not fall. States have spent less on cash aid, due to the fall in the rolls, but more on child and health care for families going to work. The federal Earned Income Tax Credit (EITC) has exploded to cost more than AFDC once did. Welfare is very much alive, although it now gives more aid to the working poor and less to the nonworking.

The leading change, rather, was that states required that rising proportions of welfare adults look for and secure work, or leave the rolls. Much of the stigma that attached to welfare before the 1960s returned. Would-be recipients now get a message that they are supposed to go to work rather than seek public aid. This deters many from applying for help, even when they would have been eligible. It was chiefly these new work tests and expectations that drove the rolls down by over 60 percent or more after 1994, although superb economic conditions and expanded wage and child care subsidies also helped.

Academic experts doubted that many recipients could work, but the reformers were vindicated when about two-thirds of those leaving welfare found jobs. Work levels among poor families rose sharply. In 1993, only 44 percent of poor female heads of family with children were employed. The rate soared to 64 percent by 1999. Like the fall in the rolls, the work rise seems due mostly to welfare reform, although other factors contributed. The work rate did fall to 55 percent by 2003, probably due to the recession (U.S. Census Bureau 1994, table 19; 2000, table 17; 2004, table POV15). Yet, despite the downturn, the welfare rates rolls did not rebound.

PRWORA also encouraged states to promote marriage as a solution to welfare and poverty, a goal alarming to many commentators. But these provisions were virtually ignored at the local level. That was because enforcing marriage is much less popular than enforcing work, and because government lacks effective measures. The Bush administration is trying to develop better programs, but there is little prospect that welfare will try to enforce marriage more seriously any time soon.

The motivation behind reform was partly to raise work levels and cut dependency. But a stronger impetus for most politicians was fear of what unconditional welfare seemed to be doing to society. An underclass unable to fulfill leading civilities, including work, was growing in American cities. Whether or not welfare was a cause, work enforcement through welfare might be one remedy. Welfare reform is really an ambitious attempt to expand the working class. Reform in Europe is more tentative but has similar goals (Mead 2001; Lødemel and Trickey 2001).

Work enforcement, I believe, signals a change in the overt meaning of citizenship. Government has set about enforcing an obligation that, studies show, most Americans think is essential to full membership in the society. It has never done this on such a scale before. Reform enforced work on several levels.

Diversion

In part, reform demanded work simply by driving off the rolls families that could support themselves, or by deterring them from coming on. This effort, known as diversion, spoke to a real problem. Traditionally, AFDC enforced financial limits on who was eligible for aid, but this did not ensure that the applicants who qualified had done all they could to avoid welfare, such as going to work or getting help from friends or relatives. The public viewed many recipients as undeserving chiefly on grounds that they did not really need aid (Gilens 1999, 61–77). Research shows that more welfare mothers worked than admitted to doing so. They often held jobs "off the books" (without telling welfare) to avoid reductions in their grants.[3] The rapid deflation of the rolls in the 1990s confirmed that many, maybe most, recipients did in fact have alternatives to aid.

Under diversion, work is enforced only indirectly. The work test demands that all claimants for aid prove their willingness to labor by looking for work or, in some cases, performing unpaid labor. The employable will then prefer to work outside welfare. Only those who truly cannot work, at least immediately, make it onto the rolls. As this suggests, diversion's focus is on people off welfare rather than on. Most of those who seek aid, it is believed, are already working, or would work if diverted.

In this understanding, rights to welfare are balanced by the rights of other people. Through the criminal law, government requires that citizens respect the rights and properties of others. Similarly, diversion requires that welfare claimants respect the taxpayers, who fund their aid. At least for claimants with alternatives, the policy aims to restore the situation before the welfare state, where people were forced to labor simply by necessity. Work is enforced by the private sector, not the public. Reciprocity exists, but it is enforced outside government, by the need to earn support in the private marketplace.

The point is to stop people who could work from exploiting the system. In Charles Murray's Harold and Phyllis story, an unwed couple with a child is driven to marry and work if welfare is denied them. But with welfare, the mother will pretend to be single and go on aid, so that neither parent has to work (Murray 1984, 156–62). What offends here is not dependency as such, but rather the casual way that some poor appear to abuse the safety net. By denying aid to the employable, then, welfare reform enforces not so much work as morality.

Reciprocity

Of course, some people have no alternative to going on aid, at least in the short term. For them, work must be enforced within the welfare system, not outside. The employable are then expected to work, not instead of aid, but in return for it. The focus now is on people on the rolls rather than off. This policy, too, addresses a real problem. Many families stay on welfare longer than they need to. Although many welfare mothers may work surreptitiously, their work levels are still well beneath those of single mothers not on welfare. Above all, they work less consistently, treating earnings as an occasional supplement to welfare rather than as their basic income.

The public demands that the adult recipients work alongside the taxpayers who are supporting them. At the level of opinion, that desire is much stronger than the desire to divert and save money, although both are present. Work is expected, not total independence. If the needy work typical hours and still need help to make ends meet, that is acceptable. The public and politicians are quite willing to spend new money on child care and other services in order to promote work (Gilens 1999, chapters 2 and 8; Farkas et al. 1996). Getting people entirely off aid is secondary.

Going back to 1967, welfare had tried to require welfare mothers to work, or at least participate in work programs, as a condition of aid. Both FSA and PRWORA raised work standards sharply compared to prior law. And work levels did rise. Under FSA, mothers with children under three years old were excluded from the work test, but under PRWORA all mothers were included, though those with a child under one year old might be excluded at state option. Under FSA, the share of mothers supposed to participate who actually were in work activities rose from 15 to 33 percent between 1991 and 1996. Under PRWORA's tougher rules, the proportion rose from 31 to 38 percent between 1997 and 1999, then fell to 33 percent by 2002, probably due to the recession and to the fact that, as caseloads fell, remaining recipients were less employable.[4]

As under diversion, reciprocity involves a work test, but the purpose is to develop recipients' capacity to work, rather than to exclude the employable. Recipients must enter work programs, perhaps prepare for work through training, and then look for work. One form of the demand is unpaid work in a government position, commonly called workfare. Employment need not preclude aid; a family may combine work with assistance if its earnings leave it below the welfare need standard. Compared to diversion, the focus is far less on keeping people off aid, and far more on obtaining some contribution from them while they are on the rolls.

The concern behind diversion is to enforce morals. With reciprocity, the concern is more about capacity. The hope is to instill enough competence in the recipients so they can leave aid and participate in the natural reciprocity of the labor market. There is little interest in finding fault, in fixing individualized blame for either poverty or dependency. Instead, the aim is accountability—obtaining effort from the recipients in the present. That implies that the responsibility for overcoming poverty and dependency is shared between the individual and society.

Under reciprocity, rights are balanced by obligations bearing on the recipients, not by the rights of others as under diversion. This assumes that clients can in fact discharge the demands made on them. That is, they must be employable. This assessment reflects two related judgments—whether the environment permits employment, and whether the recipients are able to work. The judgments are linked because ability to work can be assessed only relative to how difficult one judges employment to be. To say that work is or is not possible is a statement about the opportunity structure, but also about human nature.[5]

At the inception of AFDC, single mothers were deemed unemployable simply because they had children to take care of. After 1967, a welfare mother was judged employable after her children turned six. Under FSA that age dropped to three, under PRWORA at most to one. Disability, however, still offers a more lasting exemption. Adults can escape the work test if they can prove themselves physically or mentally unable to work. Under reform, indeed, some mothers forced off TANF have qualified for the nation's disability programs instead.[6]

Culture

Finally, welfare reform enforces work at the level of culture. Work is becoming more of an obligation within the society, rather than something left to individual choice, at least for the employable. More and more adults have sought jobs in recent decades, especially women. Policy now insists that welfare mothers do likewise, but informal pressures to work extend beyond this.

Work is one of several competences that the public views as essential to full membership of the society, what I call the common obligations. Others include obeying the law, getting through school, and speaking English. In the public mind, only people who display these civilities are really entitled to claim the rights and benefits of citizenship. The social ideal is equal citizenship, or a situation in which everyone has essentially the same rights and obligations (Mead 1986, chaps. 10 and 11).[7]

Under reciprocity, obligations are valued only as duties to others, as offsets to rights. At the level of culture, by contrast, work is seen as a positive good (Carens 1986, 45–47). It is a display of competence that can gain the poor acceptance and advancement in the wider society. The drive to introduce poor adults into that world extends far beyond getting them to work in a minimal sense. Reformers already wrestle with how to keep former welfare mothers working after they take jobs, and how to help them move up to better positions. How might unemployment insurance be changed to cover more of these workers during a recession, so that they need not go back on TANF? Training programs outside welfare are being reorganized to improve service to the whole low-income working population, which now includes the bulk of former recipients.

Government has also toughened up child support enforcement, the criminal law, and standards in the schools. This neo-Victorian policy aims to restore the higher standards of public behavior that prevailed before the 1960s and 1970s (Morone 2003, 137–46). Some fear that the effort will only stigmatize and exclude the poor, but the overt intention is the opposite—to promote the skills and self-discipline that the less privileged need to prosper. With good reason, government sees the expansion of a respectable working class as its best hope to overcome poverty.

Welfare reform integrates welfare recipients into the broader society by moving many more of them into the workplace. There they have much more contact with the self-sufficient than they did formerly. It is true that incomes did not rise, nor did poverty rates fall, by very much, at least in the short run. Equality in an economic sense hardly improved. The gains to equal citizenship, however, were substantial. The value of that can be seen in the calm satisfaction that many former recipients (and their children) take in working, despite the difficulties (Mead 2004a, chap. 10).

In social politics, the public accepts dependency provided the claimants can show some prior contribution to the society. Social insurance beneficiaries (Social Security, Medicare, unemployment insurance) hardly think of themselves as dependent on government at all, because their benefits are contributory. The same for people on veteran's benefits, who have defended the nation. Work tests aim to put welfare recipients in a similar position. In citizenship terms, fulfilling the demand to function is far more important than minimizing one's demands on the society (Mead 1986, 237–46). Indeed, functioning allows one to claim more from government than before.

The power of work to confer belonging extends far beyond welfare or any benefit program. In America, groups of all kinds find dignity in contributing to the society, above all through employment. From those obligations stem the demands they make on the regime. Various regions, industries, labor unions, and other interests generate economic output, so they expect the regime to provide them with protections and subsidies. Critics ridicule this aid as corporate welfare, but business subsidies are not welfare in the invidious sense of something for nothing. The payoffs have to be earned by remaining in business and producing. The old welfare, in contrast, aided the needy simply because they were needy, with no economic function expected at all.

The Gains of Work

Citizens are usually strangers to each other; but they still must trust each other enough to collaborate in public matters. It is those who fulfill the common obligations who earn the trust of others. Work is particularly salient. On the job, people experience one another as colleagues on which they usually can rely. Thus, to be employed certifies to the reliability of people, at least to their coworkers. Simply the fact that they were hired by employers is the most affirming response that many former welfare recipients have ever had from the society.

Work also helps to knit up the surrounding society. In families that work, the adults leave the home regularly for the workplace, and are seen to do so. Those patterns make a family more eligible to associate with others. As Pope John Paul II wrote, work "first and foremost unites people"; therefore it has "the power to build a community" (1981). Traditionally, white suburbs strongly resisted the entry of nonwhites from the inner city, because of the social problems they bring (Rieder 1985; Sleeper 1990). With higher work levels and lower crime, that resistance could well abate. Thus, employment could begin to undo the social isolation that many former recipients feel. Effectively, welfare reform uses work to rebuild ties between the poor and the rest of society (Sandel 1996, chap. 9 and conclusion).

Tolerance

Trust, in turn, permits tolerance of others. American values dictate that we bracket or ignore distinctions of gender, class, race, religion, or lifestyle when we deal with other people in the workplace or other public settings. In this we treat others as unlike us and yet as the same. We may actively disagree with what they believe or with how they live, differences that would keep us apart in private life. Yet at the same time we believe they will be honest and reliable as people we interact with in business, in public agencies, or in the streets of our cities. At least in these public realms, they will protect our interests, as we do theirs. Citizenship thus has an abstract character. It involves an "interchangeability principle," J. R. Pole writes, whereby people are seen as equally competent and worthy of respect in public matters despite private difference in class, race, or gender (1978, 293).

Religious toleration developed centuries ago when European rulers, who had enforced orthodoxy, accepted that their subjects could be loyal Englishmen or Frenchmen without espousing a particular kind of Christianity, or indeed any religion. In that spirit, the American regime abandoned religious tests early in its history. Later, the country learned that immigrants of varying cultures and races could be reliable Americans, and thus the commitment to tolerance broadened. In the past century, differences of gender and race, and, more recently, sexual orientation, have been bracketed as well. Thus, despite the long history of discrimination, we now declare that to draw distinctions between people in political or economic affairs on any of these bases is improper.

But tolerance is never unconditional. It always assumes fidelity to the common obligations, however they are understood at the time. Trust of strangers is accepted only if differences in belief and demographics really are unassociated with public reliability. When those differences become linked with civility, or incivility, then a common citizenship breaks down. This is what happened in the United States and, to a lesser extent, other Western countries after 1960. Crime and other social problems worsened, and the disorders were linked disproportionately to a dependent class and racial or immigrant minorities, although they afflicted the entire society. The loss of a sense of sameness undercut support for antipoverty programming throughout the West (Offe 1988, chap. 8).

The welfare state was originally seen as a safety net that would offset the uncertainties of capitalism. Most people faced some risk of being thrown out of work and thus needing aid. But this insurance rubric assumed that the chance of dependency was widespread, affecting workers as a class. There was then no need to notice the demographics or lifestyle of particular people. Welfare operated behind a Rawlsian veil of ignorance, paying attention only to whether claimants were economically eligible for benefits. But as welfare becomes associated with narrower subsets of the society, this insurance rationale broke down. Demanding work is now necessary, not to cut back aid to the poor, but precisely to restore a common citizenship so that welfare can be defended (Rosanvallon 2000).

Respect

In modern democratic societies, citizenship is formally universal, no longer confined to the rich or well-born, as in centuries past. Yet in practice universality is conditional on actual functioning. People are not accepted as full citizens simply because the government says so but because they live in a way that commands the respect of others. As communitarians say, citizens are constituted by the obligations they hold toward others (Sandel 1982).

Life in public involves what Hannah Arendt calls action, or the competitive display of excellence. In their interactions with others outside the home, Americans seek to win the esteem of others. Each lives in public on a stage in front of an audience of peers. Classically, the stage was politics, the Greek polis, where citizens debated the issues facing the community. Private life was essential to support citizens but too self-absorbed to be discussed in public. The family was the realm of necessity or survival, in which people were subject to "the biological life process." Only outside the home, above all in politics, were freedom and the "good life" really possible (Arendt 1958, 30, 36–37; Jaffa 1982, preface and introduction).

In modern Western societies, however, government is representative, and few citizens participate directly even at the local level. Only professional politicians and administrators usually experience competitive striving over public affairs. For average citizens, the chief arena for action is now the workplace. That is where, by displays of their own capacities, most Americans seek the affirmation of peers.[8] Employment has come to dominate American life. Many people find it more rewarding than private life. They are spending more and more time on the job, some think to the detriment of marriage and children (Hochschild 1997).

Some philosophers have grasped the enlarged importance of employment. Only the employed citizen, they say, has full standing in the society. But these interpreters tend to treat work as something that society must guarantee to its members, through measures to ensure full employment. It then becomes another right of citizenship, alongside social benefits, or voting or civil liberties (Shklar 1991, chap. 2; Arneson 1990, 1127–47). It is true that work cannot be expected unless acceptable jobs are available. But, to most Americans, work is first and foremost an obligation rather than a right. It is the chief competence that justifies claims. This means that it cannot be given to people, hence cannot be strictly guaranteed. Otherwise, it could not generate the respect, and self-respect, that it does (Moon 1988, chap. 2; Elster 1988).

Prior to welfare reform, many of the dependent poor, in effect, delegated their citizenship obligations to others. But only if people meet those duties personally do they merit respect. Work enforcement expects precisely that employable welfare recipients take back the burden to work that government has assumed for them. When they do that, a wider acceptance follows. Whether they leave welfare as a result is much less important (Mead 1986, chaps 10 and 11).

Narrowing the Welfare State

The vogue for work enforcement does imply some narrowing of the welfare state. Although traditionally welfare programs covered a variety of groups, reform suggests that Americans are increasingly unwilling to help the undeserving through government. The reason is not mainly resistance to the cost but rather the new insistence on the obligatory side of citizenship.

The usual academic view, associated with T. H. Marshall, is that the welfare state extends earlier forms of citizenship. Just as subjects obtained first civil and then political rights from rulers, so they now obtain social protections. To condition aid on work is then to revoke social rights and violate citizenship (see Marshall 1964, chapter 4).[9] But this view is plausible only if one understands citizenship to consist only of rights and claims. If we admit the obligatory side of citizenship—as Marshall did—then conditionality is consistent with an egalitarian social citizenship rather than opposed. Welfare reform enforces work precisely to reconcile dependency with the norms of citizenship (Mead 1997a).

Again, as communitarians say, equal citizenship is constituted by the obligations people recognize toward one another, not only by their rights. In an extreme form, as in Rousseau, a society of political equals might generate such strong mutual expectations that some people may be "forced to be free" (Rousseau 1755/1950, 18). Even a democratic society more wedded to freedom, such as ours, may finally have to choose between defending equal citizenship and supporting employable nonworkers. By enforcing work in TANF, America has clearly decided to value equal citizenship above the safety net, at least in this program.

The Incapacitated

Before reform, mothers received aid if they were needy and single and had children beneath a certain age; whether they had the capacity to work was not directly tested. With today's more severe work test, however, a welfare mother is normally expected to work unless disabled. Disability programs support people who can show that they are incapable of any gainful employment for at least a year. Ostensibly the standards are objective and medical, but in reality they are largely political, and some find them too lenient (Stone 1984). Thus exemption is achieved, but not without moral cost. The disabled will continue to bear some stigma unless their incapacity is physical and obvious.[10]

Even if the standards were uncontested, the claim to incapacity frees a person from work enforcement only at the level of diversion or reciprocity, not at the level of culture. A person granted disability cannot obtain the fuller acceptance that employment brings. She or he may be treated compassionately—but compassion is not egalitarian. It is the response of the fortunate to the less fortunate. It does not convey the esteem that actually meeting the work expectation does. Given public attitudes, this cost seems unavoidable.

The Undeserving

What about recipients who fail to work yet cannot establish disability? They are not deserving in either of the accepted senses—working or unable to work. The implication is that, as work tests tighten, they will get less and less aid from TANF. The same is often true in local general assistance programs, which typically cover single people who cannot prove disability. Half of the states with general assistance impose work tests; many also have recently cut benefits and eligibility, as few have done in TANF (Uccello and

Gallagher 1997). This reflects the judgment that the recipients are not unemployable and that jobs are available. That is plausible given the current low unemployment and many unskilled immigrants—legal and illegal—entering the country to take jobs. That view would change only if unemployment rose and immigration fell.

It appears that a democratic regime that takes equal citizenship seriously may simply be unable to aid the employable without violating its own standards. Aid as entitlement may simply be impolitic on any large scale as long as most Americans insist that the recipients earn their support by working. The constraint is not, as liberal commentators usually say, that the voters are ungenerous. Rather, they object morally to aiding people whose conduct appears to dishonor the society.

Fortunately, the curbing of entitlement in TANF has so far produced little hardship. Not only are most former recipients working, but the nonworkers have generally avoided destitution. One reason for this is that some other benefits, such as Food Stamps and Medicaid, are not subject to work tests. Government still treats these as an ultimate safety net unrelated to conduct. This is acceptable, in part, because in-kind aid is less subject to abuse than cash assistance.[11]

Another, more fundamental reason is that an affluent society offers sources of income other than welfare or employment—spouses, friends, neighbors, charity. In the past, these resources usually were inadequate to forestall destitution, one reason a public welfare state arose. With today's greater wealth, however, they often are adequate, as research on the finances of poor families shows (Edin and Lein 1997). Thus, the undeserving are likely to get by even if they neither work nor claim public aid. They will continue to pose an issue for society, and for those on whom they rely, but not so directly for public policy.

Charity can be a resource for the undeserving because it is often given out of religious beliefs that forbid judging the behavior of the recipients. The God who bestows life freely "on the just and on the unjust" (Matthew 5: 45) would have us do likewise. But the impulse that ignores desert cannot carry over to public assistance. That feeling, as Arendt says, is "worldless," "antipolitical," even destructive of the respect that citizens should feel toward one another (1958, 73–78, 236–43).[12]

Political Changes

Besides altering our sense of what citizenship means, welfare reform changed the tone of politics in parallel ways. The posture of demanding things from government on the basis of vulnerability has receded in favor of a more self-respecting style. Such a politics is likely to be more impersonal, more ideological, but also potentially more radical than what went before.

Curbing Complaint

Up through about 1960, American politics was conducted largely in terms of economic class.[13] The less well-off, including farmers, workers, and unionists, battled the affluent and business leaders. The first coalition favored government intervening further in the economy in order to equalize opportunities and rewards, while the second resisted. After 1960, groups defined in social rather than economic terms—minorities, women, and later gays—also sought improved treatment at the hands of government. All these causes were pressed initially by movements that arose outside government and made general arguments for greater nation action. While they appealed to hardships that government might assuage, the chief dispute was not over whether grievances existed but whether it was proper for government to respond. No one disputed that nonunionized workers earned low wages or that blacks had to use separate public facilities in southern towns. Rather, the issue was whether Washington should guarantee union rights or abolish Jim Crow. And government did concede all these claims, although gay rights are still only partially recognized.

After the civil rights era, these general issues receded in favor of complaints about concrete disadvantages. The watershed was the urban riots of the later 1960s and the sharp growth in crime and welfarism in the same years. From this point on, low-income groups such as the poor or racial minorities, or those speaking for them, rarely made broad demands for any new disposition of justice. Rather, they claimed to suffer mistreatment under the existing rules—racism or sexism, or a lack of jobs, child, or health care, or affordable housing. These problems, they alleged, were why the welfare rolls were growing and work levels falling in the inner city.

The complaining style reflected adversely on citizenship. The old claims of injustice had been voiced by sufferers who accepted some onus for changing things. They rejected how they were treated by the economy, but they accepted a responsibility to speak for themselves in politics. In this way they showed self-reliance, despite the demands they made on the regime. The gay movement displays that same style today. In contrast, claims by the poor, women, and nonwhites tend to be voiced, no longer by these groups themselves, but by self-appointed advocates. The activists appeal to the conscience of the regime, but they seldom, as in the old style, organize their followers against it. Their argument rests on the presumed vulnerability of the victims, rather than asserting some shared vision of a new society. As Wendy Brown writes, "much of the progressive political agenda in recent years has been concerned not with democratizing power but . . . with pressuring the state to buttress the rights and increase the entitlements of the socially vulnerable or disadvantaged" (1995, 5).

Complaint suffused the politics of welfare from the late 1960s through the 1980s. Advocates and most experts espoused the view that social barriers of various kinds explained the persistence of poverty and dependency. But in the political arena, the existence of these barriers was more disputed than the earlier, more visible inequities of low wages or Jim Crow. Many doubted whether the claimed deprivations were real or important. Indeed, inability to prove clearcut shortages of jobs, child care, or housing was one reason, alongside conservative politics, why government never accepted any broad responsibility to provide these things.

The larger problem was that once government accepted a wide responsibility for social problems, as it did in the 1960s and 1970s, it might well be overwhelmed with complaint. To deal with the needs of the poor or the elderly, or the entrenched problems of racial minorities, is to grapple with ultimate vulnerabilities, even with life and death. Such necessities tend to coerce the political process. They demand an immediate response, rejecting any deliberation, any balancing against other needs. Examples include the hurried expansion of antipoverty programs in the 1960s in response to urban unrest, the expansion of Food Stamps in the 1970s after the discovery of hunger in America, or the steady expansion of health access for the elderly, disabled, poor, and near-poor under Medicare and Medicaid. The expansion of Medicare to cover prescription drugs in 2003 occurred in the teeth of the looming bankruptcy of the program and mushrooming federal budget deficits. It was seen as politically imperative (Oberlander 2003, chapter 7).

A defining feature of modern politics, Arendt says, is that it has allowed such needs to flood into the public arena, which the ancients had shielded from them; "instead of carefully surrounding the human artifice with defenses against nature's elementary forces . . . we have channeled these forces, along with their elementary power, into the world itself" (Arendt, 1958, 133–34, 148–49). The result has been to foreclose action in Arendt's sense, for such needs resist deliberation. It has also been to undercut the common citizenship, for those who are known in public only for their needs cannot be the peers of those on whom they rely.

Welfare reform rebuked the complaining style. This was partly because the Republicans who took power in Washington after 1980 returned to the principled manner of the older politics. Ronald Reagan and congressional Republicans cut and reformed government on ideological grounds, rejecting activists' complaints. In PRWORA, the GOP boldly recast welfare, rebuffing predictions of hardship (Ellwood 1996; Bane 1997; Edelman 1997). The positive results of reform vindicated them against their critics. The supposed barriers did not prevent a majority of welfare families from leaving the rolls and going to work, once the work demand was clear.

Complaint is now in eclipse in social politics. Future claims to disadvantage will face a tougher burden of proof.[14] It is now once again improper to make claims in politics simply on the basis of needs. Issues cannot be framed simply in terms of victims and oppressors. Claimants must make some appeal to the interests of others, as the earlier social reform movements did. That requires a less intimate and more impersonal style. Government can do some things for the less fortunate, but it cannot bear the full weight of the human condition. Unlike charity, the main purpose of a social policy cannot be to assuage private pain. Rather, it is to sustain the capacities of citizens (Anderson 1999). This welfare reform is helping to do.

Liberating Politics

Although welfare reform curbed the politics of complaint, it also opened the door to a revived popular politics. Advocates and some liberal politicians continue to oppose reform, but most elected Democrats abandoned that cause once the good effects of change were clear. Reform, then, was a defeat for the left. At the same time, reform removed an albatross from around its neck. Democrats were freed from the need to defend traditional welfare. Rather than speaking for the dependent, they could now defend the working poor or working families, which was what many welfare cases had become. This was immensely more popular. It made exactly the appeal to a broad interest that the earlier complaints lacked. The way is open to a revived politics of economic justice focused on equality rather than social problems.

Furthermore, the new working families that emerged from reform were potentially more formidable than the old dependent class. Some authors have attempted to portray claiming welfare benefits as a form of political action (Piven and Cloward 1993; Soss 2000). But in conventional politics, recipients and the poor participate very little, as voters or otherwise. Workers are more likely to participate than nonworkers (Rosenstone 1982). They also are more troubled by barriers than the nonworking, precisely because they are moving ahead in life. They are far more able to demand help from government than nonworkers. By generating more struggling workers, therefore, welfare reform could shift political outcomes to the left.

Social politics moved that way as soon as the welfare rolls started to fall in 1994. Although the Republicans took over Congress in that year with an antigovernment agenda, they quickly moved toward the center. As part of welfare reform, Washington sharply raised subsidies for low-income wages and child care. The minimum wage was raised in 1996 and 1997. In 2000, George W. Bush was elected president as a compassionate conservative, and the school reform he championed involved significant new spending.[15] In 2003, a Republican Congress approved an expansion of Medicare to cover prescription drugs, and in 2004 Democratic candidates for president proposed expanded health coverage for children and workers.

It is true that other Bush policies are more conservative, involving tax cuts that benefited the rich and proposals to partially privatize Social Security. But public animus against big government is less heated today than it was a decade ago. Meanwhile, Democrats have moved left. They have chosen more liberal leaders in Congress. Their presidential candidates for 2004 all promised to reverse the Bush tax cuts, in whole or in part. Howard Dean became the front-runner for the nomination by taking highly partisan stances. The eventual nominees, John Kerry and John Edwards, spoke of an America divided by class much more freely than Bill Clinton would have done.

If that shift is not larger, the chief reason is that lower-income Americans do not vote and join unions or political campaigns as much as they once did. Nor do movements for social reform arise among the less fortunate outside government. This deprives the American left of the secure base that it had from the New Deal era through the 1960s. That forced Democratic leaders such as Clinton to move their party to the right. The reasons for this passivity are unclear (Bok 2001, chapters 7 and 13; Mead 2004b). Nevertheless, by shifting the focus of social policy from welfare to low-wage workers, welfare reform has helped to open the door to change.

But Is It Just?

Alongside welfare rights advocates, several philosophers argue that work enforcement is unjust. I now consider these charges, starting with the broadest and moving on to those that are narrower. While there are philosophic rejoinders, the best response, I believe, is simply that these positions are impolitic in current American conditions. Welfare reform does involve moral risks, but these seem a price worth paying to enforce common citizenship and thus help integrate the poor.

Entitlement

The most common objection to reform is that it overthrew entitlement, or the policy of giving families aid simply on the basis of need. Now welfare was available only to needy people who also behaved in specified ways, such as working. Critics feel that conditional aid is not really aid at all. Something in the nature of the welfare state requires that aid be given unconditionally. Critics appeal to the Marshallian idea that social benefits are an extension of earlier forms of citizenship. Just as civil and political rights are given without serious behavioral conditions, so should rights to welfare (King and Waldron 1988; Gaffaney 2000).[16] Or, if the welfare state is really to be a safety net against the insecurities of capitalism, it cannot demand performance as the market does. These arguments, long made by Richard Titmuss and other socialist theorists (1968; Deacon 2002), are restated in Philippe Van Parijs's recent case for an unconditional basic income (1991; 1995). Similar sentiments explain the reluctance of European socialists to work-condition welfare, although some have accepted the idea.

On the other side are philosophers who find it fair that recipients should bear some burden for what society gives them, at least if they are employable. Once obligations are brought into the picture, entitlement seems one-sided (Carens 1986; Gouldner 1960; White 2003). At most, one can contest the specific shape that reciprocity takes in welfare reform. Perhaps the obligation to work should bear on the recipients not at the time they are dependent, but at some different time, or on other people entirely (Goodin 2002).

The philosophical debate, however, fails to answer the visceral force of the public demand to enforce work in welfare. People regard the non-working poor, not just as free riders, but as parasites, even betrayers of their society. Philosophers, even those who embrace work tests, discuss the issue too antiseptically, in terms of the rights and duties of individuals. This reflects the economistic style of recent liberal political theory. The public, however, thinks in more communitarian terms, where citizens are defined by whether they honor—or dishonor—their ties to others. That demand seeks from the poor not just work but a fundamental reliability that will engender the trust and respect needed to build a common society (Bowles and Gintis 1999).

Those feelings are strong enough so that we should question whether the welfare state ever really embraced entitlement. Even T. H. Marshall, to whom the critics appeal, expressed concern that generous aid might undercut social discipline. "It is no easy matter to revive the sense of personal obligation to work," he wrote, after social rights to support are established (1964, 130). Other early theorists of welfare—such as Beatrice and Sidney Webb, R. H. Tawney, and William Beveridge—expressed similar qualms. They anticipated a need to balance rights with obligations in welfare, and thus to enforce work (White 2003, 137–40).

Indeed, in Europe as in the United States, benefit systems for the employable have long contained rules that the recipients should seek and accept work. Merely, these demands were not well enforced during the era of entitlement that followed World War II, often out of a belief that many claimants were unemployable or jobs were unavailable. But the more the dependent poor have become a separate caste, the more pressure to enforce work has revived. Although work tests are toughest in American family aid, they are stiffening in Europe too, especially for youth and the male unemployed. Here, too, the main motivation is to defend a common citizenship and avoid social division (Lødemel and Trickey 2001). Entitlement, at least for the employable, never was a principle of the welfare state but rather a mistaken practice that government is now correcting.

One can also justify entitlement on grounds other than rights. Robert Goodin argues that the needy have a claim to support on grounds of what he calls their vulnerability. This approach extends the sort of obligation people feel toward their families to encompass the distressed in the wider society (Goodin 1985, 1988). It is a secular version of the religious case for charity. The problem again is charity's worldless character, the offense it poses to equal citizenship. Churches might help the undeserving on this basis, but it is difficult to see how a popular government can do so.

Care Work

Some other advocates of welfare rights make a case distinct from entitlement. They say that a single mother should get support, not without conditions, but in return for raising her own child. Care giving is seen as a social function that should satisfy the work test, even if the task is unpaid other than by welfare.

In principle, this case is plausible. As Stuart White argues, the work obligation requires that people perform some kind of civic labor that contributes to the community. It need not be confined to paid employment. However, civic labor must meet two conditions. First, it must be accountable to the wider society. "It is not enough that I regard the work I do as valuable to others. It must indeed be so, and, indeed, it must be recognizable as such by them." Caregivers must see themselves as trustees for the wider community. Second, civic laborers must perform their task well enough to serve a public interest. In return for support, caretakers would be "responsible for raising children in ways that serve the public good," that is, by helping to "nurture the virtues and capacities relevant to effective citizenship" (White 2003, 99, 111).

The problem is that, under AFDC, the mother raising her own child was not accountable in this way. She had a child, and then claimed society's support to raise it. Society did not assign her this task. Rather, it faced a fait accompli. To save the child, in which it has a clear interest, it had to fund the mother as well. In a world where most mothers work, even single mothers, a claim to support on this unilateral basis did not strike most people as necessary or fair.

I could as well ask society to support me in some task that I find important—such as writing this essay. That claim may seem trivial next to saving a child, but the point here is its self-chosen character. For accountability to exist, civic labor must be assigned by someone other than the welfare claimant. To take jobs offered by private employers or government satisfies that standard; raising one's own child does not. For a woman to claim support to care for needy relatives or for other people's children is more justifiable, precisely because here the task is less self-chosen.

Nor does funding welfare mothers clearly serve a social interest. Currently, social oversight of mothers, either on or off welfare, is very limited. Only if they are visibly neglectful or abusive does society intervene and put the children in foster care. For government to pay single mothers to raise their own children should demand a higher standard. Whether welfare mothers could qualify is doubtful. On average, the offspring of poor single mothers emerge from childhood with significant disadvantages, for reasons going beyond the mothers' low income (Mayer 1997). White suggests that government can train the mother so that she will be a competent caregiver, but programs to improve the skills of disadvantaged mothers in any respect show very limited effects (White 2003, 111 n. 27; Maynard 1997). Further, to call for training shifts the onus for functioning to government, leaving the mother still unaccountable.

A fair conclusion, embodied in current policy, is that society has an interest in saving the children of poor mothers, diverting them to foster care if necessary. But it does not have an interest in subsidizing single mothers to raise their own children. That situation it disapproves of, on good grounds, even if it is unwilling to enforce marriage. The mother may still receive aid, but only if she establishes accountability on another basis—employment outside the home, if necessary in a government job. This work will be in addition to her care giving. Fortunately, there is no contradiction with care giving, because evaluations show that requiring mothers to work in return for aid has little effect on children. Thus, expecting work of the mothers is not inconsistent with serving the children also.[17]

What counts as civic labor is finally a political question. The need for a contribution to society in return for aid is a lot clearer than what that contribution should be (Becker 1980, 42–43, 47–49; White 2003, 113–16, 125). In Europe, the argument that child rearing is comparable to work still persuades. In America, at present, it does not.

Preconditions

One may also accept work enforcement in principle, but tie it to certain preconditions that lie outside the work obligation as such. The conditions listed by Stuart White, the main exponent of this position, are that jobs pay enough to avoid poverty and offer challenges beyond the merely menial, also that care work be recognized and that the idle rich be obligated to work as well as the poor (White 2003, 134–37).[18] I have already addressed carework and will address the idle rich. The question here is whether the jobs offered by welfare reform are good enough to justify requiring recipients to take them.

Most conservatives would say that White's conditions are already met. At least in the last decade, jobs have been widely available to most welfare recipients. Initial jobs typically pay above the minimum wage and above the poverty line, provided one works full-time and claims remaining benefits such as Food Stamps, Medicaid, and the EITC. Low-skilled women who work steadily realize wage gains over time comparable to those of better-off women (see chapter 2).[19] Many liberals, however, find the conditions unmet because the initial jobs are often menial and the workers often remain below poverty given the hours they actually work.

The real issue here is not what the labor market offers but how energetically welfare adults can respond to it. If one expects them to exploit the available jobs for all they are worth, as conservatives assume, then White's conditions are clearly met for the vast majority of recipients. But if one accepts more limited and more passive effort as adequate, then most available jobs are inadequate. Thus, whether the market is good enough already depends on the work obligation one assumes. Judgments about how demanding to be reflect, in turn, the linked judgments earlier referred to, that observers make about how feasible work is and how competent the poor are.

Liberals say jobs must be improved before the recipients will accept the work test as fair. Conservatives say the energy they expect has been normal for new entrants to employment, such as immigrants, in earlier American history. Finally, how demanding the work obligation should be is a political question. Currently, policy and opinion endorse conservative views, and these views have proven practicable (Mead 1988; 1992, chaps. 4–6).[20]

Also, preconditions about acceptable jobs assume that we can design an optimal work system from scratch. But we are not now in a state of nature, if we ever were. Society is ongoing. How attractive jobs must be is a political question to be debated by citizens in full standing. Right now, full standing for the employable requires that they work in existing jobs. As one sign of that, government is doing more for the working, not the nonworking poor, as shown earlier.

One cannot negotiate for better jobs in advance of enforcing work, which is what liberal critics attempt to do. Only after nonworkers enter existing jobs can they contest the standards for employment and try to raise them. This is what the labor movement did. In American politics, claims to equality cannot be made from outside the labor force.

Paternalism

After these more philosophic objections to work tests come several counters that have to do less with the work obligation as such than with the way it is applied. Something about making people work seems to impugn them compared to others and thus to undercut equal citizenship.

One such objection is that work enforcement is paternalist. Most often, work enforcement is justified as serving a social interest, but advocates sometimes claim that it serves the interest of the poor as well. It makes them do what they ought to do for their own sake. However, they are unable to do this on their own; they need guidance and constraint, not just opportunity. Some localities, such as Wisconsin, have monitored recipients closely to be sure they meet work expectations (Mead 1997b; 2004a, chap. 8). But to enforce work on this basis contravenes John Stuart Mill's harm principle. Mill wrote that "the only purpose for which power can be rightfully exercised over any member of a civilized community, against his will, is to prevent harm to others. His own good, either physical or moral, is not a sufficient warrant" (1859/1961, 197).[21]

One response is that Mill presumes that people have the competence to achieve their own self-interest. His rule, he notes, "is meant to apply only to human beings in the maturity of their faculties. . . . Those who are still in a state to require being taken care of by others, must be protected against their own action" (1859/1961, 197). He is speaking of children, but the same must be said of many welfare adults. Surveys demonstrate that recipients have desires to work and improve their lives that echo those of better-off Americans. But these values often fail to govern their behavior. When they are required to work, therefore, they are not being coerced but pressed to live up to their own intentions. Many recipients seem to appreciate that pressure, rather than resenting it (Mead 1997c).[22]

It is true that paternalism reflects adversely on the dignity of citizens, but a failure to work is widely judged to be worse. To require work seems the only way to restore commonality. So the regime's usual respect for autonomy is set aside in favor of enforcing the common obligations. In the end, we will subordinate freedom to functioning, became a capacity to function is the prerequisite of freedom (Mead 1986, 254–58).

Invidiousness

Even if it is constructive, however, the work demand may seem invidious because it is made only of people on welfare. To single them out belies claims that working is necessary for equal citizenship. What about the idle rich, those who need not work because of their independent income? They are shielded from work tests because they never need aid (White 2003, 136–37; King 1995, 1999).[23] This group could be said to include the minority of mothers who stay at home to raise children, because their spouses earn enough to support them.

One response is that the rich today are typically not idle. On average, they work much harder than the poor. In 2002, the last year available, only 49 percent of family heads in the bottom fifth of the income distribution worked at all, only 24 percent full-year and full-time, and there was less than one worker per family. But in the top fifth, 90 percent worked, 74 percent full-year and full-time, and there were more than two workers per household. In the top 5 percent, the last two of these figures were slightly lower, suggesting that at the very top work levels might decline slightly.[24] The vast bulk of nonworkers, however, clearly lie at the bottom of society, not the top. However, as White notes, this does not satisfy the objection of principle.

The reach of explicit work enforcement could be widened beyond welfare. Some would require that parents work if necessary to support their children, even off welfare, provided certain preconditions were met (Gutmann and Thompson 1996, 297, 300–1). Government already does this to some extent by enforcing child support payment by absent parents. In large part, these obligations impinge on the departed fathers of welfare families, so they parallel the work obligations now levied on the mothers. But again, the impact is mostly on the poor, and not everyone has to work.

The consistent response would be to enforce work on everyone, including the idle rich. Surprisingly, this was the stance taken by Russell Long, chairman of the Senate Finance Committee, when he faced the issue during hearings on welfare reform in 1971. "I am an old share-the-wealth man," he remarked, and "I would also favor sharing the burden" (U.S. Congress 1972, 2601–3). But politically, there is little support for this. Few ordinary Americans resent the rich, provided fair opportunity to get ahead is available to them (Lane 1962; Rainwater 1974). They do not demand that nonworking spouses in a family take jobs, provided the family does not draw public aid.

Americans seem to combine a communitarian ethic for the poor with a Lockean attitude above that level. That is, they insist that the dependent display recognized civilities such as working, and they accept public obligations, including aid and services, to help bring this about. The image is Rousseauian, of a society defined by a common citizenship embracing both rights and duties. But above the welfare level, individuals are presumed to pursue their own advantage, hedged in only by what Mark Roelofs calls the legal cage of the regime (1976, chaps. 2 and 4). They need only obey the law. There is much less concern about whether people behave well. If they avoid dependency, it is assumed, they must be functioning well enough. Tolerance takes over from the scrutiny visited on the poor.

The thinking is not entirely consistent, but it is realistic. Problems of coping are concentrated at the bottom of society, not the top. Work has to be enforced on the dependent, in part simply because welfare would otherwise give them a chance to avoid work that most other people do not have. The behavior of the rich does raise moral issues, but these have to do more with justice and equality. The question is whether the rich get too much out of the society, not whether they meet behavioral standards. The answer is not to make the rich work but to tax or regulate them, an issue to be resolved separately from welfare.

A partial reconciliation follows from the different levels of work enforcement mentioned earlier. Although the idle rich escape work obligations at the levels of diversion or reciprocity, they do not escape at the level of culture. They are visible figures in a society preoccupied with employment. Any that do not work are bound to confront questions from friends and associates about what they do for a living. Stay-at-home moms face no formal pressure to work, but do face informal pressure to develop careers outside the home, one reason many get involved in community activities, even on an unpaid basis.

The work test is invidious only if one believes that only government enforces work, that these unofficial pressures do not count. The public thinks they do count. The rich man who puts in long hours in an office on Wall Street is seen as morally equivalent to the welfare recipient on workfare who is made to sweep the street outside (Mead 1986, 237–40).

Discretion

A final challenge to reform concerns the discretion involved in implementing it. In applying welfare rules to cases, officials have some leeway in deciding who gets aid and who does not. The charge that welfare administration violates the rule of law was a criticism long made of AFDC. In the 1960s, the welfare rights movement aimed to restrict this discretion. Through regulatory changes and Supreme Court decisions, it largely succeeded. In the 1970s and 1980s, welfare administration became bound by rules, whose main goal was to determine eligibility and benefits accurately; motivating the recipient to leave aid secondary (Bane and Ellwood 1994, chap. 1).

Welfare reform can seem like a return to arbitrariness. Some judgment is inevitable in deciding which cases will and will not have to work for aid. And because PRWORA revoked the federal entitlement to welfare, decisions by administrators are harder to challenge in court than formerly. Will more be asked of families than they can cope with? The confusion that surrounded the institution of radical work tests in Wisconsin supports such fears (Mead 2004a, chap. 7). But evidence has not yet appeared showing that discretion has led to systematic abuses.

Administrators have more personal power over recipients than they did under entitlement, but they need it to convey work demands to clients in a forceful way. Passive administrators lead to passive clients; more active ones help raise work levels. Despite this, discretion is limited because the new work rules have been set largely by federal and state legislators, not left for caseworkers to decide. Mostly, they were added to the former rules on determining benefits, and welfare remains legalistic (Gais et al. 2001, 43–48, 62–63).

Conclusion

The objections to work tests all have some point, but do they outweigh the gains to justice and utility achieved by work enforcement, even for the poor themselves?[25] In a different society, one might conclude that. But in America as it is, the gains from having more poor adults fulfill the common obligations appear dominant. That is because in America employment has to do with citizenship, not just economics. Defending a common citizenship is an imperative of the regime, one that must be satisfied before economic goals.

When adult citizens enter the workforce, they not only obtain higher incomes; more important, they gain the trust and respect of fellow citizens. From this higher rewards will follow, from both the public and the private sectors. Create citizens first and a solution to poverty will follow. That is the implication of welfare reform to date. Politics, not economics, is the master science.

I acknowledge helpful comments on prior drafts of this chapter from my co-editor, other authors of this volume, and anonymous reviewers.

Notes

1. The following is based on chapter 1 of this volume, which summarizes many studies.
2. Quality control, or the attempt to keep ineligible recipients off the rolls, has been an important theme of reform only in New York City.
3. Kathleen Mullan Harris found that 51 percent of welfare mothers from 1984 to 1986 worked at some time while on the rolls (1993, 317–52). But according to U.S. Congress, only 5 to 8 percent claimed to be working, even part-time, from 1983 to 1994 when surveyed by the government (1996, 474). In research from 1989 to 1992, Kathryn Edin and Laura Lein report that welfare mothers often have unreported earnings (1997, chapter 2).
4. Data from the U.S. Administration for Children and Families.
5. This is a principal theme of Mead (1992).
6. These include Supplemental Security Income (SSI), which is means-tested, and Disability Insurance, which is part of Social Security.
7. The work obligation might in principle be satisfied by civic labor other than work, but the conditions for this are demanding.
8. Arendt's *Human Condition* (1958) treats labor as a threat to action because of its coercive and elemental character, focused on survival. She was thinking of physical labor or mindless, repetitive jobs on industrial production lines. Today's employment is less often physical, more likely to call for initiative and problem-solving. Even menial service jobs involve a good deal of interaction with other people. So work today, compared to the past, is likelier to elicit qualities of intellect and character that are widely admired.
9. The chapters by King and Pateman in this volume take a similar position.
10. Amy L. Wax makes a similar point in her chapter in this volume.
11. Food Stamps has work tests on the books, but they are less demanding than TANF's and they have not yet been seriously enforced (see also chapter 1).
12. For contrary views that a religious response should expect more than this of the poor, see Marvin Olasky (1992) and my chapters in Mary Jo Bane and Lawrence M. Mead (2003).
13. The following extends Mead 1992, chaps. 2, 10, and 11; 1998, 72–76).
14. Currently, the only social disadvantage that is widely credited is a lack of health coverage for over 40 million people. Lack of actual health care is less clear, because those who are not covered usually get acute care when they need it on a charity basis at hospital emergency rooms.

15. Not all the funds authorized have been appropriated by Congress, but funding still increased.
16. Carole Pateman and Desmond King make similar arguments in chapters 2 and 3 of this volume. Of course, citizenship is already conditional in ways William Galston details in chapter 5; but these conditions affect few people and are not widely perceived.
17. For child and family effects, see chapter 1. I admit the caveat that how much work can be expected of mothers early in a child's life is still open to some question (see chapters 7 and 9). One might well expect a mother to work less than normal hours, perhaps half-time, in deference to her family responsibilities. However, about half of single mothers with children already work full-time (U.S. Census Bureau 2003, table 15; 2004, table POV15).
18. For a similar argument, see Gutmann and Thompson (1996). An argument that "hard" and "dirty work" poses an issue for justice also appears in Michael Walzer (1983).
19. According to White, it is enough for job adequacy if work is meaningful "over the full course of a working life," not necessarily in every job (2003, 89 n. 23).
20. White senses this issue in saying that I assume too "thick" a theory of economic rationality on the part of the poor (2003, 149–52).
21. For a similar position, see Desmond King (1995; 1999; chap. 3, this volume).
22. Paternalism is limited under PRWORA because reliance on aid must be time-limited.
23. See also White and King's chapters in this volume.
24. A gap was clearer in 2001 than 2002 (see U.S. Census Bureau 2002, table FINC-06; 2003, table FINC-06).
25. This is a valuable question Stuart White poses in chapter 4 of this volume.

References

Anderson, Elizabeth S. 1999. "What Is the Point of Equality?" *Ethics* 109(2): 287–337.

Arendt, Hannah. 1958. *The Human Condition.* Chicago: University of Chicago Press.

Arneson, Richard J. 1990. "Is Work Special? Justice and the Distribution of Employment." *American Political Science Review* 84(4): 1127–47.

Bane, Mary Jo. 1997. "Welfare as We Might Know It." *The American Prospect.* 30(January): 47–53.

Bane, Mary Jo, and David T. Ellwood. 1994. *Welfare Realities: From Rhetoric to Reform.* Cambridge, Mass.: Harvard University Press.

Bane, Mary Jo, and Lawrence M. Mead. 2003. *Lifting Up the Poor: A Dialogue on Religion, Poverty & Welfare Reform.* Washington, D.C.: Brookings Institution.

Becker, Lawrence C. 1980. "The Obligation to Work." *Ethics* 91(1, October): 35–49.

Bok, Derek. 2001. *The Trouble with Government.* Cambridge, Mass.: Harvard University Press.

Bowles, Samuel, and Herbert Gintis. 1999. "Is Equality Passé: *Homo reciprocans* and the Future of Egalitarian Politics." *Boston Review* 23(December/January): 4–10.

Brown, Wendy. 1995. *States of Injury: Power and Freedom in Late Modernity.* Princeton, N.J.: Princeton University Press.

Carens, Joseph H. 1986. "Rights and Duties in an Egalitarian Society." *Political Theory* 14(1): 31–49.

Deacon, Alan. 2002. *Perspectives on Welfare: Ideas, Ideologies, and Policy Debates.* Buckingham, U.K.: Open University Press.

Edelman, Peter. 1997. "The Worst Thing Bill Clinton Has Done." *Atlantic Monthly*(March): 43–58.

Edin, Kathryn, and Laura Lein. 1997. *Making Ends Meet: How Single Mothers Survive Welfare and Low-Wage Work.* New York: Russell Sage Foundation.

Ellwood, David T. 1996. "Welfare Reform As I Knew It: When Bad Things Happen to Good Policies." *The American Prospect* 26(May–June): 22–29.

Elster, Jon. 1988. "Is There (or Should There Be) a Right to Work?" In *Democracy and the Welfare State,* edited by Amy Gutmann. Princeton, N.J.: Princeton University Press.

Farkas, Steve, and Jean Johnson, with Will Friedman and Ali Beers. 1996. *The Values We Live By: What Americans Want From Welfare Reform.* New York: Public Agenda Foundation.

Gaffaney, Timothy J. 2000. *Freedom for the Poor: Welfare and the Foundations of Democratic Citizenship.* Boulder, Colo.: Westview Press.

Gais, Thomas L., Richard P. Nathan, Irene Lurie, and Thomas Kaplan. 2001. "Implementation of the Personal Responsibility Act of 1996." In *The New World of Welfare,* edited by Rebecca Blank and Ron Haskins. Washington, D.C.: Brookings Institution.

Gans, Herbert J. 1995. *The War Against the Poor: The Underclass and Antipoverty Policy.* New York: Basic Books.

Gilens, Martin. 1999. *Why Americans Hate Welfare: Race, Media, and the Politics of Antipoverty Policy.* Chicago: University of Chicago Press.

Goodin, Robert E. 1985. *Protecting the Vulnerable: A Reanalysis of Our Social Responsibilities.* Chicago: University of Chicago Press.

———. 1988. *Reasons for Welfare: The Political Theory of the Welfare State.* Princeton, N.J.: Princeton University Press.

———. 2002. "Structures of Mutual Obligation." *Journal of Social Policy* 31(4): 579–96.

Gouldner, Alvin W. 1960. "The Norm of Reciprocity: A Preliminary Statement." *American Sociological Review* 25(2): 161–78.

Gutmann, Amy, and Dennis Thompson. 1996. *Democracy and Disagreement.* Cambridge, Mass.: Harvard University Press.

Harris, Kathleen Mullan. 1993. "Work and Welfare Among Single Mothers in Poverty," *American Journal of Sociology* 99(2): 317–52.

Hochschild, Arlie Russell. 1997. *The Time Bind: When Work Becomes Home and Home Becomes Work.* New York: Metropolitan Books.

Jaffa, Harry V. 1982. *Crisis of the House Divided: An Interpretation of the Issues in the Lincoln-Douglas Debates.* Chicago: University of Chicago Press.

John Paul II (Pope). 1981. *Encyclical Letter Laborem Exercens* (On Human Work). September 14. Rome: Vatican City.

King, Desmond S. 1995. *Actively Seeking Work? The Politics of Unemployment and Welfare Policy in the United States and Great Britain.* Chicago: University of Chicago Press.

———. 1999. *In the Name of Liberalism: Illiberal Social Policy in The United States and Britain.* Oxford: Oxford University Press.

King, Desmond S., and Jeremy Waldron. 1988. "Citizenship, Social Citizenship and the Defence of Welfare Provision." *British Journal of Political Science* 18(4): 415–43.

Lane, Robert E. 1962. *Political Ideology: Why the American Common Man Believes What He Does.* New York: Free Press.

Lødemel, Ivar, and Heather Trickey, eds. 2001. *"An Offer You Can't Refuse": Workfare in International Perspective.* Bristol, U.K.: Policy Press.

Marshall, T. H. 1964. "Citizenship and Social Class." In *Class, Citizenship, and Social Development: Essays by T. H. Marshall,* introduction by Seymour Martin Lipset. Garden City, N.Y.: Doubleday.

Mayer, Susan E. 1997. *What Money Can't Buy: Family Income and Children's Life Chances.* Cambridge, Mass.: Harvard University Press.

Maynard, Rebecca A. 1997. "Paternalism, Teenage Pregnancy Prevention, and Teenage Parent Services." In *The New Paternalism: Supervisory Approaches to Poverty,* edited by Lawrence M. Mead. Washington, D.C.: Brookings Institution.

Mead, Lawrence M. 1986. *Beyond Entitlement: The Social Obligations of Citizenship.* New York: Free Press.

———. 1988. "The Hidden Jobs Debate." *The Public Interest* 91(spring): 40–58.

———. 1992. *The New Politics of Poverty: The Nonworking Poor in America.* New York: Basic Books.

———. 1997a. "Citizenship and Social Policy: T. H. Marshall and Poverty." *Social Philosophy and Policy* 14(2): 197–230.

———. 1997b. "The Rise of Paternalism." In *New Paternalism: Supervisory Approaches to Poverty,* edited by Lawrence M. Mead. Washington, D.C.: Brookings Institution.

———. 1997c. "Welfare Employment." In *The New Paternalism: Supervisory Approaches to Poverty,* edited by Lawrence M. Mead. Washington, D.C.: Brookings Institution.

———. 1998. "The Politics of Disadvantage." *Society* 35(5): 72–76.

———. 2001. "The Politics of Conservative Welfare Reform." In *The New World of Welfare,* edited by Rebecca Blank and Ron Haskins. Washington, D.C.: Brookings Institution.

———. 2004a. *Government Matters: Welfare Reform in Wisconsin.* Princeton, N.J.: Princeton University Press.

———. 2004b. "The Great Passivity." *Perspectives on Politics* 2(4): 671–75.

Mill, John Stuart. 1859/1961. "On Liberty." In *The Philosophy of John Stuart Mill: Ethical, Political, and Religious,* edited by Marshall Cohen. New York: Modern Library.

Mink, Gwendolyn. 1998. *Welfare's End.* Ithaca, N.Y.: Cornell University Press.

Moon, J. Donald. 1988. "The Moral Basis of the Democratic Welfare State." In *Democracy and the Welfare State,* edited by Amy Gutmann. Princeton, N.J.: Princeton University Press.

Morone, James A. 2003. "American Ways of Welfare." *Perspectives on Politics* 1(1): 137–46.

Murray, Charles. 1984. *Losing Ground: American Social Policy, 1950–1980.* New York: Basic Books.

Oberlander, Jonathan. 2003. *The Political Life of Medicare.* Chicago: University of Chicago Press.

Offe, Claus. 1988. "Democracy Against the Welfare State? Structural Foundations of Neoconservative Political Opportunities." In *Responsibility, Rights, and Welfare: The Theory of the Welfare State,* edited by J. Donald Moon. Boulder, Colo.: Westview Press.

Olasky, Marvin. 1992. *The Tragedy of American Compassion.* Wheaton, Ill.: Crossway Books.

Piven, Frances Fox, and Richard A. Cloward. 1993. *Regulating the Poor: The Functions of Public Welfare,* rev. ed. New York: Vintage.

Pole, J. R. 1978. *The Pursuit of Equality in American History.* Berkeley: University of California Press.

Rainwater, Lee. 1974. *What Money Buys: Inequality and the Social Meanings of Income.* New York: Basic Books.

Rieder, Jonathan. 1985. *Canarsie: The Jews and Italians of Brooklyn Against Liberalism.* Cambridge, Mass.: Harvard University Press.

Roelofs, H. Mark. 1976. *Ideology and Myth in American Politics: A Critique of a National Political Mind.* Boston, Mass.: Little, Brown.

Rosanvallon, Pierre. 2000. *The New Social Question: Rethinking the Welfare State,* translated by Barbara Harshaw. Princeton, N.J.: Princeton University Press.

Rosenstone, Steven J. 1982. "Economic Adversity and Voter Turnout." *American Journal of Political Science* 26(1): 25–46.

Rousseau, Jean Jacques. 1755/1950. *The Social Contract and Discourses.* New York: Everyman.

Sandel, Michael J. 1982. *Liberalism and the Limits of Justice.* Cambridge: Cambridge University Press.

———. 1996. *Democracy's Discontent: America in Search of a Public Philosophy.* Cambridge, Mass.: Harvard University Press.

Schram, Sanford F. 2000. *After Welfare: The Culture of Postindustrial Social Policy.* New York: New York University Press.

Shklar, Judith N. 1991. *American Citizenship: The Quest for Inclusion.* Cambridge, Mass.: Harvard University Press.

Sleeper, Jim. 1990. *The Closest of Strangers: Liberalism and the Politics of Race in New York.* New York: W. W. Norton.

Soss, Joe. 2000. *Unwanted Claims: The Politics of Participation in the U.S. Welfare System.* Ann Arbor: University of Michigan Press.

Stone, Deborah A. 1984. *The Disabled State.* Philadelphia: Temple University Press.

Titmuss, Richard M. 1968. *Commitment to Welfare.* London: Allen and Unwin.

Uccello, Cori E., and L. Jerome Gallagher. 1997. "General Assistance Programs: The State-Based Part of the Safety Net." Assessing New Federalism: Issues and Options for States. Number A-4. Washington, D.C.: Urban Institute.

U.S. Census Bureau. 1994. *Current Population Survey for March 1994.* Washington: U.S. Government Printing Office.

———. 2000. *Current Population Survey for March 2000.* Washington: U.S. Government Printing Office.

———. 2002. *Annual Demographic Survey.* Washington: U.S. Government Printing Office.

———. 2003. *Annual Demographic Survey.* Washington: U.S. Government Printing Office.

———. 2004. *Annual Demographic Survey*. Washington: U.S. Government Printing Office.

U.S. Congress, House [Ways and Means]. 1996. *Green Book: Background Material, and Data on Programs Within the Jurisdiction of the Committee on Ways and Means.* Washington: U.S. Government Printing Office.

U.S. Congress, Senate, Committee on Finance. 1972. *Social Security Amendments of 1971, Hearings* before the Committee on Finance, 92nd Cong., 1971–2, February 9, 1972.

Van Parijs, Philippe. 1991. "Why Surfers Should Be Fed: The Liberal Case for an Unconditional Basic Income," *Philosophy and Public Affairs* 20(2): 101–31.

———. 1995. *Real Freedom for All: What (If Anything) Can Justify Capitalism?* New York: Oxford University Press.

Walzer, Michael.1983. *Spheres of Justice: A Defense of Pluralism and Equality.* New York: Basic Books.

White, Stuart. 2003. *The Civic Minimum: On the Rights and Obligations of Economic Citizenship.* Oxford: Oxford University Press.

Chapter 9

The Political Psychology of Redistribution: Implications for Welfare Reform

AMY L. WAX

FOLLOWING DECADES of attempts to overhaul the federal system of poor relief, President Clinton signed a bill in 1996 that repealed the New Deal program of Aid to Families with Dependent Children (AFDC) and replaced it with Temporary Assistance for Needy Families (TANF). Although the revised statute left some welfare programs untouched,[1] it transformed poor relief for most families by incorporating strict time limits and mandatory work requirements. The lifetime limit on federal cash assistance for families is now fixed at sixty months. Recipients must engage in part-time work and move toward full-time employment to remain qualified for benefits (see Bloom 1997, 74–77; Loffredo and Hershkoff 1997).[2] In the wake of these reforms, many beneficiaries have left the welfare rolls altogether, while many others receive some public assistance under various state and federal programs to supplement their (often meager) earnings at low wage jobs.

Do these reforms embody a radical shift in our nation's concept of equality, citizenship, and the role of the state? My attempt to answer these sweeping questions begins with public opinion. Popular attitudes about the redistribution of resources in our society are dominated by the idea of conditional reciprocity. This concept finds expression in the group's commitment to assist the poor, but only if those seeking help have made a reasonable effort to support themselves or are unable to contribute to their own support. I call this norm conditional because circumstances dictate how literally it is enforced (see, for example, Wax 2003b; see also Wax 2000, 2001, 2003a). This idea has had a tenacious hold on thinking about welfare in this country since its inception. It animates an array of welfare policies otherwise informed by shifting social circumstances and evolving attitudes toward economic and social life.

This piece addresses the question of whether recent reform implies any fundamental alteration in concepts of equality, citizenship, and the government's role. I conclude that no transformation has occurred. Rather, reform has responded to changes in social conditions and practices. The key shifts relate to conventions surrounding family formation, women's roles, reproductive choices, and motherhood. Such changes—and not a rejection of the conditional reciprocity paradigm itself—account for the evolution of American welfare policy.

Conditional Reciprocity

The enactment of TANF represents a revival of the distinction between the so-called deserving and undeserving poor. That distinction is fundamental to conditional reciprocity, which commands widespread support in the United States and in modern industrial societies generally. It finds expression in the popular view that the able-bodied should work, and that public assistance should be available only to those who are unable to support themselves. This precept begs many questions about how to define work, about who should be regarded as able-bodied, and about what qualifies as a sufficient contribution to self-support. The answers to these questions depend in large measure on other social values and conventions and on prevailing economic conditions.

I speculate that reciprocal expectations evolved over eons to help facilitate the development of systems of mutual aid during lengthy periods of human history that preceded the creation of strong centralized governments (see Wax 2000; Sugden 2004; Bowles and Gintis 1999, 4–10). The ability of groups to form stable insurance collectives enhances a community's chances of survival under conditions of stress and scarcity. The viability of groups, and the continuing availability of pooled resources, depends on members' willingness to cooperate by generating wealth and contributing to the pool. Game-theoretic models suggest that rational self-interested actors will cooperate in such insurance-type schemes only if others do the same. This coordination requires a mechanism for ensuring cooperation and for quelling free riding. On this assumption, evolutionary pressures would favor the development of the cohesive norms that support cooperative pooling arrangements. These mechanisms can include moral sentiments that impel group members to discipline, punish, or expel defectors perceived as unnecessarily taking advantage of the efforts of others. Similar moral sentiments inform popular attitudes today and help account for the tendency to distinguish between those who are unable to support themselves due to blameless misfortune or conditions beyond their control (the deserving) and those who refuse to make good faith efforts to pay their own way (the undeserving). In sum, this analysis predicts what social scientists in fact observe: that these categories play a central role in the political psychology of public aid for the disadvantaged.

The norm of conditional reciprocity sets parameters for the design of social welfare programs that will command popular support today. Although the community recognizes a duty to help those who cannot work at all or who cannot earn enough for an adequate standard of living, all group members must strive toward self-support. In effect, the collective assures basic subsistence on the condition that the individual make some effort to minimize the assistance that is needed.

What constitutes a sufficient effort to satisfy reciprocity requirements? There is no fixed demand but instead an expectation of reasonable contribution. What is reasonable depends on other values and on economic and social conditions. Social judgment will take into account each person's abilities, reigning social practices and conventions, and economic factors such as the overall prosperity of the group.

How do we reconcile the idea of a firm consensus about reciprocity with the sharp political disagreements we see over welfare policy? The answer is that the disputes are largely about background facts and subsidiary conventions rather than about fundamental principles. Reciprocal norms can accommodate very different fact-based beliefs about a range of social and economic conditions pertinent to desert or entitlement to help. These include views about how much economic opportunity is available to workers with low skill, how much control women have over childbearing, how hard most self-supporting families and mothers do actually work, and how much the poor already do to help themselves, among other issues. There are also normative disputes about the rules that should govern sexual conduct and family life. Should the two-parent family be recognized as the basic social and economic unit, or should mothers and their dependent children be accorded an equivalent status? Is childbearing to be viewed as a private choice within persons' effective control, as something that happens to people, or as a life-activity in which everyone is entitled to engage even at public expense? There is thus plenty of room for contention even though the principle of conditional reciprocity is widely accepted.

Conditional Reciprocity as the Animating Paradigm

What is the evidence that conditional reciprocity animates popular thinking about welfare programs? Using data from public opinion surveys, Martin Gilens asserts that the great majority of voters accept a role for government in alleviating poverty. They recognize "that people cannot always support themselves" and agree "that when individuals are in need, the government has a responsibility to help." Almost all voters surveyed express willingness to assist those who, through bad luck or disability, are unable to attain economic independence. Generosity also extends to persons who, despite trying hard to "make it on their own," fail to achieve complete self-sufficiency. Many fewer people are willing to aid persons who, despite the ability to work, fail to exert some effort on their own behalf. Most voters believe that welfare programs should be designed to avoid assisting these "undeserving" (1999).

Focus groups echo these findings (Farkas et al. 1996; Public Agenda 1995). Personal economic self-interest, as expressed in concern about program costs for taxpayers, is not a key determinant of public attitudes to welfare. Most voters are willing to expand welfare programs during economic hard times because the poor are then viewed as less responsible for their predicament. Voters are far less generous in boom times because the poor are believed to have greater opportunities for self-help (see Public Agenda 1995, 1).

Second, work requirements are wildly popular with voters. A 2002 poll asked voters to rank the importance of different goals for government welfare programs (see Lake Snell Perry 2002). The authors found that "requiring recipients to work once again tops the list—an overwhelming majority (96 percent) feel this is important, including eight in ten (82 percent) who believe it is *very* important" (2002, 6, italics in original). Another study of voter attitudes states that "Americans . . . insist that the less fortunate assume some obligation in return [for receiving benefits], that they 'prove' themselves worthy of help and work towards independence" (Farkas et al. 1996, 17).

Although voters firmly approve of work requirements, they are less certain about time limits (see, for example, Farkas et al. 1996, 26; Public Agenda 1995, 2, 14–15). Voter ambivalence about rigid deadlines for withdrawing aid goes along with approval of programs that provide a so-called "soft landing" for those who seek to move from dependency to independence. The idea of assisted or supported work extends to the core beneficiaries of cash welfare benefits—single mothers—who are deemed entitled to help with child care, transportation, and medical expenses, at least for the short term. Many voters also believe that this group's transition from welfare to work should be eased through the provision of training and skill development (see Public Agenda 1995, 2; Farkas et al. 1996, 27).

The data suggest that the public is less concerned with the precise duration and intensity of work than with ensuring that welfare recipients engage in some productive activity. Even minimally productive tasks suffice as long as recipients are expending some reasonable degree of effort. According to one study, "almost six in ten Americans (57 [percent]) say requiring 'recipients to do community service in exchange for benefits' is . . . essential. Eighty-five percent say they would be satisfied if recipients were 'required to do something in exchange for their benefits—even if it was just raking leaves or cleaning roads' " (Lake Snell Perry 2002). At the same time, solid majorities would require recipients to perform community service in exchange for benefits even when the recipients are handicapped. Although most voters do not think mothers should be exempted from paid work, they also do not think that mothers of small children should work long hours—or even a standard forty-hour week. Part-time work is viewed as sufficient. The populace recognizes that this population may need some help in getting by at first, but regards perpetual assistance with disfavor. Economic self-sufficiency is the ultimate goal for mothers, as for everyone else (see Farkas et al. 1996; Public Agenda 1995).

The Implementation of Welfare Reform

The features of state programs under TANF square with reciprocity as a moral ideal rather than as a fixed formula. Although work is considered the quid pro quo for benefits, the recipient is not seen as an employee who must literally earn his or her income, in the sense of meeting all requirements of unmediated private markets. Rather, society pledges security against destitution and recipients pledge to avoid unnecessary dependence. The group as a whole, through the agency of government, assumes the obligation of providing the needy some decent minimum. In return, the recipient must make an effort above some reasonable threshold. Although this pact requires all able-bodied persons to contribute to self-support, it leaves open how much a recipient must do in any case.

The benefit given and the work expected are loosely coupled, with many factors and circumstances potentially affecting the equation. This paradigm predicts that states requiring more work will not necessarily pay higher benefits, and those demanding fewer hours will not necessarily offer less. It also predicts that work requirements will be independent of family size, because the work effort conventionally expected from parents is not obviously tied to number of offspring. Nor should the amount of earnings disregarded in determining eligibility for cash assistance show a systematic relationship to hours required or worked or to benefits paid. In particular, there would be no reason for state-mandated earnings disregards to become less generous as state benefits levels rise and state hourly work requirements fall, as they would if minimizing taxpayer burden and government expenditures were paramount.

TANF bears out these predictions. First, there is no evidence that state welfare programs demand more work as family size grows. That is so even though states usually pay higher benefits to larger families. Second, the relationship between benefits levels, hour requirements, and earnings disregards under state programs is consistent with a system animated by a reciprocal ideal. The calculations that bear out these relationships use numbers from recent compilations of data on state welfare programs developed under TANF (see U.S. Department of Health and Human Services 2002; Center for Law and Social Policy 1990–99). Table 9.1 sets forth the pairwise correlations between the three parameters fixed by states—weekly hours of work required, benefits levels offered per month to a standard size family, and amount of earnings disregarded (based on a monthly income of $800) in computing eligibility and benefits levels. Below each correlation is its significance level.[3]

As shown, none of these correlations is significant. If anything, states with low benefits levels tend to demand slightly more work.[4] Nor do earnings disregarded to qualify for aid show any consistent and systematic correlation with hour-of-work requirements. States requiring more work do not have more generous (that is, higher) earnings disregards. Finally, low disregards are not linked to low levels of benefits, as might be expected if saving money, rather than encouraging work, was the paramount goal.[5] In sum, although the contributions considered appropriate on both sides of the welfare equation vary with locale, they obey no strict proportionality rule. And though these measures do not control for all relevant variables, they do suggest that states are not primarily concerned with reducing costs to taxpayers. Rather, a sense of minimal obligation bearing on both sides animates welfare program design.

The nature of conditional reciprocity may also contribute to state and local governments' tendency to shy away from guaranteed job or workfare programs.[6] At first blush, placing recipients in government jobs might be seen as the most straightforward way to connect welfare benefits with work effort, and some public opinion results suggest voter support for the idea. Yet few localities have insisted on workfare. That may be because workfare programs strain reciprocity in marginal cases. If benefits are conditioned on performance, standards for workfare must have some bite and jobs cannot really be guaranteed. The fact that workfare recipients are among the least employable workers and face the prospect of destitution if ejected from these programs may create reluctance to discipline participants and pressure to gut even minimal requirements. The tendency of workfare programs to degenerate into toothless entitlements adds to worries about costs, potential effects on private labor markets, and the belief that enough jobs are available in the private sector, as factors that undermine political support for government jobs programs on a large scale (Diller 1998).

Table 9.1 Pairwise Correlations

	Work Hours	Disregard
Benefits	–.084 (p = .57)	–.066 (p = .66)
Work hours		–.206 (p = .18)

Source: Author's compilation.

Reciprocity, Work Expectations, and Motherhood

The replacement of the New Deal AFDC program with a more stringent work-based federal system under TANF is best viewed as reflecting a change in a key set of social conditions rather than as a fundamental transformation in thinking about public relief. As a result of those changes, welfare mothers now face work demands that previously applied only to adult men. The nation has traditionally denied unconditional cash assistance to able-bodied men. Even during the Great Depression and other periods of economic downturn when such an offer might have been justified, no universal assistance program was enacted at the federal level. Some states and localities have created modest general assistance programs, but these have in practice been largely reserved for men impaired by mental or physical affliction or by substance abuse. These patterns reflect the long-standing expectation—consistent with conditional reciprocity—that the able-bodied should work; the community pledges to assist only those who cannot work or cannot support themselves despite a willingness to do so.

TANF extends the basic paradigm by imposing meaningful work requirements on caretakers of children—most notably single mothers. The categories of deserving and undeserving are now applied regardless of sex. But that extension does not betoken a deep transformation in the terms on which economic assistance is offered to individuals. Specifically, it represents no renewed commitment to, or repudiation of, the conditional reciprocity norm, but instead a change in how mothers are to be treated within this framework.

Nonetheless, the sweeping changes that TANF introduced illustrate how specific applications of the reciprocity principle are sensitive to evolving conditions. Since the AFDC program was first authorized during the Great Depression, the social landscape has altered dramatically. The birth control pill and other contraceptive methods have enabled many women to control their fertility. Paradoxically, and contrary to birth control advocates' predictions, the development and growing use of effective contraceptive methods coincided with a significant increase in of out-of-wedlock births. One economic model seeks to explain how the availability of birth control may have fueled this demographic change. On this account, the reduced risk of pregnancy from contraception made women more willing to engage in premarital sexual relations. Sex outside marriage became more widely available, and long-standing taboos against premarital sex began to unravel. As a result, women could no longer extract and enforce a promise of marriage in exchange for sexual favors. The higher level of sexual activity and the decline in the shotgun marriage norm increased the number of out-of-wedlock births overall, despite contraceptions' effect of preventing some pregnancies. This dynamic has led to a surge over the past few decades in never-married mothers seeking public assistance (see Akerlof, Yellin, and Katz 1996). Although out-of-wedlock births have leveled off recently, rates among poor and less educated women remain high.

Simultaneously (and perhaps for related reasons) more women have entered the workforce. Mothers no longer routinely stay home to care for their children, and most divorced and never-married mothers support themselves and their children by going to work and leaving the children in the care of others. These developments have left undisturbed the basic framework for aid, which conditions entitlement on either faultless incapacity or reasonable contribution, but have transformed how society seeks to apply that framework to poor single mothers.[7]

Formerly, single mothers achieved an exemption from the work expectation on grounds that motherhood and self-support were incompatible. Mothers must depend on someone, so if private support failed the state must take over. With today's higher wages and expanded work opportunities, however, many single women—including many single mothers—can support themselves. More important, perhaps, is the reality that many do so. Although working single parents receive the tax breaks and credits available to parents or low-paid workers generally, they do not rely on cash payments unconnected to work.[8] To be sure, their economic condition is sometimes precarious, but the fact that so many single mothers do without cash assistance vitiates society's willingness to target this group for special help. To exempt this group as a whole from work would be to license the kind of free riding that violates fundamental communal norms of cooperation. It is those norms, in conjunction with changes in women's familial and labor market conditions, that largely explain the dramatic shift in welfare policy.

Feminist Objections

The changes in mothers' status within society and their corresponding treatment by the welfare system are not without ambivalence, however. The status and claims of motherhood and of carework generally are still contested ground in our society. Feminist intellectuals have led a renewed charge toward public financing of caretakers and dependents. Although welfare reform is at odds with the pure form of this agenda, it remains to be seen how much the feminist critique will influence the precise contours of welfare programs in the future.

Advocates of public support for caretakers and their dependents draw on various arguments and analyses to advance their position. One tack is to disparage the notion of personal desert. People are ordinarily thought to deserve credit or reward for the product of their efforts. In a market economy, individuals are said to deserve the compensation, status, and other benefits that the market assigns to them. Yet political theorists and philosophers have failed to state a coherent theory of desert. Luck-egalitarians assign credit for choices individuals make but not for chance events or antecedent conditions that are outside a person's control. In applying this paradigm to real-life political decisions, theorists must contend with the difficulty of disentangling choice from chance and with the objection that everyone's contribution in some sense depends on others. This puzzle is particularly acute in the economic sphere. Because it is hard to calibrate the individual's contribution to the production of goods or services, it is difficult to argue that persons deserve the compensation they receive for jobs performed. Markets seem unfair because they assign rewards based in large part on endowments (such as looks or talent) that are the products of luck, or in response to vicissitudes of demand for which suppliers of goods and services cannot claim credit. These insights fuel a rejection of economic individualism and the embrace of a holistic view of society, where all outcomes are seen as the products of group effort (see, for example, Scheffler 2000; White 2003).

Feminists draw strength from this line of reasoning by emphasizing that every person's input—and the rewards that follow—ultimately rest on the contributions of others. The care received from parents, relatives, and friends is indispensable to everyone's ability to generate resources and to contribute to the social product. Because no one alive has failed to benefit from others' care—which has been rendered to them mostly free of charge—no one can claim entitlement to the full value of what he or she produces. By focusing on the pervasiveness of dependency within families, and specifically on the ineluctable dependence of children on parents, feminists cast aspersions on the very possibility of self-sufficiency. This further buttresses the case for a generous allotment to those who work outside the market, including single mothers and children.

Feminists note that welfare work requirements slight the kinds of domestic and caretaking tasks traditionally performed by women. The new rules threaten to burden women disproportionately and to discourage the performance of nonmonetized domestic functions. Care feminists are not asking for income as a right regardless of conduct, but for a broader view of how one may justify one's support. The crux of the debate is what should be recognized as work. Feminists note that society sanctions, and even approves, economic dependence within traditional families, including the dependence of homemaker mothers on breadwinner husbands. Similarly, no criticism is expressed when widowed mothers who never worked for pay draw Social Security benefits on accounts established by their deceased spouses (see, for example, Minow 1994). They ask why welfare mothers who perform similar tasks should not likewise receive government support.

The principal weakness of this argument is its failure to elaborate any general theory of compensable work. What counts as a productive but unpaid contribution to society and what does not? Why should the public not support other unpaid but possibly valuable contributions, such as creating graffiti art, planting gardens in public spaces, volunteering in schools, and playing classical music in subway stations?

One argument in favor of collective support for caretakers and their charges holds that parents, through their children, generate a positive externality or a public good that confers uncompensated benefits on the public as a whole (Wax 1999a; 1999b; Folbre 2001). An alternative view notes that society's obligations to children can only be properly discharged if parents undertake burdens of intensive and continuous care that go beyond their personal self-interest. If so, justice and pragmatism dictate that we subsidize parents in fulfilling this obligation (Alstott 2004). It is far from clear, however, whether these arguments suffice to distinguish caretaking from other work performed outside the market or to overcome all objections to collective responsibility for children.

Some limited political support exists for helping parents—as reflected, for example, in the enactment of modest tax credits and child care subsidies. That support, however, is tempered by at least two factors. First, a substantial body of social scientific evidence strongly suggests that single parenthood is detrimental to children (see Carbone 2000; Parke 2003; Moore, Jekielek, and Ermig 2002). In light of this, voters may be reluctant to expand programs that will make it easier for women to have children out of wedlock. Second, the belief that parenthood is a choice for which people should be held responsible is in tension with public financial support for caretakers and more consistent with the obligation to work for a living. Reciprocity recognizes an entitlement to group assistance if the need for help stems from events or forces beyond the individual's effective control. The availability of safe and reliable birth control and abortion reinforces the idea that having children should be regarded as a deliberate decision. Many people take advantage of available contraceptive methods to limit the size of their families, and many choose to do so because of a lack of income or a reluctance to work harder to support more children. Why should poor single mothers not do the same?

Even among those who accept conditional reciprocity, however, there are reservations about embracing the full implications of this reasoning. The recognition that reproduction is an individual right that everyone is entitled to exercise generates resistance to policies that, in purpose or effect, discourage women from having children. Although the distinction between negative and positive rights maintains a tenacious hold on the law, that distinction is blurred in the popular mind. Government still bears some onus to facilitate the most essential life activities. Proponents of school vouchers, for instance, claim that they seek to extend to poor parents the choices (sending their children to private schools) that are available to the wealthy. It is not enough to respond that rich people have that choice because they can afford it. Likewise, the public would like adequate health care for everyone regardless of ability to pay, though Congress has not yet managed to allocate the money to make that possible. In the same vein, voters may be reluctant to adopt policies that force the poor to make hard decisions about when and whether to have children, even though ordinary people routinely make such decisions and factor resource constraints into their calculations.

State Requirements

Although the conflicting currents of ideology and sentiment have ultimately produced reforms that require recipients of public aid to work, the precise features of state programs are informed by competing concerns and commitments. Uncertainties surrounding the social value of caretaking, the status of reproduction as a choice, the public's concern to make that choice reasonably available to most people, and the fairness and practical effects of forcing women to place small children in the (often inadequate) care of others, find expression in requirements that are surprisingly flexible, lenient, and diverse. The resulting variation is reflected in policies regarding hour-of-work requirements, the activities that are allowed to count as work, the conditions for exemption from work, and the willingness of states to use their own funds to continue benefits payments to families exceeding federal time limits.

Thirty-nine states require a set number of weekly hours of work for TANF recipients, with remaining states allowing participation to be determined on an individual basis or by localities. Of those thirty-nine, the majority (twenty-seven) fix the level at thirty hours per week, with six states demanding more (thirty-two to forty hours) and six less (twenty to twenty-nine hours). Five of the thirty-nine allow fewer hours for recipients with infant children or with basic skill deficiencies.[9]

Activities that count as fulfilling work requirements also show variation, with job search of some type authorized in all states. Subsidized employment qualifies as a work activity in forty-two states, with unpaid community service counting in thirty-four states and unpaid work experience in forty-four states. Many states permit different types of training and educational activities to fulfill work requirements, though most impose time limits on the duration of such training.[10] There are forty-four states that exempt adult recipients from work requirements if they are caring for a young child and only four states that do not have such an exemption. A bare majority of the exempting states apply the exemption to mothers of a child up to one year old, with a handful covering older preschool children and sixteen exempting caretakers of children of various ages under one year.[11] Additionally, nineteen states exempt individuals from work requirements if child care is unavailable.[12] Thirty-four grant exemptions to disabled or temporarily incapacitated adult recipients and those who are the victims of other special circumstances.[13] These figures illustrate that, against a background expectation of reciprocal contribution in some form, many commonplace situations are still regarded as absolving people—and especially mothers—of the responsibility to engage in paid employment, at least temporarily.

The pervasiveness of exemptions for mothers of very young children, however temporary, is particularly notable in light of the tough talk surrounding welfare reform. To be sure, these exemptions are generally shorter than those that prevailed under the AFDC program, which mutes the detrimental incentive effects that arose from open-ended expectations of support under the previous regime. The data nonetheless fail to support the notion that mothers of small infants must return to work immediately or that they must work much longer hours than non-welfare mothers while their children are very young.

Once again, the evidence suggests that what is deemed to satisfy reciprocation is informed by social norms, with concerns for horizontal equity and reasonableness motivating many program design features. Most working mothers—that is, those who held jobs before giving birth and who reenter the workforce while raising their children—do not place infants in daycare, so this may not be considered a fair demand on women receiving welfare either (see, for example, Hakim 2000). Likewise, most employed mothers of preschool children do not work full-time (that is, more than thirty or thirty-five hours per week), and very few mothers who work full-time work more than forty hours per week (Hakim 2000). The expectations imposed on mothers who depend on public aid reflect these dominant practices.

Also striking is the decision of most states to continue to permit welfare recipients to satisfy work requirements through training and educational activities. This is arguably in some tension with the work-first approach touted in the run-up to welfare reform. Advocates of work first cite studies and pilot programs showing that lengthy, nonspecific periods of training are much less effective than work in reducing welfare enrollment and in producing enduring employment gains. The practice of states allowing activities other than paid employment to satisfy welfare work requirements is less puzzling, however, in light of the evidence of broad public support for soft-landing policies. Despite voter awareness of the potential for misuse of these policies (see Public Agenda 1995, 3) and evidence suggesting that a more exacting work-first approach is more effective, most voters prefer to retain the option of transitional assistance aimed at preparing welfare recipients for unfamiliar and demanding responsibilities (1–2, 13–14).[14] Because job-oriented education and training are believed to enhance self-sufficiency and economic independence in the long run, allowing for training and education is justified as a rational investment that will produce fewer people on welfare and more contributing citizens in the future. Moreover, the expectation of reciprocity is not necessarily violated if taxpayers believe that recipients are preparing themselves for self-sufficiency and to give back at some later point. For all these reasons, some provision for training is still seen as a desirable feature of welfare programs.

In sum, the rules that have developed in different jurisdictions under welfare reform reflect popular attitudes toward redistribution grounded in deep-seated ideas of fairness. Welfare program design comports with reciprocal ideals informed by prevailing expectations about the conduct of productive and constructive lives. As members of society, welfare recipients must honor the rules of the game. Those rules are not, at bottom, abstract. Rather, they are shaped by dominant patterns, practices, and understandings about how decent people under similar circumstances behave and what it means to function as a responsible citizen. Although voters expect no less of welfare recipients than they expect from themselves, the specific programs and requirements imposed under welfare reform reveal that they also expect no more. Work hours, exemptions, and qualifying activities parallel expectations for persons not receiving aid. Those who have long been the main recipients of federal cash assistance—mothers of young children—are expected to do roughly as much to help themselves as many mothers in fact do today. Temporary dependency for education and training is an acceptable way to enhance future employability, but the expectation is that this status will not continue indefinitely. In this vein, social understandings that apply beyond the welfare context inevitably shape what the law requires of persons receiving support from the government.

This discussion suggests that welfare reform and the programs developed under it embody a distinct idea of equality and equal citizenship. The dominant attitude expressed by welfare program design is that to expect less, or more, from recipients of government aid than we do from nonrecipients would be unreasonable. Nonrecipients are expected to work if they can and exempted from work only if they are unable to perform any available jobs. The demands of motherhood temper these expectations to some extent, but no longer absolve from the duty to contribute to self-support. These rules now apply to everyone regardless of sex or parental status. The success and popularity of welfare reform suggest that this notion of equal citizenship, which is expressed by the range of current policies, has resonance for many voters.

Disability, Low Ability, and Supported Work

The ways of thinking discussed above have ramifications for policies toward other persons who may be unable to maintain a decent standard of living by dint of their own efforts alone. These include the working poor, the medically disabled, and the elderly.

Conditional reciprocity appears to create a sliding scale of obligation to help poor workers. Existing programs—such as the Earned Income Tax Credit (EITC)—have the effect of supplementing earnings that fall short of need. Proposed measures, including more generous credits and cash supplements for low-wage workers and their dependents, are also consistent with this goal (see Phelps 1997). The pattern of retaining and expanding the EITC program through several administrations suggests that many voters across the political spectrum accept the obligation to make up some portion of difference between what unskilled workers earn on their own and what they need for a reasonable existence. This aspect of poor relief is not currently the subject of much controversy.

The question of what policies should be adopted for the medically disabled is potentially more vexed. The practice of excusing the disabled from the obligation to work and of offering them enough cash aid to survive under the federal Supplemental Security Income (SSI) and Social Security Disability (OASDI) programs and state programs for the disabled, now coexists with the Americans with Disabilities Act (ADA), which forbids job discrimination against disabled persons and imposes on employers the affirmative obligation to accommodate those who are capable of performing the core elements of a job. The ADA assumes that many persons with medically disabling conditions can be productively employed if jobs are altered to accommodate them and that many such persons will work if suitable positions are available. But these expectations are in tension with the core assumption behind disability benefits programs, which is that disabled persons cannot work productively and will avoid paid work.

Taking reciprocity seriously makes it hard to see why persons with conventional disabilities should be entirely excused from making efforts in the job market that other people facing obstacles to job success must make. Persons with meager marketable skills or poor work habits are expected to work regardless of the cause of those deficits. In theory, of course, the disabled are those who cannot work at all. The rules of the SSI and OASDI programs stipulate that eligibles must be incapable of any remunerative work for at least a year. But in practice, many who qualify for benefits could do some existing work, especially if they were accommodated as the ADA requires. The partial overlap of the populations eligible for benefits and for ADA coverage is exacerbated by the changing nature of the disabled population. A fifth of the cases receiving OASDI and over half of those on SSI claim to be unable to work due to a mental condition—a designation that is more subjective and inherently more imprecise than disability due to a physical defect or disease (see U.S. Congress 2000, 80–81, 248).[15]

The ADA is partly designed to vindicate disabled persons' right to work (see, for example, Diller 1998; Kavka 2000; Epstein 1992; Olson 1997).

Reciprocity principles suggest that disabled persons have an obligation to work, at least to the extent possible. If so, then society would bear an onus to make work available by redesigning existing jobs. Expecting the disabled to work while accommodating them seems more consonant with society's values than exempting them from work entirely. Adopting this norm would have the added benefit of increasing social resources by harnessing disabled persons' productivity while reducing the cost of disability benefits.

That the old-age component of the Social Security program as now structured comports with reciprocal ideals has not only fueled its popularity but also generated potent obstacles to necessary reform. The quid pro quo concept at the heart of conditional reciprocity is heedless of actuarial reality and of the burden that claims by the deserving elderly place on the working population. Despite the insurance rhetoric suggesting that Social Security participants are simply drawing on earnings they set aside earlier, the program currently pays benefits well in excess of the returns retirees would receive if they had invested their contributions in private markets.[16] Those benefits are financed on a "pay-as-you-go" basis by taxes levied on working-age adults. Although some of the excess over actuarially sound returns has been financed through rising levels of productivity (Samuelson 1967, quoted in Attarian 2002, 27), there is widespread agreement that maintaining current benefit levels for future retirees will require steep tax increases or much higher government deficits to be repaid by future taxpayers. The voters' unbending commitment to the reciprocal logic of Social Security thus threatens to place a growing burden on the working population, to tilt public resources away from the needs of the young (including children), and to swamp other pressing programs and priorities for decades to come. The trends will inevitably deepen the divide in our society between the haves and the have-nots.

The Normative Implications of Conditional Reciprocity

The question of whether norms of conditional reciprocity can be defended as rational and moral remains. What most voters believe to be fair may not be. What the majority of citizens accept as reasonable may not comport with any coherent conception of equality or justice.

Because any notion that transferring earnings from workers to able-bodied nonworkers is unfair, unjust, or exploitative is difficult to derive from liberal formulations of just societies, the major liberal theorists fail to settle the question of whether liberal societies should demand work as a condition of public aid (Wax 2003b). Liberal egalitarians start from a baseline of equal dignity, rational self-interest, individual moral autonomy, equal initial resource shares, and, in many cases, skepticism about desert and the fairness of rewards assigned by markets. The skepticism derives from a group commitment to holding persons harmless for blameless misfortune. Although luck-egalitarians struggle to limit that category, their efforts are problematic. Bad upbringing, lack of talent, unproductive temperament, and even a taste for idleness (also known as laziness) affect outcomes, and it is not clear whether individuals can be held responsible in whole or in part for any of these. If no one really deserves anything, then it is difficult to say that some people deserve nothing, even if they exert no effort on their behalf. This line of reasoning suggests there is no universal obligation to work for a living (Scheffler 2000).

The liberal skepticism toward work requirements grounded in reciprocity stands in contrast to popular hostility to free riding, which yields staunch voter support for work as the quid pro quo for welfare. How can this disparity be reconciled? The tendency to disapprove of freeloaders and morally condemn free riding is widespread. Because groups that engage in mutual aid tend to outcompete less cooperative groups, these attitudes may have evolved through historical processes that pitted individuals or groups with disparate behavioral strategies against one another in repeated rounds of competition. These processes are best captured by dynamic, iterative models, not the static, idealized thought experiments that liberal theorists favor. John Rawls's famous original position (Rawls 1971) and Ronald Dworkin's primeval desert island and hypothetical insurance scheme (Dworkin 2000) will not necessarily generate conclusions that comport with our moral sentiments. These philosophical constructs do not reflect the way our ancestors lived.

Has our staunch fealty to reciprocal ideals outlived its usefulness? The political obstacles confronting Social Security reform, and the limitations and inflexibility imposed by dividing aid recipients into the deserving and undeserving, reveal the potential drawbacks of popular thinking grounded in the logic of reciprocation. As suggested, conditional norms appear to have originated in primitive periods when they were needed to hold together voluntary schemes of mutual support. In the era of strong governments and economic prosperity, the moral hazard of permitting some free riding may prove less threatening to collective well-being. The costs of supporting some group members in idleness through a centralized scheme of redistribution may now be more tolerable. If most people's rewards from working are large enough (because most jobs in the economy offer compensation well above the subsistence level), if those rewards are widely valued, and if benefits to nonworkers are not set too high, most people will continue to work hard. The state's coercive power to tax, in combination with compensation available on the market, will lure (or bribe) most people to keep working to get ahead, even if they have to transfer some of their earnings to nonworkers. The offer of unconditional benefits will not significantly threaten prosperity.

The real issue may not be so much whether the economy will collapse, but whether a society can accept the moral dissonance created by a government program that seems to turn the most productive citizens into suckers. Generating acceptance of unconditional handouts requires dislodging basic notions of equality and citizenship that include the expectation that everyone will make a good faith effort toward self-support. As explained, and contrary to what some theorists have suggested, most voters view unconditional assistance as treating the poor not as well as, but rather better than, everyone else. Handouts without obligation do not correct for inequality but instead generate unfair inequities. For most ordinary people, equality is caught up with fairness, and fairness dictates that because most people work, poor people should too. There is nothing unequal about that—quite the contrary.

Can policies that fly in the face of this outlook—an outlook that draws strength from elemental moral sentiments—ultimately succeed? The danger is not only that people will never fully accept programs that assist the able-bodied idle, but that they will change their behavior in response to such programs even in ways contrary to their rational economic self-interest. The perception of unfairness will make them less willing to strive and work hard. They will bite off their nose to spite their face.[17] Thus, even if our society is now wealthy enough to hold some people harmless for their idleness, public policies that abandon prevalent concepts of equality and equal citizenship may in the end undermine prosperity by eroding attitudes that keep people working hard and well—attitudes that are necessary to sustain prosperity in the long run. Abandoning reciprocity might usher in a wider demoralization, or it might not. How such a shift would play out is difficult to resolve in theory. The outcome would await the tests of time, experience, and political will.

Notes

1. See the Personal Responsibility and Work Opportunity Act of 1996. The statute left in place some means-tested, in-kind programs (Medicaid and Food Stamps) and maintained the basic elements of the federal program for the poor disabled and elderly (SSI).
2. Revisions to the 1996 welfare reform act are now under consideration in Congress, and President Bush has recommended strengthening the statute's work requirements.
3. The significance level is the probability that a correlation this high could have occurred when there was really no association between the variables. We usually call a correlation significant when the p value declines below .05 or .10. All the figures here are too small to be significant (for the raw data, see table 9.2).
4. The fact that some states with low benefit levels have tougher work requirements may reflect cultural factors. In particular, southern states tend to have more severe views of welfare, as reflected in lower benefits and greater demands on recipients (see, for example, Elazar 1984; Mead 2003).

Table 9.2 State Parameters from 2002 Fifth Annual Report on TANF to Congress

	Benefit Level	Hours per Week Required	Earnings Disregarded
Alabama	164	32 to 35	160
Alaska	923	30	90
Arizona	347	35	213
Arkansas	204	30	160
California	626	32	90
Colorado	356		90
Connecticut	543	25	90
Delaware	338	0	90
District of Columbia	379	30	160
Florida	303	30	90
Georgia	280	30	90
Hawaii	570	32	160
Idaho	293	20	480
Illinois	377	30	90
Indiana	288	0	90
Iowa	426	0	320
Kansas	403	30	90
Kentucky	262	30	224.4
Louisiana	190	25	120
Maine	461	30	346
Maryland	417	0	160
Massachusetts	565	0	0
Michigan	459	30	120
Minnesota	789	30	144
Mississippi	170	30	90
Missouri	292	30	0
Montana	468	30	150
Nebraska	364	30	160
Nevada	348	0	160
New Hampshire	600	30	160
New Jersey	424	30	
New Mexico	439	29	337.5
New York	577		90
North Carolina	272	35	
North Dakota	457	30	
Ohio	373	30	275
Oklahoma	292	30	340
Oregon	460	0	400
Pennsylvania	403	0	400
Rhode Island	554	20	315
South Carolina	201	30	0
South Dakota	430	30	142

(*Table continues on p. 218.*)

Table 9.2 State Parameters from 2002 Fifth Annual Report on TANF to Congress (*Continued*)

	Benefit Level	Hours per Week Required	Earnings Disregarded
Tennessee	185	40	150
Texas	197	30	224.4
Utah	451	0	350
Vermont	622	30 (average of 2)	90
Virginia	291	30	90
Washington	546		400
West Virginia	328	30	480
Wisconsin	673		0
Wyoming	340	30	200

Source: U.S. Department of Health and Human Services (2002).

5. High disregards with low benefits, if observed, would not necessarily be inconsistent with reciprocity either. The government's commitment to ensuring each family has available a minimum amount of resources might lead states with low benefits to permit individuals to keep a greater portion of their own earnings without losing qualification for a modest government supplement.
6. The Center for Community Change has predicted that the pressure on states to find jobs for welfare recipients and the lack of such jobs will lead to "a massive increase in 'workfare' in virtually every state" (1997, n.p.). This prediction, however, has not been borne out yet. Although many states and localities have created small experimental programs, only Wisconsin and New York City have established large-scale workfare. Rep. (and declared presidential candidate) Dennis Kucinich recently attributed the paucity and lack of success of government-sponsored jobs programs to their expense, the difficulty in hiring supervisors, and the potential inequities between workfare and non-workfare government and private workers (Ways and Means 2002).
7. For a discussion of how and when public opinion changed to expect much the same work of mothers as of men, see Steven M. Teles (1996, chap. 3).
8. The fact that tax breaks are available to so many people fuels the controversy about whether economic self-sufficiency is a meaningful concept or merely an empty conceit within our interdependent society and economy (see Wax 2003c).
9. Information on the range of state requirements is gleaned from the State Policy Documentation Project (Center for Law and Social Policy, note 14), which provides a concise summary of details of state programs, including hourly participation requirements, exemptions, the types of work and education that satisfy requirements, and other aspects of TANF implementation.
10. Job readiness activities and job skills training, which can include coaching for job applications, writing resumes, interviewing, and work-life skills, count toward participation in forty-eight states. Vocational educational training is

an authorized work activity in forty-seven states, and adult basic education and English as a Second Language (ESL) is authorized as a work activity in forty-seven states. Education directly related to employment is an authorized work activity in 44 states and on-the-job training is authorized by forty-five states. Postsecondary education is more complicated. Thirty-four states allow it to count in some form, although most impose time limits and some require simultaneous part-time work.

11. Of the forty-four exempting states, five have exemptions for an adult recipient caring for a child older than one year (with one state exempting for children up to eighteen months, two states for those up to two years of age and two states for those up to three years of age); twenty-three states have an exemption for children up to one year of age; sixteen have an exemption for children less than one year (eleven states for children up to three months old, one state for children up to thirteen weeks old, two states for children up to four months old and two states for children up to six months old). Two states leave exemptions to the discretion of counties for children up to one year.
12. Of these nineteen states, one exempts for children up to one year old; one exempts for children up to five years old; eleven exempt for children up to six years old; three exempt for children up to twelve years old; two exempt for children up to thirteen years old; and one has no age limit. Moreover, as the SPDP exemption summary notes, "federal law prohibits states from reducing or terminating assistance to a single custodial parent who refuses to work, if the parent is caring for a child under six and proves that he or she is unable to obtain needed child care" (Center for Law and Social Policy 1990–99).
13. These include recipients caring for a disabled household member (twenty-eight), adult recipients of advanced age (twenty-seven), victims of domestic violence (twenty-four), and pregnant recipients (twenty).
14. A "soft-landing" approach to getting people off welfare "was a prominent feature of virtually all proposals discussed" by focus group participants.
15. For the argument that disability standards are political questions, see Stone 1984.
16. Peter G. Peterson notes that "most currently retired Americans receive Social Security benefits that are two to five times greater than the actuarial value of prior contributions by employer and employee. A typical middle-income couple who retired in 1981 has already received back, with interest, not only the total value of their previous social security . . . but also *the total value of their lifetime federal income taxes*" (1993, 106, italics in original). John Geanakoplos, Olivia Mitchell, and Stephen Zeldes point out that present retirees receive "positive net subsidies and high returns," as compared to "low returns forecasted for current and future cohorts" (2000, 146). Peter G. Peterson cites several recent federal government reports stating that maintaining old age benefits programs, including Social Security and Medicare, at current levels for future retirees will require dramatic tax increases or massive borrowing (2004, 36–37). John Attarian observes that the FICA tax has doubled over the past three decades, with that amount representing more than a five-fold increase in percentage of GDP (2002, 26–29).
17. For more on these questions, including a discussion of the role of the moral sentiments in Rawls's concept of "reflective equilibrium" and literature suggesting irrational reactions to perceived unfairness, see Wax (2003b, 65–70).

References

Akerlof, George, Janet Yellin, and Michael Katz. 1996. "An Analysis of Out-of-Wedlock Childbearing in the United States." *Quarterly Journal of Economics* 111: 277–303.

Alstott, Ann. 2004. *No Exit: What Parents Owe Their Children and What Society Owes Parents.* New York: Oxford University Press.

Attarian, John. 2002. *Social Security, False Consciousness and Crisis.* New Brunswick: Transaction Publishers.

Bloom, Dan. 1997. *After AFDC: Welfare to Work Choices and Challenges for States.* New York: Manpower Demonstration Research Corporation.

Bowles, Samuel, and Herbert Gintis. 1999. "Is Equality Passé: Homo reciprocans and the Future of Egalitarian Politics." *Boston Review* 23(December/January): 4–10.

Carbone, June. 2000. *From Partners to Parents: The Second Revolution in Family Law.* New York: Columbia University Press.

Center for Community Change. 1997. *Jobs: Some Organizing Strategies* 23(May). Washington, D.C.: Center for Community Change.

Center for Law and Social Policy and the Center on Budget and Policy Priorities. 1990–99. *State Policy Documentation Project.* Washington, D.C. Available at: http://www.spdp.org (accessed July 19, 2005).

Diller, Matt. 1998. "Working without a Job: The Social Messages of the New Workfare." *Stanford Law & Policy Review* 9(winter): 19–43.

Dworkin, Ronald. 2000. *Sovereign Virtue.* Cambridge, Mass.: Harvard University Press.

Elazar, Daniel J. 1984. *American Federalism: A View from the States,* 3rd ed. New York: Harper and Row.

Epstein, Richard. 1992. *Forbidden Grounds.* Cambridge, Mass.: Harvard University Press.

Farkas, Steven, Jean Johnson, Will Friedman, Ali Bers, and Chris Perry. 1996. *The Values We Live By: What Americans Want from Welfare Reform* (Public Agenda 1996). New York: Public Agenda.

Folbre, Nancy. 2001. *The Invisible Heart: Economics and Family Values.* New York: New Press.

Geanakoplos, John, Olivia Mitchell, and Stephen Zeldes. 2000. "Would a Privatized Social Security System Really Pay a Higher Rate of Return?" NBER Reprint No. 2266. Washington, D.C.: National Bureau of Economic Research. Available at: http://prc.wharton.upenn.edu/prc/PRC/ReprintNBERno2266.pdf (accessed July 19, 2005).

Gilens, Martin. 1999. *Why Americans Hate Welfare: Race, Media, and the Politics of Antipoverty Policy.* Chicago: University of Chicago Press.

Hakim, Catherine. 2000. *Work-Lifestyle Choices in the 21st Century.* New York: Oxford University Press.

Kavka, Gregory S. 2000. "Disability and the Right to Work." In *Americans With Disabilities: Exploring Implications of the Law for Individuals and Institutions,* edited by Leslie Francis and Anita Silvers. New York: Routledge.

Lake Snell Perry & Associates. 2002. *Public Views on Welfare Reform and Children in the Current Economy* (February). Future of Children. David and Lucile Packard

Foundation. Available at: http://www.futureofchildren.org/usr_doc/lsp_welfare_survey.pdf (accessed July 19, 2005).

Loffredo, Stephen, and Helen Hershkoff. 1997. *The Rights of the Poor.* Carbondale: Southern Illinois University Press.

Mead, Lawrence M. 2003. "Welfare Caseload Change: An Alternative Approach." *Policy Studies Journal* 31(2): 163–85.

Minow, Martha. 1994. "The Welfare of Single Mothers and Their Children." *Connecticut Law Review* 26(3): 817–42.

Moore, Kristin, Susan Jekielek, and Carol Ermig. 2002. "Marriage from a Children's Perspective: How Does Family Structure Affect Children and What Can We Do About It?" *Child Trends Research Brief* (June): 1–8. Available at: http://www.childtrends.org (accessed July 19, 2005).

Olson, Walter. 1997. *The Excuse Factory: How Employment Law is Paralyzing The American Workplace.* New York: Martin Kessler Books.

Parke, Mary. 2003. "Are Married Parents Really Better for Children? What Research Says About the Effects of Family Structure on Child Well-Being." Center for Law and Social Policy. Brief #3 (May). Available at: http://www.clasp.org/publications/Marriage_Brief3.pdf (accessed July 19, 2005).

Peterson, Peter G. 1993. *Facing Up: How to Rescue the Economy from Crushing Debt and Restore the American Dream.* New York: Simon & Schuster.

———. 2004. *Running On Empty.* New York: Farrar, Straus and Giroux.

Phelps, Edmund. 1997. *Rewarding Work.* Cambridge, Mass.: Harvard University Press.

Public Agenda. 1995. *Attitudes Towards Welfare and Welfare Reform.* New York: Public Agenda.

Rawls, John. 1971. *A Theory of Justice.* Cambridge: Belknap Press.

Samuelson, Paul. 1967. "Social Security: Something for Nothing." *Newsweek,* February 13: 88.

Scheffler, Samuel. 2000. "Justice and Desert in Liberal Theory." *California Law Review* 88(965): 965–90.

Stone, Deborah A. 1984. *The Disabled State.* Philadelphia: Temple University Press.

Sugden, Robert. 2004 *The Economics of Rights, Cooperation, and Welfare.* New York: Palgrave Macmillan.

Teles, Steven M. 1996. *Whose Welfare? AFDC and Elite Politics.* Lawrence: University Press of Kansas.

U.S. Congress. 1996. *Personal Responsibility and Work Opportunity Reconciliation Act of 1996* (Enrolled as Agreed to or Passed by Both House and Senate). HR 3734. 104th Cong. 2nd sess.

———[Ways and Means]. 2000. *Green Book: Background Material, and Data on Programs Within the Jurisdiction of the Committee on Ways and Means.* Washington: U.S. Government Printing Office.

———[Ways and Means]. 2002. *Welfare Reform Reauthorization Proposals.* 107th Cong. Hearing Before Subcommittee on Human Resources of the Committee on Ways and Means, House of Representatives. Statement of Hon. Dennis J. Kucinich, Representative in Congress from the State of Ohio. Washington: U.S. Government Printing Office.

U.S. Department of Health and Human Services. 2002. Administration for Children and Families, Office of Family Assistance. TANF Fifth Annual Report to Congress.

Washington: U.S. Government Printing Office. Available at: http://www.acf.dhhs.gov/programs/ofa/annualreport5 (accessed July 19, 2005).

Wax, Amy. 1999a. "Caring Enough: Sex Roles, Work, and Taxing Women." *Villanova L. Review* 44: 495–523

———. 1999b. "Is There a Caring Crisis? A Review of Shirley Burggraf's *The Feminine Economy and Economic Man.*" *Yale Journal on Regulation* 16(summer): 327.

———. 2000. "Rethinking Welfare Rights: Reciprocity Norms, Reactive Attitudes and the Political Economy of Welfare Reform." *Law & Contemporary Problems* 63(257, winter/spring): 257–97.

———. 2001. "A Reciprocal Welfare Program." *Virginia Journal of Social Policy and Law* 8(3, spring): 477–516.

———. 2003a. "Disability, Reciprocity, and 'Real Efficiency': a Unified Approach." *William and Mary Law Review* 44(February): 1421–52.

———. 2003b. "Something for Nothing: Liberal Justice and Welfare Work Requirements." 52 *Emory Law Journal* 52(1, winter): 65–70.

———. 2003c. "Dependence, Interdependence, and Human Dignity." *Harvard Journal of Law and Public Policy* 27: 121.

White, Stuart. 2003. *The Civic Minimum.* Oxford: Oxford University Press.

Chapter 10

PRWORA and the Promotion of Virtue

JOEL SCHWARTZ

THE PERSONAL Responsibility and Work Opportunity Reconciliation Act of 1996 (PRWORA) is, I maintain, theoretically significant both because it promotes human virtue, and because its implementation suggests that our capacity to promote it is limited. In this essay, I propose that the act is justifiably seeking—with some success—to encourage the virtues that correspond with work, and contend that it can and will do little to encourage the virtues that characterize spouses and parents. PRWORA's successes and failures both have implications for our understanding of the proper scope of liberal democratic government in the United States.

By imposing a work mandate on a population of welfare recipients, many of whom have little or no work history, PRWORA in effect aims to make them employable by improving their capacities. People can find jobs only when they show that they command humble but important virtues such as reliability, cooperativeness, and punctuality. They can hold their jobs and move on to better ones only when they manifest and further develop these virtues. In this sense, PRWORA is requiring welfare recipients to acquire and to practice the virtues entailed by productive employment.

But PRWORA also seeks to promote virtue in a second sense. It aims to encourage marriage, and procreation only within marriage. To achieve those ends it must somehow foster the fidelity and responsibility that characterize spouses who successfully raise children together in wedlock. And here PRWORA's efforts have been halting and are likely to be ineffective.

Nevertheless, simply by seeking to promote virtue, PRWORA has significantly changed the goals of American welfare policy. Instead of aiming primarily to provide for the material needs of the poor, the act seeks to promote and encourage the good behavior of the poor, and the virtues or commendable habits that underlie good behavior. The expectation is that virtue and good behavior will reduce dependency and—at least in the long run—increase the prosperity and well-being of the poor. To support this contention, I begin by advancing some historical and theoretical considerations before turning to examine the enactment and implementation of PRWORA.

In some respects PRWORA returns us to an earlier—in fact, the original—understanding of the goal of American social policy. That goal was articulated by a series of influential nineteenth-century moral reformers, who administered charities and aimed to reduce dependency—and ideally poverty as well—by exhorting and helping the poor to behave in ways that would promote their self-reliance (see Schwartz 2000 for a discussion of America's nineteenth-century moral-reform tradition).

These reformers promoted virtues like sobriety, thrift, and—of greatest relevance for welfare reform—diligence. They judged that the poor needed to avoid drinking (both because it made potential workers less employable and because it cost them money that could have been spent on more essential goods), to spend within their means, and if possible to save. Most fundamentally, the poor were exhorted to work and earn.

The efforts of the moral reformers were very much in the service of a moral ideal. Thus Charles Loring Brace—who founded New York's Children's Aid Society in 1853 to assist vagrant children—asserted that all assistance to the poor was "superficial and comparatively useless," unless it "touch[ed] habits of life and the inner forces which form character" (1880/1967, 22–23). Although Brace administered a private charity and was not a government employee, this quotation nevertheless demonstrates that he consciously attempted to practice what George Will has called "statecraft as soulcraft" (1983).

If the passage of PRWORA marks a return to this nineteenth-century tradition of moral reform, it obviously follows on an earlier rejection of that tradition. In many ways America's twentieth-century history reads as a sort of referendum on the appropriateness of moral reform—a test in which moral reform was resoundingly defeated. Prohibition may have been the watershed moment, for to many it seemed to point to the folly of governmental attempts to improve the morals of American society. In addition, the Great Depression—in which destitution fell on the moral and the immoral alike—radically called into question the notion that poverty was the result of moral turpitude. Finally, the civil rights movement's focus on the gross discrimination against African Americans led many to excuse and accept the self-defeating behavior that characterized some poor blacks. It was widely believed that people living in ghetto environments—"where honesty can become a luxury and ambition a myth" (Council of Economic

Advisers, 1964, 55)—could not be expected to live up to prevailing notions of virtue.

One result of the discrediting of moral reform was a dramatic rise in the welfare rolls, which was greeted with equanimity and in some quarters even approval. In 1960 there were 3,005,000 welfare recipients, who constituted 1.7 percent of the American population. By 1972 welfare dependency had more than tripled to 10,241,000 Americans, representing 5.2 percent of the American population (see U.S. Department of Health and Human Services 2000). Because no one seriously argued that poverty was three times as severe and widespread in 1972 as it had been twelve years earlier, it was hard to ascribe a structural cause to the dramatic rise in the welfare population. Skepticism about such a cause was further fueled by Daniel Patrick Moynihan, who observed that

> during the 1950s there were quite astonishingly strong correlations between nonwhite male unemployment rates and such phenomena as the number of new AFDC [Aid to Families with Dependent Children, the pre-reform welfare program] cases opened and the number of nonwhite married women separated from their husbands, *but* that with the onset of the 1960s these relations seemed to disappear, so that, for example, the unemployment rate would decline but the number of new AFDC cases would rise. (1973, 150n, italics in original)

The surge in the welfare population instead signified the success of a welfare rights movement whose proponents vigorously denied that stigma should attach to the dependency of able-bodied people. Support by the state was viewed as a right, which needy individuals should freely exercise.

To further explain the increase in welfare dependency, Mickey Kaus has spoken of "a set of powerful new pro-dole ideas" that came to the fore in the 1960s. The beliefs were that "the poor are like the rest of us. They want to work. There is no 'poverty culture'. . . . Giving out jobs instead of money will not work. . . . The only real problem facing the poor is their lack of money; the solution is to give it to them" (1992, 114, 242–43). These ideas, predictably, had consequences. They guided policy, and as a result, as Susan Mayer has observed, "for a brief period [beginning in the 1960s] America's welfare policies were almost exclusively aimed at meeting the material needs of the poor" (1997, 5).

That period was brief, because the triumph of pro-dole ideas quickly generated a reaction. Beginning as early as the 1970s, a growing number of politicians and policy analysts questioned the wisdom of a welfare system that did little to encourage recipients to find employment. Their efforts culminated two decades later in the passage of PRWORA, which, as Mayer points out, "returned responsibility for poor families to the states, ended the entitlement to welfare, and required poor families to demonstrate suitability through work effort." Thus the passage of PRWORA made "welfare policies at the close of the twentieth century [and now at the start of the twenty-first] resemble those at the beginning of the [twentieth] century." We have returned to an era in which "states tried to break the cycle of pauperism by improving the moral character of poor families" (1997, 6).

Theoretical Considerations and Governmental Practice

Many political theorists have argued that a liberal democracy like the United States should not consciously attempt to promote the virtue of its citizenry. As William Galston notes, such theorists hold that the liberal "state must be 'neutral,' not simply toward religious professions but toward all individual conceptions of the good life. Indeed, they regard this neutrality as the defining characteristic of liberal orders" (1991, 7). For example, in his enormously influential *A Theory of Justice*, John Rawls contended that "as citizens we are to reject the standard of perfection as a political principle, and for the purposes of justice avoid any assessment of the relative value of one another's way of life" (1971, 442). According to this Rawlsian view, it is inappropriate for a liberal state's welfare policy to seek to encourage the diligence of its welfare recipients—or for a liberal state to promote virtue in any other way.

But that is not the only view of what liberal states may appropriately do, and it is certainly not Galston's view. To the contrary, he argues that liberalism is not neutral or agnostic with respect to moral questions. Instead it rests "on a distinctive conception of the human good" (1991, 8). The moral agnosticism displayed by some liberal theorists is untenable, because in practice "we actually know a fair amount about what promotes our individual and collective well-being" (11).

Because we are armed with this knowledge, Galston—with a few other political theorists such as Gutmann and Thompson and Macedo—contends that liberalism may and must legitimately seek to promote a set of liberal virtues, in that it "needs a wide range of virtues to maintain itself" (Galston 1991, 43). The liberal state is justified by "the worth of the way of life characterized by distinctively liberal or (as some would say) bourgeois virtues . . . [it is] designed to foster liberal virtues and to permit, insofar as possible, the unhindered pursuit of liberal goals" (80). Those virtues can and should be understood both instrumentally—"as means to the preservation of liberal societies and institutions"—and as ends in themselves—tied to a "conception of the virtuous or excellent individual," a conception that is valuable "not instrumentally, but for its own sake" (220, 228–29).

The views of virtue theorists like Galston have had an impact, both within and beyond the academy. Within the academy, it is significant that Rawls was decidedly less agnostic about the human good in some of his later work than he had been in *A Theory of Justice*, holding that at the least the liberal state can justly favor productive over unproductive ways of life.[1] Beyond the academy, the views of the virtue theorists are arguably reflected in the turn toward a welfare policy that more insistently seeks to encourage welfare recipients to lead productive lives.

In this context it is worth noting that Galston's canon of liberal virtues addresses the needs of a liberal market economy: to enable workers to fulfill their responsibilities, it incorporates many of the virtues that PRWORA seeks to instill. Galston contends that workers must exemplify traits such as "punctuality, reliability, civility toward co-workers, and a willingness to work within established frameworks and tasks" (1991, 223). More broadly, workers in a liberal society must also possess two other virtues.

> The first is the work ethic, which combines the sense of obligation to support personal independence through gainful effort with the determination to do one's job thoroughly and well. The second is the achievement of a mean between ascetic self-denial and untrammeled self-indulgence; call it a capacity for moderate delay of gratification. For although market economies rely on the liberation and multiplication of consumer desires, they cannot prosper in the long run without a certain level of saving, which rests on the ability to subordinate immediate gratification to longer-run self-interest. (Galston 1991, 223)[2]

In short, if only to ensure its own survival, the liberal state must somehow inculcate the economic virtues that make people diligent workers and prudent consumers and savers.

The belief that a liberal society should and must promote these virtues has obvious implications for its social policy. For Galston, the promotion of virtue places burdens on the state. Work must be demanded, but it must also be rewarded. In this vein Galston posits, I think rightly, that

> there is (at least in broad outline) a contemporary American consensus concerning just principles and institutions. Every citizen is entitled to at least a minimally decent existence. Those who are able to work receive the wherewithal to live decently in the form of wages (supplemented by public subsidies in the case of low wages). Those who cannot work—either because they are incapable of working or because they cannot find work to do—are to be compensated by the community. Those who can work but choose not to work have no valid claims against other individuals or against the community. (1991, 159)

The last sentence is particularly significant. Galston contends that "working versus shirking is a great moral divide in a liberal society," so that "individuals who are physically and mentally able to make a contribution but nonetheless fail to do so" deserve criticism (185).

In short, an entitlement to welfare is problematic if it can be shown to undermine the work ethic and promote individual improvidence.

"'Welfare' programs are morally controversial only to the extent that they are seen as allowing capable adults to avoid providing for themselves and their families or as undermining their psychological ability to do so" (188). Similarly, "the refusal to accept a decent job, or the propensity to squander resources on drugs or drink, does not generate any additional need claims that society is obliged to honor" (185).

Like Galston, James Q. Wilson also makes a case for the liberal state's need to inculcate virtue. Wilson has argued that America's social problems are likely to be reduced only to the extent that government somehow manages to encourage better behavior. Writing in an essay first published in 1985, Wilson contended that "a variety of public problems can only be understood—and perhaps addressed—if they are seen as arising out of a defect in character formation" (1991, 11). With respect to welfare in particular, Wilson claimed that the dramatic increase in caseloads during the 1960s could be understood as evidence of a failure of character: "Many persons who once thought of being on welfare as a temporary and rather embarrassing expedient came to regard it as a right that they would not be deterred from exercising" (16–17).

In Wilson's view, the welfare problem reflected a growing sense that dependency was not morally objectionable. People who had hitherto been reluctant to accept a dole were no longer dissuaded. A solution to this problem could be achieved only by "acknowledg[ing] the necessary involvement of government in character formation. The essential first step is to acknowledge that at root, in almost every area of important public concern, we are seeking to induce persons to act virtuously." People would somehow have to be encouraged to manifest "habits of moderate action," to act "with due restraint on [their] impulses, due regard for the rights of others, and reasonable concern for distant consequences" (1991, 22).

At least with respect to the citizenry as a whole (as opposed to problem populations such as long-term welfare recipients, on whom Wilson's argument focuses), American public policies have clearly attempted to promote virtue in various ways. The tax exemption enjoyed by religious institutions, to give one example, is based in part on a recognition on the part of government that the religious beliefs of many Americans promote their moral betterment, or at least discourage antisocial behavior.[3]

For a subtler and a more secular example of government policy aiming to promote virtue, consider the tax implications of home ownership. In a speech marking the fiftieth anniversary of the passage of the Housing Act of 1949, then Secretary of Housing and Urban Development Andrew Cuomo spoke of the power of home ownership to effect moral improvement:

> Housing is more than just bricks and mortar; it is the building block of community, it is powerfully tied to civic behavior—to working together with

neighbors on shared concerns, to literally making us a part of a block, a neighborhood, a town, a county, a nation. Homeownership makes us stakeholders in something grander than ourselves. (quoted in Coulson 2002, 12)[4]

Measuring "the change in behavior that arises from becoming a homeowner" (Coulson 2002, 10),[5] at least some social scientists have concluded that, compared with renters, homeowners better maintain their domiciles (10–11), do a better job raising their children because of their "stronger incentive . . . to monitor their own children and their neighbors' children" (11–12), and are more involved in their communities (12–14). Because the improved behavior of homeowners "provides benefits to people other than the homeowners themselves," (9, passage is italicized in original) to some extent at least the tax advantages enjoyed by homeowners—the exclusion from income of the imputed rent that homeowners in effect pay to themselves, and the deductibility of mortgage interest—are justifiable.[6]

If American public policy attempts in various ways to encourage citizen virtue, common sense would suggest that promoting virtuous behavior among the poor in particular would also be worth undertaking. Clearly virtue, or lack of it, is associated with social problems. A 1970 study undertaken by Edward M. Glaser and Harvey L. Ross on behalf of the U.S. Department of Labor compared two groups of men, aged twenty-one to thirty, all of whom were black or Mexican American, had grown up in a large, urban ghetto, and had been raised in families who were on welfare or lived in public housing. Thirty-two, less than half, had "made it" (had worked steadily for the last two years, had not received welfare, and had not been in trouble with the law). Not surprisingly, these men were "characterized by a work and achievement ethic"; they also valued "close family ties and loyalty, avoidance of trouble with the law, stability on the job, [and] taking responsibility for one's own destiny." By contrast, the unsuccessful were "characterized by an ethic of toughness, shrewdness, hustling, violence . . . less concern with family ties than with ties to peers . . . [and] a disposition in favor of immediate gratification." The successful men consisted of those who "told of having at least one strong parent who had high expectations for him and was effective in setting controls on his behavior" (study summarized in Banfield 1974, 249–51).

Thus if—and this is obviously an enormous "if"—public policy were able to promote a work and achievement ethic among the poor, the social problem linked to poverty would be much reduced.

Replacing AFDC with TANF

One factor leading to the passage of PRWORA and the resulting abolition of AFDC was the sense that AFDC had failed to encourage virtuous behavior among welfare recipients.

AFDC offered support for families—almost always headed by single mothers—raising dependent children. The program was driven by an understanding of care as virtuous activity: the child-raising activity of such mothers was understood to constitute socially valuable work (albeit uncompensated). But in 1996 this changed. Now it was thought morally problematic to give single mothers a stipend that enabled them to stay out of the workforce and home with their children. Why?

One answer to the question was that by 1996 it had become increasingly common for mothers raising children on their own (but not on welfare) to work. In 1995, 75 percent of formerly married women with children were either working or looking for work (U.S. Department of Commerce 1996, 400). But there is also a second—and in my view more important—answer to the question, which focuses on AFDC's effects on the children whom it was designed to assist.

Consider an argument made by one of the nineteenth-century moral reformers—Josephine Shaw Lowell, the leading theoretician of New York's Charity Organization Society, which she helped found in 1882. Although Lowell strenuously opposed doles to the able-bodied poor, she did support a program that in some respects resembled AFDC. She argued that

> widows with young children require long continued relief, and this should be given. . . . The position of a widow with small children whom she must support is most pitiful—she has to perform both the duties of father and mother, and in the nature of things she cannot do it. If she devotes herself to earning a living for her children, they suffer for her care, and if she gives them the care they need, she and they have not food sufficient. Under these circumstances, it is not only an injury to her and to her children, but to the public, to leave her unaided. (1884/1971, 102)

In short, Lowell advocated a program in which single mothers were to be given relief, which would enable them to stay out of the labor market and to remain instead at home to care for their children—precisely what AFDC was designed to achieve.

But the program that she wanted was very different from AFDC as it had developed by the 1990s. First, for good or ill, Lowell's program was restricted to widows, as opposed to wives who had been deserted—not to speak of mothers of illegitimate children.[7] Second, her program was not an entitlement, because relief was to be administered by private charities as opposed to government. Finally, and most significant, her program was not an entitlement in a second respect, in that grants were not to be made unconditionally: "No regular pension paid out week by week, *without individual supervision,* will suffice. . . . Constant oversight . . . is necessary . . . to see that all goes well, that the children are cared for and go to school" (102–3, emphasis added).

The last point is critical. Lowell insisted that a regular payment was not sufficient. True charity required proper intervention by the social worker to ensure that the widow's children were to receive the care that they needed and to go to school. This was necessary if they were one day to become able to support themselves (and their mother).

For Lowell, the objective of charity was to limit the hardship of the widow's family to a single generation. By contrast, too often the poverty of AFDC families proved to be multigenerational. Among other reasons, TANF (Temporary Assistance for Needy Families) replaced AFDC because children raised in families receiving welfare tended to fare worse in later life than did children raised off welfare. Indeed, one of the rationales for PRWORA (listed in the law's opening section) is that "children born into families receiving welfare assistance are 3 times more likely to be on welfare when they reach adulthood than children not born into families receiving welfare" (U.S. Congress 1996).[8] This is the cycle of pauperism to which Susan Mayer alludes.

Holding other factors—for example, race, family income, family structure—constant, studies have found that children growing up on welfare had cognitive abilities below those whose families received no welfare, that receiving welfare had negative impacts on the long-term employment and the earning capacity of young boys, and that young women raised in families on welfare were more likely to drop out of school than those not raised on welfare (see Rector 2001, 5).[9]

I am arguing, then, that AFDC failed because it did nothing more than maintain the poor: it did not promote the attitudes and behaviors that would enable welfare children to avoid dependency themselves. According to the Department of Labor study, parents able to set high expectations and to control their children's behavior were deemed key to the success of the minority men who made it. By the standard of whether children made it, welfare recipients—generally speaking—did not appear to raise children effectively.

Welfare reform had historically been hard to achieve, Kent Weaver observes, principally because of what he calls the dual clientele trap:

> Policymakers usually cannot take the politically popular step of helping poor children without the politically unpopular step of helping their custodial parents; they cannot take politically popular steps such as increasing penalties for refusal to work or for out-of-wedlock childbearing that may hurt parents without also risking the politically unpopular result that poor children will be made worse off. (2000, 45; passage is italicized in the original)

The force of the dual clientele trap was reduced (though not wholly eliminated), if, as the data suggest, growing up on welfare was not good for children. That conclusion helped open the door to radical reform. As Weaver notes, "the dual clientele trap . . . can be weakened if new approaches to welfare emerge that seem likely to improve the behavior of adults without hurting children" (2000, 52). Perhaps the abolition of AFDC and its replacement by TANF would aid children's development, by presenting them with better adult behavior on which to model their own.

This rationale gave many politicians a plausible basis for supporting change. PRWORA may be said to rest at least in part on the hypothesis that the example set by adults participating in the workforce will improve outcomes for the children of these adults. As Mickey Kaus states the hypothesis:

> The next generation off welfare—men as well as women, even men growing up in single-mother homes—will be better prepared not only to find jobs but to get the skills that will let them find "good jobs." That's because they will have grown up in a home where work, not welfare, is the norm, where the rhythms and discipline of obligation pervade daily life. A growing body of evidence shows that one of the most important factors in determining success at school is whether a child comes from a working home. Simply put, if a mother has to set her alarm clock, she's likely to teach her children to set their alarm clocks as well. (1992, 129)

The implementation of this policy change has largely confirmed these expectations. Evaluations of welfare work experiments from the 1990s show that children generally do better in school when their mothers are involved in these programs than children whose mothers are not subject to the requirements. The reason may be that a working mother is a better role model, or that poor children gain from being put in child care as opposed to staying home with a nonworking mother (see Duncan and Chase-Lansdale 2001). But, regardless, this evidence suggests that there is a connection between a working mother and better outcomes for her children.

More recently, discussing the outcomes of the experimental New Hope project to provide jobs and wage subsidies to the poor of Milwaukee, Lawrence Mead observed that "children from New Hope families did markedly better in school than children not in the program. . . . Why New Hope had these effects is not clear. But it is the first experimental evidence that putting poor parents to work might not just reduce welfare dependency but be connected to other, noneconomic benefits to families and neighborhoods" (2000, 27).

For good reason we tend to believe that the virtuous activity of parents is likely to set a good example for children. Insofar as PRWORA attempts to promote the virtuous activity of parents, at least as far as employment is concerned, it is not altogether surprising that it won support from politicians on both sides of the political fence.

To be sure, it is true that at least to this point participation in the workforce does not appear to have raised the family income of former welfare recipients by much. One hopes that this will change, but even if recipients' earnings do not increase significantly, their participation in the workforce can still be defended as a good example set by parents for their children. As Eugene Bardach has observed, "a job improves self-respect even if it does not pay enough to make a person economically self-sufficient" (1997, 257). Similarly, parents' holding jobs is also defensible if it improves their children's attitudes and behaviors, even if it does not significantly increase the family income.

PRWORA and Its Implementation

It would be foolish to maintain that a complicated piece of legislation such as PRWORA is devoted exclusively to promoting virtue. The legislation was surely intended also simply to reduce the welfare rolls—whether or not doing so would improve the attitudes and behaviors of welfare recipients. As it happens, these dual intentions appear to be mirrored in the differing ways in which the states implement PRWORA: caseload reduction is emphasized in some, whereas a higher level of work participation—reflecting better behavior—is emphasized in others (see Gais et al. 2001, 58–59). In any case, language within the legislation shows that the promotion of good behavior is a priority.

As I noted at the outset, PRWORA has a broad notion of good behavior; the act is clearly intended to encourage not just work but also marriage and responsible parenthood. In fact, the findings that begin the text of PRWORA focus exclusively on marriage as opposed to work: the first two of these findings are that "marriage is the foundation of a successful society" and that "marriage is an essential institution of a successful society which promotes the interests of children."[10] It is noteworthy, though, that the legislation says little about how marriage should be encouraged. In practice—a point to which I will return—the states have done little to achieve PRWORA's goal of encouraging marriage: "Because political support for employment is widespread, while debates about the means of reducing out-of-wedlock births continue, states have put more direct emphasis on the work and antidependency goals of TANF than on the goals relating to marriage and reproduction" (Gais et al. 2001, 38).

In contrast, PRWORA is fairly clear about the steps that must be taken to promote work. Thus in section 402 of the legislation each state is required to prepare a document explaining how it intends to "conduct a program . . . that provides assistance to needy families with (or expecting) children and provides parents with job preparation, work, and support services to enable them to leave the program and become self-sufficient."[11] To that end, states are subsequently enjoined to have a certain percentage of the caseload engaged in work, with work being defined to include "job search and job readiness assistance," as well as "job skills training directly related to employment."[12]

Furthermore, for each adult recipient of assistance, state welfare agencies are given the option—after consultation with the recipient—to develop an "individual responsibility plan," which is designed to "set forth an employment goal for the individual," to "set forth the obligations of the individual" (which may include "attend[ing] parenting and money management classes"), to "increase the responsibility and amount of work the individual is to handle over time," and to list the services to be provided by the state to the individual (including "job counseling") to enable the individual to "obtain and keep employment in the private sector."[13] PRWORA leaves it up to states whether to require such agreements, but all have done so (Lurie 2001, 4).

In general, observers have been surprised at the rapidity and extent of the changes made in welfare offices—changes "reflecting the employment and antidependency goals" of PRWORA (Gais et al. 2001, 36). Anecdotal evidence points to some of these changes. For example, posters are now on display in welfare offices, with texts such as "Work First So That Your Child Is Not the Next Generation on Welfare" and "Time Is Running Out/Welcome Job Seekers, Your Independence Is Our Success." The altered titles of frontline workers in welfare offices (with "new titles entail[ing] real changes in duties") also illustrate the attempt to promote the self-sufficiency of recipients. Thus Michigan has replaced its "Assistance Payment Worker[s]" with "Family Independence Specialists" (46).

In practice, caseworkers often strive to help welfare recipients become more self-sufficient through intensely personal interactions, in which they spur recipients to reshape their attitudes toward life. For example, a caseworker in Riverside, California (from one of the most successful pre-PRWORA work programs), described her message to welfare recipients as follows: "what I'm going to do for you is to teach you a better way of life, how to handle things better, to like yourself better, [but] you've got to show up every day and try your hardest" (quoted in Bardach 1997, 260). Similarly, a Manpower Demonstration Research Corporation (MDRC) study of welfare reform in Cleveland, Los Angeles, Miami, and Philadelphia found that "case managers in all four sites expressed the sense that they were responsible for helping recipients shift their opinions, habits, and attitudes about work and self-sufficiency" (Brock, Nelson, and Reiter 2002, 74). These attempts of caseworkers today to shift "opinions, habits, and attitudes" are reminiscent of Brace's nineteenth-century contention that effective work with the poor must touch "habits of life and the inner forces which form character" (1880/1967, 22–23).

According to an alternate understanding, what caseworkers do is not so much change recipients' attitudes as encourage them to live in conformity with the attitudes they already have. Thus Lawrence Mead argues:

> When asked . . . most welfare recipients and other poor people say that they want to work. If they do not actually work, the reason is that the practical

> difficulties seem overwhelming, not that they reject the idea. Not working, in fact, causes them shame and discouragement, since they are not living by their own values. This gap between intention and behavior is what makes work enforcement necessary. But acceptance of the work ethic also makes it possible. Mandatory work programs do not ask most people to do something alien to them. (1997b, 64)[14]

Attempting to inculcate virtuous attitudes—or even to encourage behavior that accords with existing virtuous attitudes—is of course not an easy task. Not surprisingly, then, many case workers seem to be uncomfortable with these newfound responsibilities. Thus Irene Lurie notes that case workers "often feel unprepared and reluctant to get involved with their clients' personal problems" (2001, 5). Furthermore, case workers often have little opportunity to interact with their clients, which may make it hard for case workers effectively to fulfill their new responsibilities. Thus the MDRC study comments that "recipients generally spend little time with their welfare-to-work case managers" (Brock, Nelson, and Reiter 2002, 76).

Nevertheless, case workers sometimes do succeed in motivating and reorienting recipients to test and—hopefully—improve themselves by entering the world of work. Summarizing evidence from Milwaukee's New Hope Project, Mead concludes that the experiment there "clearly suggests that case managers with powers both to help and obligate the dependent poor [that is, the combination of conditional restraints and moral suasion] might begin to reverse the defeatism that is the strongest deterrent to their advancement" (2000, 32).

Eugene Bardach reports that successful case managers in effect teach welfare recipients "to assume personal responsibility," which is seen not just as an obligation, but also as "liberation from a life of passivity and disorganization" (1997, 259). The case for work is also made in terms of self-improvement, nonfinancial as well as financial. Thus an Oklahoma job readiness workbook stresses that employment enables people to "set a good example for [their] children," to have "something worthwhile to do" with their lives, and to "feel like [they] belong" (quoted in Bardach 1997, 257).

In the abstract, then, a heightened sense of personal responsibility and self-worth is among the factors that enable welfare recipients to seek employment. In more concrete terms, recipients are enabled to enter the workforce by developing the virtuous habits and behaviors that are prerequisites for employment. For employment training to be successful, it must teach prospective workers

> what behaviors are important and how to demonstrate them successfully. These behaviors include getting to work regularly and on time; working well with others; accepting constructive feedback; resolving conflicts

> appropriately; and, in general, being a reliable, responsible employee. (U.S. General Accounting Office 1996, 13)

Virtues like these are admittedly modest. Nevertheless, to the extent that welfare reform inculcates them and thereby enables recipients to move into the workforce (the result being that the virtues are further enhanced over time by continued experience on the job), it is accomplishing something that is both important and praiseworthy.

Objections

It might be argued that PRWORA's attempt to promote virtue is illegitimate, because it is partial. Some of the poor are asked to manifest virtue, but not the rich; and, among the poor, women—the vast majority of welfare recipients—are asked to manifest virtue, but men are not. A third objection could be made from a libertarian standpoint: PRWORA does not produce true self-reliance, because welfare recipients (and former recipients, beneficiaries of programs like the Earned Income Tax Credit [EITC]) continue to benefit from government largesse.

The first of these objections is effectively raised in chapter 4 of this volume:

> In capitalist societies such as . . . the United States it is simply not true that, outside of the welfare system, norms of work apply to all. For example, those who inherit large sums of wealth can live off this wealth without supplying any work. Surely, then, there is objectionable inequity when we enforce work norms on welfare recipients while leaving the wealthy to share in the social product without working.[15]

Although it is true that PRWORA mandates work only among (some of) the poor, the force of White's objection is mitigated—though not eliminated, I would concede—when we realize that there is far less need to require the rich to work; in practice, the work levels of the American rich are already high.

Long ago de Tocqueville observed that wealthy Americans were ashamed to not work. "A rich man believes that he owes it to public opinion to devote his leisure to some operation of industry or commerce or to some public duty. He would deem himself disreputable if he used his life only for living" (de Tocqueville 1835–40/2000, II:18:525). It remains the case today that the idle rich are few and far between in the United States. A recent survey of individuals who have accumulated $1 million or more in assets concluded that "it is seldom luck or inheritance or advanced degrees or even intelligence that enables people to amass fortunes. Wealth is more often the result of a lifestyle of hard work, perseverance, planning, and, most of all, self-discipline" (Stanley and Danko 1996, 1–2).[16]

Census evidence tabulating family income further illustrates that the idle poor are more numerous than the idle rich. Among families in the bottom income quintile in 2002, less than half of the householders worked (49 percent), and less than a quarter (23.7 percent) worked at full-time jobs fifty weeks or more in a year (for definition of householder, see U.S. Department of Labor 2004). By contrast, in the top income quintile, 90.1 percent of householders worked and 74.1 percent at full-time jobs fifty weeks or more. Among families whose income was in the top 5 percent, 90 percent of householders worked and 73.1 percent at full-time jobs fifty weeks or more (U.S. Department of Labor 2003, table FINC-06).[17]

But even if nonwork is concentrated among the poor, does PRWORA unfairly target poor women rather than poor men (see Mead 1997b, 68)? The force of this objection, as well, is being lessened, albeit not removed, as increased efforts are made to secure child support payments from noncustodial parents of welfare children. PRWORA, following on the heels of earlier welfare legislation, seeks to toughen child support enforcement, so that more absent fathers must help support their families (see Weaver 2000, 76, 405 n. 114). For example, PRWORA includes a provision requiring states either to adopt or to have procedures to permit court or administrative orders instituting pay-or-work programs, in which noncustodial parents of children receiving public assistance must participate in work activities, if they owe child support (see Yates 1997). Less formally, welfare reform also appears to encourage female recipients to make more demands upon their male partners: a recipient who herself faces a work requirement is more likely to demand that the father of her children contribute to supporting her household (see Zedlewski and Alderson 2001; Harden 2001, 1, 30).

To enable welfare fathers to better support their children, over half the states already use some of their TANF funds to provide employment services to low-income noncustodial fathers (Miller and Knox 2001, 9). The recognition that many noncustodial fathers earn too little to pay child support has also led to the creation of experimental child support enforcement programs that encourage work effort among such men and assist them in establishing closer ties to their children and to the mothers of their children (see Mincy and Pouncy 1997).

One such program included a Responsible Fatherhood Curriculum designed to "inform participants about their rights and obligations as noncustodial fathers, to encourage positive parenting behavior, and to enhance their life skills" (Miller and Knox 2001, 18). As this suggests, the curriculum attempts to promote good attitudes and behavior. For example, it teaches that "to be successful, a father must have the desire and commitment to put the needs of his children foremost in his mind" (Hayes with Sherwood 2000, sess. 5, 2). The curriculum also aims to promote participants' self-sufficiency: "personal characteristics that foster self-sufficiency include self-discipline, motivation, and responsibility" (sess. 16, 2).

Admittedly, many fewer welfare fathers than mothers face an effective work test. Nevertheless, these mandatory experimental programs mark at least the start of attempts to promote virtue among poor men by inculcating the behaviors needed for success in the job market and by urging men to do more to assist their children and the mothers of their children.

Libertarians raise a different sort of objection. They contend that poor men and poor women who work but also receive government benefits are not wholly self-sufficient. That libertarian contention is correct, but does it point to a real problem? American public opinion does not think so. Instead, Americans by and large are untroubled by the benefits that continue to go to welfare recipients. As Kent Weaver summarizes the data, "the American people are much less concerned with getting people off welfare and reducing the costs of the system than they are with having recipients make an effort to help themselves" (2000, 186; see also 175). For the most part, Americans hope only to encourage the "responsible behavior of welfare recipients," in particular to have them "engag[e] in work effort"—not to deprive them of government benefits altogether (183).

Libertarian criticism notwithstanding, the public's approval of continued government support for welfare recipients is reasonable. PRWORA defensibly aims only to make the poor more self-reliant. It does not aim to achieve total self-reliance, a goal that is almost certainly unreachable—at least in the short run—for most welfare recipients, and rightly reflects the assumption that self-reliance and dependency are not all-or-nothing propositions: it may be impossible to be slightly pregnant, but it is possible to be somewhat self-reliant. And some self-reliance, it need hardly be said, is better than none.

The subsidies that working welfare mothers receive to pay for transportation and child care costs aim to replace their previous absolute dependency with a partial dependency that is consistent with some measure of self-reliance. By extension, a similar argument can be made on behalf of payments to the working poor from the EITC and other wage subsidies. Seeking to promote the virtue of the welfare and working poor, in other words, is not incompatible with a structural remedy for poverty such as the provision of financial aid—so long as that aid encourages work effort.

The hope underlying all such subsidies is that the welfare and working poor will gradually become more self-sufficient over time (perhaps even over generations), and the expectation is that some measure of properly targeted subsidies will assist them toward that goal. In other words, there is no contradiction in helping the poor to help themselves.

Lawrence Mead has effectively articulated this case for partial self-reliance:

> The American creed does not mandate self-reliance, in the sense of avoiding all dependency on the government. Otherwise, the 45 million Ameri-

> cans who live on Social Security could not feel good about themselves. Rather, it demands that citizens observe certain civilities, such as working and obeying the law. If they do and remain needy, the government will gladly help them. (2001, 206)

In short, PRWORA is not attempting to promote total self-sufficiency and should not be criticized for failing to achieve it. It is instead attempting to achieve something less ambitious but still quite difficult: a significantly greater measure of self-sufficiency for a population that had previously been much more dependent.

Implications

What are the broader implications of PRWORA? How should the act's attempt to promote virtue affect our understanding of American liberal democracy? In conclusion, I offer two brief responses to these questions: one response points to the great ambition of welfare reform, whereas the other suggests its limitation.

On a theoretical level, Galston has argued for a "liberal account of the good" that "constitutes, intentionally, a kind of minimal perfectionism that . . . defines a range of normal, decent human functioning" (1991, 177). PRWORA can be understood as an attempt to promote just this sort of "normal, decent human functioning" by increasing the work effort of welfare recipients. In that respect it marks a return to the efforts of nineteenth-century moral reformers, whose statecraft as soulcraft, as we have seen, sought to reduce poverty and dependency by encouraging virtuous behavior on the part of the dependent poor.

This return to statecraft as soulcraft is noteworthy, because it constitutes a notable departure from much recent liberal governmental practice. Twenty-two years ago George Will argued that liberal theory and practice are defective, precisely because of their reluctance to shape human character (1983). Believing that "government has . . . been contracting in the sphere of concern for the cultivation of character and virtue" (72), Will called for "a public philosophy that can rectify the current imbalance between the political order's meticulous concern for material well-being and its fastidious withdrawal from concern for the inner lives and moral character of citizens" (65).

Writing thirteen years after Will, Michael Sandel testified to the renewed concern with moral character that had begun to characterize the debate over welfare. Whereas conservatives like Milton Friedman had previously criticized welfare "in the name of the voluntarist conception of freedom," a "recrudescence of virtue" (Sandel 1996, 324) became apparent in the transformation of the criticisms of America's welfare system. "Welfare policy was a failure, many now argued, not because it coerced taxpayers but because it bred dependence among recipients and rewarded immoral and irresponsible behavior" (Sandel 1996, 325). Welfare reform was, the late Daniel Patrick Moynihan said, to fulfill "the central task of any society: to produce citizens" (quoted in Sandel, 326).[18]

Although PRWORA does aim to encourage virtuous behavior, I would not say that it seeks to produce citizens—or, at any rate, democratic citizens. To repeat Galston's formulation, the "normal, decent human functioning" that PRWORA elicits is subpolitical behavior—behavior that characterizes workers under authoritarian regimes as well as liberal democracies.[19] Nevertheless, I believe that work is a necessary though not a sufficient condition for citizenship; democracy requires that all citizens share the responsibilities of sovereignty, and that sense rests on the knowledge that one is, in Stuart White's words, doing one's bit. Moreover, in a liberal democratic regime such as ours, one can speculate that in the long run welfare reform may also help promote citizenship. That is, individuals better integrated into society (as a result of joining the workforce) may eventually be more likely also to vote and otherwise to participate in the political process.

But regardless of whether PRWORA produces citizens, its passage is significant in that it constitutes a much more direct effort to promote virtue—admittedly in exchange for benefits—than the tax exemptions accorded religious institutions or the deductibility of mortgage interest. The enactment of PRWORA signifies a newfound recognition of the need for public policy, in Will's words, to "nurtur[e] people so they can be comfortable and competent in society" (1983, 145), to "reward and thereby nurture the attributes essential to strength (industriousness, thrift, deferral of gratification) and . . . [to] discourage the attributes inimical to economic vitality (idleness, dissipation, self-indulgence)" (123).

To attempt to reduce poverty by promoting virtuous behavior—as opposed to attempting to reduce poverty by redistributing income—is a remarkably ambitious undertaking. In his controversial and influential study of urban problems Edward Banfield posited that the urban lower class was characterized by "an outlook and style of life which is radically present-oriented and which therefore attaches no value to work, sacrifice, self-improvement, or service to family, friends, or community." He also hypothesized that "if . . . the lower class were to disappear—if, say, its members were overnight to acquire the attitudes, motivations, and habits of the working class, the most serious and intractable problems of the city would all disappear with it" (1974, 235).

The ultimate aim of PRWORA, I would say, is precisely to lead a significant subset of the members of the lower class to "acquire the attitudes, motivations, and habits of the working class," though obviously not overnight. Banfield quite rightly noted that "no one knows how to change the culture of any part of the population" (1974, 263), and that fact should cause us to temper our expectations. Attempting to promote employment to mothers with no work history—or responsible fatherhood to the men who fathered their children—is surely difficult. It is inconceivable that the task will always be accomplished well; it is more than conceivable, on the other hand, that it will sometimes be accomplished well. In my view it is better to achieve occasional success in promoting virtue than not to seek to promote virtue at all.

Marriage?

PRWORA's attempt to change hearts and minds by inculcating a work ethic among a population previously characterized by nonwork makes it a radically ambitious piece of legislation. We can reasonably hope that it will accomplish at least some good. In another respect, however, PRWORA's effort to promote virtue is arguably not all that ambitious. In practice PRWORA is doing much to achieve one of its two chief goals (encouraging work), but little to achieve the other (encouraging marriage).

As noted earlier, the implementation of PRWORA has focused almost exclusively on getting welfare recipients to work rather than to marry—notwithstanding the findings with which the text of PRWORA begins, which emphasize the importance of marriage rather than work. And the start of PRWORA's text focuses on marriage for good reason. Thus James Q. Wilson has argued that the family is the foundation of public life, so that the problems besetting the urban underclass principally reflect the scarcity of two-parent families in inner cities. To make this case Wilson summarizes familiar evidence like this: when raised in single-parent families, children are much more likely to drop out of school, boys are much more likely to be both out of school and out of work, and girls are much more likely to give birth out of wedlock (2002, 7).[20]

Wilson further contends that this evidence should temper the enthusiasm of PRWORA's proponents:

> It is not obvious why our fears about families should make [PRWORA] seem a solution. If implemented as intended, it will enforce a work requirement on women seeking welfare. In short, it will tell young mothers to be employed, away from their children[,] for much of each week. These children, already fatherless, will now become partially motherless. They will be raised by somebody else. A grandmother? A neighbor? An overworked day care manager? Or they will be left alone. (15)[21]

Wilson's observation—like that of Josephine Shaw Lowell, quoted earlier—points to what is arguably a contradiction between the two sets of virtues that PRWORA attempts to promote. To some extent at least, the virtues of the caring parent (who would like to maximize the time spent with his or her children) conflict with the virtues of the productive employee (who is willing to spend as much time on the job as is necessary to accomplish his or her work successfully). This conflict is not, of course, unique to welfare recipients. It is instead common to all working parents, who must regularly attempt to balance their conflicting obligations at home and on the job. In this sense, what welfare reform is doing is to normalize the welfare population, by requiring recipients to carry out the complicated balancing act that is familiar to working parents.[22]

That balancing act tends to be negotiated far more easily by married parents than by single ones. The relevant question, then, is whether welfare reform is succeeding or can succeed in promoting the raising of children by married parents. As it happens, there is some evidence showing that welfare reform at least correlates with—whether or not it has caused—a modest decline in the percentage of children raised in single-parent families, as well as modest increases in the percentages of children raised by cohabiting and married couples (see Zedlewski and Alderson 2001; Harden 2001; Dupree and Primus 2001, table 2).[23]

Nevertheless, it is still striking that the problem of single-parent families has really been addressed only indirectly, with the work requirement—as we have seen—arguably spurring the increased involvement of welfare fathers in raising their children. To put the question starkly, why is it that we are willing to introduce and enforce a work mandate, whereas we could not conceivably introduce and enforce a comparable marriage mandate?

A sufficient answer to that question is that we know much more about promoting work than we do about promoting marriage (see Horn and Bush 1997, 40). First, there are bureaucratic obstacles that make it hard for the states to promote marriage. James Q. Wilson notes that

> although many states have created programs to reduce illegitimacy, for most bureaucrats who deal with the women who apply for benefits, work trumps legitimacy. . . . Getting women to work is a readily measured goal, saves the state money, and can readily be discussed. By contrast, getting them to have babies only after they are married produces no immediate gains, may cost more time and effort, and requires bureaucrats to talk about delicate matters. (2002, 198)

But it is important to add that to some extent we also lack the will or the desire to promote marriage. As Wilson (2002) goes on to observe, "the elite culture of the United States . . . remains deeply divided about marriage. To some, it is wrong to prefer it to other forms of sexual contact; marriage should not be 'privileged' (by which is meant, endorsed)" (198).

The ambivalence about marriage characterizing the American elite may be reflected in the frequency with which better-off Americans divorce one another. If Wilson is right to contend that fatherlessness is the root problem confronting the urban underclass, we should realize that it is also a problem facing many children of prosperous Americans—admittedly in a less severe form. After all, there are two major sources of fatherlessness in contemporary America: out-of-wedlock births and divorce. It is true that births out of wedlock are far more common among the poor than among others (see Wilson 2002, 211; Sawhill 2003, 91).

Divorce, on the other hand, is far from uncommon among the well-to-do.[24] The American divorce rate is far higher than any other in the industrialized world, with roughly half of all first marriages ending in divorce (see Popenoe 1996, 5). And, in practice, children of divorced parents almost always live with their mothers, with less than half of divorced fathers (according to 1987 and 1988 data) seeing their children more than several times a year (31). Evidence along these lines led William Galston to contend in 1997 that the problems of familial pathology in the inner city are "far from . . . aberrant" but instead only "intensified versions of trends clearly visible throughout society" (153).

Those considerations point to the limits of government's capacity to promote virtue. In practice PRWORA is significant because it mandates work and therefore encourages the development of the modest virtues that work entails. In this respect it represents a governmental effort to foster virtue—if only on a small scale, if only among a small subset of the American population. But the theory underlying PRWORA (as expressed in the legislation's introductory findings) suggests that marriage is more important than work in solving the problems of the urban underclass. Unfortunately, government seems to lack the capacity to do much to promote marriage, and many Americans seem also to be of two minds on the issue.

On the whole, Americans are not comparably divided about the desirability of promoting work. They thus approve government's enjoining the poor. The government, though competent to foster diligence, lacks both the mandate and the competence to promote virtues such as premarital chastity and marital fidelity—among the poor or anyone else.

Notes

1. See chapter 4 for Rawls's account of "surfers[, who] must somehow support themselves."
2. Note that these two virtues correspond to the moral reformers' virtues of diligence and thrift. Galston goes on to speak of a third virtue, adaptability, necessitated by the likelihood that economic change will require most employees to shift jobs and careers several times in the course of their lives (223–24). I omit mention of this because it is of limited relevance to the condition of welfare recipients with little or no experience as jobholders.
3. Religious institutions are also exempt from taxation because taxing them would arguably infringe on Americans' free exercise of religion, guaranteed by the First Amendment to the Constitution.
4. See also Alan Charles Raul, "Undermining Society's Morals," *Washington Post*, November 28, 2003, p. A41: "Favoring home ownership over renting

has . . . certain utilitarian justifications. But the fact is that we collectively believe that the country benefits from the moral strength growing out of families owning and investing in their own homes."

5. Coulson notes that the researchers whose work he summarizes "have taken great care to overcome the objection that it's the type of people who choose ownership that makes the difference, and not the fact of owning or renting" (14).
6. I say to some extent because it is unclear that the improvement in homeowners' behavior justifies the size of the tax advantages that they enjoy (Coulson 2002, 14).
7. "Deserted wives with children must not be treated as widows, for it has been found that to deal as tenderly with them as sympathy would dictate, leads other men to desert their families" (106). Lowell did not discuss the issue of relief for mothers of illegitimate children, presumably because of the rarity of illegitimacy in her day. If a child was conceived out of wedlock, generally speaking either a shotgun wedding took place or the child was given up for adoption.
8. H.R.3734, Personal Responsibility and Work Opportunity Reconciliation Act of 1996 (Enrolled as Agreed to or Passed by Both House and Senate) [hereafter "PRWORA"], Section 101(9)(C). The complete text of PRWORA is available online at http://thomas.loc.gov/cgi-bin/query/z?c104:H.R.3734.ENR: (accessed July 22, 2005). The scholarly source for this statistic may have been M. Anne Hill and June O'Neill (1993). Summarizing evidence from the National Longitudinal Survey of Youth tracking individuals from 1979 through 1987, Hill and O'Neill report as follows: "Among white women from welfare families 31 percent ever go on welfare themselves, compared to only 5.4 percent from non-welfare families. Among black young women these proportions were 55 percent for those from welfare families compared to 25 percent who were not from welfare families and for Hispanic women 38 percent versus 12 percent" (44).
9. Rector's testimony, it should be made clear, summarizes articles that have appeared in refereed scientific journals, such as the *Journal of Human Resources* and the *Social Science Quarterly*.
10. PRWORA, Section 101(1)-(2).
11. PRWORA, Section 402(a)(1)(A)(i).
12. PRWORA, Section 407(c)(2)(d)(6) and Section 407(c)(2)(d)(9).
13. PRWORA, Section 408(b)(2)(A)(i–iv).
14. For discussions of paternalist attempts to get the poor to live in accordance with their values, see Mead (1997a).
15. Note, however, that in Stuart White's view the existence of the idle rich does not obviously invalidate the imposition of a work requirement on welfare recipients. See where he defends a work requirement in principle, hypothesizing that it might "legitimate the claims [and thereby improve the lot] of the worst-off."
16. They define millionaires as those with $1 million in assets (12). They report that 80 percent of the millionaires whom they surveyed are "first-generation affluent" (9); two-thirds work "between forty-five and fifty-five hours per week" (10); "more than half never received as much as $1 in inheritance" (16).
17. Here I summarize data for work experience of householders. Of the 10 percent of top-quintile householders who did not work in 2002, in all likelihood

many were retirees. The data for age of householders show that there were 1,005,000 householders age 65 or higher in top-quintile families in 2002. It is reasonable to suppose that there was a substantial overlap between that group and the 1,493,000 nonworking householders in these families. By contrast, there was a much larger group of householders age 65 or higher—3,602,000—among bottom-quintile families in 2002. But those retirement-age householders can account for less than half of the 7,710,000 bottom-quintile families in which the householder did not work at all in 2002.

18. Moynihan, ironically, was to fiercely oppose the passage of PRWORA.
19. In chapter 8 of this volume, Mead speaks of "several competences" that are viewed as components of citizenship in addition to work, including "obeying the law, getting through school, and [obviously only in the context of Anglophone polities] speaking English." In my view, adding Mead's other competences to work still does not constitute democratic citizenship, for which some measure of political participation is necessary.
20. The research on the harmfulness of being raised by a single parent is reminiscent of the research on the harmfulness of being raised on welfare (summarized on p. 231 of this chapter).
21. Wilson's concern about overworked caretakers is well taken. Nevertheless, it is not clear that placement in day care is generally harmful to children of welfare mothers (see p. 232 of this chapter).
22. It might be more accurate, though, to say that welfare reform is mandating a balancing act that was already being carried out—for the most part surreptitiously—before the reform. A survey of single mothers who received prereform welfare (at a time when a recipient's stipend was often lowered if she reported earnings) found that 46 percent of the recipients worked; only 5 percent of all the recipients reported their earnings, whereas 39 percent of all recipients did not report their earnings. These earnings helped welfare mothers cover their expenses by supplementing the meager payments that welfare offered them (see Edin and Lein 1997, 43–45).
23. In 1995, 34.8 percent of black, non-Hispanic children lived with married parents, 47.1 percent lived with single mothers, and 2.9 percent lived with cohabiting mothers. In 2000, by contrast, 38.9 percent lived with married parents, 43.1 percent lived with single mothers, and 4.2 percent lived with cohabiting mothers.
24. "Divorce is common among better-off people. It is not hard to see why. In the first place, they are more likely to be married and hence to have divorce as an option. Even more important, they can more easily afford divorce. Though women tend to be made worse off by these splits, their own earning power makes it easier for them to get by than is the case for their poorer, unskilled sisters" (Wilson 2002, 212).

References

Banfield, Edward C. 1974. *The Unheavenly City Revisited.* Boston, Mass.: Little, Brown.

Bardach, Eugene. 1997. "Implementing a Paternalist Welfare-to-Work Program." In *The New Paternalism: Supervisory Approaches to Poverty,* edited by Lawrence M. Mead. Washington, D.C.: Brookings Institution.

Brace, Charles Loring. 1880/1967. *The Dangerous Classes of New York and Twenty Years' Work among Them,* 3rd ed. Montclair, N.J.: Patterson Smith.

Brock, Thomas, Laura C. Nelson, and Megan Reiter. 2002. "Readying Welfare Recipients for Work: Lessons from Four Big Cities as They Implement Welfare Reform." New York: Manpower Demonstration Research Corporation. Available at: http://www.mdrc.org/Reports2002/UC_ReadyingWelfare/UC-Full Report.pdf (accessed July 22, 2005).

Coulson, N. Edward. 2002. "Housing Policy and the Social Benefits of Homeownership," *Business Review* (of the Federal Reserve Bank of Philadelphia). Second Quarter 2002: 7–16.

Council of Economic Advisers. 1964. *Economic Report of the President.* Washington: U.S. Government Printing Office.

Duncan, Greg J., and P. Lindsay Chase-Lansdale. 2001. "Welfare Reform and Children's Well-Being." In *The New World of Welfare,* edited by Rebecca M. Blank and Ron Haskins. Washington, D.C.: Brookings Institution.

Dupree, Allen, and Wendell Primus. 2001. "Declining Share of Children Lived with Single Mothers in the Late 1990s: Substantial Differences by Race and Income." Washington, D.C.: Center on Budget and Policy Priorities. Available at: http://www.cbpp.org/6-15-01wel.htm (accessed July 22, 2005).

Edin, Kathryn, and Laura Lein. 1997. *Making Ends Meet: How Single Mothers Survive Welfare and Low-Wage Work.* New York: Russell Sage Foundation.

Gais, Thomas L., Richard P. Nathan, Irene Lurie, and Thomas Kaplan. 2001. "Implementation of the Personal Responsibility Act of 1996." In *The New World of Welfare,* edited by Rebecca M. Blank and Ron Haskins. Washington, D.C.: Brookings Institution.

Galston, William A. 1991. *Liberal Purposes: Goods, Virtues, and Diversity in the Liberal State.* Cambridge: Cambridge University Press.

———. 1997. "A Progressive Family Policy for the Twenty-First Century." In *Building the Bridge: 10 Big Ideas to Transform America,* edited by Will Marshall. Lanham, Md.: Rowman and Littlefield.

Gutmann, Amy, and Dennis Thompson. 1996. *Democracy and Disagreement.* Cambridge, Mass.: Harvard University Press.

Harden, Blaine. 2001. "Two-Parent Families Rise After Change in Welfare Laws." *New York Times,* August 12, 2001, pp. 1, 30.

Hayes, Eileen, with Kay Sherwood. 2000. "The Responsible Fatherhood Curriculum: A Curriculum Developed for the Parents' Fair Share Demonstration." New York: Manpower Demonstration Research Corporation. Available at: http://www.mdrc.org/inpractice/FatherhoodCurriculum/FatherhoodContents.htm (accessed July 22, 2005).

Hill, M. Anne, and June O'Neill. 1993. *Underclass Behaviors in the United States: Measurement and Analysis of Determinants.* New York: Center for the Study of Business and Government, Baruch College, City University of New York.

Horn, Wade F., and Andrew Bush. 1997. "Fathers and Welfare Reform." *The Public Interest* 129(fall): 38–49.

Kaus, Mickey. 1992. *The End of Equality.* New York: Basic Books.

Lowell, Josephine Shaw. 1884/1971. *Public Relief and Private Charity.* New York: Arno Press and The New York Times.

Lurie, Irene. 2001. "Changing Welfare Offices." Welfare Reform & Beyond. Policy Brief No. 9. Washington, D.C.: Brookings Institution. Available at: http://

www.brook.edu/dybdocroot/wrb/publications/pb/pb09.pdf (accessed July 22, 2005).

Macedo, Stephen. 1991. *Liberal Virtues: Citizenship, Virtue, and Community in Liberal Constitutionalism.* Oxford: Clarendon Press.

Mayer, Susan E. 1997. *What Money Can't Buy: Family Income and Children's Life Chances.* Cambridge, Mass.: Harvard University Press.

Mead, Lawrence M., ed. 1997a. *The New Paternalism: Supervisory Approaches to Poverty.* Washington, D.C.: Brookings Institution.

———. 1997b. "Welfare Employment." In *The New Paternalism: Supervisory Approaches to Poverty,* edited by Lawrence M. Mead. Washington, D.C.: Brookings Institution.

———. 2000. "The Twilight of Liberal Welfare Reform." *The Public Interest* 139(spring): 22–34.

———. 2001. "The Politics of Conservative Welfare Reform." In *The New World of Welfare,* edited by Rebecca Blank and Ron Haskins. Washington, D.C.: Brookings Institution.

Miller, Cynthia, and Virginia Knox. 2001. "The Challenge of Helping Low-Income Fathers Support Their Children: Final Lessons from Parents' Fair Share." New York: Manpower Demonstration Research Corporation. Available at: http://www.mdrc.org/publications/104/full.pdf (accessed July 22, 2005).

Mincy, Ronald B., and Hillard Pouncy. 1997. "Paternalism, Child Support Enforcement, and Fragile Families." In *The New Paternalism,* edited by Lawrence M. Mead. Washington, D.C.: Brookings Institution.

Moynihan, Daniel Patrick. 1973. "The Crises in Welfare." In *Coping: Essays on the Practice of Government.* New York: Random House.

Popenoe, David. 1996. *Life Without Father: Compelling New Evidence that Fatherhood and Marriage are Indispensable for the Good of Children and Society.* New York: Free Press.

Raul, Alan Charles. 2003. "Undermining Society's Morals." *Washington Post,* November 28, 2003, p. A41.

Rawls, John. 1971. *A Theory of Justice.* Cambridge, Mass.: Harvard University Press.

Rector, Robert. 2001. *The Effects of Welfare Reform.* Testimony before the Subcommittee on Human Resources of the Committee on Ways and Means of the United States House of Representatives, March 15, 2001. Washington, D.C.: The Heritage Foundation. Available at: http://www.heritage.org/Research/Welfare/Test031501b.cfm (accessed July 22, 2005).

Sandel, Michael J. 1996. *Democracy's Discontent: America in Search of a Public Philosophy.* Cambridge, Mass.: Belknap Press of Harvard University Press.

Sawhill, Isabel V. 2003. "The Behavioral Aspects of Poverty." *The Public Interest* 153(fall): 79–93.

Schwartz, Joel. 2000. *Fighting Poverty with Virtue: Moral Reform and America's Urban Poor, 1825–2000.* Bloomington: Indiana University Press.

Stanley, Thomas J., and William D. Danko. 1996. *The Millionaire Next Door: The Surprising Secrets of America's Wealthy.* Atlanta, Ga.: Longstreet Press.

de Tocqueville, Alexis. 1835–40/2000. *Democracy in America,* translated, edited, and with an introduction by Harvey C. Mansfield and Delba Winthrop. Chicago: University of Chicago Press.

U.S. Congress. 1996. *Personal Responsibility and Work Opportunity Reconciliation Act of 1996* (Enrolled as Agreed to or Passed by Both House and Senate). HR 3734. 104th Cong. 2nd sess. Washington: U.S. Government Printing Office.

U.S. Department of Commerce. U.S. Census Bureau [Census Bureau]. 1996. *Statistical Abstract of the United States 1996.* Washington: U.S. Government Printing Office.

U.S. Department of Health and Human Services. 2000. "Temporary Assistance for Needy Families (TANF) Percent of Total U.S. Population, 1960–1999." Washington, D.C.: Administration for Children and Families. Available at: http://www.acf.hhs.gov/news/stats/6097rf.htm (accessed July 22, 2005).

U.S. Department of Labor. U.S. Bureau of Labor Statistics [CPS]. 2003. *Current Population Survey.* "Percent Distribution of Families, by Selected Characteristics Within Income Quintile and Top 5 Percent in 2002." Table FINC-06. Available at: http://ferret.bls.census.gov/macro/032003/faminc/new06_000.htm (accessed July 22, 2005).

———. 2004. *Current Population Survey—Definitions and Explanations.* Washington: Population Division, Fertility & Family Statistics Branch. Available at: http://www.census.gov/population/www/cps/cpsdef.html (accessed July 22, 2005).

U.S. General Accounting Office. 1996. *Employment Training: Successful Projects Show Common Strategy.* HEHS-96-108. Washington: U.S. Government Printing Office.

Weaver, R. Kent. 2000. *Ending Welfare as We Know It.* Washington, D.C.: Brookings Institution.

Will, George F. 1983. *Statecraft as Soulcraft: What Government Does.* New York: Simon & Schuster.

Wilson, James Q. 1991. *On Character: Essays by James Q. Wilson.* Washington, D.C.: AEI Press.

———. 2002. *The Marriage Problem: How Our Culture has Weakened Families.* New York: HarperCollins.

Yates, Jessica. 1997. "Child Support Enforcement and Welfare Reform." *Issue Notes* 1(5). Washington, D.C.: Welfare Information Network. Available at: http://www.financeprojectinfo.org/Publications/childsupportresource.htm (accessed July 22, 2005).

Zedlewski, Sheila R., and Donald W. Alderson. 2001 "Before and After Reform: How Have Families Changed?" Washington, D.C.: Urban Institute.

Chapter 11

The Deeper Issues

LAWRENCE M. MEAD AND CHRISTOPHER BEEM

WELFARE REFORM represents a sea change in American and British domestic policy. This volume demonstrates that political theory offers valuable resources for understanding that change and the controversy surrounding it. Each of our authors appraises the shift and asks how it affects our understanding of citizenship and democracy. Here we identify eight issues that seem to cut to the heart of the debate, and we summarize what our authors say about them. These disputes seem to capture what is most deeply at stake in welfare politics. They explain why it is so profoundly divisive for political actors and interpreters alike.

Seven of the issues are fairly specific, but crosscutting them we find a deeper question—the meaning of citizenship. Some of our authors see the citizen as the autonomous self of liberal theory, in which individuals make demands on government. But obligations from either government or society are minimal and arise only out of pragmatic agreement. Others assert a more ambitious, communitarian vision in which citizens are defined not only by their rights, but also by their obligations toward others.

In the first conception, rights come first because justice comes first. In terms most clearly defined by John Rawls, individuals must agree about what justice requires before the state can make any demands for individual behavior. This also means that concerns about equality before the law, about the equal enforcement of those rights, become paramount. Welfare, therefore, is about protecting the rights of society's most marginalized individuals.

In the second conception, good behavior is grounded in facts about the human condition that transcend the social and political fabric.[1] Certain civilities are deemed essential before human beings can even associate. Therefore these virtues must be required first. Only after human community is possible does justice become an issue. Welfare then is about what is due to the poor, and what can be expected from them, as a result of their membership in society.

We take up our seven more specific issues starting at the broadest and ending with the narrowest. We suggest places where further inquiry might help to resolve the differences or, at least, understand them more fully. Some of these directions involve empirical research and some theoretical reflection. By these means, theorists and policy analysts alike may pursue welfare politics to a deeper level. At the end, we return to the core issue of citizenship, which appears throughout.

Entitlement

Perhaps the most heated issue in welfare politics is the criteria families must meet to receive assistance. Before reform, eligibility was usually granted based on entitlement, meaning that the rules took account only of whether families were financially needy. This philosophy became dominant in the 1960s, when virtually all stipulations about how recipients had acted or should act in return for aid were abandoned. In that period, as Susan Mayer observes, "America's welfare policies were almost exclusively aimed at meeting the material needs of the poor" (1997, 5).

Opponents of AFDC attacked entitlement, saying that it promoted dysfunctional lifestyles among the poor (Mead 1986). At the core of reform, accordingly, is the opposed philosophy of conditionality. Now to get aid, recipients have to meet not only financial criteria but behavioral tests meant to promote constructive behavior. In particular, they must either be working, looking for work, or, in some cases, in training for future work.[2]

Opponents of reform, such as Pateman or King, reject this change as threatening to democratic citizenship. Following T. H. Marshall, they see citizenship as something equal and universal, and in tension with the inequalities meted out by the economy (Marshall 1964, chap. 4). To enforce work in welfare is to impose those economic inequalities on citizenship. In King's words, it turns recipients into economic participants rather than citizens.

Instead of requiring work, the opponents say, government should guarantee people the resources needed to participate fully in the society regardless of their economic position. Entitlement welfare was one way to do that. But Pateman would do more than simply restore AFDC. She advocates a wider form of entitlement proposed by Philippe Van Parijs—an unconditional basic income that would go to all adults regardless of need or work effort (1991, 1995). A guaranteed income is the only way to ensure what King calls "the social bases of democratic participation and inclusion" (this volume, p. 66). For Pateman and Van Parijs, this assurance is thus a necessary feature of a genuinely democratic society.

The advocates of conditionality, in contrast, see citizenship as rooted in economic function rather than in tension with it. This position claims a pedigree from classical liberal thought. In Locke, labor creates property, and property creates the need for government. That is, labor is not just about supporting oneself; it is the foundation of any claim to citizenship. Thus those who do not labor inherently have less standing in a liberal society that those who do. Locke, as White notes, would have conscripted welfare recipients into the military rather than leave them idle.

In that spirit, Galston, Mead, Wax, and White criticize entitlement as a form of free riding. Those who are guaranteed an income depend on the labor of other citizens and need not labor themselves. Fairness requires that they have to work alongside the taxpayers, on whom they rely. To end entitlement is not to threaten equal citizenship but to revoke an unjustified privilege. Galston argues that democratic citizenship is and always was conditional on good behavior in several respects. Serious lawbreaking, for example, is a disqualification, so that in every state but Vermont felons lose the right to vote. Wax cites research suggesting that the popular insistence on work is buried deep in the human past. Strong feelings against free riding were perhaps vital to sustaining the earliest efforts at human social cooperation. Galston and White contend that, under the scheme of mutual cooperation imagined in much contemporary liberal theory, one may demand some effort from the dependent in return for support, at least in principle.

What really separates the two sides? One issue is how democratic citizenship relates to the economy. Is the workplace a threat to equal citizenship or its embodiment? In part, the question is empirical. As Pateman notes, classical and early modern thinkers doubted whether people who had to work for a living had the autonomy to be citizens, because they were subject to the authority of employers. The idea that the market prevents political equality lived on in the severe images of capitalism formed by nineteenth-century social democrats, and by Marx. John Edwards's campaign theme in 2004 that there are two Americas evoked similar notions. But in today's economy, almost everyone labors in a workplace where they are subject to the authority of others. If classical doubts apply to all of us, they apply to none of us. What is more, labor is frequently less physically arduous than it was a century or more ago, and the insecurities of the market are cushioned by social programs, some of them unaffected by welfare reform. As Mead notes, most Americans now find employment fulfilling. In this view, working is not opposed to citizenship but an aspect of it.

Another, more theoretical issue concerns the relative role of rights and obligations in constituting citizenship, as suggested already. The defenders of entitlement evoke a liberal image in which citizenship consists entirely of rights. These claims counter the burdens and inequities stemming from the economic order. The defenders of conditionality are more communitarian. For them, working and other social duties are incorporated within citizenship. The capacity to fulfill what Mead calls the common obligations, including work, becomes essential to the equal respect that citizenship is supposed to bring. In one conception, to protect people from the inequities of the labor market is part of the promise of democracy, in the other a denial of it.

A further theoretical issue—perhaps the most fundamental—is the notion of fairness that drives welfare reform. Why do those who work see not working—if one draws aid—as unfair? Why is working regarded as an obligation, not simply as a preference? Public support for reciprocity, which is forceful, seems to go beyond mere opposition to free riding, to demand reliability of a more fundamental kind. But what is the substance of that demand, and are its roots anthropological, cultural, or what?

What Should Be Enforced?

Following the general issue of entitlement comes the question of what specific behaviors should be demanded as a condition of aid. The disputes here are somewhat more practical.

Chiefly, conditionality means that recipients must work in exchange for benefits, but what does this mean in practice? Wax shows that states have implemented the work test flexibly; many allow exemptions and reduced obligations depending on the circumstances of mothers. This suggests that even among supporters of conditionality, work is a principle, but not something that society defines rigidly. Alternatively, opponents of welfare reform accept that a burden to work must bear on someone, but they resist the idea that it has to bear on the recipients of aid at the time they are dependent. Rather, it might bear on them at a different time, as in social insurance, where beneficiaries contribute toward benefits in advance of claiming them. Or it might bear on other people entirely. At the extreme, the taxpayers bear the burden, and we are back to entitlement.

Pateman makes the further argument that, even if society depends on employment from its members, welfare need not enforce it. Everyone is to some extent dependent, and to some extent functional, in a complex web of interdependence. Once people appreciate this, they will willingly share the burdens of the society. Different people will work or be dependent at different times, without government explicitly mandating it.

Interestingly, some of the proponents accept this idea, although they still endorse work tests. Deacon cites research on the way people juggle their many obligations. They clearly are aware of social duties, even if they balance them against personal needs. Wax suggests that employment today is attractive enough so that most people would continue to work even if it were not required. This internal drive to work might make the costs of free riding tolerable and sustain the work ethic even if entitlement welfare lived on.

Beyond the work test, Schwartz mentions child support as an obligation to be enforced. Deacon and White would require that parents educate their children, because this is important for the formation of citizens. Society might even intervene in parenting, because it is even more important than schooling for creating functioning adults. Under Deacon's mutualist philosophy, what society demands of its members could be quite extensive, but these duties are largely left undefined. And in all these cases, it is unclear whether, or how far, society needs to do more than trust parents to act in the best interests of their children. Were that trust enough, families would generate able citizens with little special attention by government, as classical liberalism always assumed.

Where do the two sides differ? The empirical issues include which competences society must assume in its members, and how fully these are achieved without explicit enforcement. Inquiry would no doubt return a mixed verdict, with some civilities in decline, especially among lower-income people, and some not. The public response to the question of competence is complex. Americans seem to adhere to a hybrid ethos, insisting on explicit obligations below the poverty level, at least for people dependent on government. But above that level, there is little attempt or desire to enforce good behavior beyond the criminal law. Perhaps it is assumed that if people are competent, self-interest as well as social mores will motivate them to behave well. Alternatively, perhaps nonpoor Americans simply oppose any enforcement that might curb their behavior. Thus, at low levels of the society, Americans seem to be communitarians, while above that they are classical liberals. They thus affirm both the images of citizenship about which philosophers disagree.

The more theoretical question is what competences we ideally would want citizens in a liberal society to have, aside from practical necessity. The public insists that certain obligations be demanded of the dependent, especially work and child support payment. To the voters, it is not enough to say that norms are informally observed, let alone that noncompliance is tolerable. Rather, these civilities are seen as ends in themselves that government must affirm. Again, that reflects a communitarian vision, an idea that good behavior comes before claims to social justice. Why is that feeling so strong, and how can society defend it, particularly if such explicit demands are made only of the dependent?

Care Work

The moral legitimacy of the work test is perhaps most disputed when considering whether welfare mothers can satisfy it by taking care of their own children. The claim here is not the same as entitlement, or receiving aid without behavioral conditions. Rather, it is that, in caring for their children, single mothers already meet the chief condition that society might set. That is, they are already performing beneficial work, and welfare is compensation for that labor.

As Beem and Pateman note, the original rationale for family welfare was the assumption that a single mother could not both raise her children and work. Under welfare, her caring responsibility took precedence over the normal obligation to support her family financially. At least part of the reason for the demise of AFDC is that, after 1960, this assumption came into question. More and more mothers who were not poor entered the paid work force, and Western society began to discard the idea that motherhood and working were incompatible. And if middle-class mothers had to work, it seemed right, at least in America, that welfare mothers should have to do so too.

Opponents of welfare reform continue to maintain that care work should satisfy the work test. Pateman, for instance, argues that there is a need for "social reproduction" that cannot be squared with the capitalist economy's demand for labor. A single mother is therefore entitled to receive support outside the marketplace.

Several other authors endorse this idea, even if they also affirm the work test. Beem advocates a form of guaranteed support for needy mothers, although he limits it to those who have shown an attachment to the workforce. At our authors' meeting, Galston noted that stay-at-home mothers are not seen as social parasites. Most Americans accept their uncompensated work as a worthy social contribution. Thus, care work remains an important social value, and the vogue for mothers working has not totally eclipsed it.

Stuart White has provided a general argument that citizens in a liberal society can be supported outside paid employment provided they perform civic labor, meaning that they contribute to the society in unpaid ways. Two conditions must be met: the task they perform must be assigned by people other than themselves, and they must perform it well enough to serve a social interest (2003, chap. 5).

The proponents of reform might accept civic labor in principle, but they deny that a single mother caring for her own children qualifies. Mead and Wax argue that White's conditions are not met. Society never commissioned welfare mothers to raise their children at public expense; rather, it faces a fait accompli when they have children and expect support. Nor, on current evidence, do they perform that task well enough to serve a social interest. Therefore, if single mothers are to draw aid, they must show their accountability to society by working in private or public jobs, as other mothers do.

More generally, skeptics note that advocates of care work do not present any general theory about what tasks society should accept as civic labor.

Why should single mothers have special claims for support? "Why," Wax asks, "should not other unpaid but possibly valuable contributions also get public support, such as creating graffiti art . . . and playing classical music in subway stations?" Perhaps caring for a child has greater moral claims than these tasks, but why does that entitle the mother to aid without questions? Deacon accepts that to provide adequately for care may require extensive social benefits, but he still doubts that such support should be given without conditions.

Wax also questions whether the caring function is in fact threatened if public support is denied. Most mothers, including single mothers, are already working substantial hours and apparently raising their children adequately. Why should not poor single mothers do the same? Just as the opponents of reform question whether entitlement welfare really threatens the work ethic (see above), so here the proponents of reform ask whether welfare reform really threatens caring. To the contrary, as chapter 1 shows, they can argue on current evidence that when single mothers work the effects on children are mostly negligible or positive. As Wax also shows, society enforces the work norm in welfare flexibly to help reconcile it with the caring burden. Work and caring are thus served together and are not seen as opposites as they were a century ago.

One empirical question that divides the two sides is how adequately caring is performed without entitlement welfare. The idea that single mothers must no longer choose between market work and care work assumes that both tasks are easier to perform than they once were. A century ago, to make a poor single mother work seemed impracticable or inefficient. The only alternative to funding her to raise her children without work was to put the children in foster care, a drastic and costly alternative. With today's higher real wages, however, employment is a viable alternative for the mother. Both the family and government are better off if she works, even if she still needs some public subsidies. The vast expansion of the child care system also makes this possible. Whether the quality of this care is good enough for optimal child development is another question.

As Beem argues, however, there is reason to doubt whether society can responsibly enforce work during the first year of a child's life. His broader argument is that well-raised children constitute public goods that we cannot assume the private sector will produce. Thus, even under contemporary conditions, we cannot assign the entire onus of care to the mother, any more than we expect the marketplace to produce aircraft carriers for national defense.

The theoretical issue behind care work is whether obligations can be self-chosen. Few would say that rights can be determined solely by those claiming them. But society every day allows people to assume obligations on its behalf, for instance by joining or contributing to charities or community organizations. Those bodies receive support, directly or indirectly, from society. Why shouldn't a welfare mother claim support on the same basis? If there is a difference, it is that the community organization tackles problems not of its own making, while the mother creates her own task by having the child. The key may be whether we regard the caring task as an obligation—or as a claim to entitlement in disguise. The issue reveals a perennial dilemma in welfare policy. Do we focus on the child, who is innocent and whose future well-being is a clear social interest, or on the mother, whose predicament is frequently compounded by her own mistakes.

Preconditions

Another issue is whether conditionality in welfare should have to satisfy any preconditions about the rest of the social order. Conditionality must be viewed not only as just in itself, but as fair given the conditions prevailing outside welfare. Conceivably, one might accept work enforcement in principle but reject it for the society we have.

All our authors set some conditions like this but do so to very different degrees. At one extreme, the opponents of welfare reform use the presence of social injustice to reject conditionality. The very need for welfare, they argue, arises from the structural impediments associated with class, race, and gender. These obstacles make it difficult or impossible for the poor to support themselves. Benefits are thus necessary to compensate for the inequities. To the opponents, then, the idea that the poor must face unique standards of conditionality because of certain behaviors obfuscates or, worse, ratifies the true social realities.

Somewhat further right, Deacon's mutualism assumes that inequality is limited enough to make a common society imaginable, as Tawney earlier argued (1952). White embraces work requirements in principle but opposes them in practice if their enforcement would tend to consolidate the structural disadvantages of the poor. He finally judges the British New Deal as it stands to be unacceptable because its generous elements, such as job training, are insufficient to offset consolidation. He advocates such further steps as tougher taxation of inheritance and mandatory service for all youth, so that not only the poor bear work obligations (2003).[3]

Other proponents of reform, however, set much more limited conditions that largely comport with present policy. Mead admits that work cannot be demanded of aid recipients unless they are employable and jobs exist. Galston insists that to demand work requires that government be willing, if necessary, to guarantee employment in public jobs. Recipients put to work also have to achieve some minimum income and have a chance to improve their skills. Wax says that government must provide surrounding social benefits, such as education, health care, and wage subsidies.

To some extent the differences are empirical. How serious are the barriers that deter the welfare poor from supporting themselves? On this question, recent evidence favors the conservatives. The American caseload fall demonstrated that most recipients of entitlement aid could work. But as Mead argues, the situation is not so simple. How imposing the barriers are really involves two related judgments, one about the demands of working and the other about how capable the poor are of meeting them. Liberals typically find the impediments more onerous and doubt the ability of poor adults to make headway, while conservatives are more optimistic on both counts. Especially, opponents of reform doubt that the low-wage jobs most available to welfare leavers allow them to earn enough to live or to improve their earnings over time, while conservatives say they do. Both sides have a case, in that welfare mothers who work typically do improve their lot, but not by a great deal.[4] Hence, the opponents conclude that society is not just enough to permit welfare reform, while the proponents say that it is.

The judgment about capacity might seem to be no less empirical than the question of barriers, but we believe it has a strong philosophic element because of the judgments about competence involved. Debates among American experts about barriers tend to be statistical and impersonal, but those who do and do not see opportunity for the poor often differ about the personality they impute to unskilled jobseekers. Typically, liberals think that social injustices have left poor people less able to find and keep jobs. Conservatives argue, as President Bush says, that liberals consign the poor needlessly to a tyranny of low expectations. Each of these views reflects a different notion of the ability of the poor to handle their environment. The grounding of such views in divergent visions of agency, or the ability to cope, is more recognized in British debates, in which political theorists have played a larger role.[5]

Preconditions raise the question about whether the quest for justice must come before or after welfare reform. The opponents of reform say before. Convinced as they are that the economy is threatening and unfair, they think that to inflict work on the dependent in advance of a broader social reform would simply institutionalize unfairness. The advocates of reform say that social reform must wait. In part, their case is practical, in that the poor will be in a stronger position to make claims to justice after they are employed than before. White, for one, gives some weight to this contention.

But ultimately, the preferred sequence also reflects the question of citizenship. Does one think justice takes precedence over good behavior, or vice versa? The opponents of reform effectively say that the conduct of the poor cannot be criticized until society is more just. The proponents say the opposite—that only better functioning makes a more egalitarian society imaginable. Mead, for instance, treats justice as an open question, to be decided by the citizens in full standing. But in contemporary society, full standing requires working, at least for the employable. Therefore, welfare adults must work before they can ever enter into the debate about what justice should mean (1992, chap. 11).

Moral Neutrality

A question closely related to entitlement is moral neutrality. The liberal state was designed to limit the moral cognizance of the state, and to set wide latitudes for acceptable behavior. Violation of the criminal law was the only thing that aroused the judgmental potential of government. The rejection of entitlement, however, extends public judgments about lifestyle beyond criminality into other realms of conduct. At least for welfare recipients, government now judges some behaviors so desirable that they must be encouraged and even enforced among people who do not manifest them. That is a change from the recent past.

The defenders of entitlement reject the change and defend moral neutrality. They would have government go on ensuring income to the poor, regardless of how they live. Pateman asks why we should view single motherhood as a problem, and King asks why nonwork should be blamed on the poor rather than on the surrounding society. Such defenses act to fence off the dependent from invidious questions. This reflects the commitment of liberalism, as Wax notes, to defend a "baseline of equal dignity" and "individual moral autonomy." As systematized by John Rawls in *A Theory of Justice*, this sort of liberalism requires that government be impartial among its citizens' plans of life. Justice is not to be based on personal desert but on general rules decided in an original position before individual attributes such as desert are known (1971). Van Parijs takes this to mean that people must be given an income whether they choose to work or not (1991, 1995).

Those who question entitlement also question moral neutrality. Mead treats the setting of collective behavioral norms as a legitimate exercise of democracy. White argues that a liberal government can disallow some lifestyles and affirm others provided it gives practical and not religious or perfectionist reasons for doing so. In other writing, Galston rejects Rawls and contends that liberalism cannot be value-free. To the contrary, it rests on a distinctive conception of the good, a form of minimalist perfectionism that affirms such values as individual rationality and self-reliance (1991).[6]

Following *A Theory of Justice*, Rawls reversed or clarified himself on desert to the extent of excluding voluntary nonworkers from a claim to public support. He concluded that for people not to work when they could violated his assumption that individuals cooperate in society for mutual advantage.[7] White thinks that this reconciled Rawls with earlier liberal thinkers who had no trouble demanding that all citizens contribute to the community. Galston, however, finds that the fix is superficial because Rawls's basic idea of justice still excluded desert. That stance "deprives political philosophy of resources essential to its success."

The real issue here recalls the fault line around citizenship. The question is not desert as such but whether desert or justice has priority over the other. Even in Rawls, desert of a kind can exist. After the basic principles of justice are set, society derives detailed institutions, programs, and policies from them. The latter may well define desired and undesired behaviors, and individuals may well be rewarded or penalized accordingly.[8] Desert in this sense, however, is overshadowed by justice and can have only limited moral standing. One can always argue, as Van Parijs does, that the Rawlsian principles of justice do not permit enforcing desert. Or, like White, one can accept conditionality in principle yet question it in practice because society is not yet just enough.

The other view, reflected in Galston and our more conservative authors, is that desert is part of a broader understanding of social morality that comes before justice. That is, certain civilities are so essential to social cooperation that they must be assumed under any conceivable scheme of justice. Even a liberal society otherwise dedicated to freedom must assume a work ethic, law-abidingness, and so on. Even Mead, who treats the common obligations as a political question and thus changeable, assumes that citizens trust each other enough to cooperate in politics. Only such citizens can have the standing to enter into a debate about what justice should mean. This implies that some civilities have to be expected from the very start. There can be no Rawlsian original position where citizens deliberate about justice knowing nothing about their own characteristics. To the contrary, they must know and trust each other before they can even discuss other political questions, including justice.

Two of our authors go still further, in effect questioning the idea of individual autonomy at the core of liberalism. In Deacon's mutualist vision, government is simply an instrument of society, and thus only one of many means by which society may make moral demands on its members. Those strictures could in principle touch any behaviors that affect others, even in private life. Deacon affirms the right of society to punish any behavior that disturbs others.

Joel Schwartz embraces James Q. Wilson's idea that an orderly society depends, not just on specific good behaviors, but on character, or a general self-restraint. He contends that, in pursuing work as a means of inculcating virtue, welfare is returning to the moralistic cast it had in the nineteenth century. This shift has created a more effective antipoverty policy. Following Galston, Schwartz insists that while these virtues have a practical value, they are also right and good in themselves, and the belief that they are is one reason society pursues them. Thus, social policy must be to some extent perfectionist—the very thing that White, as well as Pateman and King, disallow.

The divisions partly reflect differing empirical judgments about what values or virtues society must enforce to maintain itself, the same question that emerged earlier. Can the inculcation of certain central virtues be left to private society, or must government apply its more heavy-handed suasions? The more philosophic issue is again the nature of citizenship. What values or virtues do we assume when we speak of a liberal political order? Can that conception ever be as value-free as it may appear? The defenders of moral neutrality believe that, given the insurmountable divisions over morality, policymakers should be as noncommittal as possible. The detractors see all kinds of assumed values lurking between the lines. They deny that all knowledge about the human good is contestable. There are at least basic truths here, they believe, that we can know and act on. And these values come in advance of justice.

Marriage and Family Life

Closely related to moral neutrality is the question whether welfare should intervene in family life, meaning the relationships between parents and between them and their children. Although the core of welfare reform has been work enforcement, PRWORA added the declaration that "Marriage is the foundation of a successful society." Specifically, the "prevention of out-of-wedlock pregnancy and reduction in out-of-wedlock birth" could prevent poverty and dependency and thus were "very important Government interests" (U.S. Congress 1996, sec. 101, para. 1 and 10). The act instituted bonuses for states that reduced unwed births. As noted in chapter 1, to date most states have done little to promote marriage, and government does not yet possess programs with a proven ability to do so. Nevertheless, the recent debate on TANF reauthorization featured proposals from both Congress and the White House that would spend more on supporting marriage, especially by developing pilot programs.

This, too, is a significant change. In classical liberalism the family was the realm, above all others, that was protected from government intrusion. Although marriage and the family were regulated by government as legal statuses, family life was shielded from official intrusion by a strong presumption of privacy. Precisely because liberals hesitate to address issues of moral formation through the law, they typically give a wide berth to those private institutions that perform this function, including the family. They might well conclude that for government to intervene in private life, even to promote virtue, would do more harm than good. In short, they presume that—in American as in England—one's home is one's castle.

Defenders of traditional welfare are even more alarmed by marriage promotion than by work enforcement. That policy offends the right to privacy that they see as central to a liberal society. It means the intrusion of a particular moral code into the most private of decisions. Critics also see the traditional family, like capitalism, as potentially oppressive. In the last generation, feminism liberated women to some extent from that structure by asserting their right to control their reproduction, work outside the home, and demand more from their spouses, even at the expense of rising divorce rates. Feminists frequently see any attempt to restore marriage, even to deal with poverty, as a conservative ploy to reassert traditional gender roles. Pateman notes that unreformed welfare, while offensive to many people, still had advantages from the viewpoint of poor women. Not only did it give them assured support for care work, but it strengthened their bargaining position relative to men. It gave them an alternative to relying on neglectful or abusive spouses.

Some of our authors support the principle of governmental intervention to encourage marriage among welfare recipients. However, none of us is yet confident that policy can accomplish this. Most Americans feel similarly. If we fail as yet to enforce marriage, Joel Schwartz suggests, the reason is not that it is unimportant but that the public is ambivalent. Most Americans work hard, and are therefore prepared to enforce work on the poor. They feel markedly less confident about marriage. About half of marriages end in divorce, and marital problems are common even among the affluent. Americans fear anything that would make marriage vows more binding, and they blanch at any idea of enforcing marriage—on the poor or anyone else.

Similarly with parenthood. As noted earlier, Deacon, White, and Beem think government might legitimately seek to improve parenting in order to improve the formation of children. Advocates for the poor long argued that needy single-parent families share burdens and responsibilities among themselves, so as to raise children acceptably despite the absence of fathers (Stack 1974). However, studies show that the children from such families do worse on average, in terms of schooling and avoiding social problems such as early pregnancy or crime, than children raised in two-parent homes. That shortfall must be tolerated or made up by the society.

Social opposition is also prompted by the free riding involved. Single mothers—and their absent husbands—presume that the surrounding community will pick up some of the burden of supervising their children. They assume that "it takes a village to raise a child." For any one such family, it is rational to make this demand, but collectively it is irrational. When single-parent families come to dominate a neighborhood, supervisory resources are overwhelmed. Then children become uncontrolled and order breaks down, helping to generate gangs, crime, unwed pregnancy, and the other ills of the inner city. That is unfair to the adults as well as bad for child development.

The empirical issue is how much free riding is tolerable. How well does the private sector do in incubating marriage and parenthood, and thus the formation of citizens? Even if it seems necessary for government to intervene, what evidence is there that it can do so effectively and without causing greater harm? The philosophical—really ethical—issue comes down to whether, and in what circumstances, our commitments to others can trump our personal rights and freedoms. Thus again, the nature of citizenship appears as a crucial question.

Invidiousness

A further set of issues concerns differential treatment. Even if one accepts welfare conditionality as fair on other grounds, one may still resist it because it involves treating the poor differently than other people.

The view of opponents, as King states broadly, is that equal treatment of people is essential to the equal respect citizenship is supposed to command. If only some people face invidious questions about their conduct in order to get social support, this undercuts equal standing and thus equal belonging in the society. King appeals especially to the British working class experience, in which the conditions placed on aid—means tests as well as work tests—became hated because they created distinctions and undermined solidarity. Jim Crow, similarly, separated whites and blacks in the United States.[9] To minimize such differences, welfare should remain an entitlement.

On the other hand, Mead, White, and others think that the behavior of welfare recipients has already set them apart. Their failure to work when employable has separated them from at least one sine qua non of citizenship. By failing to put forth an effort toward pulling their own weight, nonworking recipients infringe the basic social standard of reciprocity—the demand, in White's words, that everyone do their bit. Conditionality may create a stigma by treating the poor distinctively, but it also removes one by putting them to work.

But what about people who have enough income to support themselves without working? White, for one, finds it unjust to enforce work on the poor but not on the idle rich. Mead and Schwartz counter that the rich, on average, work much harder than the poor, not less, but the issue of principle remains. The inequity occurs, White points out, not only among the rich but at any income level where people inherit enough support to have a choice about working, when others do not.

To remove the inequity, White and Galston favor heavier taxation of inheritance. White also favors requiring national service for all. But Galston argues that there is a "protected right not to work" under the Constitution. That is, short of a draft, people cannot be required to work except, like welfare recipients, in return for some benefit. If so, people of independent means cannot legally be made to work. The fallback is Mead's position that work is enforced in America at several different levels. Although only the poor are formally required to work in connection with welfare, the culture puts strong pressure on everyone, including the rich, to be employed. Whether that suasion is morally equivalent to the explicit work tests in welfare is an issue among us.

How essential is it that social standards be publicly enforced on everyone? Few would doubt that equal enforcement is essential to the criminal law, where penalties are severe and strongly stigmatizing. With other obligations, society's practice has varied. The duties people face to pay taxes and serve on juries vary widely by residence. In other cases enforcement may seem too rigid, as in government's insistence that virtually all workers regardless of income pay the Social Security tax, even though it is regressive.[10] The military draft is a case in which attitudes have changed. Enforcement was highly discretionary during the Vietnam War because of the use of student deferments, but this came to be seen as unjust.

Is there a necessary relationship between differential treatment and political inequality, as King and others assert? Why, to these opponents of reform, does unequal enforcement necessarily imply that citizenship is unequal? And if differential treatment is not always objectionable, what features render it so?

The Meaning of Citizenship

Ultimately, all the specific questions reflect to some degree the core dispute over citizenship. How do we understand the status of citizen that everyone thinks must be in some sense equal? Especially, does citizenship consist centrally of rights and claims that enable the individual to stand apart from the society? Or does the concept center on obligations to that society? Is society a compact among individuals formed in advance of government, or are citizens formed by their relationships with others, in part shaped by government?

In the spirit of John Stuart Mill, King and Pateman treat citizenship as a set of protections for individual autonomy. The goal is that people should retain even in society much of the freedom to decide their actions and beliefs that they had in a state of nature. To that end government observes limits on what it expects of them. And, given a welfare state, it also extends positive benefits to them. Negative rights join with positive claims to help people live out their Rawlsian plans of life. In this light, government's ability to shape individual lives is and ought to be strictly limited. Any extension of public power, or any conditions placed on benefits, appears to compromise citizenship.

In this conception, there may be pressures on the individual, but they come from the private sector, especially the economy and the family. In those realms, individuals cannot avoid all subservience and inequality. But a liberal polity can mitigate those pressures by constructing a political realm where people are equal. Hence the Marshallian conception that citizenship is egalitarian and in tension with the private sector, which is inegalitarian. In Pateman's vision, democracy means not just elected government but a wider-ranging process of democratization that gradually frees people from all the inequities of private life.[11]

Others among us retain a liberal conception of citizenship, but are willing to enforce good behavior in some respects. Of course, in the classical liberalism of Hobbes, Locke, or John Stuart Mill, there already is a willingness to enforce the law against actions by individuals that infringe the rights of others. Galston reminds us of that tradition with his discussion of legal restrictions on citizenship. Essentially, he and other proponents extend that same logic to welfare reform. They present conditionality, not as alien to the liberal conception, but as necessary to avoid free riding by individuals in the areas of economic support or child rearing. When Beem and Pateman advocate public support for care work, they also appeal indirectly to the liberal tradition. Government's role, they assume, is to support social functions that the market does not in a society otherwise based on reciprocal exchange.

Our other authors, however, lean toward a nonliberal or communitarian conception, in which citizenship means obligations to others as much or more than rights. In this idea, Michael Sandel argued, citizens are not defined against social pressures but constituted by them, meaning the burdens they assume on behalf of others. The good citizen is not aloof from the society but accepts its proprieties. Individuals are then not autonomous or separate but intersubjective, each one present to the others in terms of the duties he or she has accepted (1982).

Mead assumes some such bonding in his argument that individuals must gain the respect of others through functioning before tolerance is possible. The more freedom there is in the public sphere, the more obligation there must be in private life, where people must willingly undertake duties for others and minimize free riding. A liberal society absolutely depends on the personal discipline that its members show. The very possibility of autonomy within society depends on self-command. "Society cannot exist unless a controlling power upon will and appetite be placed somewhere," Edmund Burke wrote, "and the less of it there is within, the more there must be without" (1791/1967, 282). Self-control comes from socialization. Those who would be free must first be bound.

Wax expresses a similar idea with her speculative anthropology about how the social opposition to free riding arose. Because groups that provided mutual aid in times of misfortune were the most successful, society evolved to view itself as a collectivity with a shared destiny. Because that vision is threatened by free riding, solidarity may not extend to those who seem undeserving. As Mead suggests, these communitarian sentiments are particularly activated by poverty. It is among the poor and dependent that we especially want to make sure that there is community. We are thus willing to proclaim common duties and to support them with social benefits. Above that level, we are less concerned, even libertarian, because we assume that competent individuals will behave well out of both social mores and self-interest.

Deacon and Schwartz are the most communitarian, interestingly, even though they are well apart politically. Deacon's mutualism imagines a community in which individuals might embrace far-reaching obligations toward others simply because everyone's life is affected by the good or bad behavior of others. A similar ideal of a peaceable kingdom, Frank Field suggests, lies behind recent moves to discipline antisocial behavior in Britain (2003).[12] Schwartz summons precedents from nineteenth-century welfare, in which social elites unashamedly sought the moralization of the poor. Deacon would like to see more redistribution than we have, whereas Schwartz's Victorians focused far more on the misbehavior of the needy, although they accepted a public role in helping the poor. Yet both conjure up worlds where good behavior is considerably more salient than classical liberalism's concern for individual autonomy, or for justice.

The empirical difference behind these competing visions concerns how threatening the social disorders linked to welfare are to be considered. To deal with them, can we maintain liberalism's image of the autonomous, rights-bearing individual, or must we abandon it in favor of a tutelary image of people driven into civility by the duties imposed on them? In the first conception, personal competence is an assumption, in the second a project. Is the self-restraint of the good citizen something natural, or easily acquired, as liberal theorists tend to assume? Or is it the painful product of inhibitions imposed by civilization?[13] Society apparently believes both things about different classes, given the two-level approach to competence suggested earlier—an assumption of civility above the poverty level coupled with a more demanding, communitarian attitude to those below.

The theoretical issue is the same as under entitlement: the relative balance of rights and obligations in the constitution of the citizen. A priority for rights leads toward entitlement and opposition to welfare reform, and a priority for obligation leads toward conditionality and a paternalist social policy.

Conclusion

Of these issues among our authors, we think that entitlement, care work, moral neutrality, and citizenship are the most far-reaching. These questions seem especially to underlie the deep divisions that welfare reform provokes, among political actors as well as political theorists.

The entitlement question is really about accountability. Should recipients who are employable have to answer to anyone for living on aid? The essence of entitlement is not to press such questions, out of the view that citizens, under pressure from an unjust society, require the right not to answer. The whole point of rights is that one need not explain oneself to the authorities. The opponents of entitlement think, to the contrary, that the dependent, like other people, must be accountable for their support, and that failure to demand this made welfare into a corrupting force.

The appeal of care work as a justification for welfare is that it appears to accept accountability rather than evading it. It portrays traditional welfare as functional rather than dysfunctional. But once non-welfare mothers entered the work force, the claim of compensation for care work looked like another form of free riding. So it was rejected. This explains much of the bitterness expressed by welfare advocates and the feminist theorists who defend them. Even if, as Beem argues, care work might still justify support, some conditions must now be set about work connection and parental competence.

Moral neutrality presents many of the same divisions as entitlement, but focused more on the proprieties of private life rather than the work test. Traditionally, whether democratic citizenship would be helped or harmed was an important criterion in the making of domestic policy. That concern faded during most of the twentieth century. But in its war against poverty, government is once again defining desired ways of life. Welfare reform seems to say that contemporary liberalism has abandoned Sandel's procedural republic, which coordinates self-seeking individuals without passing judgments on them (Sandel 1996). Critics doubt whether such an effort can avoid caprice and thus unfairness.

The question of citizenship is the bottom line for this entire book. Our authors have held welfare reform to be good or bad by various criteria. In the end, all these judgments point toward a rebalancing of citizenship, either toward more rights or more obligations. The opponents of reform restate a vision of the political individual as a rights-bearing claimant to various benefits and protections against the wider society. Entitlement welfare, they think, continues a process of democratization that stretches back centuries. The proponents of reform seek rather to vindicate assumptions about obligation and competence that they say liberal citizenship always presumed. We must now pay explicit attention to them through welfare reform, this argument runs. When all citizens are indeed competent a democratic society will be the stronger for it. But because we now make functioning assumptions explicit, it will be a more Spartan society than what we have known.

We have stressed the need for political theory to address actual policy issues. The citizenship issue dramatizes the difference this makes. In early theorizing about the welfare state, the advocates of generosity often made collectivist assumptions about the society. Individuals were seen as common citizens who banded together through the welfare state to protect themselves against the insecurities of capitalism. That image is still found in the social democratic writers to whom White appeals. Conservative critics of big government, on the other hand, asserted an individualist vision in which people were entitled to their property and redistribution from rich to poor was unjust. That was one issue between Rawls and Nozick, for instance (Rawls 1971; Nozick 1974).

But because welfare reform focused more on work than on changing the generosity of welfare, in this context conservatives became the statists and liberals their opponents. Thus, in our chapters, it is the opponents of reform who assert the more individualist vision, seeing entitlement welfare as a right of citizenship. It is the proponents who are the more communitarian, asserting public authority to demand good behavior from the dependent—just the reverse of the earlier pattern.[14]

Concerning all these issues, an overriding division is how serious the disorders linked to welfare are. What civilities must society assume in its members, and how fully are these generated by the private sector, without special enforcement by government? Despite the problems of poverty and dependency, can we muddle through with a liberal conception of society and welfare that assumes that people are functional and responsible? Or must we reject it in favor of a more collectivist vision in which citizenship is enforced by public action and individuals must accept more explicit responsibilities toward each other? The presumption of the liberal conception is personal competence. When that premise comes into question, nonliberal conceptions inevitably come to the fore.

Notes

1. Alternatively, one might describe this contrast as that between a thinner and a more perfectionist understanding of liberalism.
2. As explained in chapter 1, entitlement also has a budgetary meaning.
3. White sets out preconditions for conditionality in somewhat broader terms: Jobs must be available and pay above poverty, care work must be recognized, and the work obligation must extend to all (2003, 134–37). Under various headings we consider all these criteria in this chapter.
4. See chapter 1 for evidence on this point.
5. See, for instance, Deacon and Mann (1999) and Hoggett (2001).
6. See also Beem (1998).
7. Rawls's fix was to include leisure outside a normal working day as among the primary goods of which everyone must be assured a minimum share. Therefore, people who do not work consume more leisure than this and thus cannot claim as much of other primary goods; therefore, they cannot claim public support (see 1974, 654; 1988, 257 note 7; 2001, 179).
8. We owe this point to one of the Russell Sage autonomous reviewers.
9. See also King (1995, 1999).
10. At most, we offset this tax for the low-income through the Earned Income Tax Credit and other subsidies.
11. The idea that economic inequalities should not invade other social realms such as politics is developed in Michael Walzer (1983).
12. See also *The Economist* (2004).
13. For divergent visions of personality consistent with these images, see James Q. Wilson (1993) and Sigmund Freud (1930/1961).
14. We owe this point to John Tambornino.

References

Beem, Christopher. 1998. *Pluralism and Consensus: Conceptions of the Good in the Liberal Polity.* Chicago: CSSR Press.

Burke, Edmund. 1791/1967. "Letter to a Member of the National Assembly." In *Reflections on the Revolution in France.* London: Everyman's Library.

Deacon, Alan, and Kirk Mann. 1999. "Agency, Modernity and Social Policy." *Journal of Social Policy* 28(3): 413–35.

The Economist. 2004. "The War on Incivility." *The Economist.* July 24, 2004, pp. 53–4.

Field, Frank. 2003. *Neighbours from Hell: The Politics of Behaviour.* London: Politico's Publishing.

Freud, Sigmund. 1930/1961. *Civilization and its Discontents,* trans. James Strachey. New York: W. W. Norton.

Galston, William A. 1991. *Liberal Purposes: Goods, Virtues, and Diversity in the Liberal State.* Cambridge: Cambridge University Press.

Hoggett, Paul. 2001. "Agency, Rationality and Social Policy," *Journal of Social Policy* 30(1): 37–56.

King, Desmond S. 1995. *Actively Seeking Work? The Politics of Unemployment and Welfare Policy in the United States and Great Britain.* Chicago: University of Chicago Press.

———. 1999. *In the Name of Liberalism: Illiberal Social Policy in the USA and Britain.* Oxford: Oxford University Press.

Marshall, T. H. 1964. "Citizenship and Social Class." In *Class, Citizenship, and Social Development: Essays by T. H. Marshall,* introduction by Seymour Martin Lipset. Garden City, N.Y.: Doubleday.

Mayer, Susan E. 1997. *What Money Can't Buy: Family Income and Children's Life Chances.* Cambridge, Mass.: Harvard University Press.

Mead, Lawrence M. 1986. *Beyond Entitlement: The Social Obligations of Citizenship.* New York: Free Press.

———. 1992. *The New Politics of Poverty: The Nonworking Poor in America.* New York: Basic Books.

Nozick, Robert. 1974. *Anarchy, State, and Utopia.* New York: Basic Books.

Rawls, John. 1971. *A Theory of Justice.* Cambridge, Mass.: Harvard University Press.

———. 1974. "Reply to Alexander and Musgrave," *Quarterly Journal of Economics* 88(4): 633–55.

———. 1988. "The Priority of Right and Ideas of the Good," *Philosophy and Public Affairs* 17(4): 251–76.

———. 2001. *Justice as Fairness: A Restatement,* edited by Erin Kelly. Cambridge, Mass.: Harvard University Press.

Sandel, Michael J. 1982. *Liberalism and the Limits of Justice.* Cambridge: Cambridge University Press.

———. 1996. *Democracy's Discontent: America in Search of a Public Philosophy.* Cambridge, Mass.: Harvard University Press.

Stack, Carol B. 1974. *All Our Kin: Strategies for Survival in a Black Community.* New York: Harper and Row.

Tawney, R. H. 1952. *Equality,* 4th ed. London: Allen and Unwin.

U.S. Congress. 1996. *Personal Responsibility and Work Opportunity Reconciliation Act of 1996* (Enrolled as Agreed to or Passed by Both House and Senate). HR 3734. 104th Cong. 2nd sess.

Van Parijs, Philippe. 1991. "Why Surfers Should Be Fed: The Liberal Case for an Unconditional Basic Income," *Philosophy and Public Affairs* 20(2): 101–31.

———. 1995. *Real Freedom for All: What (If Anything) Can Justify Capitalism?* New York: Oxford University Press.

Walzer, Michael. 1983. *Spheres of Justice: A Defense of Pluralism and Equality*. New York: Basic Books.

White, Stuart. 2003. *The Civic Minimum: On the Rights and Obligations of Economic Citizenship*. Oxford: Oxford University Press.

Wilson, James Q. 1993. *The Moral Sense*. New York: Free Press.

Index

Boldface numbers refer to figures and tables.